University of Nebraska Press • *Lincoln and London*

SOCCER STORIES

Anecdotes, Oddities, Lore, and Amazing Feats

Donn Risolo

Library of Congress
Cataloging-in-Publication Data
Risolo, Donn.
        Soccer stories : anecdotes,
oddities, lore, and amazing feats /
Donn Risolo.
p. cm.   Includes bibliographical
references.
ISBN 978-0-8032-3014-9
        (pbk. : alk. paper)
1. Soccer—Miscellanea.
2. Soccer—Anecdotes. I. Title.
GV943.2.R57 2010
796.334—dc22   2010011139

Set in ITC New Baskerville and
Scala Sans Pro by Kim Essman.
Designed by A. Shahan.
Cleats © 2007
iStockphoto.com/sasimoto

CONTENTS

INTRODUCTION

I like soccer.

That puts me in a highly unexclusive club made up of billions of members spanning the globe, including a mushrooming legion of Americans just as misguided as me. We're not all on a first-name basis, but once a game starts, we all speak the same language.

I suppose that if your country's national soccer team is strong, if your country's national soccer league is rich in tradition and loaded with stars, if you grew up supporting your father's club like his father before him, you're likely to find the pull of soccer irresistible, regardless of whether you've ever kicked a ball in anger. All of the above will generate not just interest but also passion. And a rivalry—from a pair of neighboring town teams in a Brazilian Amazon backwater to Glasgow's famous, or infamous, Auld Firm, the bitter meetings of the Roman Catholic–backed Celtic and the Protestant-backed Rangers— can only fan the flames. I recall an acquaintance, an American who during a business trip to Madrid was invited by a local associate to the latest renewal of one of the greatest rivalries of all, Real Madrid versus FC Barcelona. He was taken to Santiago Bernabeu stadium, sat among the capacity crowd of ninety thousand, and experienced the pageantry, the atmosphere, the us-against-them partisanship, and he came away like a wide-eyed hermit who'd been dragged to a Rolling Stones concert: he wasn't quite sure what he'd seen, but whatever it was left a deep impression. He also came away convinced that, back home, the ill will between, say, fans of the Green Bay Packers and the Chicago Bears could never begin to compare with the sheer hatred between Real Madrid's Castillians and FC Barcelona's Catalans, whose common history includes, of course, a civil war.

In the United States soccer lacks such bells and whistles. Oh, we host a World Cup once a lifetime, but there is no steady drum beat that makes the sport a part of American life week after week, the success of the U.S. National Women's Team, the remarkable progress of the U.S. National Men's Team, and the dogged survival of Major League Soccer notwithstanding. Instead, the game, raw and unadorned, has had to sell itself, and in that respect it has not failed. There's an estimated 18 million men, women, boys, and girls playing organized soccer in the United States, a country that until recently was overwhelmingly hostile to the sport, proof of sorts that the siren song that long ago hypnotized Europe, South America, Central America, Africa, and Asia hasn't sounded a sour note here, at least among listeners with an open mind. For those willing to meet soccer halfway, they just have to play it, or play at it. Chances are, anyone who has ever knocked a ball around for more than five minutes at a family picnic (and was never forced to play a crude version of the game by an unenthusiastic P.E. teacher) will find soccer engaging, challenging, alluring. For those who don't play, it only takes a short time on the sidelines, pulling for a son or daughter or sister or uncle, to appreciate it. Instead of ninety minutes of seemingly random moves, a soccer match for those with a rooting interest suddenly becomes a living, breathing, undulating drama that alternates between danger and hope as the ball is played from one end to the other.

I like the simplicity of soccer. On its most primitive level, all that's required is an object to kick and a plot of land. The goals can be made up of whatever's handy—on one end, a couple of rocks placed a few feet apart, on the other a tree trunk and a trash can, and the game is on. That basic set of ingredients made it the sport of the masses long ago, and it continues to be the sport of the urban alley in Bratislava, the rock-strewn lot in Tehran, the open beach in Bahia, the jungle clearing outside Abidjan, and that rare flat patch in a Tibetan mountain village. Go up a notch, where what's being kicked is a genuine ball and the players are in uniform, and the game remains relatively basic: two goals, four corner flags, two goal lines, two touchlines, two penalty areas, and a center circle. The referee blows the whistle once to signal the opening kickoff, twice for halftime, and three times to end the game. There is no need to keep track of timeouts because there are no timeouts; if there is a delay to tend to an injured player or retrieve an errant ball, the ref adds the missing minutes to the end of the half; you don't need a separate timekeeper to account for that missing 1:39:05. Because the deciding goal can be scored in the first minute or the ninetieth, few spectators budge during a match, and thus halftime is the time for a run to the concession stand or restroom, not a midfield performance of a two-hundred-member marching band. There's no set number of times a player is allowed to misbehave; once the ref loses patience with a miscreant he's warned or sent off. If he's sent off, his team plays shorthanded for the rest of the game—the perfect punishment for any player who puts his lack of self-control ahead of his teammates' welfare. (Imagine a four-man basketball team, or a baseball team minus its shortstop.) If there's a foul, the fouled team sets the ball down in the vicinity of the infraction and quickly restarts play without the help of a chain gang. Soccer's rules, the Laws of the Game, number only seventeen, and when it comes to any gray areas, the referee is expected to exercise simple common sense. As for the macho factor, for all their rib-rattling collisions, knee-wrenching slide tackles, and repeated banging of heads, the protective equipment worn by soccer players is limited to a pair of shin guards, about a quarter inch thick.

I like the fact that soccer is played—with one exception, the goalkeeper—without the hands. The game's critics have long contended that the United States is a nation of throwers and catchers, and that this restriction is the major reason many Americans haven't embraced the sport (hard to hug something when you can't use your arms). To the rest of the planet, "no hands" makes soccer unique and a terrific test of skill. Forty-yard passes are produced with the foot and caught by a teammate using the instep, thigh, or chest. Dribbling requires not just quick feet but imagination, and tackling the ball away from that dribbler requires timing and even quicker feet. For those who must have hands, the player who leaps above two opponents to head-flick a cross past the goalkeeper and six inches inside the far post probably does so despite a friendly elbow to the throat or an errant arm draped over his shoulders, and he certainly uses his arms after the fact, to throw them into the air in celebration of a goal. Soccer players don't give a wit about being handcuffed, just as athletes in other sports can live with restrictions such as traveling, illegal procedure, blue line violations, and the balk. In fact, in a world of sports in which scoring is often the result of a play imposed by a coach and rehearsed countless times in practice, it is the soccer player, relying on intuition and improvisation to create most goals, who is truly unfettered.

I like soccer's value system, one in which 2–1 is considered a fine final score and 4–3 an offensive orgy. Someday, those who consider soccer too low-scoring will acknowledge that other spectator sports might just be dizzyingly high-scoring . . . but I won't hold my breath. Do you want your scoring in drip-drip-drip fashion (basketball), in a sporadic blast of machine-gun fire (gridiron football's six points per touchdown), or in soccer's occasional nuclear bomb blast? It's all a matter of taste, or the ability or willingness to wait for something worth waiting for.

I like the fact that soccer is dominated by players who are lifelike. The sport has no implied height or weight requirement, but anyone freakishly large will have his great height or weight turned to disadvantage in short (or tall or fat) order. Pelé stands 5'8". Diego Maradona remains an unimposing 5'6". Both, extraordinarily inventive, exploited their terrific balance and low center of gravity to torment a generation of defenders who, relatively speaking, towered over them. Moreover, Pelé, with his remarkable leaping ability, was a lethal header of the ball. On the other hand, the goalkeeper, usually the biggest man on his side, is effective between 5'11" and 6'3", but get into the area of 6'5" and he becomes a liability, a man who might not be able to get down to a grounded shot often enough to hold onto his job. Thus, soccer is like the real world: the guy who's a power forward–like 6'9" or a defensive tackle–ish 375 pounds has as much of an advantage in this game as he has in banking or auto repair or contract bridge.

Finally, I like the universality of soccer. Ask a foreign tourist wearing a replica jersey about his favorite club and you've immediately reached out hundreds and possibly thousands of miles. Make a crack about the tourist's club's biggest rival and you've made an instant friend. And while you or I may not have a real connection with this fellow's club, we are all linked by the World Cup. Every four years I watch the World Cup secure in the knowledge that this tournament is the one true championship in team sports. Not only did about two hundred nations fight it out through a Byzantine system of regional playoffs for the chance to be among the thirty-two finalists, but each national team involved represents a population, large or small, in which a good number of the citizenry played soccer at one point or another, and, whether they knew it or not, made themselves a candidate to wear the national team jersey. We will never know if the true successor to Nolan Ryan is a farm boy in Finland who spends his summer days pitching hay instead of baseballs, just as, potentially, the greatest skater ever is a girl living hand to mouth in the steaming jungles of Congo, destined never to see an ice cube. It is doubtful, however, that a great soccer player has gone undiscovered, not on this earth. Ultimately, 0.0003 percent of the planet's regular players appear in a World Cup, and a still more infinitesimal number, twenty-two, play in a World Cup championship match. But looking on will be a television audience in the billions, a good number of them would-be World Cup stars who are not just watching but down on the field in spirit.

A fast-growing number of those who tuned in to the 2010 World Cup in South Africa were from the United States, where, as in 1994, 1998, 2002, and 2006, records for televised soccer were shattered—just one more indication that soccer is slowly but steadily becoming a part of American culture. Wall-to-wall live TV coverage of the entire monthlong tournament, in English, without commercial breaks during the action, was unthinkable just twenty years ago. So were the handful of soccer-only stations that now dot the TV menu, as well as the vast ocean of websites that enable Americans, isolated from the soccer mainstream, to follow the latest news without being at the mercy of the hidebound conventional U.S. media and its traditionally dim view of the sport.

This progress has come at a dizzying pace for those who remember other days, when the fledgling high school soccer team would have to battle the school's gridiron football coach for playing space, when the only soccer on television might be a two-week-old match from Europe with Spanish commentary. Hence *Soccer Stories*, a pause during this inexorable march for some of the interesting, amusing, odd, and amazing tales that help flesh out soccer and give the game its color. Some of the items that follow are weighty, a few appear mostly for their entertainment value, but they all are necessary, because there's so much more to any sport than X's and O's; if not, there's no place in our consciousness for Roy Riegels's wrong-way run in the 1929 Rose Bowl, the tragic demise of Lou Gehrig, the 1980 USA hockey team's Miracle on Ice, or the humor that launched a thousand bad golf jokes. A handful of the items herein will be familiar to some, but for most readers they represent a chance to see what they might have been missing, the stories and anecdotes that make soccer such a rich and wonderful game.

SOCCER STORIES

Five days shalt thou labour, as the Bible
says. The seventh day is the Lord
thy God's. The sixth day is for football.
ANTHONY BURGESS, English playwright,
composer, critic, translator, linguist, and author
of *A Clockwork Orange*, from the comic novel
Inside Mr. Enderby

It's not whether you win or lose.
It's whether you play.
JAMES CAAN, actor and American
youth soccer coach

1 EVERYONE, EVERYWHERE

*Soccer is a universal game, enjoyed everywhere by people regardless of age,
gender, size, skill level, color, creed, or station in life. Along with youth
leagues, school leagues, amateur adult leagues, multidivision professional
leagues, national cups, regional international competitions, and the World
Cups—male and female—there are major championships for the deaf, for
the blind, and for players with intellectual disabilities. Versions of soccer
are played on grass, beach sand, cinders, hardwood, asphalt, and ice.
Elephants have played it, as have robots. A tournament held in a pool in
Germany as part of 2006 World Cup festivities featured players wearing
weights for ballast while kicking away at a heavy soccer ball. Clearly,
soccer's debut in outer space is only a matter of time.*

The Homeless World Cup

While horse racing is known as the sport of kings, soccer is the sport
of the working class. Make that the sport of the indigent class as well,
officially beginning in July 2003 in Graz, Austria, where eighteen
teams took part in the first Homeless World Cup. The event was
played out over seven days in two of the city's major squares. Clad in
the colors of their home countries, ten-member teams of homeless

men and women, from teens to those in their mid-fifties, played a series of fourteen-minute games (thirty minutes for the placement rounds) with three field players and a goalkeeper per side. The field was blacktop surrounded by hockey-style dasher boards, with a small goal at each end.

Sponsored by the International Network of Street Papers, the Graz homeless street newspaper, and the charity group Caritas, the tournament was intended to lift the self-esteem of the players and help them feel a part of society while in turn improving society's perception of the homeless. The idea for the event was born in Cape Town, South Africa, during an international meeting of editors of street newspapers, which are sold by homeless people around the world. Mel Young, cofounder of *The Big Issue Scotland,* joined forces with Harald Schmied, editor of Australia's *Megaphon,* after Young came across a childhood chum and avid soccer player who had become a street beggar.

Among the nations represented in Graz was the United States, whose team was a group of New Yorkers hastily assembled by the local street paper *BIGnews.* Despite the team's lack of soccer experience, their scrappy play won over fans and opponents as the United States finished ninth.

As in most World Cups, the home team, Austria, enjoyed a distinct advantage and won the tournament, beating England in the final, 2–1.

There were several other winners as well, according to a follow-up survey conducted by organizers. Of the 141 players in Graz, 31 later secured full-time jobs and 12 signed with pro clubs as players or coaches. Forty-nine reported that their life situation had changed "significantly."

On the other hand, there were the three Swedish players who slipped out of the boarding school being used for housing for the participants and went on a drinking binge. Although the tournament had not yet kicked off, the trio, who were voted off their team, blamed the pressure of the competition for their relapse.

The 2004 Homeless World Cup was played in Sweden with twenty-six teams; Italy defeated the defending champion Austria, 4–0, in the title match in Stockholm.

New York was originally chosen to host the 2005 tournament, but the games ultimately went to Edinburgh, where the Princes Street Gardens and the imposing Edinburgh Castle provided an impressive frame for the twenty-seven-team competition. There was controversy from the outset, however, as, in an irony of ironies, the players from five African nations—Burundi, Cameroon, Kenya, Nigeria, and Zambia—were refused visas to enter Britain because they were deemed unable to support themselves during the tournament. This coming two weeks after a G8 summit up the road in Perthshire that addressed, among other issues, fighting poverty in Africa. Said disgusted tournament organizer Young, "To deny homeless people access to the UK on the basis that they are too poor is ridiculous."

In the final, despite the chants of "Polska, Polska," Italy shaded Poland, 3–2, to retain its crown. As the Italians hoisted their trophy, they were serenaded by the crowd with, appropriately, The Proclaimers' hit, "500 Miles."

In 2006 the Homeless World Cup, sponsored by the Union of European Football Associations (UEFA), Nike, and the South African tourist authority, arrived at its founding home, Cape Town, with forty-eight contestants. The host team, Bafowethu ("Our Brothers"), defeated Chile, 2–0, in the opener. And the competition produced further irony in the title game: a matchup of two former members of the Soviet Union, a workers' state where unemployment, theoretically, was unknown. Russia, which had beaten Kazakhstan 2–1 earlier in the week, again nipped its former fellow socialist republic in the final, 1–0.

Once again, a poll by organizers of the previous year's participants produced positive numbers: 94 percent expressed a new motivation, 62 percent of alcoholics and drug addicts claimed to be coping better, 40 percent had improved their housing, 38 percent had found employment, and 28 percent had returned to school.

The fifth installment attracted another five hundred players representing forty-eight nations, this time to Copenhagen. In the final in City Hall Square, the 2005 host, Scotland, and 2005 finalist Poland met before a packed crowd that included the prince of Denmark. With the Danes' most prominent referee, Kim Milton Nielsen (best known for sending off David Beckham in the 1998 World Cup), officiating, the Scots rolled to a 9–3 victory.

As organizers continued to hope that each succeeding Homeless World Cup would be minus most of the previous year's individual participants, the 2008 edition in Melbourne, Australia, attracted more than five hundred players and a record fifty-six teams, among them eight all-female teams, necessitating a first-ever women's division. The homeless of war-torn Afghanistan, driven by chants of "A-F-G" by a large contingent of expatriates, defeated Russia, 5–4, in Federation Square for the championship. In the ladies-only title match, Zambia met the representatives of another embattled African nation, Liberia. Hit by injuries, the Liberians enlisted three local Aussies but lost, 7–1.

No Escaping *This* World Cup

France won the 2002 World Cup. The Thailand Prison World Cup, that is. A French team defeated Nigeria on penalty kicks, 7–6, to win the championship of a Thai prison that is home to thirteen hundred foreign inmates. Italy, England, and Germany were among the eight nations represented in the event. The winners received new soap and toothbrushes.

Four years later, in a less-representative penal World Cup, Sweden played Ivory Coast at Ciudad de La Plata Stadium in an Argentine prison final before a small crowd that included diplomats from the two nations involved, as well as hundreds of security guards.

One team each from thirty-two prisons in the province of Buenos Aires adopted the names of the 2006 World Cup finalists and battled it out over three months. In the end the "Swedes" of Unidad Penal de Campana defeated the "Ivorians" of Mar del Plata, 2–0. Fittingly, "Sweden" won the tournament's fair play award.

Soccer Makes Its Polar Debut

Despite subfreezing temperatures, fog, and polar bears scientists on three icebreakers anchored along an ice floe some three hundred miles from the North Pole in late 2001 decided to play a bit of soccer.

Three twenty-minute matches were played among the Healy (United States), Oden (Sweden), and Polarstern (Germany). A meteorologist and licensed referee, Hilger Erdmann of Germany, officiated. His pregame field inspection included a check of the thickness of the ice that would serve as the pitch, which was limited to fifty yards by twenty-five yards because of melt pools.

Guards were posted after polar bear tracks were discovered in the snow nearby.

The German ship took first ahead of the Swedish ship on overall goal difference, while the American ship dropped both of its matches and finished last.

Six years earlier eight men's amateur teams from Russia staged a tournament at the North Pole itself, making it the first organized team sport played on top of the world. Winner of the tournament was a team representing a refrigerator plant in Biyusa.

Canada, Where Ice Hockey Used to Be King

Unfathomable but true: there are more soccer players than ice hockey players in Canada.

It became a reality in 1997 when the Canadian Soccer Association announced that its player registration had reached 536,000, more than the number of Canadians practicing that country's unofficial religion, hockey.

A 13 percent jump in registrations helped soccer vault to the top in Canada, population 27 million. Ten years later the number of registered soccer players had grown to 867,869 while hockey participation figures remained flat, at 545,363.

The milestone was reached in the face of a long history of Canadian failure on the international level and an inability to maintain a successful pro league. Despite its strong British ties, Canada's lone major soccer achievement remains its appearance in the 1986 World Cup, where it was eliminated in the first round. The Canadians' biggest regional honor was the 2000 CONCACAF Gold Cup. Canada also hosted the first-ever FIFA Under-19 Women's Championship in 2002, but with a world title within reach and the support of a partisan crowd of 47,784 at Edmonton's Commonwealth Stadium, the Canadian teens lost to the United States in the final, 1–0, in overtime.

A Ship-to-Shore Championship

In addition to six continents and one of the two poles, soccer is played on the mighty oceans as well.

The Seven Seas Football Series pits teams representing ships from throughout the world in an annual world nautical championship.

One edition in the mid-1970s attracted 975 vessels; in 2008 crews from 133 ships played three hundred matches.

Actually, the matches are played on shore, not ship decks. But the size of the event and the maze of schedules of the ships involved demand superhuman planning skills on the part of the series organizers.

Another Soccer Title for Brazil: Amputee Champs

Except for that elusive Olympic gold medal, Brazil has won every men's world soccer championship—the World Cup, World Youth Championship, Under-17 World Championship, World Futsal Championship . . . and the Amputee Soccer Championship.

In November 2000 the Brazilians won the twentieth annual amputee title in Seattle, site of the series' first competition, beating Russia in the final on an own goal in overtime. Brazil also beat the Russians in the final in the previous year's tournament in Kiev.

Many of the field players play on one leg and use forearm crutches. Rules forbid players from using the crutches or their residual limb to play the ball. Goalkeepers are limited to arm amputees who can use only the nonresidual arm.

Brazil's prowess also extends to the soccer portion of the Paralympics, an Olympic-style, seven-a-side competition for ambulatory athletes suffering from cerebral palsy or who have experienced a stroke or traumatic brain injury.

In September 2004 the Brazilians added another chapter to their long-running rivalry with neighboring Argentina during the semifinals of the Athens Paralympics soccer tournament. Brazil was leading Argentina, 4–1, when the match was marred by a bench-clearing brawl in the fifty-sixth minute. One Argentine and three Brazilians were ejected, including goal-scoring hero Luciano Rocha. A verbal bout between Mario Sosa of Argentina and Flavio Pereira of Brazil broke out after Rocha's third goal, touching off the free-for-all.

The red cards left Argentina with a player advantage of 6–4, but it could only close to 4–2, thanks to a Brazilian own goal.

1881: Women's Soccer Is Born; "What next?"

Today, women have their own World Cup, under-20, and under-17 world championships, and Olympic soccer tournament, plus continental championships. There was a time, though, when the (male) soccer establishment considered organized women's soccer something of an outrage.

Perhaps not in the Scottish town of Iveresk, Midlothian, where, in the late eighteenth century an annual match was played between the married and unmarried fishwives of Fisherrow. From the first such contest in 1795 area bachelors would watch the bachelorettes in action and decide on a potential bride based on the young woman's soccer skills.

But that open-mindedness had shut tight nearly a hundred years later, as evidenced by the account of a female version of Scotland versus England played in 1881 in nearby Edinburgh:

So it has come at last! What next? Two teams of young women have just played a game under Association Rules in Edinburgh.

Several years ago there was a rage for silly displays of certain kinds of athletics by women, but we thought the time had passed for another outburst in the form of Association football. It had been whispered some weeks ago that twenty-two young women were practicing the dribbling game in a hall in Glasgow for the purpose of "coming out," and that eventually they had applied to several of the Glasgow clubs for the use of their ground, but not one would grant it for such purpose. Somehow or other, however, the Edinburgh Association players are not so particular about the arrangement of matches, if there is any chance of a gate, and the ground at Eastern Road belonging to the Hibernians was given without much ado.

To give the arrangement the semblance of an international event the girls had the "cheek" to designate the farce, England v Scotland, and, as a matter of course, it suited them best to allow Scotland to win by three goals to none.

The "Scottish Eleven" wore blue jerseys, with crimson sashes round the waist, knickerbockers, blue and white hose, and high laced boots, while the English team had on crimson jerseys, with blue sashes, white knickerbockers, and crimson and white hose, and badges with the English lion. The football shown was of the most primitive order, and reminded one of a couple of A B C classes of schoolboys engaged in a "big side."

It is said that other matches are about to come off, one in Glasgow this afternoon. If it does come off in that city it will most probably be on some of the professional running grounds, for no football club with any regard for its good name would encourage such a humiliating spectacle made of the popular winter pastime.

The account concluded with the lineups of both teams. For the record, Scotland's enormous head start in women's soccer hasn't been parlayed into success today. Scotland failed to qualify for the first four Women's World Cups and in December 2003 was ranked No. 30 by FIFA in the first installment of its worldwide women's rankings.

The Groundhoppers, Soccer's Super Fans

Hopelessly devoted soccer fans of the world can take heart: they're not as hopeless as Carlo Farsang of Germany.

Farsang is far and away the leader of the group of soccer fanatics known as the "Groundhoppers," fans who are more interested not in following one particular club or national team but in visiting as many soccer grounds as possible.

From 1991 through 2003 Farsang attended 1,038 matches at 800 stadiums in 104 countries.

A close second is fellow countryman Franz Jasperneite, who has taken in up to 210 matches in 150 days in a single year (705 games in 45 countries and counting), leaving the international business graduate with no time to pursue a career. He does, however, edit the bible of this odd hobby, *Groundhopping Informer*.

As of June 2004 there were more than two thousand registered groundhoppers worldwide, including one thousand in the United Kingdom, where the favorite reading was England's *The Football Ground Guide*.

Just as England is the birthplace of modern soccer, so it is the place where groundhopping can be traced, to October 1974. An Englishman, Geoff Rose, suggested in a soccer periodical that an award be given to anyone who visited the ninety-two clubs in the four-division English League, inspiring the creation four years later of the "92 Club."

In 1993 the Germans raised the bar with their own groundhopping club, which recommended that its members visit three hundred stadiums in thirty countries.

Groundhoppers are expected to witness at least forty-five minutes of a match, and on their own they document each visit with photos and a written account. For all their dedication, however, no groundhopper has ever attended a match in all 204 FIFA-member nations. Even FIFA President Sepp Blatter tops out at 180.

But Farsang, a former apprentice baker who has become a travel guide for soccer fans, would no doubt believe it can be done. "The Internet and budget airlines have made groundhopping far too easy these days," Farsang told the *FIFA News*. "It has taken away the sense of adventure."

Man of the Cloth, Man of the Match

Pope John Paul II was known in his youth as an enthusiastic goalkeeper, and during his nearly three-decade reign as pontiff he occasionally watched a match on television. But Il Papa the player never reached the heights of a humble Spanish priest from Ecuador in the 1971 Copa Libertadores.

That April, Estudiantes of Argentina, holder of the South American club cup three years running, traveled to Guayaquil to meet Barcelona of Ecuador in the opening match of its three-team semifinal group. Estudiantes won, 1–0, on a goal by Juan Miguel Echecopar, and although Barcelona bounced back to beat Union Española of Chile by the same score in its next game, the Ecuadoran side seemed certain of elimination later that month during the return match against Estudiantes at La Plata.

Notorious for their brutal style and backed by a sellout crowd at Paseo del Bosque, Estudiantes was expected to brush aside the Ecuadoran upstarts, but in the seventeenth minute midfielder "Pibe" Bolanos and inside left Alberto Spencer combined to set up a chance for the Ordained One, Father Juan Manuel Basurko, and the young priest, playing inside right, scored to give Barcelona a 1–0 triumph.

A holy goal, perhaps, but there was no salvation for Barcelona. A 3–1 defeat at Union Española in Santiago in its fourth and final semifinal-round game left Father Basurko's team two points behind Estudiantes. There was redemption of sorts, however: Estudiantes lost to Nacional of Uruguay in a third-game tiebreaker, 2–0, and has never won another South American club championship. In fact, it suffered through eleven years before winning its next Argentine title.

So are the ranks of the Roman Catholic clergy an untapped source of soccer talent?

An answer was provided in 2007 when sixteen teams, made up of priests and seminarians from fifty countries studying at pontifical universities in Rome, took part in the first Clericus Cup, which ran from late winter through midspring.

Matches were limited to one hour to encourage older seminarians to join in. Each team was allowed a time-out, and players who misbehaved were shown not a yellow or red card but a "blue card" and banished to a "sin bin" for five minutes of reflection. In addition, matches were not played on Sundays, unlike the Italian Serie A.

Inspiration for the tournament was that other state religion, Italian professional soccer. The end of the 2005–6 season was rocked by a major match-fixing scandal, and the campaign that followed opened with fan violence in Sicily that claimed the life of a police officer. In between was the 2006 World Cup final in Berlin, where Italy's Marco Materazzi goaded France's Zinedine Zidane into a head-butting incident in overtime that helped pave the way to the Italians' ultimate triumph in a penalty-kick tiebreaker.

According to the Vatican's second-highest official, Cardinal Tarcisio Bertone, the cup should "reaffirm the educational and pastoral value of sport" and "strengthen feelings of true friendship and fruitful sharing."

The Clericus Cup opener, played in the shadow of St. Peter's Basilica, pitted Gregorian University, a team of Brazilians, and the Collegio Mater Ecclesiae, a collection of Africans, Asians, and Latin Americans. Said Cardinal Pio Laghi to the players before kickoff, "You are playing in view of St. Peter's cupola, so behave well."

Play throughout the event wasn't exactly scintillating, and some of the players, particularly the Gregorians, were a bit overweight, but there also were participants who had given up promising soccer careers to answer a higher calling, and harsh play wasn't unknown.

Alas, gamesmanship came to the fore in the final.

In May, after four months of competition, Redemptoris Mater College met Pontifical Lateran University at the massive Olimpico

Stadium in Rome. Redemptoris Mater had not surrendered a goal throughout the tournament and was in the second half of a scoreless tie with Pontifical Lateran when a Redemptoris forward from Costa Rica drew a penalty kick with what Pontifical Lateran players regarded as a dive. The incident triggered a flurry of blue cards, but Redemptoris converted the ensuing spot kick for the win.

"Priestly footballers? Worse than Materazzi," tut-tutted the Italian daily *La Stampa.*

Among the casualties at the Clericus Cup was the U.S. representative, the Pontifical North American College. The aptly named NAC Martyrs lost to the top-seeded Neocatechumenal Way's Redemptoris, 1–0, and missed the final round. As in many things soccer, the Americans were regarded as long shots to lift the cup.

Also missing from the final—and the tournament itself—was the Vatican team. Composed mostly of Swiss Guards, the team has represented the tiny papal state on numerous occasions, including a 2002 "international" in which it held the principality of Monaco to a scoreless draw, its greatest accomplishment. But the Clericus Cup was exclusively for men of the cloth, not those wielding a halberd.

In announcing the tournament Cardinal Bertone raised the notion of the Vatican fielding a team of priests—clad in the yellow and white of the papal flag—that could compete in Serie A. Said Bertone, a loyal Juventus fan who, as Archbishop of Genoa, once doubled as a TV soccer commentator, "If we just take the Brazilian students from our Pontifical universities, we could have a magnificent squad."

The Holy See versus the likes of AC Milan? There are miracles, and then there are miracles.

2 HISTORY

*Soccer's existence could be seen as almost inevitable: the kicking motion is,
physiologically, one of the most natural among those used in sports, while
others, such as throwing a ball overhand, are not. No wonder kicking
games have been around for thousands of years. Here is not a complete
history of soccer but a look at some of the more notable, revealing, or odd
moments in the sport's evolution.*

A Tale of Two Universities

Cambridge University and Harvard University. One in Cambridge,
England, one in Cambridge, Massachusetts. One nicknamed the Light
Blues, the other the Crimson. One played a leading role in creating
soccer, the other changed the course of soccer in America.

The sport owes an enormous debt to Cambridge University. Although many of England's exclusive schools were playing a form of
the game in the early nineteenth century, it was Cambridge whose
rules helped form the framework for the modern game.

Eton, Winchester, Charterhouse, Westminster, Uppingham, Shrewsbury, and other elite public schools (what Americans would call private schools) tried to bring order to what was little more than a street

13

brawl centered around a ball by codifying rules. What those schools created, unfortunately, was a sporting version of the Tower of Babel as the lack of uniformity in the rules made it difficult if not impossible for the schools to play one another, while the expansion of rail transport in Britain during the era turned the prospect of interscholastic athletics into reality. The famous episode—or myth—at Rugby School in 1823 in which a student startled all by picking up the ball and running with it only underlined the challenge at hand. (William Webb Ellis was the young lad, and a plaque marking the spot notes that Ellis, "with a fine disregard for the rules of football as played in his time, first took the ball in his arms and ran with it, thus originating the distinctive feature of the rugby game.")

That began to change in October 1848 when the first widely accepted code, the so-called Cambridge Rules, was drafted at a meeting of fifteen schools at Cambridge's Trinity College called by John Charles Thring, a master at Uppingham School, and fellow Cambridge graduate Henry de Winton. Although English football had split into "dribbling" and "handling" camps, most of Cambridge's players happened to be graduates of prep schools that favored dribbling. The final rules were influenced by those of Harrow School, which by 1830 was playing an eleven-a-side game whose object it was to send the ball over a goal line between a pair of twelve-foot-high posts; the ball was moved with the feet, and hacking (kicking an opponent below the knee) was forbidden. Interestingly, the finished product at Trinity did not stipulate the number of players per team, and "barging" and catching were made legal. It did, however, forbid holding, pushing, tripping, and hacking; its version of offside closely resembled the modern offside; and a string serving as a crossbar was required on each goal. To the chagrin of soccer historians, an original copy of the "Laws of the University Foot Ball Club" has not survived.

The game still had a long way to go, but the Cambridge Rules formed the basis in 1856 for the Sheffield Club Rules, which helped introduce soccer to northern England. That influence resurfaced in 1862, when Thring concocted an updated football code he called "The Simplest Game" (aka the Uppingham Rules). In 1863 Cambridge revised its rules and addressed several basics, including size of the field (150 yards by 100 yards maximum), duration of game, number of participants (to be agreed on by the captains), corner kicks, and free kicks.

Weeks later, on October 26 at the Freemasons' Tavern on London's Great Queen Street, representatives from fourteen leading teams, schools, and clubs first met. After extensive debate over a series of meetings, the London Football Association was formed on December 8, with the Cambridge, Harrow School, and Eton College (1862) rules providing the basis for the original fourteen laws of what would become known as "Association Football." Representatives who favored handling and hacking—Blackheath School, Blackheath FC, and Perceval House of Blackheath—walked out and eventually formed the Rugby Union.

Ironically, no Cambridge representative was present when the seven remaining "dribbling game" parties approved the final rules.

It took years for the country to be unified under the new code, but a major hurdle was cleared in 1877 when the London F.A. and the rival Sheffield F.A. in the north agreed on a common set of rules. Meanwhile, the Factory Act of 1850 ended the six-day, seventy-two-hour workweek, thus creating the weekend and paving the way for the spread of soccer beyond the privileged old boys of Marlborough and Cheltenham to the average British mill worker, clerk, and tradesman. The first (unofficial) international match—England versus Scotland—was played in 1870, and the first English F.A. Cup, a knockout competition for clubs, followed two years later. By the time the first English League championship was played in 1888–89, British engineers, miners, railroad workers, sailors, and other emissaries of Queen Victoria were introducing soccer in the Americas, Asia, Africa, and the Middle East.

Harvard, meanwhile, was already introducing a form of soccer across the pond with its annual mass football game between freshmen and sophomores that came to be known as "Bloody Monday," an event in which pummeling an opponent was more important than the whereabouts of the ball. The battles, which were first mentioned in a humorous poem published in 1827, predated the appearance of football-like games in neighboring colleges such as Yale, Brown, and Amherst. Harvard administrators put an end to "Bloody Monday" in 1860, and the game wouldn't reappear there until 1871. Nevertheless, Harvard's version of soccer/rugby helped make the Boston area a hotbed of the sport and inspired the formation in 1862 of the first soccer club outside Britain, the Oneida Football Club. A collection of high schoolers, Oneida FC, which called the Boston Common its home, went undefeated before the side was disbanded in 1865.

All this activity paved the way for the first intercollegiate football game, played by Rutgers and Princeton on November 6, 1869, in New Brunswick, New Jersey. The winner was to be the first side to score six goals, and the Scarlet Knights of Rutgers defeated the Tigers of Princeton, 6–4. In this more genteel time Rutgers' student-athletes met their Princeton counterparts at the railway station, escorted them to the playing field, and hosted them later in a postmatch banquet. (Although the Rutgers-Princeton game has since been regarded by the NCAA and in other quarters as the first collegiate gridiron football game, the rules that day were based on those of the London F.A.)

Yale, Cornell, Columbia, and other Ivy League schools played one another in this form of soccer for the next six years. But Harvard, swept up in the Muscular Christian movement of the times, held out for the "Boston Game," a more "manly" hybrid that combined dribbling with carrying the ball.

Out of this confusion would come a chain of events that would alter the course of soccer in the United States. In 1873 representatives of Yale, Princeton, Columbia, and Rutgers met in New York (Harvard was invited but declined to attend) and embraced a set of rules resembling those of the London F.A. That autumn Yale, whose own version of Bloody Monday, the Annual Rush, had centered on dribbling, defeated a team of graduates from England's Eton School in a match played with Eton's preferred eleven players to a side and one point for each goal scored (the margin of victory was 2–1). The dribbling game's future in the Colonies seemed assured.

Harvard, however, looked outside the country for an opponent who favored the handling game and found one in McGill University of Montreal. Harvard met McGill in a two-game series, the first played under Boston Game rules, the second played with an oval ball under Rugby Union rules. The Crimson, predictably, won the opener, 3–0, but despite being held to a scoreless deadlock in the second, the Muscular Christians of Harvard were sold on this strain of football and turned their backs on the dribbling game for good.

In 1875 Harvard agreed to meet Yale in football and demanded that the game include rugby-like tries, touchdowns, and the like. Although the Elis lost the contest, it reversed course and took up this new form of football. A year later, Harvard, its prestige and influence irresistible, was joined by Yale, Princeton, and Columbia at the Massasoit Convention in forming the Intercollegiate Football Association (IFA), which was based on Rugby Union rules. Soccer, as BMOC in America, suddenly was doomed.

The rugby football played in the IFA and on other college campuses soon morphed into a game viewed by the media as a reflection of the healthy, hearty, rough-and-tumble character of the United States. In 1880 Yale coach Walter Camp pushed through several rule changes that further distanced the IFA game from anything played before. In a young nation seeking an identity separate from the Old World, this football was now uniquely American, and one thing it was *not* was English. Just as there couldn't possibly be a connection between English cricket and the game of baseball (see the tall tale of Abner Doubleday, who in 1839 created our national pastime from whole cloth in Cooperstown, New York), gridiron football had to be a wholly American invention, and it would be. Now sportswriters trumpeted the increasingly violent American football as an improvement over both English soccer and, after several more rule changes, rugby.

(Ironically, Harvard's championing of rugby probably allowed soccer to live to fight another day on American soil. Had soccer been the IFA sport of choice, it might have been soon morphed out of existence. "In the colleges, rugby was soon swallowed up by the Americanization process," wrote longtime U.S. soccer columnist Paul Gardner in the book he titled—with a nod to Thring—*The Simplest Game.* "Within ten years a stream of changes had produced a new sport—football—that bore only the slightest likeness to rugby. Soccer, surely, would have suffered the same fate, producing heaven knows what kind of hybrid sports monster.")

Soccer, the sport that was sweeping the rest of the world, was consigned in the United States to the shadows. It would be played from the late 1880s until well into the next century in industrial centers by immigrant Brits and Irish, the huddled masses from continental Europe, Latin American transplants, and the occasional open-minded native son. Gridiron football, meanwhile, would flourish as the sport played by the finest young men from our prestigious institutes of higher learning.

Ironically, Harvard, which touched off the gridiron football boom, helped soccer gain a second life on U.S. college campuses. On April 1, 1905, the Crimson played Haverford College of Pennsylvania in the first official collegiate soccer match in history, losing, 1–0. (A championship featuring several Ivy League schools, the Intercollegiate Soccer Football League, made its debut that year; Harvard managed to finish first in 1912–13 and 1913–14, but not again until 1930.)

Also in 1905 eighteen young men were killed playing football, and an appalled President Theodore Roosevelt (Harvard class of 1880) threatened to ban the gridiron game, thus prompting its backers to scramble to create what would become the National Collegiate Athletic Association. In this atmosphere soccer was being viewed in a better light, and it began to be promoted in some quarters as the safer alternative for America's young men. But that campaign only helped paint the kicking game as a benign exercise for physical education classes rather than a sport to be taken seriously. Already damned as an ethnic pastime, soccer became regarded in the United States as a game for those not tough enough for the manful, masculine, and manly game of gridiron football.

Soccer, as an interscholastic sport, never truly recovered. Ever so slowly, colleges and universities across the country added the non-revenue sport, but it wasn't until 1959 that the NCAA organized its first national soccer championship.

Today, soccer is surprisingly similar at Cambridge and Harvard universities.

In England, Cambridge and some seventy other schools field teams, but the rise of professionalism eclipsed the collegiate game long ago. Nevertheless, Cambridge proudly points to an early history in which it produced forty-one English National Team members.

Cambridge plays before crowds in the hundreds. Highlight of the season is the annual "Varsity Match" with traditional rival Oxford University, a series that dates from 1874. That showdown is part of a full day of sports; the marquee events are the soccer game, played at cavernous Wembley Stadium, and the University Boat Race, which takes place just outside Wembley on the Thames.

Harvard, too, plays soccer before modest crowds, and its Oxford is Yale, the ancient enemy. The Crimson soccer team has won zero national championships to the gridiron football team's seven, although the first of those came in 1890 and the last in 1919. Meanwhile, Harvard has reached the NCAA Division I soccer semifinals four times since 1968, not bad for a school that offers no athletic scholarships.

Why Soccer Fields Aren't as Long as a Landing Strip

What if certain changes had never been made in certain sports? Imagine gridiron football played without the forward pass and stuck with a field marked like, well, a gridiron. Or baseball, with eight balls for a walk and runners retired when plunked by a thrown ball. Or basketball, with someone scaling a ladder to fish the ball out of a peach basket over and over.

Although soccer's rules have always been relatively simple, the sport has undergone several important changes since 1863, when representatives of England's leading clubs met in London to form the Football Association and draw up the original Laws of the Game.

The very first rule, or Law, involved the size of the field: "The maximum length of the ground shall be 200 yards, the maximum breadth shall be 100 yards . . . ."

Two hundred yards?

Fortunately, the rule eventually was amended to the still outrageous 130 yards maximum by 100 (or a minimum 100 yards by 50). Most professional matches are played on fields that approximate World Cup specifications: 115 yards by 75 yards.

Other key changes through the years that seem to have been inspired by, well, common sense:

- Tape is used to create a crossbar, at a height of eight feet, in 1865.
- A player is declared offside if he is closer to the opponent's goal line than three opposing players when the ball is played to him, in 1870.
- The fair catch (a ball caught on the fly after being played by an opponent) and all other handling is eliminated, in 1866.

- The number of players per side is set at eleven and the length of a match is fixed at ninety minutes, in 1896.
- The direct free kick awarded for major infractions and the "advantage clause" (no harm, no foul) are introduced, in 1903.
- The offside rule is amended to reduce the number of opposing players between the attacking player and the opposition's goal line from three to two, in 1925.
- Substitutions are first sanctioned for consenting national teams, in 1932.
- A player is required to play a goal kick beyond the penalty area before it can be played again (preventing a player from tapping a goal kick to his goalkeeper), in 1937.
- The goalkeeper is not allowed to handle a ball in his penalty area if it is intentionally played to him by the foot of a teammate or thrown in to him, in 1990.

When There Was as Much Action off the Field as On

The sidelines on a soccer field are properly known as touchlines, and a ball that has crossed a touchline out of bounds is said to be "in touch."

The name seems to make no sense, unless one goes back to the first Laws of the Game. According to the original Law V: "When the ball is in touch the first player who touches it shall kick or throw it from the point on the boundary line where it left the ground, in a direction at right angles with the boundary line." In other words, when a ball crossed a sideline, the team whose player was first to touch the errant ball was awarded possession and allowed to restart play.

Two problems. First, no doubt spectators were in danger whenever players from both sides came flying off the field in pursuit of a loose ball. Second, there was nothing preventing a partisan spectator from doing what he or she could to make sure that the loose ball was first touched by a player from his or her favored side. In 1895 the rule was changed, giving possession to the "team opposite to that of the player who last touched it."

There also was the matter of the restart, made with a throw. Back then, the throw could be a one-handed heave. All was well and good until, eventually, the right-angle aspect was dropped. At that point the throw-in could go in any direction on the field—perfect for the likes of English international William Gunn, who, it was said, could hurl the unwieldy and heavy round ball of the day the entire length of the field. Gunn, who represented England three times in 1884, was reduced to mere mortal status in 1882 with the rule change calling for two-handed throw-ins from behind the head, the present-day method.

Native Americans as Soccer Pioneers

The birthplace of modern soccer is, of course, England, while the United States until recently has been known primarily for its indifference, even hostility, to the sport.

Nevertheless, the original Americans may have been playing a version of soccer long before the nineteenth century, when the young gentlemen attending the elite schools, colleges, and universities of England began to hone the rules of what would become the football we know today.

After the Pilgrims dropped anchor at Plymouth Rock in 1620, they soon found the local Indians playing a game called Pasuckquakkohowog (loosely translated, "They gather to play football"). Pasuckquakkohowog was played during low tide on the broad beaches of what were later named Cape Cod, Lynn, and Revere, Massachusetts.

The playing field stretched a mile long and a half-mile wide, with goal posts at each end. The ball, made of deer hair encased in deerskin, was about the size of a handball. Teams of thirty to forty men battled for an entire day, sometimes two. Injuries were common, so players disguised themselves with paint and ornaments to keep retaliation to a minimum. Gambling was central to the proceedings, and teams often played for prizes such as otter skins, beaver skins, or wampum.

Wrote an early area settler, William Wood, in his *New England Prospect*, in 1634: "Apparently, the tribes of New England were the only Indians on the continent of North America who played this type of ball game. [In fact, another English settler, William Strachey, found the Indians in Virginia playing another football-like game, Pahsaheman, near the Jamestown settlement, in 1610.] Usually, the Indians played football during the summer months with a varying number of players involved, depending upon the circumstances. Village played village and a large amount of property changed hands, depending upon the outcome of the game. Surprisingly, there was little quarrelling."

Pasuckquakkohowog, however, could only have drawn frowns from most newcomers, who had no tolerance for sport, the theater, or other forms of entertainment. Wrote Philip Stubbes in his 1583 pamphlet "Anatomie of Abuses in the Realme of England," "Lord, remove these exercises from the Sabaoth. Any exercise which withdraweth from godliness either upon the Sabaoth or on any other day, is wicked and to be forbidden." That would cover all seven days of the week.

Despite the relatively sporting nature of Pasuckquakkohowog, Roger Williams, the founder of the Rhode Island colony, was not impressed: "I feared the distractions of the games, and would not attend them in order that I might not countenance and partake of their folly after I saw the evil in them."

Ironically, while Williams saw evil in the game played by what many settlers considered savages, the version of football believed to have been first played on the British Isles, in the third century, by the Anglo-Saxons centered on the severed head of a vanquished Danish prince. Only a myth, but nevertheless . . .

Other primitive versions of soccer include the following:

Tsu Chu. The earliest known version of a football-type game, Tsu Chu was first played in China's Shandong province in 2500 BC, also transcribed Tsu'Chu, Tsu-Chu, and Cuju.

Tsu chu later was known to have been played during the Ts'in Dynasty (255 to 206 BC) in front of the royal palace as part of the birthday celebration for Huang-Ti, China's renowned "Yellow Emperor." It was highly popular during the Han Dynasty (206 BC to AD 220) and even played by one of the emperors, Han Wu Di. Tsu chu literally received a bounce during the end of the Tang Dynasty (AD 618 to 906) with the introduction of a ball with an air-filled bladder, and it enjoyed a revival during the Song Dynasty (AD 960 to 1279), when it spread from the wealthy to the average Chinese.

The object of the game was to send a ball of leather or brocade silk through a one-foot gap in a net stretched between thirty-foot bamboo poles. Hence the name tsu ("kicking a ball") chu ("ball stuffed with feathers"). Teams of six players each were allowed to use their feet, chest, back, and shoulders to play the ball.

The Chinese military played a form of tsu chu as part of its training;

the game was seen as the ideal cool-down for horse soldiers after a long ride. Confucian scholar Liu Xin (circa 50 BC to AD 23) referred to Taju bingshi ("Football strengthens the fighting power of soldiers") in his seven teachings. Tsu chu players trained to perform before the royal court were the world's first professional football players, and the tsu chu organizations set up in major cities, known as Qi Yun She or Yuan She, could be considered the first football clubs.

Tsu chu faded during the Ming Dynasty (1368 to 1644) and soon was all but forgotten.

Notable innovations: propelling a ball into a goal without the use of hands; juggling and general skill on the ball; set number of players; referees; and an assistant official.

Kemari. Introduced to Japan by China during the seventh century BC and played until AD 200 Kemari, also known as Kenatt, involved teams of eight players who, positioned in a circle, kept a deerskin ball—nine to ten inches in diameter and filled with sawdust—from touching the ground for as long as possible.

Goals were scored by sending the ball through a pair of fifteen-foot-high bamboo stakes. The field was rectangular, and each corner was marked by a sapling of pine, maple, willow, or cherry. Participants wore colorful kimonos, formal headgear, and special shoes. A game more ceremonial than competitive, kemari, played in places such as the Asukadera Temple, was an important part of religious and political life.

It is believed that Chinese tsu chu players and their Japanese kemari counterparts battled in 50 BC, which would make that meeting the first international match in football history.

A later version of the Japanese game, Kemari Asobi, was popular among the samuri into the 1400s; by the Edo era (1603 to 1867) it was being played by both commoners and wealthy landowners. Twenty-minute matches were contested on courts about fourteen meters wide with a ball measuring twenty-two centimeters in diameter.

For reasons unknown, kemari lost its appeal in the 1800s, although Emperor Meiji kept the game alive with the founding of the Kemari Preservation Society, an effort to maintain Japan's noble court traditions.

Kemari today is played as part of New Year's celebrations (Kemari

Hajime, or "First Kick") and at an annual festival at the ancient capital of Nara.

Notable innovation: soccer-like goals.

Episkyros/Harpastum. Episkyros was a team game vaguely similar to rugby played in Greece as early as 600 BC whose objective was to throw a ball over the heads of the opposing players and ultimately force all of them over their own goal line. The play centered on catching and throwing, not kicking. Harpastum, a similar ball game played in the second century AD by the Romans throughout their empire, including Britain and France, appears to be a form of dodge ball.

Notable innovations, via harpastum: teams of twenty-seven players each attempting to move a ball up and down a field rather than a small court; a center line dividing the field into halves.

Polynesian games. Pacific islanders were among the first to play ball with the feet and hands, although the genesis of their games has not been pinpointed. In addition to some Polynesians, tribes of the Philippine archipelago, the Maoris, were enthusiastic players of these games.

Notable innovation: use of a pig bladder for a ball (islanders also used oranges and coconuts).

Aqsaqtuk. Date of origin unknown, this game was played by the Eskimos of Alaska and Canada for several hundred years. Matches were held on snow and ice and involved kicking a ball stuffed with grass, caribou hair, and moss through goals situated several hundred yards apart. A game began with opposing teams facing one another in parallel lines; the players attempted to kick the ball through the other team's line, then toward its goal. According to Alaskan legend, one match was played between neighboring villages with the goals separated by ten miles. Men and women played together, and teams sometimes pitted married people against singles.

Notable innovation: the concept of defense—the object of aqsaqtuk was to keep the ball away from one's own goal.

Pokyah. Traced to the seventh century and played by the Maya, pokyah is similar to games played by the Aztecs (tlachtli) and Zapotecs (taladzi).

The pokyah playing area was a court forty to fifty feet long that was shaped like an *I*, with a stone or wooden ring, mounted vertically, at each end. Goals were scored by shooting a hard rubber ball through the opponent's ring using only the feet, legs, hips, or elbows. Players were dressed in colorful costumes, headdresses, and leather protection for the hips, groin, thighs, and elbows. The game was played under the supervision of the king and high priests. The most important pokyah court was at Chichen Itza, the Mayan ceremonial center in Yucatan.

Variations of pokyah spread as far as Arizona and Honduras before the game came to a halt with the arrival of the Spanish conquistadors. All versions were an important part of religious life. The Aztecs' was best known for the fate of the members of the losing team: death at a sacrificial altar.

Notable innovation: the rubber ball (the rubber used to make the ball eventually was introduced to Europe by the returning Spaniards).

La Choule. This was a mass football game that came to Britain via the Norman Conquest in 1066. There is scant evidence of football-like games credited variously to the Romans, Anglo-Saxons, Celts, and other residents of the British Isles in the first millennium. La choule, however, inspired the first literary reference to a football game, by William FitzStephen in 1175. Wrote FitzStephen, the clerk to Thomas Becket, archbishop of Canterbury, in his *History of London,* after observing youngsters playing a Shrove Tuesday match: "After lunch all the youth of the city go out into the fields to take part in a ball game. The students of each school have their own ball; the workers from each city craft are also carrying their balls. Older citizens, fathers, and wealthy citizens come on horseback to watch their juniors competing, and to relive their own youth vicariously: you can see their inner passions aroused as they watch the action and get caught up in the fun being had by the carefree adolescents."

La choule (believed to come from the normal verb *chouler*—"to jostle or fall over one another"—in the Breton or Norman languages) was probably adopted by the Normans during their earlier invasion of Brittany and came to be an important part of Shrovetide, a pre-Lent celebration. The field of play was often the distance between neighboring towns, and mobs of men and boys, unfettered by formal rules, attempted to score by advancing an inflated pig's bladder via the hands and feet to a goal—sometimes a landmark in the enemy village, such as a church balcony. The result was utter chaos as the participants smashed through fences, forded streams, trampled crops and hedgerows, caused livestock to scatter, and, as the goal came into view, shattered shop windows.

Many attempts were made in Britain to snuff out la choule, the first by King Edward II in 1314, to no avail. In 1389 King Richard issued a royal decree forbidding the playing of la choule, or foot balle, on the grounds that it was luring his subjects away from the patriotic and practical sport of archery. Invading hoards lurked everywhere at the time, and the number of available defenders had been decimated by the Black Death; the reasoning went that it was more effective to shoot the enemy with an arrow than to tackle him.

The popularity of what could be called early soccer/rugby continued to grow in Britain, and it received two boosts to its image, first in 1620 when the first matches were organized by the students of Cambridge University, then in 1681 when King Charles II sanctioned the sport for his servants.

As the game became more civilized, mass football died out, and by the early 1800s the exclusive schools of England and the gentlemen sporting clubs they fostered would take the game into the modern era. Nevertheless, the game known as la choule is still played in Ashbourne in Derbyshire and other pockets of Britain to mark Shrove Tuesday.

Notable innovation: a soccer-like game as contact sport and public spectacle.

Giuoco del Calcio Fiorentino. Played by the young among the aristocracy in Florence, Venice, and elsewhere in Renaissance Italy, marking the period between the Epiphany and Lent, the game involved kicking and carrying a ball and was markedly more organized than la choule. Players dressed in brightly colored silken livery (the first true uniforms, perhaps?) engaged in a football game in which it was permissible to kick an opponent or deliver a blow below the belt.

Born as a form of military training, the Italian game made its most notable appearance in 1530. With the troops of the Holy Roman Emperor, Charles V, on the Florentine doorstep, the locals organized a calcio match as a show of defiance. Fifty years later, Count Giovanni de'Bardi di Vernio penned *Discorso sopra l'giuoco del Calcio Fiorentino,* possibly the first written rules of any football game. Calcio Fiorentino ("Florentine Kickball") died out by 1739 but was revived in 1930, when it was played to commemorate the notoriously spiteful match of four hundred years earlier. The game continues to be played in Florence for the benefit of tourists.

As for Calcio Fiorentino's contribution to the evolution of soccer, fortunately its most distinctive original feature—a decapitated human head of an enemy serving as the ball—did not become an innovation.

Soccer by the Numerals

At first glance the numerals on soccer jerseys are as simple as 1-2-3. There are eighteen to twenty-two players on most rosters, and the numbers run as high as the midtwenties.

In soccer's early days in Britain, players simply wore colored caps so that participants and spectators could tell the sides apart, a practice abandoned in the latter part of the nineteenth century as colored uniforms became the norm.

In 1933 England experimented with uniform numerals at the F.A. Cup final to better identify the individual players, and six years later the numbers were made mandatory throughout the English league. The attack-minded 2-3-5 formation was in vogue (two fullbacks, three halfbacks, five forwards), so numbers were assigned to players based on their positions, reading right to left as the players faced upfield: (1) goalkeeper, (2) right fullback, (3) left fullback, (4) right halfback, (5) center halfback, (6) left halfback, (7) outside right forward, (8) inside right, (9) center forward, (10) inside left, (11) outside left forward.

Rather than keep each player in the same uniform throughout a season, though, the jerseys were handed out to the players prior to a match based on the starting lineup. Thus, if a player moved between right halfback and inside right forward from game to game, he'd wear No. 4 one day and No. 8 on another; the longtime substitute who finally won a job as starting center half would turn in his No. 12, 13, or 14 jersey and get No. 5.

Under this system, you couldn't tell the players with or without a program. While the system helped spectators immediately identify the positions of the players, it did nothing to help them with their names. Fans were expected to be familiar with the entire squad and pay close attention when the starting lineups were announced and, years later, when substitutions were made. The 1-through-11 system was finally undone when formations evolved from the 2-3-5 to the more defensive 4-4-2 or 4-3-3, and the No. 8 who used to be the right winger in one formation became the inside left halfback, or midfielder. Within time, players were wisely assigned numbers for the season, not the afternoon. It came just in time, because Holland's introduction in the early 1970s of "Total Soccer," the approach that freed players from rigid positions and demanded that they play interchangeable roles, ended the era for good.

Holland's solution at the 1974 World Cup was simply to assign its numbers in alphabetical order, from Ruud Geels, No. 1, to Harry Vos, No. 22, with goalkeeper Jan Jongbloed sporting No. 8. The lone exception was the exceptional Johan Cruyff, who would have worn No. 1 but was allowed to don the No. 14 he made famous while playing for his club, Ajax Amsterdam. Argentina did likewise, although starting goalkeeper Daniel Carnevali was given No. 1; the alphabetical order started with forward Hugo Ayala, No. 2.

Today, the tradition of the original numbering system continues on an informal basis, with a team's regular defenders often wearing low numbers and the attackers wearing slightly higher numbers. But the goalkeeper might sport No. 0 or 00 or, if he is the backup, the highest number on the squad, such as No. 22. Some starters could have numbers in the high teens or low twenties. As for the player with the No. 10 made famous by a certain inside left—Pelé—it is likely that he's not the team's goal scorer but its playmaker, a central midfielder.

Things since Holland's "Total Soccer" haven't been the same on the national team level, not to mention the club level. Today, the player/position/number system has gotten downright weird. Some examples:

FC Porto goalkeeper Vítor Baía, No. 99
Chivas Guadalajara's Adolfo Bautista, No. 100
Aberdeen striker Hicham "Zero" Zerouali, No. 0
Inter Milan striker Iván Zamorano, No. 1+8 (assigned to the Chilean star after Brazilian superstar Ronaldo was signed in 1997 and given his customary No. 9, Zamorano's old number)

Bayern Munich defender Bixente Lizarazu, No. 69 (the French standout was born in 1969, stands 169 centimeters tall, and weighs 69 kilograms)

The First Celebrity Player: Henry VIII

Soccer's celebrity friends range from Michael Schumacher to Placido Domingo and Rod Stewart. Both President George H. W. Bush and 2004 presidential candidate John Kerry (ironically, a right winger on the field) played for Yale University. Its first name enthusiast, however, was King Henry VIII.

In 1526 the English monarch, according to researchers, ordered the royal cordwainer, Cornelius Johnson, to make him a pair of hand-stitched boots "to play football," according to the National Archives at Kew. The shoes cost four shillings (about $200 today) and were probably made of especially strong leather.

Concluded one historian, Dr. Maria Hayward of Southampton University, in 2004, "He wasn't a serious player. I don't think he would have played on a regular basis. I certainly don't think he was out there every Saturday."

Regardless of how often or how well Henry VIII played what was a wild and occasionally savage game, his participation marked a break in a long lineage of English and Scottish authorities who waged war against foot balle.

King Edward II was the first. In his 1314 ban in London of this unruly game, Edward proclaimed, "Forasmuch as there is great noise in the city caused by hustling over large balls from which many evils may arise which God forbid; we command and forbid, on behalf of the King, on pain of imprisonment, such game to be used in the city in the future."

A partial list of the prohibitions of foot balle, or la choule, by British authorities following Edward II's ban:

1331, 1349, and 1365, in London, by Edward III
1389, in London, by Richard I
1401, 1409, and 1410, in London, by Henry IV
1414, in London, by Henry V
1424, in Perth, by James I of Scotland
1450 and 1454, in Halifax, by James I of Scotland

1457, in Perth, by James II of Scotland
1467, in Leicester, by James II of Scotland
1471 and 1491, in Perth, by James III of Scotland
1474, 1477, and 1478, in London, by Edward IV
1488, in Leicester, by Edward IV
1491, by James IV of Scotland
1496, in London, by Henry VII

The reign of Henry VIII began in 1497, and after Henry's initial participation, he joined in with his own ban in 1540 in an effort to maintain the peace. Hayward notes that along with foot balle His Majesty also issued restrictions on carrying firearms and the playing of his beloved tennis, "neither of which would have applied to him, so it is not that contradictory. It is the old scenario of one rule [for] him and one for everyone else."

Official disapproval continued from 1570 until 1667, as the game was prohibited in Peebles and Shrewsbury as well as three more times in London and five times in Manchester. At Derby, the city fathers issued a number of bans between 1731 and 1841, finally invoking riot laws to give their efforts some teeth.

La choule finally was vanquished not by royal decree but by the spread of Puritanism, which frowned upon the game and other frivolous endeavors as threats to the peace on the Sabbath. Mob football, all but extinct by the seventeenth century, would not resurface until the early 1800s, when it was resurrected under a different guise by Britain's elite schools, which began to promote pastimes like football as beneficial to the mind, body, and spirit, as well a distraction from more base pursuits.

While Henry VIII may have been a soccer enthusiast, the Bard apparently was not.

Football makes an appearance in at least two of William Shakespeare's plays:

"Nor tripped neither, you base football player."—*King Lear*, Act I, Scene 4

"Am I so round with you as you with me, that like a football you do spurn* me thus? You spurn me hence, and he will spurn me hither:

*Spurn, in this instance, means to kick away.

If I last in this service, you must case me in leather."—*A Comedy of Errors*, Act II, Scene 1

This made Shakespeare either the world's first sportswriter or just soccer's first critic.

The Ageless Sir Stanley Matthews

Stanley Matthews never won a World Cup medal. He never scored more than a dozen goals in a season. Yet so great were his skills as a winger, so long was his reign, that Matthews was simply a legend, one of a small handful of players who would be named to anyone's all-time team.

Matthews, who in 1956 was voted the first-ever European Footballer of the Year at the age of forty-one, played in the English League for an incredible thirty seasons, retiring at age fifty.

Unlike American sports heroes such as gridiron football place-kicker George Blanda and baseball's knuckleball pitcher Phil Niekro, who beat the clock and plied their highly specialized trades well into their forties, Matthews's craft involved quickness, a calculated feint, a burst of speed. Typically, the unimposing Matthews would dribble to the corner flag, work his way toward the goalmouth, and suddenly loft the ball over the goalkeeper to the far post or scald a pass along the turf to a teammate crashing into the penalty area. Almost without fail, Matthews would sell his marker on a move to the left, only to dart to the right and past the man. Hence his nickname, "The Wizard of the Dribble." As time wore on, it was more and more likely that the defender he beat had been born after Matthews turned pro.

One of his contemporaries was the great Brazil defender Nilton Santos, who was famously put on his backside by a Matthews feint during a 4–2 England victory in a 1956 friendly. Matthews played a part in all four England goals that day against a Brazil side that Santos would help lead to its first World Cup crown two years later.

Matthews, born in 1915, signed his first pro contract in 1932, with Stoke City. After sixteen seasons Stoke, believing its star right winger was a mere mortal and close to retirement, transferred Matthews to Blackpool for $20,000. And it was with Blackpool that he experienced his greatest triumph.

The Matthews-led Seasiders lost both the 1948 and the 1951 English F.A. Cup finals, and when Blackpool reached the 1953 final against Bolton it appeared that all of England was rooting for Matthews in what would surely be his last stab at the brass ring. Bolton took a 3–1 lead into the final twenty-two minutes, but it only set up one of the greatest flourishes in soccer history. Matthews, then thirty-eight and with a receding hairline that made him look that much older, set up two goals, including Bill Perry's winner in the dying moments to spark Blackpool to an astonishing 4–3 triumph. Although "the Other Stan," star forward Stanley Mortensen, scored Blackpool's first three goals to become the first man to post a hat trick in an F.A. Cup final at Wembley, the game would forever be known as "the Matthews Final."

Matthews, who made his last international appearance in 1957 at age forty-two, returned to Stoke in 1961 and played until 1965. In his final game—the 709th of his league career—he scored the goal against Fulham that clinched the Potters' promotion to the first division. He was fifty years and five days. Later that year, he was knighted for "services to football," the first player so honored.

Sir Stan could credit his longevity on the soccer field in part to his father, Jack Matthews, an accomplished boxer known as "the Fighting Barber of Hanley." The elder Matthews imposed on his son a rigorous fitness regimen, one that included deep-breathing exercises at an open window on cold winter mornings. Jack's influence made Stan one of the game's most fitness-conscious players, a man who religiously set out on long-distance runs on the sands of Blackpool and fasted every Monday during the season.

Matthews, who retired to Malta, was a giant in England, but his fame could have been greater. He was at his peak during soccer's pretelevision age. He also lost seven good years to World War II, and he lost several starts for England immediately after the war to Tom Finney of Preston North End, another great right winger who was seven years Matthews's junior. (The committee that selected England teams in those days finally chose Finney to play left wing and Matthews right for a 1947 match against Portugal; England won, 10–0). Matthews also did not play for any of England's glamour clubs, and England's decision to shun FIFA in the 1930s and 1940s cost the world's greatest dribbler the opportunity to play in two of the first three World Cups. Nevertheless, his tremendous skills, longevity, and sportsmanship—he was never cautioned, let alone sent off—made him one of a kind.

Matthews died in 2000. His final tally over those remarkable thirty seasons was an unremarkable seventy-one goals for his clubs and a more impressive eleven goals in fifty-four games for England. But while goals decide games—and Matthews set them up by the bushel—soccer is mostly about what goes on between the end lines, where, in Matthews's case, the game was reduced to an attacking player, an uncertain defender, a gentle bump-bump of the ball, and a sudden, brilliant burst of speed.

Traffic Light Inspires Red, Yellow Cards

Red and yellow cards, introduced to soccer in the late 1960s and used to eject and caution millions of players since, were inspired by a traffic stop at a London intersection in 1966.

Longtime English referee Ken Aston, chief of officials for that year's World Cup, hosted by England, came up with the idea while sitting in his car, waiting for a light to change. "As I drove down Kensington High Street, the traffic light turned red," said Aston. "I thought, 'Yellow, take it easy; red, stop, you're off.'"

Earlier that day he was at Wembley Stadium for the infamously ill-tempered quarterfinal between England and Argentina, a match marred by several bookings (warnings) and the sending off of Argentine captain Antonio Rattin, who argued with West German referee Rudolf Kreitlein for ten minutes before taking his sweet time in leaving the field.

Aston also believed that many of the players booked that day didn't realize they had been cautioned. In fact, newspapers later reported that Bobby Charlton and Jack Charlton had been booked, but Kreitlein did not clearly indicate that the English brothers had been admonished.

Aston's cards, which FIFA eventually approved, made their debut at the 1968 Olympic soccer tournament in Mexico City, and players worldwide who've run afoul of the referee have been seeing red—and yellow—ever since.

Only five yellow cards and zero reds were shown at the 1970 World Cup in Mexico, but at West Germany '74 the dubious distinction of earning the first red in World Cup history went to midfielder Carlos Caszely of Chile, who was sent off by Turkish referee Dogan Babacan in the sixty-seventh minute of the Group 1 opener in Berlin for kicking West Germany's Berti Vogts.

The tightly packed Chileans lost that day, 1–0, on a long-range bomb by Paul Breitner in the seventeenth minute, but the visitors could take some solace in the news that greeted referee Babacan later that day: while his wife and daughter in Istanbul watched the match on a neighbor's television, the Babacan family home was burglarized.

Red and yellow cards, which incidentally weren't incorporated into the Laws of the Game until 1992, were only the best known of Aston's innovations and ideas. In 1966 he instituted the practice of appointing the senior linesman to take over if the referee is unable to continue and proposed that the air pressure of the ball (600-1,100 grams per square centimeter at sea level) be spelled out in the Laws of the Game. And in 1974 he introduced the numbered board held up by the fourth official during a substitution to indicate which players are moving on and off the field.

It was Aston again who proposed changes to the linesman's flags to improve their visibility, and he introduced the black referee uniform, featuring white cuffs and collar, that became standard issue worldwide during the latter part of the twentieth century. He also tried to introduce white shoes for referees, believing it made the referee easier to pick out by players focused on a ball on the ground. He planned their debut for his last match, the 1963 English F.A. Cup final, but the F.A. rejected the idea, and Aston wore his white shoes only during noncompetitive matches. Another Aston idea that landed in the dustbin: settling a match tied after overtime by awarding the win to the side with the fewer ejections, cautions, and fouls committed.

Aston died in 2001 at age eighty-six. A schoolteacher by profession, he devoted considerable time late in his life to the improvement of refereeing in America, and in 1997 he was appointed a Member of the British Empire for "services to U.S. football."

The First Night Match, 1878

Night soccer has been around almost as long as the modern game itself, replete with primitive illumination and a whitewashed ball.

Although soccer after dark didn't become common in Britain until the 1920s, the first match played under floodlights was staged October 14, 1878, at Bramall Lane, Sheffield, England, between two selections from the Sheffield Football Association.

Four banks of lights, each with the power of eight thousand candles, were mounted on thirty-foot poles around the field. Two Siemens dynamo engines, one behind each goal, supplied the power.

A crowd of twenty thousand—a world record at the time—turned out, firing the imagination of club directors everywhere. The English F.A. didn't sanction floodlit games until 1887, however, and repeat performances were few and far between in Britain. One such occasion was a game played Christmas night in 1893 between host Glasgow Celtic and Clyde.

Hungary, Part I: Match of the Century

There have been more unlikely upsets in the history of soccer, but none had greater repercussions than the match that turned the sport on its ear more than fifty years ago: England 3, Hungary 6, on November 25, 1953, before a full house of one hundred thousand in London in a mere friendly that's still called the "Match of the Century" in Hungary.

Since inventing modern soccer in the middle of the nineteenth century, the English had been de facto kings of the game, even though they had agreed to play in just one World Cup to that point, in 1950, where they crashed in the first round, thanks in part to a humiliating 1–0 upset loss to the United States.

Safely back at home, they deigned to take on the team known as the "Magic Magyars" at Wembley Stadium. Playing in an international tournament in far-off Brazil during the English close season (or off-season) was one thing; putting the latest European challenger in its place on home ground was another.

This was no pretender, however. Hungary had reached the 1938 World Cup final and played well in a 4–2 loss to defending champion Italy. The Hungarians went 11-3-8 during the upheaval of World War II, then hit their stride beginning in 1950, as they reeled off a 50-1-7 mark—including an international-record twenty-nine-game winning streak and 215 goals scored—before the team was left in pieces by the 1956 Hungarian Revolution. They also captured the gold medal at the 1952 Helsinki Olympics and came to England with nineteen wins and three ties in their previous twenty-two matches.

That the Hungarians emerged from the players' tunnel at Wembley wearing strange, lightweight boots, cut below the ankle, should have made the English curious, if not concerned. They also lined up in coach Gusztáv Sebes's more progressive 4-2-4 formation to counter the English's conventional 2-3-5 (the old "W-M" system). For England, its record of never having lost at home to an opponent from continental Europe was about to end.

Hungary took the lead within sixty seconds through withdrawn center forward Nandor Hidegkuti, and the Magic Magyars' ninety-minute clinic in ball movement and positional interchange was on. Though England equalized on a goal by Jackie Sewell, the Hungarians shot ahead, 4–1, within twenty-eight minutes thanks to another strike by Hidegkuti and two by Ferenc Puskás, the first one of the most impressive ever scored at Wembley. Stan Mortenson allowed the English to hope against hope with a goal in the thirty-eighth, but József Bozsik upped the Hungarian lead to 5–2 five minutes after halftime, and Hidegkuti applied the clincher in the fifty-third. Alf Ramsey scored a consolation goal for England from the penalty spot in the fifty-seventh.

Hungarians would've loved to have seen it, but there was no television in the country at the time. To prove it wasn't a fluke, Hungary flattened England, 7–1, in the return match in Budapest the following May.

But while those twin humiliations forced England and the rest of the world to scramble to adjust to a totally new approach to the game, the not-so-distant future belonged to the English, who won the 1966 World Cup.

Hungary stormed into the 1954 World Cup in Switzerland, where it reached the final against West Germany, a team it had humbled, 8–3, in the first round. Despite taking a 2–0 lead after just eight minutes, Hungary tumbled, 3–2, in one of the greatest cup upsets in history, and the Hungarians would never again get within touching distance of the cup. The defeat ignited riots back in Hungary, and the players, fearing punishment from the communist government, had to be talked into returning home.

Two years later thousands fled during the prodemocracy uprising, including the heart of the Hungarian team, Puskás, Bozsik, and Zoltan Czibor, all of whom landed in Spain. Among those left behind during the 1956 Hungarian Revolution was goalkeeper Gyula Grosics, who was accused of spying and placed under house arrest for thirteen months while the secret police investigated the bogus charges. Grosics published a book on the team in 1963, but censors reduced it by some fifty pages by removing all mention of the players who fled during the revolution.

Worse still, the Hungarian National Youth Team was on tour during the revolt and simply dispersed, costing the country its next generation of Magic Magyars.

Hungarian soccer would never recover. It would eventually settle among the lower ranks of Europe. The national team bowed out in the first round of the 1958 World Cup and reached the quarter-finals in 1962 and 1966, then failed to survive the opening rounds of the 1978, 1982, and 1986 World Cups. It hasn't been back since. Its greatest club feats were Ferencváros' triumph in the 1965 UEFA Cup and semifinal appearances in the European Cup by Vasas Budapest (1958), Vasas ETO Györ (1965), and Ujpest Dózsa (1974).

The victory at Wembley, however, will remain a burst of sunshine for a generation of Hungarians who lived in the gray world ruled by Stalinist dictator Mátyás Rákosi.

The people of Budapest still patronize the "6–3" wine bar in Budapest, where the walls are graced with photos of Puskás and Hidegkuti. Hungarians also set a postcommunist box-office record with 6–3, a movie not about the game but about the everyday lives of ordinary people who were glued to the radio in 1953 for a remarkable afternoon of soccer.

Hungary, Part II: The Miracle of Berne

One of the most popular movies screened in Germany in 2003 was a film that captured a brief, bright moment in the country's long road back from the shame of Nazi atrocities and the humiliation of defeat in World War II.

Das Wunder von Bern (*The Miracle of Berne*) recounted the triumph of the then–West Germany at the 1954 World Cup in Switzerland, an unlikely victory that some historians credit with marking the beginning of the country's "Economic Miracle."

Das Wunder tells the story of the friendship between an eleven-year-old boy from Essen and star West German international winger Helmut Rahn, who becomes the youngster's father figure until his real father returns home after a decade in a Russian POW camp. In the tear-jerking finale, father and son limp to Berne in a borrowed car and see Rahn, recalled to the national team just before the World Cup, score the winning goal.

Among those unabashedly admitting to getting choked up while watching the film were Chancellor Gerhard Schroeder, who attended the premier, and German National Team coach Rudi Völler, born six years after the Miracle of Berne, who viewed it three times.

Director Sönke Wortmann could have gone without the father-son plot device, however, and elicited the same emotional reaction from his audience. The story of the victory was sufficiently dramatic.

Germany fielded solid but not dominant national teams in the years before World War II, the high point being an unexpected third-place finish at the 1934 World Cup in Italy. The 1938 World Cup was a disappointment: a first-round elimination at the hands of Switzerland (1–1 and, in a replay, 4–2) despite the addition of four Austrian stars following the German annexation of that country three months earlier. Despite the war, the national team continued to play through 1942 with a string of friendlies against conquered and neutral nations, and the annual German Cup survived to 1943. But the devastation of the war, the division of the country into East and West, and the two Germanys' ouster from FIFA in 1946 left the game there at a standstill.

Undeterred, both Germanys were playing separate national league schedules by 1948, and soon FIFA readmitted both back into the fold (the West in 1950, the East in 1952).

The West had always boasted the strongest clubs in prewar Germany, and it was that talent pool that lifted West Germany into the 1954 World Cup in Switzerland. There, the West Germans and the rest of the field were supposed to bow before Hungary, the juggernaut that was undefeated (23-0-4) over the previous four years.

West Germany had the misfortune of being grouped with Hungary for the first round, and when the two sides met in Basle, the "Magic Magyars," behind four goals by Sandor Kocsis, rolled to an 8–3 win and clinched first place in Pool 2.

The defeat was deceiving. Sepp Herberger, who had coached Nazi Germany since 1936 and continued on as West German boss, studied the tournament's quirky format, saw a clear path to the semifinal, and took it. By making seven changes from the side that topped Turkey, 4–1, in its opener and sending a weakened team out to absorb the pounding at the hands of the Hungarians, Herberger avoided the formidable Brazil and got the quarterfinal matchup he wanted, against the weaker Yugoslavia. West Germany beat the Yugoslavs, 2–0, then crushed Austria in the semifinal, 6–1.

West Germany's opponent in the final would be Hungary, marking the first time that two teams met twice in the same World Cup. The Hungarians had the much more challenging path to the championship match. The Magyars first eliminated Brazil, 4–2, in one of the ugliest games in World Cup history. They then beat defending champion Uruguay by the same score on two headed goals by Kocsis in the second overtime period in a semifinal regarded as Hungary's finest performance and a match worthy of a final.

Although Herberger fielded his best possible lineup for the title decider, the Hungarians, who scored a staggering twenty-five goals in their first four matches, were clear favorites. The crowd of sixty thousand at Wankdorf Stadium anticipated a comfortable victory after star striker Ferenc Puskás scored on a counterattack in the sixth minute and midfielder Zoltan Czibor ran onto a poor back pass by West German defender Werner Kohlmeyer and doubled the lead two minutes later.

What happened next has been blamed by observers on Hungarian overconfidence, a steady rain that left the ball heavy and slowed the skillful Hungarians, and/or the overall ineffectiveness of stubborn captain Puskás, who insisted on playing despite an ankle injury—courtesy of West German defender Werner Liebrich's two tackles from behind—suffered in the opener that caused him to miss Hungary's next two games.

In the tenth minute West German forward Maximilian Morlock stabbed the ball into the net after a sequence that included crosses by left winger Hans Schaefer and Rahn and an errant deflection by Hungarian midfielder József Bozsik. Right winger Rahn then produced the equalizer from a corner kick by German legend and captain Fritz Walter in the eighteenth, thanks in part to an ill-timed leap by Hungary goalkeeper Gyula Grosics.

Four goals before a quarter of the game was gone—ample time for many more. But there would be none the rest of the half and only one more after intermission. In the second half Hungary's Nandor Hidegkuti sent a shot off the post, Kocsis headed off the bar, Kohlmeyer made amends by clearing forward József Tóth's shot off the line, and West German goalkeeper Anton Turek pulled off a number of clutch saves. The stage was set for Rahn.

With the game six minutes away from becoming the second World Cup final to go to overtime, Schaefer, against the run of play, sprinted down the left wing and lofted a cross. Hungarian defender Mihaly Lantos's headed clearance was pounced on by Rahn, just beyond the right corner of the penalty area. He calmly touched the ball twice and, from the penalty arc, fired a low shot past Grosics and inside the left post.

"I just hit the ball as hard as I could," said Rahn, who died three months before the premier of *Das Wunder von Bern*. "I didn't see where the ball was going but I knew it was in the net."

A goal by Puskás with two minutes left was controversially flagged for offside, and Turek thwarted a blast by Czibor to preserve the West German win, perhaps the biggest upset in a World Cup final.

Moments later, referee Bill Ling of England blew the final whistle and radio play-by-play man Herbert Zimmermann told his West German audience, "Over, over, over . . . the game is over! Germany are world champions!" For many West Germans, more than a game was over.

A much more prosperous West Germany would play host to and win the 1974 World Cup, beating Holland in the final at Munich's Olympiastadion, which featured a grassy hill nearby made of the rubble from World War II. Sixteen years later, with the Soviet bloc crumbling and reunification with East Germany within sight, West Germany won its third World Cup, edging Argentina at the Italia '90 finale in Rome. As for that first world championship, however, it has been said that Germans born in the 1920s and 1930s—still living— share one characteristic: almost without exception, they can recite the starting lineup of the team that pulled off the Miracle of Berne.

Hungary, Part III: "Little Brother"

During Hungary's brief reign as undisputed master of international soccer, the superstar on this team of stars was the stumpy, inventive forward with the devastating left foot, Ferenc Puskás, who scored a then–world record eighty-four goals in just eighty-five international games.

Born April 2, 1927, Puskás learned the game on the streets of his native Budapest and played his first pro match at age sixteen with Kispest, coached at the time by his father, a former Kispest player. He made his international debut for Hungary a year later. Following the war, Kispest, renamed Honvéd, became the official Hungarian Army team, and Puskás was soon surrounded by the country's finest players, including forwards Sandor Kocsis and Zoltan Czibor, midfielder József Boszik and goalkeeper Gyula Grosics. He also rose to the rank of major—without ever touching a rifle.

The Hungarian National Team, meanwhile, was on the rise, proving itself by stunning mighty England by lopsided scores in 1953 in London and Budapest.

With Puskás scheming and finishing, the "Magic Magyars" went 40-1-7 from 1950 to 1956, but that one loss came in the 1954 World Cup final.

Two years later Honvéd was at Athletic Bilbao for the first leg of its opening European Cup series when the Hungarian Revolution broke out. The second leg was moved to neutral Brussels, and afterward the Honvéd players, now with nowhere to go, scattered and assumed new nationalities. Though widely reported at one point to have been killed in the fighting in Hungary, Puskás landed in Italy and sat out a two-year ban imposed on him by FIFA for jumping Honvéd. He resurfaced in 1958 in Spain with the Alfredo Di Stéfano–led Real Madrid, which was busy winning the first five European Cups.

Following an initial chill, he and new teammate Di Stéfano became friends, and Europe's greatest one-two punch thrived. Puskás led Spain in scoring four times before his retirement in 1966. He is probably best remembered in Spain for his performance in the 1960 European Cup final against Eintracht Frankfurt, a match regarded by many as one of the greatest ever. In a 7–3 goalfest played before

135,000 at Glasgow's Hampden Park, Di Stéfano scored three goals and Puskás four.

Puskás eventually became a Spanish citizen and played four games for Spain's national team, a development that the Hungarian news media was not allowed to report.

Like his nearly goal-a-game pace for Hungary, Puskás ended his club career with 514 goals in 529 league games and 35 goals in 39 European Cup matches. The man known as Öcsi (Hungarian for "Little Brother") and dubbed by the press as the "Galloping Major" went on to coach in Europe, Canada, and Australia. His greatest feat from the bench was guiding Panathinaikos of Greece to an appearance in the 1971 European Cup final, but like many star players before and since, Puskás was better at playing the part of soccer great than bringing great soccer out of those in his charge.

One of his last coaching stints was as temporary boss of the Hungarian National Team after his homeland, in 1993, granted him a full "pardon." He later worked for the Hungarian soccer federation, but Puskás soon was engaged in his greatest battle, with Alzheimer's disease, and died in Budapest in November 2006 at age seventy-nine. He was laid to rest under the dome at St. Stephen's Basilica in Budapest.

The government called him "the best-known Hungarian of the twentieth century" and declared a day of mourning. Quite a change of heart by a government that, in other hands, had once significantly altered the official biography of its "Little Brother."

Ultimate Betrayal: Goalkeeper Invents Penalty Kick

Goalkeepers everywhere who have rued the day that the penalty kick was invented can blame one of their own. William McCrum, goalkeeper for a charter member of the Irish league, Milford Everton, is the guilty party.

McCrum proposed the "penalty kick" to the Irish Football Association, of which he was a board member, in 1890. A true sportsman, McCrum was fed up watching players from both sides engaging in gamesmanship in front of their own goal, and he sought a method that would not only punish the offending player but his entire team as well. (The fact that Milford gave up sixty-two goals while scoring only ten in the 1890–1891 season may have helped motivate Mc-Crum as well.)

Naturally, it was a goal scorer who seized upon McCrum's idea—Jack Reid, center forward for both the Cliftonville Club and the Irish National Team. Reid also was general secretary of the Irish F.A. and held a seat on the International Football Association Board (IFAB), the body charged at the time with supervising the Laws of the Game in Britain.

Reid presented the proposal to the IFAB, but it was withdrawn after a cool reception from board members. Later made public, the idea was attacked from all sides. After all, soccer was a gentleman's game; it was inconceivable that a player would resort to deliberate foul play in an effort to prevent a goal.

Reality said otherwise, and it was an incident in the following season's English F.A. Cup quarterfinals that tipped the scales in the penalty kick's favor. Notts County held a 1–0 lead over Stoke City in the final minute when a Notts defender, positioned inches from his goal, stopped a Stoke shot with his hand. Stoke was awarded a free kick at the spot of the infraction, and some award it was: the Notts goalkeeper simply stood in front of the ball and successfully blocked the ensuing free kick without moving a muscle.

In June 1891 in Glasgow, the International Board approved what only months earlier had been dismissed as the "death sentence." Mc-Crum and Reid were on hand to argue in favor of the proposal.

Text of the original law read as follows:

"If any player shall intentionally trip or hold an opposing player, or deliberately handle the ball within twelve yards from his own goal-line, the Referee shall, on appeal, award the opposing side a penalty kick, to be taken from any point twelve yards from the goal-line, under the following conditions:—All players, with the exception of the player taking the penalty kick and the opposing goal-keeper (who shall not advance more than six yards from the goal-line) shall stand at least six yards behind the ball. The ball shall be in play when the kick is taken, and a goal may be scored from a penalty kick."

What eventually became Law XIV has undergone a long evolution, as have attitudes toward the penalty kick itself.

In the beginning, goalkeepers, in a misguided demonstration of sportsmanship, often stood to the side of the goal during a penalty-kick attempt; a likeminded shooter would respond by aiming his shot high or wide of the mark. Common sense soon returned to both sides, however, as shooters began to take advantage of the open net and goalkeepers began to actually try to stop the shot. The 'keepers also capitalized on the odd rule that allowed them to advance as much as six yards off the goal line during the taking of the kick. As a result, an overwhelming percentage of PKs were thwarted.

Finally, in 1905, two years after the present-day penalty area markings were introduced, the International Board stipulated that the goalkeeper must stand on the goal line between the posts during a penalty kick. He was still allowed to move from side to side before the kick, but that ended in 1929 when a rule change ordered the 'keeper to stand on the line and not move his feet until the kick had been taken—surely a formula for success for the shooter.

But that rule became one of the most widely violated in soccer as goalkeepers routinely moved a split second, or more, before a PK was struck. It took a rare official to uphold the rule, such as the referee of a Scottish league game in 1945. Kilmarnock's Tommy White was awarded six tries from the penalty spot because the Partick Thistle goalkeeper moved early each time. The seventh was saved.

The rule was amended in 1997 to allow goalkeepers to move before a PK as long as they remained on the goal line. Now that rule is one of the most widely violated in soccer.

Americans Blameless for Coining the Word *Soccer*

"Football, or what you Americans call 'soccer' . . ."

Who hasn't heard that line? One would think that Americans actually dreamed up the word *soccer* in a misguided effort to avoid confusion with gridiron football, a sport in which the foot seldom comes into play.

But no, it was the English who invented the word back in the nineteenth century, when football was split between those who favored the dribbling game governed by the London Football Association and rugby football, the so-called handling game.

According to legend, the word was coined by Arthur Fitzgerald Kinnaird, the son of the Tenth Baron Kinnaird of Perthshire, a founder of the English Football Association and proud holder of one cap for Scotland (a 4–2 loss to England in 1873). Kinnaird also earned five

English F.A. Cup winner's medals and, later, was a member of the House of Lords, president of the YMCA, director of Barclays Bank, thirty-three-year president of the English F.A., and Lord High Commissioner to the Church of Scotland. One day, the young Eleventh Lord Kinnaird was asked which game he would be playing and he replied "soccer," a shortened version of association football. Kinnaird led with the second syllable in the word *association*, thus giving his game a nickname with, um, punch.

The veracity of the Kinnaird story is questionable because around that time English students were fond of replacing the last syllable of a word with an *er*; "rugger" became slang for the sport of rugby and association football became "soccer," apparently without Kinnaird's help. (According to FIFA, the word *soccer* first became common among the student-athletes at Oxford; Kinnaird was a Trinity College man, by way of Eton.)

While those in countries where futbol, futebol, fussball, or football is played cringe at the mention of "soccer," the United States isn't the only offender. The game in the Great White North is governed by the Canadian Soccer Association, and the sport's ruling body Down Under was called the Australian Soccer Federation for its first four decades until a recent change to Football Federation Australia. One of the most respected monthly magazines covering the sport is *World Soccer*, which is based in London.

And Italy, winner of four World Cups, does not call the game "soccer." Nor does it call it "football." Instead, the sport Italians play is calcio, which loosely translated means "kickball." Thus, Italy's national soccer, or football, association is the Federazione Italiana Giuoco Calcio.

The First of Many Wrongheaded Tiebreaker Ideas

Perhaps soccer wouldn't allow for ties if an attractive and fair method for settling draws had been devised. Seemingly everything has been tried, from limited and unlimited overtime to the dreaded penalty-kick duel to the shootout and even—at some youth tournaments—total number of corner kicks. But no method has been found to be satisfactory. As a result, draws universally have been allowed to stand and a tiebreaker employed only when a match absolutely must have a winner.

Efforts to break ties go all the way back to the mid-nineteenth century in Sheffield, England, an area that was at the forefront of the development of modern soccer. In September 1867, the same year the influential Sheffield Football Association was formed, the Sheffield Wednesday Cricket Club decided to add football to the club menu in an effort to keep its members together during the winter months. (The "Wednesday" comes from the day each week that members left work early to play cricket.) A month later Sheffield Wednesday FC played its first match and defeated the Mechanics Club of Norfolk Park, 3–0.

Not figuring in the final score was the tiebreaker that was at the ready had the match ended in a deadlock. Wednesday's goals that day were made up of a pair of nine-foot posts positioned four yards apart, with no crossbar on top. Four yards to the outside of each post was a so-called rogue post. Any ball that passed between a goal post and an outer post was scored as a rogue, and if a match ended in a tie, the team with the most rogues would be declared the victor. (For the record, Wednesday had outrogued the Mechanics, 4–0.)

Rogues wouldn't survive infancy, however. The goal was reconfigured the next year to the more familiar eight yards wide by eight feet high.

No Photographic Record of the First International Match

The 1872 meeting of England and Scotland in Glasgow has been recorded by illustrators, who depict players sporting handlebar moustaches, knickerbockers, and caps, but there is no photograph of that first official international competition in the history of team sports.

The host Scots had arranged for a photographer, but the gentleman's demand that the players purchase his photos afterward was rejected and he walked out on the assignment.

The two teams met the following March in London, but efforts to capture the English squad on film were abandoned "because some of the team persisted in pulling faces at the camera."

The team England played in Glasgow—and tied, 0–0—was actually Scotland's oldest club, Queen's Park, founded in 1867. The Scottish Football Association, the second in the world after the English F.A., wasn't born until three months after the match.

The Umpire Gives Way to the Referee

For those players, coaches, and fans who agree that officials blow a minimum 50 percent of their calls, thus ruining 100 percent of all matches, here's a trip back to the good ol' days.

In mid-nineteenth century England, where modern soccer was undergoing a rapid evolution, the only official at a match was the umpire. The umpire made decisions only when a team captain lodged an appeal. Thus, the umpire did not need a whistle and did not even have to be on the field.

The umpire, however, was a luxury, not a necessity. There was no mention of an umpire in the original Laws of the Game in 1863. The players, after all, were gentlemen. Cheltenham College, however, was not so trusting, calling in the rules it drew up in 1867 for two umpires, one chosen by each side, plus a third official who was to be consulted if the umpires disagreed.

Apparently the game wasn't so gentlemanly after all, because in 1871, in the rules for the first Football Association Cup, Cheltenham's two umpires and that third official were required. This third official needed a name. A player with a complaint over a play took his beef to his captain, who in turn took it to the two umpires. If they couldn't agree, the umpires referred the matter to the third official, who became known as the "referee."

Still, it took several years for the referee to become the soccer icon that he, or she, is today. Umpires were not written into the Laws until 1874, and the referee wasn't officially created until 1880 with this addition to the Laws: "By mutual consent of the competing clubs in matches, a referee shall be appointed whose duty shall be to decide in all cases of dispute between umpires. He shall also keep a record of the game and act as timekeeper, and in the event of ungentlemanly behavior on the part of any of the contestants, the offender or offenders shall, in the presence of the umpires, be cautioned, and in the case of violent conduct, the referee shall have power to rule the offending player or players out of play, and order him or them off the ground, transmitting name or names to the committee of the Association under whose rules the game was played, and in whom shall be solely vested the right of accepting an apology."

Soccer in Britain went another eleven years before the umpires were jettisoned and replaced by two linesmen—that's right, the Brits killed the umpire. And in 1894 the referee was moved onto the field of play so as to better view the action.

Today, the referee makes all the calls. The linesmen, renamed "assistant referees" in 1996, continue to advise and, when called on, consult with the referee, but all decisions remain in the hands of the man—or woman—in the middle.

Meanwhile, across the pond in the nineteenth century, baseball killed the referee.

An umpire—one who would settle disputes between the two team captains—was a part of baseball rules as early as the 1830s. Two decades later some ballgames were officiated by two umpires, each representing one of the two clubs, and an impartial referee. The referee would step forward only if the two umpires—or team advocates—disagreed on a call. Something had to give, and in 1858 the rules were changed to leave things up to a single umpire. However—shades of soccer—it wasn't until after the Civil War that this lone official had evolved from appellate judge to active decision maker.

The White Horse Final

It's regarded in some quarters as soccer's greatest legend, and for a sport that seemingly wears a permanent black eye because of its long string of violent incidents on the field and in the stands, that's a very good thing.

In 1922 work was begun on the Empire Stadium in the London suburb of Wembley, a structure that would showcase the 1924 British Empire Exhibition. Its leading advocate, the Prince of Wales, saw the 100,000-capacity stadium as a home to soccer and a sporting venue that would "appeal to all Britishers," although original plans called for it to be demolished after the exhibition.

The building became the storied Wembley Stadium, the symbolic home to soccer. It was the site of some of the game's biggest matches, and many a player felt his heart race as he set foot on the emerald turf of Wembley.

Completed in twelve months, the stadium held its first major event in 1923 with the English F.A. Cup final between West Ham United and Bolton Wanderers, a game later dubbed "the White Horse Final."

Official attendance that April afternoon was 126,047—including King George V—but it is believed that as many as 200,000 squeezed into the stadium, and another 100,000 milled about outside. By kick-off time, the entire field was jammed with people, and officials decided to postpone the match.

Before an announcement could be made, however, police constable George Storey appeared atop his white stallion Billie and gently but firmly began to nudge the crowd back, leading efforts to clear the field.

The players eventually emerged from the dressing rooms and the match kicked off an hour late with spectators tightly packed around the field's perimeter. At one point, a goal was disputed because a fan sitting along the goal line appeared to keep the ball in play with his foot.

Bolton won, 2–0, and the next day photos of Storey and his mount Billie were on the front page of every newspaper in Britain.

END OF THE WORLD

DAILY MIRROR. Banner headline
that topped the London tabloid the
day after England was eliminated in the
qualifiers for the 1994 World Cup

3 WORLD CUP

*For passion and sheer drama—not to mention number of eyewitnesses—the
World Cup is the greatest show on earth. Since it began in 1930 the quadrennial world championship of soccer has grown into a sporting behemoth
that, over four weeks, attracts a cumulative global audience of more than
26 billion. Nearly two hundred nations take part in regional qualifying
rounds, most of whom have precious little hope of making it into the thir-
ty-two-nation finals; from there, only a handful have a realistic chance of
surviving the sixty-four-match battle to lift the World Cup trophy. Here's a
sampling of the legends and lore from the event that has been both blamed
for heart attacks and credited with lifting the self-image of entire nations.*

Brazilian Chutzpah

"You Brazilians, whom I consider victors of this tournament . . . you
players who in less than a few hours will be acclaimed champions by
millions of your compatriots . . . you who have no equals in the ter-
restrial hemisphere . . . you who are so superior to every other com-
petitor . . . you whom I already salute as conquerors."

That was a portion of the speech delivered by the governor of the
state of Rio de Janeiro at the brand-new Maracanã Stadium *prior* to

kickoff of the last game of the 1950 World Cup between host Brazil and Uruguay.

Given that spirited send-off, Brazil lost.

Indeed, Brazil needed only a tie to claim the title because, for the first and only time, a World Cup concluded with a four-team round-robin playoff—no semifinals, no true final. The Brazilians had flattened Sweden, 7–1, and Spain, 6–1, while their opponent in that last game, neighbor and rival Uruguay, had tied Spain, 2–2, and edged the Swedes, 3–2. Twenty-two gold medals with the name of each Brazil player had been struck, and a Brazilian victory song, composed days earlier, was to be performed after the final whistle. Even FIFA President Jules Rimet, caught up in the prematch frenzy, prepared a congratulatory speech in the Portuguese of Brazil, not the Spanish of Uruguay.

Nevertheless, Brazil tumbled in unthinkable fashion as a world-record crowd of 199,850 (unofficially, 220,000, thanks to standing room) saw Uruguay claw its way back from a one-goal deficit and emerge with a 2–1 victory.

While Uruguay collected its second world crown, Brazil would have to wait eight more years to win its first World Cup. Four more would follow, and Brazil, the only nation to have taken part in every World Cup, is now nothing if not serene when it comes to its standing in international soccer. Regardless of the coach or the current selection of players, Brazilians expect their team to not only win World Cups but entertain while doing so. Yet before the shock of 1950, Brazilian overconfidence surfaced at the 1938 World Cup in France, the last played before World War II caused the next two tournaments to be canceled.

Brazil had stumbled in the first round of the 1930 and 1934 World Cups, but '38 was to be different. Led by the great Leónidas da Silva, supposed inventor of the bicycle kick and known as "the Rubber Man" for his flexibility, Brazil got off to a flying start with a wild, 6–5 extra-time win over Poland in Round 1. Leónidas scored four of the goals, matching the four by the Poles' Ernst Willimowski, an unprecedented output by two players in one World Cup match.

In the quarterfinals, Brazil was held to a 1–1 tie by 1934 runner-up Czechoslovakia in a brutal match in Bordeaux (four ejections, two broken limbs), forcing a replay two days later. With their passage to the semifinals in doubt, were the Brazilians worried? Hardly. They sent their main delegation to Marseilles, site of the semifinal, to await the expected semifinal match with Italy.

Brazil had to rally from an early deficit to finish off the Czechs, 2–1, in the replay, but that scare did nothing to shake the South Americans' confidence. Before the Italy game they booked every seat on the only available flight from Marseilles to Paris, where the final would be played, making no provisions for a possible trip to Bordeaux for the third-place match. Italy's coach, Vittorio Pozzo, paid a visit to the Brazilian delegation and proposed that the flight go to whichever team won, but that idea was rejected out of hand by the amazed South Americans. After all, losing simply hadn't occurred to them.

The topper proved to be the lineup Brazil trotted out for the Italy game, one missing Leónidas, who had suffered a minor injury in the first Czech match. Coach Adheniar Pimenta explained before the match that he preferred to save his star goal scorer for the final.

Alas, the Brazilians lost to Italy, 2–1, giving up two goals in a five-minute span early in the second half. This was long before substitutes were allowed, so Leónidas, scorer of six goals in Brazil's first two games, could only watch helplessly as his replacement, Peracio, missed two late chances. Back in action in the third-place game in Bordeaux three days later, Leónidas scored twice more as Brazil defeated Sweden, 4–2.

That same day in Paris, the Italians, knowing they had already dispatched their toughest opponent in Brazil, outlasted Hungary in the final, 4–2.

Such hubris has its victims, and while the 1938 team took its defeat as a team, one man unfairly took the lion's share of the blame for the Maracanã disaster.

In 1950, two minutes after intermission, Brazil, which had bombarded the Uruguayan goal throughout the first half, broke up a tense scoreless deadlock through right-sided forward Albino Cardoza Friaça. Needing only a tie to claim the championship, Brazil nevertheless continued to attack and paid the price. In the sixty-sixth minute, Friaça's Uruguayan counterpart, Alcides Ghiggia, beat Brazil left back João Ferreira Bigode and crossed for unmarked center forward Juan Alberto Schiaffino, who equalized. Then, with Brazil eleven minutes away from a glorious celebration, Ghiggia again beat Bigode and, instead of the expected cross, slotted a shot between Brazilian goalkeeper Moacir Barbosa and the near post for the stunning go-ahead goal.

Among those in denial was Radio Globo play-by-play man Luiz Mendes, who first announced "Gooool do Uruguay!" Mendes then repeated the phrase as a question— "Gol do Uruguay?"—then several more times with different intonation to express emotions ranging from shock to resignation.

At game's end, the enormous crowd gave the stout, fearless Uruguayans a warm round of applause. But the surprise and disappointment throughout Brazil was palpable, and there were several suicides.

There had to be a scapegoat, and it fell not to Bigode but to Barbosa, and the man voted the tournament's best goalkeeper was never allowed to live it down.

Barbosa was a gifted, athletic star for Rio de Janeiro's Vasco da Gama. Though his international career ended with the Uruguay game, he didn't retire as a goalkeeper until 1963, when he was forty-two. That year he was given the wooden goal used at Maracanã at Brasil '50. He took it home and burned it, but it gave him neither solace nor absolution as he continued to be reviled by the press and public as the man who had snatched defeat from the jaws of certain victory.

Ghiggia's goal, or Barbosa's apparent gaffe, and its aftermath inspired books and films; one book touched on the race of the black Barbosa, noting that Brazil reverted to white goalkeepers thereafter— it didn't win a World Cup with a black 'keeper until its fifth, in 2002, with Dida between the posts. Meanwhile, Brazil dumped the white jerseys it wore that day against Uruguay and has appeared in its famous yellow or its alternate shirt, blue, ever since.

In 1993, with Brazil preparing for USA '94, superstitious assistant coach Mario Zagalo barred Barbosa from a training session, fearing that the ex-goalkeeper would bring bad luck. That same year, the head of the Brazilian soccer federation prevented Barbosa from serving as a TV commentator during a Brazil match.

Barbosa lost his wife of fifty years to bone cancer in 1997 and died virtually alone three years later. On his seventy-ninth birthday, in 2000, he lamented, "Under Brazilian law, the maximum sentence is thirty years. But my imprisonment has been for fifty years." He died of a heart attack a week later.

Barbosa also spoke for all goalkeepers with another quote regarding 1950: "I'm not guilty. There were eleven of us."

Europe's Cold Shoulder

Like the rest of the world, Europe comes to a standstill every four years, glued for a month to telecasts of the World Cup. It was the Europeans, however, who nearly smothered soccer's world championship in its crib.

FIFA discussed the idea of a world championship for national teams at its first Congress, in Paris in 1904. By the 1920s, when the rise of professionalism was removing the best players from the all-amateur Olympic soccer tournament and the rise of South America was bringing Europe's superiority into doubt, FIFA, at the urging of its president, Frenchman Jules Rimet, and French Football Federation General Secretary Henri Delaunay, decided to act, voting at its 1928 Congress in Amsterdam to organize a tournament open to all players, whether professional or amateur. At the following year's Congress in Barcelona, Uruguay was selected host nation by a landslide vote of 27 to 5.

Uruguay, which had proved in winning the 1924 and 1928 Olympic gold medals with flair that Europe held no monopoly on soccer skill, was selected not only for its high profile on the playing field but also for a healthy domestic climate that would prove to be virtually untouched by the Great Depression. And as part of their bid, the Uruguayans, seeking to make the cup the centerpiece of their nation's centennial celebration, promised not only to pay the travel and lodging expenses of all participating teams but also to build what would be the massive one-hundred-thousand-capacity Estadio Centenario in Montevideo for the occasion.

Ultimately, however, only thirteen countries—including just four from Europe—accepted invitations to what had been intended to be a sixteen-team competition.

FIFA knew two years in advance that its first world championship would go forward without Great Britain. England, regarded as the unofficial reigning soccer superpower, had quit the world soccer governing body along with Scotland, Wales, and Northern Ireland in a dispute over the definition of Olympic amateurs and broken-time payments (money paid to players for the time they missed at their jobs while taking part in athletic activities). This self-imposed exile would ultimately keep that foursome out of the 1934 and 1938 World Cups as well.

Italy, Spain, Holland, and Sweden had all offered to host the first tournament but couldn't match Uruguay's generous offer. And when FIFA chose little, obscure, far-off Uruguay, they and other European nations, including the continent's best, Austria and Czechoslovakia, soon lost all interest.

It appeared that the first World Cup would instead be an Americas Cup, with only Argentina, Bolivia, Brazil, Chile, Mexico, Paraguay, Peru, and the United States headed to Uruguay. In March, Rimet and Enrique Buero, Uruguay's ambassador to Holland and Belgium and the head of the Uruguayan World Cup organizing committee, met in Paris to discuss the possibility of half-world cups, with the winners of separate Europe and Western Hemisphere tournaments meeting in an overall championship match. By May, two months before kickoff and long after the official World Cup entry date of January 19, not a single European nation had budged. But thanks to some last-minute arm-twisting by Rimet, four second-tier European nations—Yugoslavia, Belgium, Romania, and Rimet's native France—agreed to enter. The World Cup would be a World Cup, after all.

The Europeans' enthusiasm might have been greater had it not been for the severe economic crisis sweeping the continent. Romania, for one, would not have taken part but for the efforts of King Karol II. Karol, who as prince helped form his country's soccer federation in 1910 and served as its general secretary, personally selected the Romanian squad and persuaded the players' employers to rehire them upon their return from Uruguay.

The prospect of a fourteen-day voyage to Montevideo didn't help, either. As it was, three of the European sides made the trip on the same ship, the Italian steamer SS *Conte Verde*. The Romanians boarded at Genoa, the French at Villefranche-sur-Mer, and the Belgians at Barcelona. Also on board was Rimet himself, as well as three referees and the World Cup trophy. The *Conte Verde* made one last stop, at Rio de Janeiro, to pick up the Brazilian team before proceeding to

Montevideo. (The Yugoslavs sailed solo, out of Marseille aboard the mail steamship *Florida*.)

A competition minus all of Europe's star attractions was no way to launch a world soccer championship, and the Uruguayans were insulted. They avenged the slight by winning the tournament.

Uruguay and its rival, Argentina, both strolled through to the championship game, setting up a rematch of the 1928 Olympic gold medal showdown, an all–South American affair in Amsterdam won by the Uruguayans. This time, with the support of a packed Estadio Centenario behind it, Uruguay rallied from a 2–1 halftime deficit to win, 4–2. The next day was declared a national holiday in Uruguay, while in Buenos Aires the Uruguayan consulate was stoned by an angry mob before being dispersed by police gunfire.

The tournament, despite averaging just 24,139 spectators for its eighteen matches (including some in the hundreds for those not involving the host nation), pulled in $1 million, enabling the Uruguayan organizers to turn a profit after fulfilling their promise to pay all expenses of the visiting teams. But the absence of so many leading soccer powers made it a diluted World Cup.

Still miffed by Europe's reluctance to embrace their tournament, the Uruguayans boycotted the 1934 World Cup, which had been awarded to Italy—the only time a champion has refused to defend its title. The 1934 tournament, run by Italy's fascist government, became something of a preview of the 1936 Nazi Olympics in Berlin as Mussolini turned the event into a propaganda bonanza for his regime. And despite the dark undertones, Europe was won over by the World Cup movement. Twenty-two European nations sought entry, requiring qualifying rounds for the first time.

Elsewhere, four North American countries played qualifiers (the United States won out over Haiti, Cuba, and Mexico), and Egypt won the right to represent the Middle East after beating Palestine in a playoff. As for South America, the response was nearly as tepid for Italy '34 as Europe's was for Uruguay '30: Brazil and Argentina were the only representatives, qualifying after their respective playoff opponents, Peru and Chile, withdrew.

Europeans weren't alone in their lukewarm reception to the 1930 World Cup, a first-time event that no one at the time could have imagined would become the global phenomenon it is today. Argentine center forward and captain "Nolo" Ferreira, known as "the Maestro," thought so little of the competition that he returned home after his team's opener against France to take a university exam. Guillermo Stabile, who would score one goal in the final en route to a tournament-leading eight, took his place, and Ferreira was shifted to inside left upon his return, where he went goal-less in three matches.

Also skipping Uruguay was the United States' finest player, Archie Stark. Scotland born and New Jersey raised, Stark scored 277 goals in 274 American Soccer League matches for the New York Field Club and the powerful Bethlehem Steel from 1921 to 1930, including an amazing 67 in 44 games for Bethlehem in 1924–25. But Stark, dubbed by then–newspaper columnist Ed Sullivan as "the Babe Ruth of Soccer," stayed home because he had just launched a new business. With the United States playing precious few games during his prime, Stark's international career was short but sweet: two games against Canada in 1925, four goals scored.

Monti's Two Shots at a World Championship

The great Johan Cruyff never won a World Cup. Nor did Michel Platini, Alfredo Di Stéfano, Eusébio, or Roberto Baggio. George Best never even played in one. Meanwhile, the honor roll of those given championship medals ranges from all-time greats to long-forgotten bench riders. And among the first recipients was one of the game's first true rogues, the infamous Luisito Monti, who played in World Cups for two different nations before pocketing his medal.

Monti, a tough-as-nails center halfback, was the lynchpin of the Argentine team that fully expected to reach the final of the first World Cup, in 1930 in Uruguay, and he didn't disappoint. In the opener against France he showed his guile with a quickly taken free kick that beat a disorganized French wall and led to the game's lone goal, and in the semifinals he scored the first goal in Argentina's 6–1 romp past the United States. Monti's primary mission, however, was search and destroy, a role he played with relish, and his crunching tackles soon made him the tournament's most notorious player. His high (or low) point came in Argentina's last opening-round match, a 3–1 win over Chile, in which one of his fouls touched off a free-for-all just before halftime.

The win over the United States put Argentina into the final against Uruguay, giving it the opportunity to avenge its bitter loss to its smaller neighbor in the 1928 Olympic final in Amsterdam. But it was feared that another typical Monti effort might incite what would be an overwhelmingly partisan Uruguayan crowd of ninety-three thousand at the Estadio Centenario in Montevideo, so Argentine Football Association officials ordered Monti to be on his best behavior. He was, Argentina squandered a lead and lost, 4–2, and Monti, for his trouble, was later roasted by the Argentine critics for his angelic performance.

The night before the final, an armada of boats set sail across the River Plate from Buenos Aires, bound for Montevideo, containing hundreds of Argentine supporters who chanted, "Argentina, sí! Uruguay, no!" and "Victory or death!" Monti didn't buy into the latter. In fact, he took his quest for a world championship across the Atlantic.

When Argentina lined up to play Sweden in the first round of the 1934 World Cup in Italy, Monti was not around, and neither were any of the other players from Uruguay '30. The Argentines tumbled, 3–2, and under that tournament's harsh format they were eliminated after one game.

Some of those departed from the 1930 team were victims of natural turnover. But Monti had gone to Italy after the loss to Uruguay to sign with Juventus, and he eventually was called up to the Italian National Team as an *oriundo*, a foreigner of Italian descent.

Given a second chance, Monti played in all five of the Italians' World Cup matches, including their 2–1 victory in overtime over Czechoslovakia in the final in Rome. Another Argentine *oriundo*, Raimundo Orsi, scored Italy's first goal. Looking on, sporting a spiffy yachting cap, was Il Duce himself, Benito Mussolini. Monti's most notable performance came in the semifinals, where he brutally marked Austrian star forward Matthias Sindelar out of the game and Italy won narrowly, 1–0.

Not a bad career move, because had Monti not joined Juventus and Italy after the 1930 World Cup, he might not have represented Argentina in 1934 anyway. Several top players, including 1928 Olympic silver medalist Orsi, had already been poached by Italian and Spanish clubs, so AFA officials purposely sent a weak national team to the tournament to prevent another generation of Argentine stars from being gobbled up by the hungry clubs of Europe.

Since Monti, only four other players have made World Cup appearances for two nations. Defender José Santamaria was a starter for the Uruguay team that reached the 1954 semifinals; at the 1962 World Cup in Chile, he donned a Spain jersey and didn't survive the first round. Midfielder José Altafini was known as "Mazola" when he played three matches for champion Brazil in the 1958 World Cup in Sweden, then made the mistake of adopting a new home; as a newly minted Italian, he tumbled in the first round four years later in Chile. The immortal Ferenc Puskás was a runner-up in 1954 while with Hungary and, after the Hungarian Revolution, a first-round victim with Spain in 1962. And after helping Yugoslavia reach the 1990 quarterfinals, goal-scoring star Robert Prosinecki was part of the Croatia team that finished third overall in 1998 and third in its opening-round group in 2002.

Barefooted India Says No to World Cup Berth

Despite a population that now tops a billion, India has never appeared in a World Cup. Poverty and the popularity of field hockey and cricket there have been major contributors to the Indians' wafer-thin soccer résumé.

However, they could have made their World Cup debut as early as 1950. India and Burma were the only nations to enter the Asian qualifiers the previous year, and when Burma, a longtime province of India, withdrew, the Indians were in without kicking a ball. Then, at the last minute, India withdrew also.

Why did India back out? According to one account, the All India Football Federation pulled its team because of financial and organizational problems. According to another, the Indians balked when FIFA forbade the team from playing in a World Cup barefoot, as was its custom.

Two years earlier, in fact, Indian players—some wearing socks, others barefoot—lost to France, 2–1, in the first round of the 1948 London Olympics and were eliminated. India's performance impressed, but as a later FIFA account noted, the choice of footwear (or lack thereof), "raised questions about the Laws of the Game."

The Indians reached the semifinals of the 1956 Melbourne Olympics, claimed their lone international honor at the 1962 Asian Games, and haven't been heard from since.

World Cup Trophy: Most Precious Icon in Sports

It's not an Olympic gold medal, nor is it the Super Bowl trophy, the Stanley Cup, or the green jacket that goes to the winner of the Master's golf tournament.

More precious than any of those by far, it's soccer's World Cup trophy, the most coveted prize in sports. The golden icon, measuring thirty-six centimeters high and weighing 4,970 grams, goes to the one true world champion, the team that is number one in the world's most-played team sport.

The original trophy, the one awarded to Uruguay, champion and host of the inaugural World Cup in 1930, was designed by French sculptor Abel Lafleur. Thirty-five centimeters tall and weighing 3.8 kilograms, the statuette was made of sterling silver and gold plating, with a blue base made of the semiprecious stone lapis lazuli. In the best art deco tradition, the trophy featured Nike, the ancient Greek goddess of victory, holding aloft an eight-sided chalice. The winners of the first nine World Cups were engraved on the four sides of the base (Uruguay, Italy, Italy, Uruguay, West Germany, Brazil, Brazil, England, Brazil).

After Italy's twin triumphs in the 1930s, World War II prevented another World Cup from being played until Brazil '50. What of the trophy during that twelve-year gap? According to folklore, a FIFA vice president from Italy, Dr. Ottorino Barassi, removed the precious hardware from a bank vault in Rome and hid it under his bed for the duration to keep it out of the hands of the Nazis. Another tale places the trophy under the bed of FIFA President Jules Rimet.

The trophy was finally named for Rimet in 1946 in recognition of his twenty-five years as FIFA president and status as the father of the World Cup. "Coupe Jules Rimet" would have enjoyed a long public life had not Brazil, in the 1970 final, beaten two-time winner Italy to become the first nation to win three World Cups. As FIFA had promised, the trophy was retired and permanently awarded to the South Americans.

A new trophy was needed, and FIFA approved a design by Italian sculptor Silvio Gazzaniga, chosen over fifty-two other entries. It is made of 18-carat gold and features a base containing two layers of semiprecious malachite. Seventeen small plaques on the base are reserved for all the winners through the 2038 World Cup.

According to Gazzaniga, "The lines spring out of the base, rising in spirals, stretching out to receive the world. From the remarkable dynamic tensions of the compact body of the sculpture rise the figures of two athletes at the stirring moment of victory."

West Germany, winner of the 1974 World Cup it hosted, was the first to lift what is properly known as the Copa Mundial de la FIFA, which has since gone to Argentina, Italy, Argentina, West Germany, Brazil, France, Brazil, Italy, and, in 2010, Spain.

As for the Jules Rimet Trophy, Brazil proved to be a poor custodian. In 1983 the cup was stolen by thieves in Rio de Janeiro, melted down, and sold off. Two accomplices, gold dealers Antonio Pugliese and Carlos Hernandez, were convicted and imprisoned for ten years each.

The Gazzaniga-designed World Cup trophy will remain the property of FIFA regardless of how many times a nation wins the championship. The national soccer federation of the winning country receives a replica, and in an effort to deter thieves, it's only gold plated.

1966: Pickles, the Pilfered Ball, Hurst's Hat Trick and Caviar Dreams

England hosted and won the 1966 World Cup, as any Englishman will be happy to point out, but according to popular belief, were it not for a black-and-white mongrel dog named Pickles, the victorious English team would have had nothing to show for it.

The grand prize, the perpetual Jules Rimet trophy, was delivered to the English Football Association's headquarters at Lancaster Gate in London in January 1966, five months ahead of the eighth World Cup. On Saturday, March 19, it was placed on display at an exhibition at Westminster Abbey's Central Hall. But the very next day the trophy, valued at $47,000, was stolen despite the stipulation that it be under guard at all times. The thieves entered the rear of the building and forced open the glass display case before fleeing with their booty sometime before noon. The hall was used for Methodist services on Sundays, perhaps explaining the lax security on that fateful day.

Embarrassed FIFA and English F.A. officials cringed at the thought of a World Cup in which the captain of the winning team was handed a coupon redeemable for a trophy to be cast later.

What followed was something out of the British movie *The Lavender Hill Mob*.

Two days after the theft, Joe Mears, chairman of both the F.A. and Chelsea FC, received a package containing the removable lining from the top of the trophy along with a written demand for $30,000 in one- and five-pound notes.

"Dear Joe kno [*sic*] doubt you view with very much concern the loss of the world cup. . . . To me it is only so much scrap gold. If I don't hear from you by Thursday or Friday at the latest I assume it's one for the POT."

If the police were not alerted and the demand was met, it continued, the trophy would be returned Friday, March 25; otherwise, it would be melted down and never seen again.

Per the instructions in the ransom note, Mears arranged a rendezvous through a newspaper advertisement ("Willing to do business. Joe"). Mears, however, also contacted Scotland Yard, which turned the case over to the vaunted Flying Squad unit. On deadline day, the authorities were poised with a suitcase filled with bank notes sandwiching bundles of ordinary paper, but Mears was at home in bed, suffering from stress brought on by the drama. So at Battersea Park, suspect "Jackson" climbed into a Ford Zodiac purportedly to be Mears's (license plate "CFC 11") with a man introduced to him as Mears's Chelsea assistant "McPhee" (aka Detective Inspector Len Buggy) on the pretext that suspect Jackson would lead the way to the trophy. After a ten-minute drive around south London, a suspicious Jackson spied a van containing a backup team of police and leaped out of the moving Zodiac, but he was quickly apprehended by Buggy. Jackson was later identified as Edward Betchley, age forty-six, a used-car salesman convicted in 1954 of theft and receiving stolen goods, namely cans of corned beef. Betchley, who served honorably in Egypt and Italy during World War II as a member of the Royal Armoured Corps, denied having stolen the trophy and claimed a man known only as "the Pole" had offered him $1,000 to serve as middleman.

On Sunday, March 27, the trophy was found three miles from Westminster on Beulah Hill in the suburb of Norwood, although the circumstances remain in dispute, with the Scottish border collie mix, Pickles, at the center of it all.

According to popular accounts, the canny canine's keen nose unearthed the trophy from a rubbish heap, or a garden, or a garden hedge, while out on an evening walk with his master, twenty-six-year-old David Corbett. The cup was wrapped in a newspaper and tied with string. Pickles's master handed over the trophy at the Gypsy Hill police station, and Corbett, originally considered a suspect, was then taken along with the cup to Cannon Row police station, where a relieved Harold Mayes of the F.A. identified the trophy. Questioned until 2:30 a.m., Corbett was released; he returned home and was up for work at 6:00 that same morning.

According to Corbett, however, his four-year-old companion wasn't quite the hero he was made out to be. He told the *Observer* on the fortieth anniversary of the theft that he walked Pickles across the street from his ground-floor flat to make a call from a pay phone when he found a suspicious package in the street near the front wheel of a parked car. This differed from his original statement to police, in which he described being at his front gate, putting the leash on Pickles, when he spotted the package "at the side of a bush." Pickles once again assumed a minor role when the *Sunday Mirror* interviewed Corbett a month after the *Observer* story: "Although Pickles sort of led me in the direction of the cup, it was me who found it. There were all these stories at the time that he dug it up from under a bush. Well, it wasn't quite like that."

Despite the bungling thieves (or was it *thief*, as in Betchley, acting alone?), the 1966 World Cup tournament would not have gone without its grand prize. Before the theft became public, a local silversmith, George Bird, was secretly asked by F.A. secretary Denis Follows to produce a replica of the Jules Rimet trophy. Bird's fake, fashioned from base metal, made countless public appearances after England's triumph while the real thing was kept under wraps by the F.A.

So Pickles wasn't quite the hero, but the aftermath wasn't happy for any of the principals in the caper.

For Mears, the theft and resulting tension proved fatal. Ten days before England would play Uruguay to a dull scoreless draw in the World Cup's opening match, an angina attack claimed the F.A. boss's life.

Betchley, convicted of "demanding money with menaces," served a two-year prison sentence and died of emphysema in 1969—without offering any information on how the trophy was unceremoniously dumped on David Corbett's street.

And Pickles's fame was short-lived, as was his life. With the help of an agent, he starred in the movie *The Spy with the Cold Nose* and appeared in several British TV shows; he also received a year's supply of chow from a dog food company and was honored as Britain's Dog of the Year. The evening of England's victory over West Germany in the final, Pickles and Corbett were guests at the English players' celebration party at a hotel in Kensington, an affair from which the players' wives were barred. But a year later, Corbett's six-year-old son was walking Pickles when the dog bolted after a cat. An hour later Pickles was found dead, hanging by his choke chain from a tree branch.

Corbett buried Pickles in the backyard of the $7,000 house in Surrey he bought with the reward money he received for the cup's recovery. Although it all happened some three hundred dog-years ago, "People still ask me if Pickles is still alive," said a bemused Corbett.

The English, who nearly lost the World Cup before the tournament even kicked off, also had problems with the ball used in their 4–2 overtime victory over West Germany in the title game, which was played July 30, 1966, at London's Wembley Stadium.

What should have been a prized English souvenir from a famous triumph became instead the very private property of West German midfielder Helmut Haller, who, before ninety-six thousand potential witnesses, stuffed the ball under his jersey during the chaos that followed the final whistle. Haller smuggled the ball out of the stadium and brought it home, then gave it to his five-year-old son, Jürgen.

The ball became something of a Holy Grail to the English, but Haller, who scored the game's opening goal in the twelfth minute, rejected several requests to return the ball to England. The oblivious Jürgen, meanwhile, forgot about his valuable gift. It wasn't until 1996, when a Duesseldorf man claimed to have the ball, that the younger Haller rummaged through his cellar and found it in a box.

At long last, in an odd ceremony at English F.A. headquarters in London, Jürgen Haller turned the ball over to the winners, thirty years after his father's petty theft.

So Germany gave back the game ball. But was England striker Geoff Hurst willing to give his deciding goal back to the Germans?

Ten minutes into overtime, with the score England 2, West Germany 2, a shot by Hurst slammed off the underside of the crossbar, caromed straight down, and then bounced back onto the field. Swiss referee Gottfried Dienst wasn't sure what to call, but after a dramatic and prolonged consultation with Soviet linesman Tofik Bakhramov, he ruled it a goal.

The goal demoralized the Germans, who had saved themselves from defeat in the dying seconds of regulation through an equalizer by defender Wolfgang Weber scored off a goalmouth scramble. And the twenty-four-year-old Hurst, who had answered Haller's early goal with a strike of his own in the nineteenth minute, scored his third goal in the 119th minute to become the only man to produce a hat trick in a World Cup final. Not bad for a fellow who rode the England bench during the group stage and became a starter only after star striker Jimmy Greaves was injured in the quarterfinals.

But Hurst revealed second thoughts thirty-five years later in his autobiography *1966 And All That.*

"Everyone understood the frustration felt by the Germans," wrote Hurst. "They believed they had been robbed of the most prestigious prize in world football. Perhaps they were. They genuinely believed the ball had not crossed the line and they may be right.

"Having listened to all the arguments over the decades and watched the replay hundreds of times on TV, I have to admit that it looks as though the ball didn't cross the line."

The man beaten by Hurst that day, West German goalkeeper Hans Tilkowski, seemed amused by the admission. He told the German newspaper *Bild,* "My friend Geoff only confirmed what I always said: His shot bounced off the crossbar and onto the line and not behind it. It shows he is a good sport. I hope they don't pillory him in England for it. Otherwise, he might have to seek asylum in Germany."

Surprise World Cup winners in 1954, the West Germans went on to add world championships in 1974 and 1990. But the '66 final continues to haunt Germany, where the phrase *Wembley Tor* ("Wembley Goal") means something phony. Backing German sentiment was a University of Oxford study conducted in 1995 in which an examination of computer-enhanced footage of Hurst's shot led to the conclusion that the ball did not wholly cross the goal line.

Hurst's admission, meanwhile, put his English teammate and fellow striker, Roger Hunt, temporarily back in the spotlight. After Hurst's shot had bounced off the bar, Hunt ignored the loose ball and leaped into the air in celebration. Had Hunt, left alone with Tilkowski beaten and the net at his mercy, simply pounded the ball home, there would have been no controversy.

What, then, separated England and West Germany that day? It may have come down to caviar.

Nikolai Latyshev, who refereed Brazil's 3–1 victory over Czechoslovakia in the 1962 World Cup final in Chile, claimed in an interview shortly before his death in February 1999 that fellow Soviet official Tofik Bakhramov was at Wembley only because two jars of the Russian delicacy were quietly delivered to a Malaysian member of the World Cup officiating committee before the assignments for the '66 final were made.

For his pivotal role in one of the most dramatic moments in soccer history, Bakhramov later saw a stadium in Baku, in his native Azerbaijan, named for him. In October 2004, prior to a World Cup qualifier between Azerbaijan and England, a statue of Bakhramov was unveiled outside the stadium. Among the dignitaries on hand were Hurst and FIFA President Sepp Blatter.

Kuwaiti Prince Makes a World Cup Cameo

Kuwait, with its population of 2.2 million, fourteen registered clubs, and 2,500 registered players, isn't likely to become a World Cup regular anytime soon. But its one and only World Cup appearance, in 1982, won't soon be forgotten.

The Kuwaitis, representing an Arab Gulf city-state smaller than the island of Fiji, qualified along with New Zealand from a combined Asia and Oceania playoff, and neither nation was expected to make a dent at España '82.

But while New Zealand, also in its first World Cup, was losing all three of its first-round games, Kuwait, with its mascot, a camel, in tow, was proving to be a pleasant surprise, particularly in its opener as it tied Czechoslovakia, 1–1, in Valladolid.

It was in their second game—a lopsided loss to France, also in Valladolid—that the Kuwaitis made an indelible impression. The French were coasting with a 3–1 lead in the seventy-sixth minute when Alain Giresse, who had set up his side's second goal, ran onto a through ball by Michel Platini and easily scored from close range. Easily, because the Kuwaiti defense was motionless during the goal, the players claiming that they had heard a whistle for offside.

Soviet referee Miroslav Stupar awarded the goal, touching off a vehement protest by the Kuwaitis. Then, from the stands, Prince Fahid, one of the world's richest men and president of Kuwait's soccer federation, appeared to beckon his players off the field. But just as the players obeyed, the prince, clad in a resplendent pink burnoose, made his way down onto the field. His appearance and words of persuasion apparently affected Stupar because, incredibly, the referee reversed his decision. In all, the match was held up for eight minutes. Once the game resumed, France scored a "second" fourth goal and went on to win, 4–1.

Asked at the postgame press conference about the incident, Kuwait coach Carlos Alberto Parreira, who would go on to lead his native Brazil to the 1994 World Cup crown, said that the prince was trying to prevent his players from abandoning the field. Skeptical media members believed that once Stupar reversed his decision, His Highness was forced to reverse his decision to pull his team. "So when he goes like this," said a German journalist, imitating Fahid's original beckoning gesture, "he is telling the players to stay on the field?"

FIFA had the last word, fining Kuwait $12,000—chicken feed to Fahid.

Kuwait's World Cup adventure ended bravely four days later with a 1–0 loss to England in Bilbao.

Fahid, who had spent millions to transform his nation from a soccer minnow into a regional force, would not live to see his country play in another World Cup. He was killed during the 1990 Iraqi invasion of Kuwait.

Orsi Can't Remember How to Duplicate Memorable Goal

The 1934 World Cup is remembered for host Italy's victory, which would be followed by a second victory four years later in France.

What it is not remembered for is the recorded image of left winger

Raimundo Orsi scoring a late equalizer to help enable the Italians to edge Czechoslovakia, 2–1, in overtime in the final in Rome.

As the Czechs clung to a 1–0 lead through a goal by left winger Antonin Puc in the seventieth minute, Orsi scored a goal that has been described as half genius, half fluke. With fewer than ten minutes remaining in regulation, Orsi took a pass from Enrique Guaita and roared through the Czech defense. Within range, he feinted a shot with his left foot and fired with the outside of his right, sending a wildly swerving shot that grazed the fingertips of goalkeeper František Plánička and spun into the net.

Momentum had swung dramatically to the Italians, and with a crowd of fifty-five thousand at Stadio del Partido Nacional Fascista urging them on, they completed their comeback through midfielder Angelo Schiavio's goal seven minutes into overtime.

The talk later, however, was of Orsi's goal. Stung by the suggestion that the goal was more the result of luck than skill, the indignant Orsi, born in Argentina to Italian parents, assured the press he could do it whenever he wished. The next day, with a crowd of photographers at the ready and no goalkeeper to stop him, Orsi tried twenty times to duplicate his feat and failed to find the net each time.

England: How *Not* to Win Hearts and Minds

After winning the World Cup on home soil in 1966, England knew that a lot of things would have to go right if it was going to defend its title at the 1970 World Cup in Mexico. Instead, everything went wrong as the English rewrote Murphy's Law.

Alf Ramsey, England's prickly coach, committed the first of what proved to be a string of diplomatic blunders long before Mexico '70.

While eking out a 1–0 victory over Argentina in the '66 quarterfinals at Wembley Stadium, England was subjected to a madding series of chippy fouls that destroyed whatever flow the game might have had. Each booking by West German referee Rudolf Kreitlein evoked protests from Argentine captain Antonio Rattin, and finally, in the thirty-sixth minute, Rattin was sent off. The hulking defender at first refused to go and argued with Kreitlein and other officials for ten minutes. The entire Argentine team appeared poised to exit in protest before Rattin gave up and leisurely strolled to the dressing room with his trainer, exchanging insults with spectators along the way.

At the final whistle, Ramsey physically prevented his players from exchanging jerseys with the opposition, and he later called the Argentine players "animals." The English Football Association eventually pressured Ramsey to withdraw the comment, but the damage had been done as seemingly all of Latin America took offense.

And so England, sporting its world crown, approached Mexico under a cloud, and the first of many pretournament faux pas was committed in 1969.

Despite frequent pronouncements that he intended for England to win hearts and minds among the locals to help pave the way to a second straight World Cup title, Ramsey was at his diplomatic worst following a scoreless draw with Mexico in a friendly in Mexico City. Asked at a press conference afterward if he had any comment, the coach replied: "Yes. There was a band playing outside our hotel 'til five o'clock this morning. We were promised a motorcycle escort to the stadium. It never arrived. When our players went out to inspect the pitch, they were abused and jeered by the crowd. I would have thought the Mexican public would have been delighted to welcome England. Then, when the game began, they could cheer their own team as much as they liked.

"But, we are delighted to be in Mexico, and the Mexican people are a wonderful people."

Too little, too late, and England's nightmare was just beginning.

A few days later England beat a Mexican selection, 4–0, in Guadalajara. After the governor of the state of Jalisco made a presentation to Ramsey, the England coach led his team into the stadium's underground dressing room, with Mexican press a step behind. Seconds later, the media members were scurrying back to ground level, sent packing by Ramsey. "*You've* got no right in here," he hissed.

The incident cemented the England team's status as the number one target of the Mexican media thereafter, and the people of Guadalajara eventually were given a second crack at the English when the World Cup draw placed them back in Mexico's second-largest city for the first round along with Romania, Czechoslovakia, and Brazil. The stage had been set.

In May 1970, a month before the World Cup, England beat Colombia, 4–0, in a tune-up in Bogota. But beforehand there was a major controversy the English could have done without as legendary defender Bobby Moore, the captain of England's 1966 triumph, was accused of stealing a $1,200 bracelet from a jewelry store inside the team's Tequendama Hotel.

A shop clerk and a witness fingered Moore, who was lounging with teammate Bobby Charlton outside the Green Fire Jewelry Shop. No action was taken, and England and its second team played their games in Bogota, then played another pair of games in Quito, Ecuador, four days later. Upon England's return to Bogota en route to Mexico, Colombian police placed Moore under house arrest at the home of the president of the famous club Millonarios.

The shop proprietor, the clerk, and the witness (who would subsequently disappear) all accused Moore of lifting the bracelet. But English and Colombian officials worked out an arrangement in which the player was freed to play in the World Cup, and the case later exposed a string of incidents in which innocent bullfighters, singers, and other visiting celebrities were similarly ensnared. Two years later Moore's accusers were charged with conspiracy.

In June England landed in Mexico for the World Cup, and the team staff, suspicious of Mexican cuisine but ignorant of Mexican law regarding imports, brought along their own food and bottled water. Upon the team's arrival, the food and water were destroyed by authorities. *Bienvenida, Inglaterra.*

"We do not fear any team; we are going to be champions for a second time," proclaimed Ramsey on the eve of the cup, and his players got their quest underway with a 1–0 win over Group 3 opponent Romania.

Mexicans among the crowd of fifty thousand at Jalisco Stadium roundly jeered the English, and Ramsey further roiled the waters by criticizing the state of the field.

It was Brazil, meanwhile, that was winning over the Mexicans, staging a successful public relations campaign that was variously described as "beads for the natives."

By the time England and Brazil met in the match that would determine the winner of Group 3, the people of Guadalajara were solidly behind the Brazilians, who would go on to become the people's choice nationwide after Mexico was knocked out in the quarterfinals.

England had chosen the Guadalajara Hilton for its first-round stay, and instead of serving as an oasis the hotel's downtown location made the English sitting ducks. The night before the Brazil game, hundreds of locals gathered in and around the hotel, chanting "Bra-zil!" "Bra-zil!" Others in autos and on motorbikes circled the Hilton, honking their horns incessantly. The police did not intervene, and the din grew in the wee hours, depriving the players of a good night's sleep before what for many would be the game of their lives.

The match itself was a classic, won by Brazil, 1–0, on a goal by Jairzinho, set up by Pelé, in the fifty-ninth minute before a capacity crowd of sixty-six thousand at Jalisco Stadium.

It could have been worse for England. In the tenth minute, only a save by goalkeeper Gordon Banks, widely regarded as the greatest stop of all time, prevented an early Brazil score. On that play Jairzinho drove a cross from the right for Pelé, who leaped high and pounded a header just inside the foot of the left post; Banks, guarding his near post, threw himself across the goalmouth and parried the ball on the bounce up and over the crossbar.

"At that moment I hated Gordon Banks," said Pelé. "I just couldn't believe it. . . . It was the greatest save I have ever seen."

While Brazil nursed its one-goal lead, England couldn't produce the equalizer, despite chances by midfielder Francis Lee, his substitute, Jeff Astle, and, on three occasions, midfielder Alan Ball.

The game wasn't the only thing lost by the English: all the starters, playing ninety minutes in withering ninety-eight-degree heat, dropped a minimum ten pounds.

After bowing to Brazil in the match considered in some quarters as the "real" final of the 1970 World Cup, England bounced back to nip Czechoslovakia, 1–0, in its last group game and set up a quarter-final showdown in Leon with West Germany.

But, aiming to both earn a possible second shot at Brazil and deny the West Germans revenge for their loss at the final four years earlier in London, the English did neither and suffered a tough 3–2 defeat.

Banks fell ill the morning of the game, costing England if not the world's best goalkeeper then certainly the tournament's hottest. If that was a bad omen, it didn't appear to affect Banks's teammates, who jumped out to a 2–0 lead after forty-nine minutes on goals by Alan Mullery and Martin Peters. But the Germans came back. "Der Kaiser," Franz Beckenbauer, slipped a shot under Banks's replacement,

Peter Bonetti, and a back-header by Uwe Seeler in the seventy-sixth evened the score at 2–2. Three minutes into the second overtime period, Gerd Müller's close-range volley off a cross by key substitute Jürgen Grabowski put the Germans ahead for good, and England's collapse was complete.

Bonetti, who hadn't played a competitive match in more than a month, was harshly criticized, as was Ramsey, whose tactics and substitutions came under intense scrutiny by the English press. This was considered in many circles an England team superior to the '66 champs.

And so England exited Mexico without its crown. But the English also returned home without its king. One of Ramsey's substitutions involved Bobby Charlton, who came off after Beckenbauer's goal. It was Charlton's 106th international appearance—an English record at the time—and the last of his storied career. No one in England has managed to replace him.

Mysterious North Korea's Remarkable World Cup

There are plenty of choice Italian curse words and oaths, but to Italians old enough to remember the 1966 World Cup in England, none can make them shudder like the name "Pak Doo-Ik."

Pak Doo-Ik is the man who scored the goal in North Korea's famous 1–0 victory over Italy in Middlesborough, a result considered the biggest World Cup upset since the United States' win over England sixteen years earlier.

The North Koreans were lucky just to be at the '66 World Cup. Seventeen Asian and African entrants withdrew from the qualifying rounds in protest of FIFA's allotting just one berth total to those two continents, leaving two holdouts, North Korea and Australia, to play off for the trip to England. The Koreans won, 6–1 and 3–1, in neutral Phnom Pehn, Cambodia.

Little was known about the secretive North Koreans, but, drawn into Group 4 with the USSR, Italy, and Chile and scheduled to play all three of their first-round matches in Middlesbrough, they were considered the longest of long shots. Nevertheless, oblivious to what the oddsmakers thought of them, the Koreans showed plenty of spirit in losing their first-ever World Cup match, a 3–0 decision to the group favorite Soviet Union. By the time they tied Chile, 1–1, three days later, thanks to an eighty-eighth-minute goal by Pak Seung-Zin, they were clearly the sentimental favorites of Middlesbrough.

At Sunderland, meanwhile, Italy, which beat Chile in its opener, 2–0, saw its defensive tactics backfire in a 1–0 loss to the USSR, but it figured to brush aside the Asian mystery men and reach the quarterfinals as group runner-up.

How the Koreans won, however, was no mystery. Despite their short stature (tallest player: 5'8"), they demonstrated the same quickness, deft short passing, relentless tackling, and utter lack of gamesmanship that made them the darlings of the group.

In the thirty-fourth minute, Italy was reduced to ten men when midfielder Giancomo Bulgarelli reinjured a gimpy knee while attempting to foul an opponent. Seven minutes later forward Pak Seung-Zin back-headed a loose ball for Pak Doo-Ik at the top of the Italian penalty area, and Pak touched the ball forward before rifling it into the net.

Italy, starring Giacinto Facchetti, Gianni Rivera, and Sandor Mazzola and gunning for a third world championship, was out. But there was a further indignity to endure. Seeking to slip back into Italy quietly, the humiliated Azzurri flew not into Rome at midday as scheduled but into the Genoa airport at one o'clock in the morning. It must have been the worst-kept secret in Italy because the team was greeted at the airport by a hostile press and a hail of rotten vegetables and verbal abuse hurled by hundreds of irate fans.

It would be months before the players could appear on the street without hearing insults. Among the favorite taunts was the chant of "Kor-e-a" whenever a veteran of Italy's 1966 squad appeared in an Italian stadium.

As for the Koreans, they nearly did it again four days later in one of the most amazing World Cup games ever. Facing Portugal in Liverpool, North Korea jumped out to a three-goal lead thanks to goals by Pak Seung-Zin in the first minute, Li Dong-Woon in the twentieth, and Yong Seung-Kook in the twenty-second. The crowd of 51,780 was in shock—except for the few thousand fans from Middlesbrough who had followed their new heroes to the Merseyside.

Unsure of what to do with their good fortune, the Koreans naïvely continued to attack and paid dearly at the hands of the tournament's finest player and Europe's answer to Pelé, the legendary striker Eusébio.

Known as "the Black Panther," Eusébio scored his first goal in the twenty-seventh minute, converted a penalty kick three minutes before halftime, hit the equalizer in the fifty-fifth, and netted his second PK in the fifty-eighth after being fouled following a brilliant run.

Midfielder José Augusto, with Eusébio's help, closed out the scoring in the seventy-eighth minute to give Portugal a harrowing 5–3 victory.

Portugal lost to eventual champion England, 2–1, in the semifinal at Wembley Stadium (Eusébio scored another PK, his tournament-leading ninth goal). By then, the North Koreans were back home and back behind their own particularly thick version of the Iron Curtain. While their estranged cousins to the south have appeared in eight World Cups and even cohosted the 2002 tournament, the North Koreans hadn't come close to qualifying for a second World Cup until they won their way into South Africa 2010.

The 1970 Italy–West Germany Goal Fiesta

Often in a World Cup one or both of the semifinals are more dramatic than the final that follows. Such was the case in 1970, when Brazil's brilliant, exhilarating 4–1 triumph over Italy couldn't quite compare with the wild Italy–West Germany semifinal played four days earlier, a goalfest that left the crowd of 102,444 at Mexico City's Estadio Azteca nearly as wrung out as the participants.

For an hour and a half the game pitted Italy's innate ability to gird its loins and protect its goal against West Germany's reputation for the comeback. After that, in overtime, all hell broke loose.

In the seventh minute Italy center forward Roberto Boninsegna bulled his way goalward and found the net with a left-footed shot, and for the next eighty-three minutes the Germans were faced with an Italian stone wall. Three minutes into added-on time, however, the wall cracked as West German sweeper Karl-Heinz Schnellinger drove Jürgen Grabowski's cross home, and the score was level at 1–1.

The momentum now was with the Germans heading into overtime, despite the fact that legendary captain Franz Beckenbauer had dislocated a shoulder in the sixtieth minute and courageously played on with his arm strapped to his chest.

In the ninety-fifth minute midfielder Uwe Seeler's header fell to striker Gerd Müller, who gave West Germany's its first lead.

Midfielder Tarcisio Burgnich used a free kick by substitute Gianni Rivera to equalize for Italy, and forward Luigi Riva put the Italians ahead, 3–2, two minutes before the end of the first OT with a low, left-footed shot inside the right post.

Fifteen minutes, and another two goals, remained.

In the 110th minute Seeler, at the far post, headed a right-sided centering pass across the goalmouth, and the stumpy Müller leaped to nod the ball home for his tournament-leading tenth goal. Three to three. Penalty kicks loomed, but in the 111th Rivera put the Italians safely into the final by scoring the fifth goal of overtime. Boninsegna escaped down the left wing and pulled the ball back for Rivera, who drilled it past West German goalkeeper Sepp Maier.

Italy–West Germany '70 will never be remembered as a work of art, but it nevertheless was voted the greatest World Cup match of all time in a 1997 poll of fifty star players, including Pelé, Beckenbauer, Johan Cruyff, Stanley Matthews, Alfredo DiStéfano, and Bobby Charlton, conducted by the French sports newspaper *L'Equipe*.

Each player was asked to name his top three favorite World Cup matches under a point system. Thirteen named Italy versus West Germany number one, including five players who were on the floor of the Azteca that day. Seven of the top ten games chosen were played in soccer's color TV era that began with the 1974 World Cup.

The results:

1. 1970 semifinal, Italy 4, West Germany 3 (OT)
2. 1970 final, Brazil 4, Italy 1
3. 1982 second round, Italy 3, Brazil 2
4. 1982 semifinal, West Germany 3, France 3 (West Germany on PKs, 5–4)
5. 1966 final, England 4, West Germany 2 (OT)
6. 1958 final, Brazil 5, Sweden 2
7. 1954 final, West Germany 3, Hungary 2
8. 1974 final, West Germany 2, Holland 1
9. 1970 first round, Brazil 1, England 0
10. 1986 quarterfinal, France 1, Brazil 1 (France on PKs, 4–3)

The Indifferent Lions Give Up Salenko's Five Goals

Does a record-setting performance count if it comes against an indifferent opponent?

It is doubtful that Russian striker Oleg Salenko bothered to ponder that question after he struck for five goals in a 6–1 rout of Cameroon in the opening round of the 1994 World Cup. The outburst at Stanford Stadium in Palo Alto, California, shattered the single-game World Cup record of four goals shared by Gustav Wetterstrom of Sweden (1938 versus Cuba), Leónidas da Silva of Brazil (1938 versus Poland), Ernst Willimowski of Poland (1938 versus Brazil), Ademir de Menezes of Brazil (1950 versus Sweden), Juan Schiaffino of Uruguay (1950 versus Bolivia), Sandor Kocsis of Hungary (1954 versus West Germany), Just Fontaine of France (1958 versus West Germany), Eusébio of Portugal (1966 versus North Korea), and Emilio Butragueño of Spain (1986 versus Denmark). But it wasn't quite the glorious feat it should have been.

Salenko, then a member of the modest Spanish club Logroñes and a player who will never be mistaken for one of soccer's immortals, scored Russia's first five goals, in the sixteenth, forty-first, forty-fifth, seventy-third, and seventy-fifth minutes. A disappointment in the Russians' 2–0 loss to Brazil in their tournament opener, Salenko started against Cameroon only because of star striker Sergei Yuran's falling out with coach Pavel Sadyrin.

Three of the goals were not exactly feats of genius. The second one came after Russia took a quick free kick while the Indomitable Lions argued with the ref over a foul call. The third was from the penalty spot, and the fifth was on a gentle lob after Salenko spied Cameroon goalkeeper Jacques Songo'o absent-mindedly drifting off his line.

Cameroon was ripe for just such an embarrassment. The darlings of the 1990 World Cup in Italy, the Lions were hardly troubled in qualifying for their second consecutive cup. They had plenty of internal troubles, however. First, a disputed election in the Federation Camerounaise de Football nearly caused FIFA to award the Lions' berth to another nation. Then the team itself unraveled after it became embroiled in a battle with its federation over bonuses the players claimed they had been promised for qualifying for USA '94.

After a 2–2 tie with Sweden at the Rose Bowl in their first match, the Cameroon players nearly boycotted their second game. Faced with setting an ugly precedent, the Lions reluctantly agreed to take the field but shouldn't have bothered as they were comprehensively beaten by eventual champion Brazil, 3–0, in Palo Alto. Veteran goalkeeper Joseph-Antoine Bell, who went public with the Lions' pay revolt before giving up all three goals, quit the team before coach Henri Michel could drop him.

By then, the demoralized Cameroon players needed a win over Russia and a Swedish upset of Brazil to be assured of advancing to the round of sixteen. The Russians, missing many top veterans who had refused to play for Sadyrin, were all but eliminated and certainly lined up against the now Indifferent Lions feeling no pressure.

Salenko, whose previous best on any stage was a hat trick for Dynamo Kiev in the 1990 Soviet Cup final, ended his stay in the United States with six goals in three games and eventually was tied for the tournament lead by Bulgarian hero Hristo Stoichkov, who played in the maximum seven games.

The all-time record for goals in a World Cup tournament is thirteen by Just Fontaine, who sealed his place in World Cup history by scoring four goals in the 1958 consolation match to lead France to a 6–3 victory over West Germany. Career leader is Brazil's Ronaldo (1998, 2002, 2006), whose three goals at the '06 World Cup gave him fifteen, one ahead of the previous leader, West Germany's Gerd "Der Bomber" Müller (1970 and 1974).

Italian Scandals a Precursor to World Cup Triumphs

Just days after its national team hoisted the World Cup trophy for the fourth time, beating France on penalty kicks in the final in Berlin, a match-fixing scandal that had smoldered in Italy for months reached its climax in July 2006 as the boom was lowered on four prominent clubs and several top officials and referees.

A domestic sports tribunal stripped Juventus of its 2004–5 and 2005–6 Serie A titles, dropped the Turin giant into Serie B, and docked it thirty points—later reduced to seventeen—to start the 2006–7 season. Fiorentina, Lazio of Rome, and AC Milan were penalized nineteen, eleven, and eight points, respectively.

Twenty-six nonplayers were implicated. Nineteen were punished, including two who were given lifetime suspensions after they had resigned.

Although the mess included charges of fraud, illegal wagering, and creative bookkeeping, the heart of the scandal was the network of contacts with Italian league officials masterminded by two Juventus officials to influence referee assignments and, in turn, yellow and red cards issued players. Those two officials, who both were slapped with five-year bans, resigned, along with the rest of the Juventus board, in May.

Of the twenty-three members of the Italian World Cup team, thirteen played for the four clubs sanctioned, but they managed to blot out the drama back home long enough to conquer Germany '06.

Scandal, however, seems to bring out the best in Italy when it comes to World Cups. The Italians won the second and third World Cups, Italia '34 and Francia '38, but didn't triumph again until España '82—when they were coming off another match-fixing scandal.

Central figure in that tempest was center forward Paolo Rossi, who scored three goals in Italy's fourth-place finish at the 1978 World Cup in Argentina. Rossi, on loan from Lanerossi Vicenza to Perugia, followed those heroics with his alleged involvement in a fixed-odds betting scheme in 1980. Despite scoring two goals in the game in question—a 2–2 draw with Avellino—he was hit with a three-year suspension.

Rossi protested his innocence long and loud, and subsequently his ban was conveniently commuted to two years, making Rossi, since transferred to Juventus, free to play in the final three games of the 1981–82 Italian season, giving him a valuable tune-up for the World Cup.

The '82 World Cup had been expanded from the customary sixteen teams to twenty-four. Rossi did little to distinguish himself in the first round, but the offensively challenged Italians got a major break: they finished tied for second in their group with Cameroon, behind Poland, at 0-0-3 but advanced on total goals scored (Italy scored two and gave up two; the hard-luck Cameroon side was 1-1).

That put Italy into one of four three-team second-round groups. Coach Enzo Bearzot was under fire to replace Rossi, but his patience was rewarded as his striker began to stir in a tough, 2–1 victory over

Argentina in Barcelona. Rossi's breakaway shot in the sixty-eighth minute was turned away by the goalkeeper but driven into the net by Antonio Cabrini for what proved to be the winning goal.

Back in Barcelona six days later against favored Brazil, the Rossi steamroller began. Brazil needed only a tie to edge the Italians for the semifinals, so when Roberto Falcao's sixty-eighth-minute goal evened the score at 2–2, the Brazilians appeared to be home and dry. But Rossi, who had scored with a header in the fifth minute and through a defensive blunder in the twenty-fifth, took advantage of a weak clearance by Junior in the seventy-fifth to complete his hat trick and drive a dagger into the heart of the Brazilians, who seemingly let their attacking instincts get the best of them.

But there was more to be done. In the semifinals, again in Barcelona, Rossi scored both goals against Poland in a 2–0 win, wiping out the memory of the punchless Italy that had played the Poles to a scoreless draw in the opener. And in the final against an injury-hit West Germany in Madrid, Rossi's header in the fifty-seventh minute snapped a scoreless deadlock and Italy roared on to a 3–1 triumph.

The rehabilitation of Rossi, the tournament's scoring leader, was complete. In fact, in the eyes of his countrymen, it came earlier, with the conquest of Brazil. A day after the Azzurri's semifinal win, the once-disgraced Rossi was honored by his government with the prestigious Commendatore de la Repubblica.

A final note: Italy became the first nation to be winless in its first three games and go on to a championship.

World Cup's Back Door Opens for Wales

England, Scotland, Northern Ireland, and Wales have made twenty-five World Cup appearances among them. Only once, however, did all four members of the United Kingdom play in the same World Cup, and that took some doing.

None of the four played in the first three World Cups because of Great Britain's on-again, off-again relationship with FIFA. The two sides made up after World War II, and it was decided that every four years the winner and runner-up of the annual Home International Championship would represent Great Britain in the World Cup, thus ensuring that two of the four would be on the outside looking in. After Brasil '50 and Switzerland '54, however, the doors were thrown open and the English, Scots, Northern Irish, and Welsh were placed in the general European population for the qualifiers for the 1958 World Cup, making all four eligible for the finals.

England, Scotland, and Northern Ireland all won their European groups, knocking out the likes of Italy and Spain along the way. Incidentally, England's first-place finish eliminated the Republic of Ireland.

But Wales never recovered from a 2–0 loss at Czechoslovakia and finished second to the Czechs in a group that included East Germany. The Welsh were resigned to watching the cup on TV—until a major break developed far away.

The Asia-Africa region was allotted one berth in the '58 finals, and eight nations were entered. In Group 2, Israel was to have met Turkey in a home-and-home playoff, but the Turks refused to play the Israelis and withdrew. In the second phase, Israel was snubbed twice more as two other Muslim states, Group 1 winner Indonesia and Group 3 winner Egypt, withdrew. That left Asia-Africa with a showdown between Israel and Group 4 winner Sudan. But Sudan, yet another Muslim state, likewise withdrew, putting the Israelis into the World Cup finals without their having played a game.

To FIFA, this would not do, and it was decided that Israel would have to beat *somebody* to get into the cup. So it held a lottery among the runners-up from Europe's nine qualifying groups to find an opponent for Israel, and Wales won. The Welsh then took the playoff, 2–0 in Tel Aviv and 2–0 in Cardiff, making it a cockeyed clean sweep for the United Kingdom.

But Wales did not go to Sweden as a tourist. Led by the legendary John Charles and strikemate Ivor Allchurch, the British minnows were bound and determined to make their mark, which they did by tying Hungary and Mexico by 1–1 scores and host Sweden, 0–0, forcing a playoff with the Hungarians to decide who from Group 3 would advance along with the first-place Swedes. Though the Magic Magyars had been depleted by age and defections during the Hungarian Revolution, Wales was given no chance, so only 2,832 were on hand in Stockholm to see a 2–1 upset that put Wales into the quarterfinals.

There, they had the misfortune of facing powerful Brazil in Gothenberg. Yet despite missing the injured Charles, the highly organized

Welshmen muffled Garrincha, Didí, and company for seventy-three minutes before seventeen-year-old Pelé scored the first World Cup goal of his career to give the relieved Brazilians a 1–0 decision.

Wales, the team that wasn't supposed to be in Sweden, had bowed out after giving the eventual champion Brazilians what they later considered their toughest game of the tournament. And making it all the sweeter was that the Welshmen finished, unofficially, tied for fifth in the tournament while Northern Ireland (2-2-1) was outclassed by France, 4–0, in the quarterfinals and England (0-0-3) and Scotland (0-2-1) failed to survive the first round. Not bad for a small country where rugby is king and the list of soccer clubs includes the likes of Merthyr Tydfil, Chirk, and Druids.

That Wales would be given a back door to begin with is just one example of the curious history of World Cup formats, one rife with loopholes, inequities, and downright bone-headedness.

The formula for the world's soccer championship is fairly simple, or at least it was at its debut in 1930 in Uruguay, where thirteen nations—three shy of the desired sixteen—were divided into four groups, and after round-robin play the four group winners advanced to the knockout semifinals. No third-place match was played, and it was all over after just eighteen games in as many days.

Clean and efficient was this combination of league and cup play, but then FIFA had a difficult time suppressing the temptation to tinker.

In 1934 (Italy) and 1938 (France), the entire sixteen-nation competition was changed to a knockout affair, so the first-round winners advanced to the quarterfinals and the losers, after just one match, went home. For the United States and Brazil ('34) and the Dutch East Indies ('38), that was a return trip of several thousand miles.

In 1950 (Brazil) round-robin group play was back as FIFA killed off single elimination entirely: the four group winners advanced to a second round-robin playoff, thus depriving the public of a true final. Fortunately, the last match was contested by that playoff's top two teams, host Brazil and Uruguay.

From 1954 (Switzerland) the format was relatively stable for the next seven tournaments. Sixteen teams were placed in four groups of four for round-robin play. In the first five the group winners and runners-up advanced to the knockout quarterfinals; semifinals, consolation game, and the final followed.

In 1982 (Spain) the World Cup was expanded to twenty-four teams as FIFA tried to extend its party beyond Europe and South America while better milking what had become its rapidly swelling cash cow. The four-team first-round groups jumped from four to an unwieldy six, with the first- and second-place finishers advancing to one of four three-team groups, the winners of which would play in the semifinals.

In 1986 (Mexico), 1990 (Italy), and 1994 (USA), the six group winners and runners-up and four best third-place finishers formed a knockout round of sixteen, which was followed by the quarterfinals and so forth. It was a somewhat clumsy route to the sixteen, but the various battles for third place guaranteed that, happily, the last game of nearly every group was significant.

In 1998 (France) FIFA, under increasing pressure from Asia, Africa, CONCACAF, and Oceania, expanded the field yet again, to thirty-two teams, thus opening the World Cup doors further beyond Europe and South America. The winners and second-place teams from what were now eight first-round groups advanced to the elimination stage, and while purists decried what they considered a diluted competition, the World Cup format had been made easier to follow.

Such was not the case in 1954 (Switzerland), when FIFA's hand became unusually heavy: sixteen teams, four first-round groups—and a remarkable, unnecessary twist. Instead of round-robin play among the group opponents, which would have resulted in two dozen games played, the FIFA brain trust decided that each group would have not one but two seeded teams. The seeded teams would play only the two unseeded teams, and if two teams tied at the top of a group, regardless of goal difference, they would draw lots to determine their places in the quarterfinals. (If teams tied for second, a playoff match would be held.)

Each team would thus play just two first-round games, and for the only time in World Cup history group matches tied after ninety minutes went to thirty minutes of overtime. (Only two games ended in a deadlock, and in both cases extra time failed to produce a winner.)

This daft format not only denied fans the opportunity to see matches between the two best teams in each group, but also by reducing the number of first-round matches—a total of sixteen, rather than twenty-four—FIFA increased the likelihood of ties in the group standings.

Group I cowinners Brazil (+5 goal difference) and Yugoslavia (+1) drew lots, as did Group III cowinners Uruguay (+9) and Austria (+6). In Group IV England finished first and Switzerland (-1) broke its second-place tie with Italy (+2) by winning a playoff, 4–1.

As for Group II, there was Turkey, which had "defeated" Spain in the European qualifiers.

Spain, not Turkey, was supposed to go to Switzerland. Spain, after all, had finished fourth at the 1950 World Cup in Brazil, while Turkey had skipped the first three World Cups, then qualified for Brazil '50, only to withdraw. So impressed was FIFA that it gave the Spaniards a group seeding in the World Cup finals even before the qualifiers were played. In January they opened European Group 6 against their one and only opponent, Turkey, with a 4–1 victory in Madrid. The Turks took the return leg, 1–0, two months later in Istanbul. But aggregate goals did not apply in this series, so, three days after, the two sides met again in neutral Rome and deadlocked, 2–2. Amazingly, there would be no overtime, no penalty kicks. There would be a drawing of lots. The Spaniards lost, giving Turkey not only a World Cup berth but Spain's World Cup seeding as well.

Turkey was placed in the same group with perhaps the biggest pre–World Cup favorite ever, Hungary, as well as what should have been the group's other seeded team, West Germany, plus the long shot South Korea. The West Germans thumped the Turks, 4–1, in Berne before taking their expected whipping at the hands of the Hungarians, 8–3, in Basle. Turkey hammered South Korea, 7–0, in Geneva, but because, again, goal difference was not a factor, the Turks (+4) and Germans (-2) were forced to meet in a playoff in Zurich.

West Germany won, 7–2, and thus took a softer route through the quarterfinals (2–0 over Yugoslavia in Geneva) and semifinals (6–1 over Austria in Basle), while Hungary had to fight its way past Brazil and Uruguay. The less-battered Germans then shocked the Hungarians, 3–2, in the final in Berne.

Goose Eggs for That Goal-Scoring Machine from Brazil

For all of its attacking flair, Brazil holds a World Cup record for offensive futility when it's all on the line. The Brazilians played Italy to a 0–0 tie at the 1994 final in Pasadena before eking out a victory via penalty kicks. In 1998 they were humbled by France, 3–0, in the final in Saint-Denis outside Paris. That's two consecutive world championship games, plus overtime ('94), without scoring a single goal. Throw in the last four minutes of the 1970 World Cup final in Mexico City, where Brazil routed Italy, 4–1, as well as the first sixty-seven minutes of the 2002 final, before Ronaldo scored the first of his two goals, and the South American giants, with the whole world watching, went 281 consecutive minutes without scoring a goal.

This from a country that has scored a World Cup–record 201 goals in its first ninety-five games, an average of 2.1 per match, as well as the most goals in a final, five, in its 5–2 romp over Sweden in 1958 in Stockholm. (On the other hand, Brazil had the dubious distinction of playing in the first-ever scoreless tie in a World Cup, in 1958 against first-round opponent England in Gothenburg.)

The only other teams shut out in a final are Argentina in 1990, Italy in 1994, of course, Germany, which lost to the Brazilians, 2–0, in 2002 in Yokohama after the South Americans regained their scoring touch and Holland, a 1–0 overtime victim to Spain in 2010.

Brazil's drought, however, came during an era in which winning a World Cup final takes a backseat to not losing it. From Jorge Burruchaga's winner late in Argentina's 3–2 victory over West Germany at Mexico '86 until Zinedine Zidane's first-half strike in the 1998 World Cup hosted by champion France, not a single goal was scored from anywhere but the penalty spot for 244 minutes, or more than four hours.

It also should be noted that in addition to its five world championships, Brazil, which once went unbeaten for thirteen World Cup games (1958 to 1966), has been eliminated by the eventual World Cup winner five times: 1938 by Italy (semifinal), 1950 by Uruguay (last game of championship pool), 1978 by Argentina (second-round pool), 1982 by Italy (second-round pool), and 1998 by France (final). The Brazilians also went down to the eventual runner-up five times: Hungary, in 1954 (semifinals), Holland twenty years later (second-round pool), Argentina in 1990 (second round), France in 2006 (quarterfinals), and Holland again in 2010 (quarterfinals).

Things like that are bound to happen when you're the only country to have participated in every World Cup and have gone into most of them as a favorite, if not *the* favorite.

Drop Trou', Score Goal

Brazil was trailing Italy, 1–0, an hour into its 1938 World Cup semi-final in Marseilles when star right back Domingos Antonio da Guia made his only mistake of the afternoon, bringing down Italian center forward Silvio Piola in the penalty area.

Most accounts agree that although Piola made a meal of the foul, Swiss referee Hans Wuthrich had already made up his mind and pointed immediately to the penalty spot. One report, however, describes Piola, lying on the turf, convincing Wuthrich to award the PK by pointing to Domingos like a man on his deathbed fingering his assailant.

What happened next inspired a variety of accounts:

Giuseppe Meazza stepped up to take the kick and beat Brazilian
    goalkeeper Walter without incident, or
Just before Meazza took his shot, he intentionally dropped his
    ripped shorts to his ankles, distracting Walter, or
Meazza dropped his shorts before the shot and beat Walter, who
    was doubled over with laughter, or
The elastic in the waistband of Meazza's shorts had broken. He
    placed the ball on the spot with his right hand while holding
    up his shorts with his left, then drilled his shot past Walter, or
Meazza converted his kick a moment before his ripped shorts
    accidentally fell around his ankles.

Italy held on for a 2–1 win, then beat Hungary, 4–2, in the final in Rome without any further wardrobe malfunctions on Meazza's part.

(Go with the fifth version. It's hard to believe, with a capacity crowd of thirty-five thousand looking on and millions of Brazilians on pins and needles back home, that goalkeeper Walter would blithely laugh at Meazza and allow the Italians their clinching goal.)

Market Forces at the World Cup Turnstile

Germany '06 and Mexico '70 are considered the two most festive World Cups in history, tournaments marked by generally attractive soccer, enthusiastic fans, and a warm welcome from the respective host nations. The two events, however, show that market forces can affect the cost of happiness.

Ticket prices for the final of the 2006 World Cup at the 66,021-seat Olympiastadion in Berlin ranged from about $166 to more than $800 for the best seats. For the group matches, the cheap seats cost nearly $50, the best seats $140.

At the 1970 World Cup, the least expensive group-round ticket cost . . . 40 cents (5 pesos). Wish you could have joined 107,000 fans in watching Pelé and his mates dismantle Italy in the final at Mexico City's Estadio Azteca from the comfort of a reserved seat? That would've cost you $12.80 (160 pesos).

> Everything I know surely about morality and the obligations of man, I owe to football.
> **ALBERT CAMUS,** French novelist and former goalkeeper for the Algerian club Oran

> If you'd given me a choice of beating four men and smashing in a goal from thirty yards against Liverpool or going to bed with Miss World, it would have been a difficult choice. Luckily, I had both. It's just that you do one of those things in front of fifty thousand people.
> **GEORGE BEST,** Northern Ireland legend, Manchester United great, and international playboy

4 MISBEHAVIOR

What would soccer be without players, coaches, team officials, fans, even the media, behaving badly? With so much seemingly at stake, getting an edge has become the game within the game. Whether it's an obscure youth match or a World Cup final, what goal-bound player, in hopes of drawing a penalty kick, hasn't tumbled to the earth after brushing by an enemy defender? Poor sportsmanship, or "ungentlemanly conduct" as it is referred to in the Laws of the Game, and its many cousins are an integral part of soccer. It may be maddening to some, but it also helped produce one of the longest chapters in this book.

Conspiracies? What Conspiracies?

FIFA has frequently tweaked the format of its World Cup in an effort to keep its marquee competition fair, competitive, and above board. However, there have been cracks, most notably Argentina-Peru at Argentina '78 and West Germany–Austria at Spain '82.

Brazilians continue to claim that the second-round match between Argentina and Peru in 1978 was a sham, that the Peruvians laid down so that the host Argentines could reach the final at Brazil's expense.

No proof was ever uncovered, and in fact there were reports before the match in the Argentine press that Brazil had attempted to bribe Peru to play well. Either way, the game had a curious odor to it.

Under the World Cup format that year, the winners and runners-up from the four first-round groups advanced to the second round, where they were divided into two groups for another round-robin playoff. The two second-round winners would advance to the final in Buenos Aires, the runners-up to the third-place match.

In the second round, Argentina landed in Group B with Brazil, Poland, and Peru. The Brazilians thumped Peru, 3–0, in their group opener in Mendoza, and the Argentines blanked Poland, 2–0, that same day in Rosario, setting up a critical showdown between the hosts and their perennial rival four days later in Rosario. That tense, emotional match, marred by a series of savage tackles, ended in an inconclusive 0–0 draw. Argentina and Brazil were now tied at three points apiece (two for a win, one for a tie in those days), with Brazil holding the edge in the first tiebreaker, goal difference, +3 to +2. Group B would be decided June 21: Brazil versus Poland in Mendoza and Argentina versus Peru in Rosario.

Brazil, behind two second-half goals by forward Carlos Roberto, took care of business with a 3–1 victory, but the game kicked off hours ahead of Argentina-Peru, giving the favored Argentines the advantage of knowing how many goals they would need to overhaul the Brazilians.

As a result the Argentines lined up with a five-man front line and attacked relentlessly for ninety minutes. Despite the backing of a rabid capacity crowd of 40,567 at New Rosario Stadium, Argentina didn't score until Mario Kempes broke through in the twentieth minute with a shot past Peru goalkeeper Ramón Quiroga. Three more chances went wanting before Alberto Tarantini doubled the lead two minutes before halftime. Kempes scored again in the forty-eighth minute to level the goal difference with Brazil at +5, and Peru then collapsed, allowing goals to Leopoldo Luque in the forty-ninth minute, Rene Houseman in the sixty-eighth, and Luque again in the seventy-second for a 6–0 rout.

As one Brazilian sportswriter lamented, "If Brazil had won 50–0 against Poland, Argentina would have won 52–0!" And rumors swirled after the match that fascist Argentina subsequently shipped thirty-five thousand tons of grain to fascist Peru free of charge while the Argentine Central Bank unfroze $50 million in Peruvian credits.

Peru's battered goalkeeper, Quiroga, published an open letter defending his side's effort in the Group B finale, but his credibility, to Brazilians at least, was suspect. Quiroga, after all, was a naturalized Peruvian, born in Rosario, Argentina. The man known as "El Loco" also had once again shown his eccentric side in Peru's previous match by fouling Poland winger Grzegorz Lato on *Poland's* half of the field.

Argentina defeated Group A winner Holland in the title game, 3–1, in overtime for its first world championship; Brazil beat Italy, 2–1, for third.

The final records of the two South American giants, with goal difference in parentheses: Argentina, five wins, one loss, one tie (+11); Brazil, four wins, zero losses, three ties (+7).

Four years later, having the advantage of knowing ahead of time what needed to be done would allow not one but two teams to advance in a World Cup.

The 1982 World Cup in Spain kicked off with twenty-four finalists—an increase of eight from Argentina '78—and a format in which the winners and runners-up from the eight four-team groups would move on as well as the four best third-place finishers. Nevertheless, FIFA, seemingly oblivious to the Argentina-Peru debacle four years earlier, still failed to give the last two matches in each group the same kickoff time. In fact, it didn't even have the last games of each group played on the same *day*.

Algeria, a Group 2 long shot, pulled off an early stunner in Gijon when it upset West Germany, 2–1, in its opener. The Algerians lost to Austria, 2–0, in Oviedo five days later but closed out their first-round slate by beating Chile, 3–2, also in Oviedo. That result left the North Africans tied on points with Austria and two ahead of West Germany; on goal difference, the Germans and Austrians were both +2 and the Algerians 0.

The next day in Gijon, six days shy of the twentieth anniversary of Algeria's independence, West Germany and Austria met in Group 2's last match and engaged in the biggest farce in World Cup history.

The Germans opened the scoring in the tenth minute on a header by hulking striker Horst Hrubesch. Knowing that a 1–0 West German win would see the two neighbors through at Algeria's expense, the Germans and Austrians proceeded to aimlessly pass the ball around for the next eighty minutes. Algerian supporters on hand, convinced the match was fixed, booed and whistled in disgust; some tried to invade the field to halt the game. In the stands, a West German burned his nation's flag.

FIFA rejected out of hand an Algerian call to disqualify West Germany and Austria on sportsmanship grounds, and Algeria's first World Cup adventure ended in bitter disappointment. Final group standings (with goal difference): West Germany 2-1-0 (+3), Austria 2-1-0 (+2), Algeria 2-1-0 (0), and Chile 0-3-0 (-5).

West Germany later bowed to Italy, 3–1, in the final in Madrid. Austria lost to France and tied Northern Ireland in its second-round group and was eliminated. Algeria qualified for Mexico '86, crashed in the first round, and didn't make it back to the World Cup for twenty-four years.

How distasteful was the game derisively called a second German-Austrian *anschluss*? French coach Michel Hidalgo, anticipating a second-round meeting with the Austrians, scouted the match and didn't take a single note. Hidalgo later suggested that the two sides be awarded the Nobel Peace Prize.

Money *Can* Buy You Goals

Can't get enough scoring in soccer? Perhaps you need a scoring fix. Here's not one but four examples.

- In February 2004 Wilfred Leisure and Curtorim Gym of the third division in India were tied on points on the last day of the season, so it was possible that goal difference would determine which side would be promoted to the second division.

  Unbeknownst to the players from either side was the fact that both season finales—Wilfred versus Dona Paula Sports Club and Curtorim versus Sangdolda Lightning—had been fixed.

  And so, for ninety minutes, team officials planted at the rival teams' matches made frantic phone calls back to their respective home grounds, giving updates and thus inspiring a scoring frenzy as the compliant Dona Paula and Sangdolda defenses gave up more and more goals.

In the end, Wilfred crushed Dona Paula, 55–1, only to be outdone by Curtorim, which scored sixty second-half goals for a 61–1 victory. That's 116 goals scored—or given a welcome mat—in two games.

"It is really unfortunate," said a spokesman for the All India Football Federation. "We have suspended all four teams for one year and recommended that they should be expelled permanently."

- Mere slackers were the two teams that were paid to lose matches in September 1999 and help determine a regional championship in Paraguay.

  Needing lopsided victories to improve their goal differential, the two contenders got their money's worth as one, behind a thirty-five-goal effort by one of its players, posted a 75–0 victory and the other won 37–0. That's only 112 goals.

  A giveaway that something was up: both losing teams showed up with the minimum seven players.

- Renaissance Daoukro of Ivory Coast's second division was ordered by authorities in August 2004 to spend at least two seasons in the third division because of a match-fixing scandal. Renaissance entered its final game needing to beat AS Tanda by sixteen goals to qualify for the promotion playoffs, and it led, 8–0, less than fifteen minutes after the opening kickoff. At one point, a half-dozen Tanda players walked off, disgusted at the lack of effort by certain teammates. Renaissance won, 20–0.

- Mumias Sugar was stripped of its 1999 Kenyan first-division crown after it was learned that its final match had been fixed—for all of $535.

  The last-place Kisumu All Stars were paid in installments—before, during, and after the match—to give Mumias a runaway victory and the championship over Tusker FC on goal difference. Mumias needed a ten-goal win and got it, 10–0.

  Player-coach Nick Yakhama and his assistant, Patrick Mugata, arranged the fix, according to the Kenyan Football Federation, which suspended both Mumias and Kisumu for a year.

A Penalty Kick as an Own Goal

There are own goals, and then there's the own goal scored in a fit of pique in March 1998 in an English amateur league match in Scarborough between Tap and Spile FC and Rangers Reserves.

Incensed by a penalty kick awarded to Rangers by referee Steve Ripley, Tap and Spile captain Paul Flack, age twenty-two, stepped up and drilled the PK past his own goalkeeper.

"I thought if he was stupid enough to do it, I'd give the goal," shrugged Ripley.

Thus inspired by Flack's act of insurrection, Tap and Spile went on to lose, 5–4.

Turkey's Answer to Howard Cosell Pays a Price

TV soccer commentator and former referee Ahmet Cakar was notorious for his acerbic criticism of the Turkish league's players and teams. He once claimed that the mafia controlled soccer, personally called the president of Turkey's biggest club, Galatasaray, a liar, and engaged in a running battle with the head of the Turkish soccer federation.

Cakar was asked in February 2004 if he feared physical retribution. "The worst they can do is kill me," he replied defiantly. "Whoever dares can come and try to take my life. But it's not that easy. . . . He who has the guts to shut me up, he who has the heart, the courage to do this, please let him come. But my flesh is thick. It's not so easy to bite."

Quite true. Days after daring his critics to kill him, Cakar was visiting a hospital when an assailant, concealing a pistol behind a bouquet of flowers, shot the commentator five times in the stomach and groin.

Cakar survived.

Malfeasance Puts Greek Team in the Cellar

National soccer leagues routinely dock clubs points in the standings for various transgressions, from failure to control an unruly home crowd to financial misadventures. Usually the penalty is three points or so, based on the universal system of three for a win and one for a tie, and rarely does such a punishment have a major impact on the final standings.

The Greek league (EPAE), however, proved to be absolutely merciless in its handling of PAS Giannina in April 2003. The cash-strapped team's mountain of debt included more than $1 million owed to no less than eighteen former players, and the exasperated EPAE dropped the hammer with four rounds remaining in the 2002–3 Greek championship. It subtracted ninety points from the Ioannina-based club, three for each game it would play that season, leaving it at the bottom of the division with *minus* sixty-five points.

At the time of the sanction, the team was in fifteenth, or next-to-last, place with nineteen points. PAS Giannina finished last, of course, and was relegated to the Greek second division for 2003–4. It could have been worse, however. Earlier in the season the EPAE deducted twelve points from Giannina for debts to other clubs, but that sanction was overturned on appeal.

Camera-Throwing Fan Caught on Film

To catch a thief—make that a minor hooligan—just check the film in his camera. Such was the fate of the Turkish fan who tossed his disposable camera at Ronaldinho as the Brazilian star exited the field following Brazil's 2–2 draw with Turkey in Saint-Etienne in the first round of the 2003 FIFA Confederations Cup in France.

French police recovered the camera and developed the film, finding one exposure of the fan himself, proudly standing in front of his car. The authorities tracked down the man through the license plate on the car in the photo and soon made an arrest.

Chilean Goalkeeper Busted for Bad Acting

Attacking players are notorious for their bad acting as they try to convince the referee that they not only were fouled but were nearly killed by an opposing player. Their antics are usually ignored by the referee or, on occasion, met with a yellow card for play acting.

The worst-ever soccer thespian made his grand appearance at Maracana Stadium in Rio de Janeiro in 1989 during a World Cup qualifying match between Brazil and Chile. This central figure was not a forward but a goalkeeper.

In August the two sides tied in their first meeting, 1–1, in Santiago.

Brazil coach Sebastião Lazaroni complained that his Chilean counterpart, Orlando Aravena, had whipped the home crowd into a frenzy, and Brazil subsequently lodged a protest with FIFA.

Three weeks later in the return leg in Rio, Brazil was clinging to a 1–0 lead on a goal by Careca when, in the sixty-ninth minute (or sixty-fifth or seventy-eighth, depending on the account) a lighted flare was hurled from the stands and landed at the feet of Chile goalkeeper Roberto Rojas, who threw himself to the turf holding his face.

As smoke billowed from the flare, Rojas was stretchered off the field, covered in blood, and his teammates, seemingly fearing for their safety, walked off the field. The match was abandoned.

Any hopes the Chileans may have had that they would be awarded a forfeit victory or a replay at a neutral site were dashed by FIFA, which gave the win to Brazil, barred Chile from the 1994 World Cup, fined the Chilean soccer federation $31,000, and slapped Rojas with a lifetime ban from international soccer for faking the injury. Rojas had indeed sustained a cut during the incident, but it turned out to be self-inflicted: he'd been slipped a blade by a trainer during the confusion caused by the flare.

As for the person who threw the flare, Rosemary de Mello, a twenty-four-year-old secretary, she made the most of her fifteen minutes of fame. Dubbed "Rocket Rosey," she posed nude for the Brazilian edition of *Playboy* and appeared in several TV commercials.

A very late postscript: A benevolent FIFA finally showed Rojas mercy in April 2001, when it granted him a pardon. The move came at the urging of the Chilean players union, which found that Aravena, via walkie-talkie, ordered the goalkeeper as he was being treated to stay on the turf and await a stretcher. By the time of Rojas's pardon, he had retired as a player and become a trainer in, of all places, Sao Paulo, Brazil.

The Chilean debacle apparently went unnoticed in Tunisia, where one of its leading clubs, Esperance, tried in December 2000 to succeed where Chile and Rojas had failed.

Esperance, a 2–1 loser to Ghana's Hearts of Oak in Tunis in the first leg of its African Champions Cup final, was leading in the seventy-fifth minute of the second leg, 1–0, in Accra and pressing for the critical second goal when rioting erupted, prompting police to fire tear gas into the crowd. One canister landed in the VIP box, forcing African soccer confederation chief Issa Hayatou of Cameroon and other dignitaries onto the track surrounding the field.

During the confusion a Tunisian fan ran to Esperance goalkeeper Chokri El Ouaer and handed him an object, which he used to gash the side of his face. Referee Robin Williams caught the Tunisian international in the act, however, and ejected him, ignoring El Ouaer's claims that he had been injured by a missile hurled by Hearts supporters.

When play resumed, Esperance, having made its three substitutions, curiously replaced El Ouaer in goal with midfielder Hassen Gabsi, who had scored his team's goal with a diving header in the tenth minute.

With a midfielder now in goal, Hearts of Oak took full advantage. Captain Emmanuel Osei Kuffour scored in the eighty-third and eighty-ninth minutes and Ishmael Addo added a third goal during injury time to give the Ghanan side a 3–1 second-leg victory and the title by a 5–2 aggregate.

Thirteen years after the Rojas/Rosie incident, Brazil benefited from some bad acting by one of its own. At the 2002 World Cup, in the Group C opener in Ulsan, South Korea, Brazil was tied with an upset-minded Turkey, 1–1, with five minutes remaining. The Turks' Alpay Ozalan was then sent off for a controversial shirt-pulling foul on Luizão in—or rather, near—the penalty area. Rivaldo converted the resulting PK to put the Brazilians ahead for good.

However, Rivaldo, who first stung the Turks by setting up Brazil's equalizer shortly after halftime, wasn't done. Two minutes into added time, while Rivaldo waited to take a corner kick, Hakan Unsal petulantly kicked a ball that struck the Brazilian in the leg. Rivaldo went down in a heap, clutching his *face*, and South Korean referee Yung Joo Kim bought it, showing Unsal his second yellow card and with it a red.

The incident was shown repeatedly on the stadium video screens, drawing boos from the Munsu Stadium crowd. Rivaldo was fined $7,350 by FIFA for "simulation," but he was unrepentant. "Obviously, I exaggerated the incident for the guy to be sent off. It didn't hit me in the face, but that kind of [action] must not be allowed on the field. He deserved to have a red card."

Brazil won Group C and, eventually, the World Cup. Turkey recovered to finish second in the group and a surprising third overall.

Croatian Players Not Worthy of Their Jerseys

NK Dinamo Zagreb players were left topless in October 2004 after some fifty supporters of the Croatian club stormed a team training session.

The fans, irate after their team stumbled to just three wins in its first eleven matches, claimed that the Dinamo players were not fit to wear the team's blue jerseys and forced them to hand them over. The players, coming off a 2–1 loss at home to the mediocre Slaven Belupo, meekly complied, and they completed practice in plain shirts.

Dinamo president Mirko Barisic was left shaken by his team's capitulation. "It's interesting that the players showed no resistance," he said. "That tells you something about their mentality. That is also the way they were behaving on the field."

A year earlier Dinamo led Croatia in goals scored and finished second in the championship to NK Hajduk Split by a mere two points. This Dinamo team finished the first stage in seventh place and dropped to the relegation stage, but it managed to remain in the top division by going 3-2-5. Perhaps that dissuaded the fans from stripping the players of their shorts as well.

Elsewhere in Croatia, two defeats left one team dead and buried. That was the message delivered by some angry supporters of Hajduk Split a month into the club's 2003–4 season when they climbed a fence surrounding Poljud Stadium, eluded security cameras, and dug graves on the field for each Hajduk player, coaching staff member, and club official.

Hajduk, runner-up for the championship and winner of the Croatian Cup the year before, had kicked off its new campaign with a 4–1 loss at home to the newly promoted Inker, then dropped the first leg of its first-round UEFA Cup qualifying series at FC Haka of Finland, 2–1.

Thus inspired by its "supporters," Hajduk rallied to beat Haka, 1–0, back at Split to take that series on away goals, and although it was eliminated in the third round by AS Roma on aggregate, 2–1, months later Hajduk rolled to its fourth Croatian league title in twelve years.

Run Over by a Taxi

A certain taxicab driver in Cordoba, Argentina, probably thought he had heard it all from his customers until Talleres striker Claudio Gonzalez hopped into his hack in April 2003. Gonzalez told the cabbie not only that he had recently faked an injury but also that the Talleres players were doing what they could to get rid of their coach, ex-Uruguayan international Luis Cubilla. The cab driver sought out Cubilla, presented his Club Atlético Talleres membership card, and told the coach of his revealing conversation with the player. Gonzalez was promptly suspended by Talleres.

No Doctor in This House When Italy's on TV

In November 1987 a group of employees at San Gennaro Hospital in Naples abandoned their stations to watch a telecast of Italy's 2–1 victory over Sweden in a qualifying game for the 1988 European Championship. Authorities arrested thirty-nine hospital staffers, and criminal charges were filed against twenty.

Brazil Club Prompts Fans to Turn About-Face

Just when it needed them most, fans of Fluminense turned their backs on the team. Spectators sitting in a section of Laranjeiras Stadium in Rio de Janeiro stood and faced away from the field during the latter part of Fluminense's 3–0 loss to Sport Recife in a September 1997 home match. What triggered the demonstration was Recife's third goal, the result of a Fluminense defensive error. The loss left Fluminense next-to-last in the twenty-six-team Brazilian national championship. Flu's coach, Carbone, was dismissed two days later.

One Italian Club's Answer to Racism

More than eight decades after a mixed-race Uruguay team dazzled Europe in winning the 1924 and 1928 Olympic soccer tournaments, racism remains one of continental soccer's most embarrassing problems. Racist taunts and bunches of bananas hurled from the stands are only part of the indignities many black players have had to endure.

At the end of Italy's 2000–1 Serie B season, one club decided to respond. The players of Treviso appeared in blackface in support of teammate Akeem Omolade for a home match against Genoa. The eighteen-year-old Nigerian entered the game to half-hearted applause from Treviso fans and scored his side's second goal in a 2–2 tie. Omolade's heroics, unfortunately, weren't enough as the draw condemned Treviso to relegation to Serie C.

A week earlier, Omolade made his debut with Treviso and was booed by the team's fans. One section of supporters left the stadium in protest.

Paraguayan Medics Add Injury to Injury

Players and team officials engaged in a ten-minute free-for-all during a Paraguayan playoff match in October 2001 in Luque after stretcher bearers from host Sporting Luqueño dropped a Sportivo San Lorenzo player.

San Lorenzo players attempted to get at the stretcher bearers, who they believed intentionally caused injured striker Gerardo Traverso to tumble to the ground as he was being carried to the sidelines. Luqueno players tried to protect the stretcher bearers, and the brawl was on. At least one player was head-butted, and four were shown red cards.

The match, the second leg of the quarterfinals, ended 0–0 and San Lorenzo advanced on aggregate, 1–0.

Brazilian Teammates Sent Off for Fighting

Two teammates begin fighting late in a match. How do you, the referee, handle the situation?

The referee of an April 2001 game in Rio de Janeiro between Vasco da Gama and Fluminense, faced with just such a predicament, correctly sent off both players for violent conduct.

The bizarre battle began while Vasco goalkeeper Helton was being treated for an injury. Paulo Miranda accused teammate Viola of failing to mark his man. Viola, a veteran of Brazil's 1994 World Cup championship, took exception, and the two Vasco players exchanged punches.

After being shown red cards, Miranda and Viola continued to scrap on the way to the dressing room, and Vasco officials were forced to pull them apart.

Despite being reduced to nine men, Vasco held on for a 3–3 tie.

That punch-out came three and a half years after another scrap between Brazilian teammates, this time in a national championship game at Maracanã Stadium in Rio. Coritiba was playing Flamengo when forward Jaja made a poor pass. Defender Guiherme complained, and the two came to blows. Both were sent off and a grateful Flamengo went on to win, 1–0.

The bad behavior of Miranda and Viola was exceeded in April 2005 as Newcastle United teammates Lee Bowyer and Kieron Dyer got their marching orders for fighting one another during an off-the-ball incident.

Bad enough that the Magpies were already trailing in their English Premier League match, at home, to Aston Villa by a decisive 3–0, but when the two England international midfielders left in the eighty-first minute, they had been preceded by substitute defender Stephen Taylor, who had been ejected earlier by referee Barry Knight for an intentional handball that helped give Villa its third goal.

Eight-man Newcastle lost. Villa's hero that day was Gareth Barry, who scored his side's last two goals, both from the penalty spot, and separated Bowyer and Dyer during their punch-out.

At the postgame press conference, Bowyer and Dyer, seated on either side of stone-faced coach Graeme Souness, apologized to anyone within the vicinity of the Magpies' St. James Park.

What If the Combatants Are Bench Personnel?

Liga de Quito found out what happens when bench personnel begin brawling in September 2003. Its physical trainer, Alejandro Valenzuela, and team physician, Juan Barriago, traded punches during an Ecuadoran first-division match at Tecnico Universitario, much to the surprise of Liga players, coaches, and the crowd of five thousand. Both were red-carded by the referee, who later had to halt play after a police officer accidentally fired a tear gas canister onto the field.

Italian Club Offers Its Fans Hooligan Insurance

Fear of hooligans keeping you from watching your favorite club in person? Modena, a northern Italian club playing at the time in Serie B, came up with a solution in November 1990 with an offer of free insurance to its 1,265 season-ticket holders. "If fans get punched, get bottles smashed on their heads, get bitten by (security) dogs in the stadium, they now have insurance," said Modena president Francesco Farina, who allowed that the coverage cost just 25 cents per spectator per game.

In addition to the in-stadium protection, the fans were insured against traffic accidents up to an hour before and after every home match. Not a bad idea for sports spectators everywhere.

A Very, Very Late Red Card

It's true: a player left a match for a substitute and was ejected nearly a half hour later.

Cremonense and Treviso were playing an Italian Serie B match in April 1999. Mattia Collauto of Cremonense was replaced in the sixty-sixth minute. Treviso equalized late in the game with a disputed goal, and at the final whistle Collauto, who hadn't played in more than twenty-five minutes, was shown a red card for arguing with the officials.

His sending off went down in the books as coming in the third minute of added-on time.

You Can't Watch Your Team, but You Can Play for It

It's also true that a man can be allowed to play in a game that he would otherwise be prevented from watching as a spectator.

Veli Hakki, age twenty-three, was convicted of hooligan activity for his role in a riot during an English match in 2002. He was sent to prison for a year and banned from attending professional matches in England for six years. Hakki served his time, and in November 2003, when the professional Blackpool played the semipro Boreham Wood in an F.A. Cup first-round match at Blackpool's Bloomfield Road Ground, Hakki was there. That's because part-time hooligan Hakki also was a Boreham Wood player.

Blackpool, then part of the English second division, brushed aside Boreham Wood, 4–0, and Hakki, a carpenter, went back to hammering nails and sitting out his exile as a pro soccer spectator.

Mexican Club Made Relegation Proof

The owners of Club Puebla de la Franja sure showed the Mexican league after their team was relegated following the 1999 summer season. Thanks to Mexico's complicated promotion/relegation system, Puebla was on the precipice in the closing weeks along with fellow strugglers Atlético Celaya and Monterrey. In the end Puebla sank to the second division based on goal difference (-15 to Monterrey's -13 and Celaya's +3).

Rather than go quietly from the Campeanato, or first division, down to Division 1-A, however, the Puebla bosses pulled a remarkable end run. Owner Francisco Bernat announced the purchase of CD León, another struggling first-division club, with the intention of moving it to Puebla, where it would continue to play in the top flight as Puebla FC. León owner Victor Aguirre and León fans protested, however, and the Puebla bosses backed down, only for a new scheme to be revealed two days later. This time another León-based club, Union de Curtidores, promoted to the top division by virtue of its Division 1-A championship, was purchased by Aguirre and would play in the Campeanato as a reconstituted Puebla FC with a mix of Puebla and Leon players. CD León would continue in the top division with a roster made up of Curtidores players. And the relegated Puebla FC would be represented in Division 1-A by a new team, Angeles de Puebla, populated with Puebla reserves.

The plan nearly backfired immediately when Angeles de Puebla won its 1-A division group going away during the 1999 winter season, but it lost in the playoff quarterfinals to San Luis by a 5–2 aggregate, ending the possibility that two Puebla sides with the same owners would end up in the top flight.

Angeles again knocked on the first-division door during the 2000 summer season, finishing first in its group again. But it was eliminated once again in the playoffs, and the Puebla bosses' web remained not quite so tangled.

Magic Charm Does the Trick for Rwanda

A juju is a magic charm cherished—and feared—in West Africa. It can only be created by a witch doctor, and it takes many forms, whether a spirit, an aura, or an actual object, like a monkey's paw.

Whether good or bad, juju also bedevils soccer in that region, and one juju nearly caused the abandonment of an African Nations Cup qualifying match in June 2003 between host Uganda and Rwanda in Kampala, a game already politically charged because of those two countries' clashes in recent years over the war in the neighboring Democratic Republic of Congo.

Six weeks earlier, the two sides met at the Rwandan capital, Kigali, and Rwanda goalkeeper Mohammud Mossi pulled off a string of spectacular saves to preserve a scoreless draw that further tightened the three-team Group 13, which included Ghana. The Ugandan players were convinced that Mossi had employed juju, burying it in the turf inside his goal or applying it to his gloves.

With the return leg in Kampala, the Ugandans were on guard. But first, there were some prematch complications.

Rwanda, which was seeking its first berth in the African Nations Cup finals, appeared to be headed for a forfeit the day of the game as the bus taking the team from its Kampala hotel to the national stadium was stopped dead in snarled traffic. The president of the Rwandan soccer federation, Brigadier General Cesar Kayizari, exited the bus and strode nearly two miles to the source of the problem, an impossibly tangled intersection. The imposing Kayizari, who took a bullet in the mouth during a Rwandan guerrilla war a decade earlier, assumed the role of Ugandan police captain and ordered the startled traffic officers in charge to get things moving, which they did with a frantic due diligence. The Rwanda bus arrived at Nakivubo Stadium two hours late, and for his second act, Kayizari convinced the Ethiopian referee to allow the game to go on.

A crowd of 60,000, some 15,000 beyond capacity, jammed the stadium, and Mossi repeated his first-leg routine, igniting a magic something in his goal area. Mossi let the Ugandan players know that he had, in his words, "electric juju" on his side, and he "proved" it early with yet another excellent save. That triggered a free-for-all as one Ugandan player tried to tear off Mossi's gloves and another dug frantically around the Rwandan goal in search of the offending juju. Among the blows landed as the players skirmished was one by a Ugandan reserve who used his shoe to put a gash in the head of Rwanda striker Jimmy Gatete. A charge onto the field by Ugandan police only worsened the situation, and match officials eventually got the two sides separated. A half hour later, play resumed, and shortly thereafter Gatete, sporting a large bandage around his head, scored the game's only goal.

Before the second half began, the Ethiopian linesman walked to the goal area vacated by Mossi, made the sign of the cross, and removed the Rwanda 'keeper's juju.

All of Rwanda—eight million strong, most of whom live on a dollar a day—went wild, and after the Wasps' flight touched down in Kigali around 1:00 a.m. the players were greeted by President Paul Kagame, Prime Minister Bernard Makuza, and cabinet members, then driven to a packed Stade Amahoro ("peace stadium") for a middle-of-the-night celebration.

Rwanda apparently got by without the power of the juju in its final qualifier that July back at Amahoro, against Ghana, a four-time champion of Africa. Uganda had finished group play with five points, and Ghana and Rwanda were tied at four, with the Black Stars, ahead on goal difference, needing only a draw to win the group. But Gatete scored again in the second half and Rwanda—No. 119 at the time in the FIFA world rankings—eked out another 1–0 victory to become the smallest country to reach the African Nations Cup since Mauritius in 1974.

A Very, Very Early Red Card

Players have been known to be red-carded in the minutes after a match for jawing with the referee or picking a fight with an opponent on the way to the dressing room, but here's an ejection forty minutes *before* a game.

A backup goalkeeper for host Real Betis, Joaquín Valerio, was talking with players from his previous club, Albacete, prior to a Spanish second-division match between the two teams in December 2000, when referee Fidel Valle Gil overheard Valerio insult him. Valle Gil pulled out his red card, and Valerio was done for the day, well before most spectators had arrived.

Zidane's Infamous Head-Butt a Top-40 Hit

The sight of Italian players celebrating their nation's historic fourth world championship should have been the lasting memory of the 2006 World Cup final, but instead it's that of French superstar Zinedine Zidane suddenly burying his head into the chest of Italy's Marco Materazzi in overtime of a tense 1–1 battle.

Zidane was red-carded and the short-handed French, minus their captain, playmaker, and best penalty-kick taker, went on to lose in a PK tiebreaker.

No choir boy, Materazzi had been ejected five minutes into the second half of Italy's 1–0 second-round win over Australia for a sloppy tackle against midfielder Marco Bresciano; the defender was thus suspended for the quarterfinals and missed Italy's 3–0 victory over Ukraine.

It took Materazzi more than a year to reveal what he said to trigger the head-butt seen 'round the world; it went like this: Zidane, exasperated by Materazzi's hands-on marking throughout the game, sneered, "If you want my shirt that badly I'll give it to you at the end of the match," to which the Italian retorted, "I'd prefer your whore of a sister." Zidane, whose family came to France from Algeria, was livid—Materazzi had besmirched the honor of a Muslim woman in the presence of her Muslim brother.

While the truth was long in coming, it was just the blink of an eye after the final itself for "Coup de Boule" ("Head Butt") to be written, recorded, and on its way to the top of the French music charts. "Watch out, it's the head-butt dance," goes the ditty, composed in thirty minutes by two producers from La Plage Records, while the chorus "Zidane, he hit him," plays over an African beat. The record sold sixty thousand copies in France just nine days after ZZ's infamous hit.

The "Head-Butt Dance" came and went, and so did Zidane, winner of the FIFA World Player of the Year trophy in 1998, 2000, and 2003. "Zizu," who had already announced that Germany '06 would mark his international swan song, not only turned in his France jersey that summer but walked away from his club, Real Madrid, as well. He was all of thirty-four. Despite his ignominious exit, Zidane was awarded the Golden Ball as the 2006 World Cup's most valuable player and, at year's end, nearly missed being named the best player on the planet for an unprecedented fourth time as he finished second to Italy's Fabio Cannivaro in the voting for the '06 FIFA World Player of the Year award.

He hasn't played a competitive match since.

The Ugly Legacy of the Late, Unlamented Intercontinental Cup

There have been far too many ugly soccer matches over the game's long history, but the ugliest *big* match was, arguably, the climactic game of the 1967 Intercontinental Cup series between Glasgow Celtic of Scotland and Racing Club of Argentina.

The annual home-and-home playoff between the reigning European (Euro Champions Cup, now UEFA Champions League) and South American (Copa Libertadores) club champions for the unofficial world club championship had been plagued by cynical play, questionable calls, and fan violence from its launch in 1960, so neither side could have been startled when there was trouble. But this one . . . .

Celtic, on a sixty-ninth-minute goal by Billy McNeill, won a relatively uneventful opening leg, 1–0, in mid-October before a crowd of one hundred and three thousand at Hampden Park in Glasgow. Two weeks later at Estadio Mozart y Cuyo in Buenos Aires, as the teams warmed up for the second leg, Celtic goalkeeper Ronnie Simpson was knocked cold by one of several stones hurled from the stands. John Fallon was hastily inserted to fill in, and Racing beat the shaken Scots, 2–1, in front of one hundred thousand as forward José "El Chango" Cardenas scored a brilliant goal three minutes into added-on time.

The Argentines' last-gasp victory tied the series at a win apiece and set up a third and deciding game, which was scheduled for the semineutral Montevideo three days later.

The showdown at Estadio Centenario was ill-tempered from the start, and by the twenty-fifth minute Paraguayan referee Rodolfo Perez Oserio, on the brink of losing control, called together the two captains and issued a warning.

Within twelve minutes, elusive Celtic winger Jimmy Johnstone was fouled down by Racing midfielder Juan Carlos Rulli. Defender (and future Argentine National Team coach) Alfio Basile of Racing then spat on Celtic winger Bobby Lennox, triggering fights among the players. Police rushed in and order was restored after five minutes as Oserio ejected both Basile and Lennox.

Three minutes into the second half, the diminutive Johnstone was fouled again, and he retaliated by punching Racing defender Oscar Martin, earning an expulsion. Eight minutes later, Racing striker Cardenas pounced on a through ball by Rulli and scored the game's lone goal with a thirty-five-yard blast.

It was all over except for the brawling. Celtic forward John Hughes was ejected for a blatant foul on Racing goalkeeper Agustin Mario Cejas, leaving the Scots with eight men. Then Rulli was given his marching orders in the eighty-sixth minute, reducing the Argentines to nine. Finally, with two minutes remaining, a free-for-all broke out. Oserio apparently ejected Celtic midfielder Bertie Auld, but Auld was still on the field when the game came to its merciful end. Racing left the chaotic scene as world club champions.

The five players sent off set a record for a professional match involving a British team, and an apoplectic Celtic management fined its offending players 250 pounds each. The mess helped convince organizers by 1969 to replace the original format—total points for two games, followed by a playoff, if necessary—with aggregate goals. But the Intercontinental Cup's image was further tarnished by the violent play of a new Argentine power, Estudiantes de La Plata, which beat Manchester United in 1968 and lost to AC Milan in 1969 and Feyenoord of Rotterdam in 1970.

Lowlights included a punch-out between United great George Best and José Hugo Medina that got both players ejected; and an elbow thrown by Aguirre Suarez that broke the nose of Milan's Argentine-born striker, Nestor Combin, and ignited a player melee.

The Europeans couldn't have been taken by surprise: most of Estudiantes' leading players were graduates of the club's under-19 team, a band known as La Tercera que Mata ("The Killer Juveniles"), and the violent game encouraged by coach Osvaldo Zubeldia was dubbed El Antifutbol.

So bad was the behavior of Estudiantes in the Milan series—the spitting, the shoving, topped by an incident in which Milan's Pierino Prati was kicked in the back by Estudiantes goalkeeper Alberto Poletti while being treated for an injury—that the Argentine president, General Juan Carlos Ongania, appalled by what he saw on television, had the entire team arrested. Poletti was suspended for life but later pardoned. The following year, after substitute Joop van Daele scored a second-half goal to give Feyenoord a 1–0 second-leg victory and the series on aggregate, 3–2, Estudiantes' Oscar Miguel Malbernat responded by ripping off the glasses of Feyenoord coach Ernst Happel and stomping on them; Malbernat later explained that the wearing of spectacles was not allowed in South American futbol.

(Estudiantes ironically included two players who completed medical degrees while in the red and white stripes of Los Profesores, midfielders Raul Madero and captain Carlos Bilardo, who would go on to coach Argentina to the 1986 World Cup title and a runner-up finish in 1990. Bilardo's assistant at Mexico '86 was ex-Estudiantes teammate Carlos Pachame.)

By 1971 Europe's Intercontinental Cup participation became a running question. European Cup holder Ajax Amsterdam refused to meet Libertadores Cup holder Nacional of Uruguay and was replaced by Euro runner-up Panathinaikos of Greece, which lost. Ajax conquered Europe again in 1972, changed its stance, and defeated Independiente by an overall 4–1, but the Argentines' rough play, which resulted in an injury to superstar Johan Cruyff, led the Dutch club to declare that it would never play another match in Argentina.

Independiente repeated as Copa Libertadores winner the next year, and Ajax, again the Euro champion, was true to its word. Juventus of Turin filled in and was beaten by Independiente in a single-match playoff in Rome, 1–0. In 1974 Bayern Munich and Independiente were the finalists, but the German side, concerned by the competition's violent reputation and by possible financial losses, bowed out; Atlético Madrid, the replacement, defeated Independiente on aggregate, 2–1. Ironically, it was newly acquired Argentine Reuben Ayala who scored the winner for Atlético in its 2–0 second-leg victory in Spain.

So bad was Independiente's reputation in Europe by then that in 1975, when South America was once again represented by the Argentine club, both European Cup winner Bayern and runner-up Leeds United turned down the chance to take part, and the Intercontinental Cup was not contested.

The competition received a jump-start in 1976 when Bayern agreed to meet a new South American champion, Cruzeiro of Brazil. Only 22,000 skeptical Munich fans showed up to watch their club take the home leg, 2–0, but a throng of 114,000 in Belo Horizonte was on hand for the 0–0 tie in the second leg.

The European withdrawals, however, continued. Liverpool opted out in 1977—Borussia Moenchengladbach of West Germany stepped in and lost handily to Argentina's Boca Juniors by a 5–2 aggregate— and in 1978 Liverpool gave Boca Juniors the cold shoulder, once again interrupting the series.

The following year, another Euro champ from England, Nottingham Forest, failed to show, leaving it to FF Malmö to take over and bow to Olimpia of Paraguay, 1–0 in Sweden and 2–1 in Asunción.

Something had to be done, and it was in 1980 that the automaker Toyota stepped in as principal sponsor, turning the annual event into a single-match playoff that would be held at a most neutral site, Tokyo's National Stadium, in late autumn. That first year Nacional of Montevideo defeated Nottingham Forest, 1–0, before a capacity crowd of sixty-two thousand, and the Intercontinental Cup was saved.

The cup, also known as the Toyota Cup, became an occasionally interesting test of top teams from the world's leading soccer-playing regions. Some finalists took it seriously; some regarded it as a distracting exhibition foisted on them in the middle of the league season. It was no longer, fortunately, the passionate, chaotic showdown it was in the days of Celtic-Racing as European and South American clubs buried the hatchet.

FIFA never officially recognized the Intercontinental Cup—it couldn't be considered a world club championship, after all, because it didn't involve the continental champions of Africa, North America, Asia, and Oceania. The FIFA chief, first Dr. João Havelange and later Joseph Blatter, found a way to attend in later years, but the competition's days became numbered with the creation in 1999 of the FIFA Club World Championship as a sop to the weaker continental soccer confederations. Despite its dark chapters and status as the true world club championship, the Intercontinental Cup whimpered to a close after 2004 as FC Porto of Portugal edged Once Caldas of Colombia on penalty kicks after a placid scoreless tie at Yokohama's International Stadium.

You're Never Too Old to Be a Hooligan

Soccer hooliganism is a young man's occupation—with at least one exception. Raymond Everest, age fifty-six, was sentenced by a London judge in January 2003 to five years in prison and banned from all soccer stadiums in England and Wales for eight years for a kung fu–style kick landed on a police horse following an English first-division match between Millwall and Birmingham City the preceding May.

Everest, a self-proclaimed Millwall supporter from the age of three, was caught by closed-circuit TV cameras laughing following a fan rampage outside Millwall's New Den Stadium. A total of 157 police officers and twenty-six police horses were hurt.

"You have brought shame on your family and on the club you purport to support," Judge Philip Statman told Everest. "It is difficult to imagine a worse example of behavior by a man in his mid-fifties than that you displayed on that particular evening."

The opposite wing of the English hooliganism hall of shame would have to include a fourteen-year-old Portsmouth fan who became the youngest female to be punished for misbehavior at a match. In July 2004 a local court found Felicity Thorpe guilty of violent disorder for her role three months earlier in an incident following a Premier League game against Southampton.

Thorpe, who had a record of seventeen previous offenses, admitted to being a part of a crowd of three hundred that ran amok outside Fratton Park Stadium. The pony-tailed girl was captured by television cameras dressed in a Portsmouth jersey and hurling at least sixteen rocks and other missiles at police. She claimed to be retaliating after an officer struck her with a baton earlier in the evening.

Thorpe was banned from matches for six years and ordered to spend eight months in a juvenile detention facility.

Seen on the telly with Thorpe was an unnamed boy engaged in similar mayhem. He was barred from matches and referred to detention by magistrates. At age ten, that made him the youngest convicted hooligan in England.

The Irrepressible Vinnie Jones

Vinnie Jones was well known—make that infamous—for being the toughest of the English League's tough guys during a stormy career that reached its peak—or nadir—in the 1990s. The onetime captain of the Welsh National Team left many an attacker writhing on the turf in agony on his way to thirteen career red cards.

As Jasper Rees wrote of Jones in the *Independent* in October 1992, "The image people have of him is of a player who regards it a matter of personal honour to intimidate the nation's finest, to castrate them with a shattering, late tackle early in the game, to rip their ears off and spit in the hole." Jones described himself in simpler terms five years later: "I can't run, can't pass, can't tackle, can't shoot, but I'm still here."

Jones pulled off one of the quickest ejections in soccer history when in February 1992 he was sent off three seconds into a fifth-round English F.A. Cup match between Chelsea and Jones's former club, Sheffield United. That topped the red card shown Jones after a mere five seconds the preceding season.

But Sheffield Wednesday goalkeeper Kevin Pressman outdid even Jones when it comes to getting a quick hook. Pressman managed to be shown a red card in the thirteenth second of his team's English first-division game against Wolverhampton in August 2000 for an intentional handball committed outside his penalty area. While that missed Jones's mark by ten seconds, it came during Sheffield Wednesday's 2000–1 *season opener.*

Then there's Jason Crowe of Arsenal, who was red-carded thirty-three seconds after coming on as a substitute in an English League Cup game against Birmingham in October 1997. Crowe was making his English debut in that match, so the ejection came slightly more than a half-minute into his *professional career.*

The all-time champ, however, is Walter Boyd. In November 1999, with Swansea and Darlington of the English third division tied, 0–0, the Jamaican international forward entered the game in the eighty-third minute as Darlington prepared to take a free kick. But before referee Clive Wilkes could whistle to restart play, Boyd, in the midst of some pushing and shoving at the top of the Swansea penalty area, punched Darlington's Martin Gray and was sent off. Time elapsed: zero seconds.

As for the master of sustained misbehavior, it's central defender Agim Shabani of Fredrikstad FK, a Norwegian of Albanian descent. In June 2007 Shabani was given his marching orders in the last minute of stoppage time in a 2–1 loss to Stromsgodset in a Norwegian Premier League match. The next day he was sent off while playing for the Fredrikstad reserves in the second division, and two days after that he was ejected during Fredrikstad's loss to Nybergsund IL in the Norwegian Cup. Three red cards in three different competitions in four days.

A postscript on Jones: Vinnie, who in 1992 was suspended by the English F.A. for six months for bringing the game into disrepute, parlayed his reputation as the baddest of soccer bad boys into an acting career. No Olivier, he, but Jones did receive rave reviews for his movie debut in *Lock, Stock and Two Smoking Barrels,* ultimately winning an award as the British screen's best newcomer. Stars in his eyes, he retired as a player months later at age thirty-four. Jones followed that with a costarring role in the Brad Pitt film *Snatch*. Both films were directed by the future Mr. Madonna, Guy Ritchie. Within three years of his acting debut, Jones was named British Actor of the Year. Usually the heavy, Jones appeared in dozens more films—among them *Gone in Sixty Seconds* and *X-Men: The Last Stand*—appearing alongside the likes of John Travolta and Nicolas Cage. In a bit of perfect casting, Jones also narrated the English video *Soccer's Hard Men*, which included shots of players yanking armpit hair and grabbing the genitals of opponents.

Israeli Fans Jump the Gun

Impatient fans of Hapoel Tel Aviv nearly caused their club to lose an Israeli championship because of a premature celebration. In the next-to-last round of the 1999–2000 season, second-place Hapoel Petach Tikva lost, leaving Hapoel Tel Aviv needing only a point to clinch its first national title in twelve years. And Tel Aviv appeared to have it in its hip pocket as the seconds ticked away during a 1–1 tie with Bnei Yehuda.

But overeager fans invaded the field and tore down one goal, forcing the match to be abandoned. A week later, the Hapoel Tel Aviv players, unfazed, calmly beat Maccabi Herzliya, 2–0, to clinch the crown.

The Reason Soccer Players Don't Wear No. 88

Italian international goalkeeper Gianluigi Buffon changed the number on his Parma jersey in September 2000 after being accused by the country's Maccabi Association of having neo-Nazi leanings. Buffon had selected the unusual No. 88, a numeral that is used by neo-Nazis as a code for "Heil Hitler," *h* being the eighth letter in the alphabet. The pressure to drop 88 was somewhat justified: Buffon had been spotted earlier wearing a T-shirt with the fascist slogan, "Death to those who surrender."

A Soccer Brawl on the Floor of the Italian Parliament

Please don't disturb the Italian Parliament when it's addressing important affairs of state.

Italy's legislative body apparently had nothing better to do than discuss soccer one day in April 1998, in particular what had become a nationwide debate over whether a penalty should have been award-ed to Inter Milan after Ronaldo was fouled by a Juventus player in a key Serie A match played the previous weekend in Turin. Deputy Prime Minister Walter Veltroni found himself in the middle of the storm as MPs denounced the match's referee as having a longtime pro-Juventus bias.

The climax was an explosion by right-wing MP Domenico Gra-mazio, who was restrained by ushers before he could attack left-wing MP Massimo Mauro, a former Juventus player who taunted him by repeatedly calling him a clown.

The members could be excused for their impassioned remarks on the floor. After all, Juventus' 1–0 win that weekend gave the team a four-point lead over Inter with three matches remaining in the 1997–98 season. Two weeks later the side known as "the Old Lady" clinched its second *scudetto* (Italian championship) in a row, its third in four years, and the record twenty-fifth in club history.

The Inter fans among those in Parliament had watched Inter hold on to the top spot throughout the fall until it was caught by the hard-charging Juventus in January. A week before the late April showdown with Inter, Juve, which had lost only two matches at home all season, visited lowly Empoli and escaped with a 1–0 win after a seemingly valid goal by the hosts was disallowed. That put Juve ahead of Inter by one point.

Never mind the Parliament. What about the Vatican?

In October 2004 the official radio station of the tiny Roman Catho-lic state premiered "Not Only Sports," a program that gave the priest-hood a forum to weigh in on all matters soccer. One of the show's first guests was Cardinal Florenzo Angelini, who implied that the Italian National Team selection process was corrupt. Host Luca Col-lodi wholeheartedly agreed.

Accustomed to abuse from press and public, this was too much for Italy coach Marcello Lippi. "I understand that Italy is a Catholic country, but now we've got cardinals talking out about football," the exasperated Azzurri boss said. "I'm having a hard time understand-ing this."

Perhaps Angelini absolved Lippi upon Italy's triumph at the 2006 World Cup.

Bogus Telegram Causes Goalkeeper to Miss Match

In 1904 the goalkeeper for Bristol East, an English club, received a telegram from the team secretary informing him that a match with Warmley had been called off. The goalkeeper stayed home and Bristol East was lucky to scrounge a replacement in time for the game. It was later learned that the telegram had been sent by Warmley. Three Warmley officials were later punished by the English F.A.

Player Argues *Against* Favorable Penalty Kick Call

The controversial career of talented striker Robbie Fowler hit a high note of sorts in March 1997 when he pleaded with the referee not to award his side, Liverpool, a penalty after he collided with Arsenal goalkeeper David Seaman during an English Premier League game. Referee Gerald Ashby insisted on giving Liverpool the PK, and Fowler took it, making a tame attempt that Seaman parried. To Fowler's chagrin, the loose ball rebounded to Liverpool teammate Jason McAteer, who had no disagreement with his conscience and drilled it home for a 2–1 victory. The reaction of Fowler's teammates was mixed, but his sportsmanship was widely praised from FIFA President Sepp Blatter on down.

Fowler was less sporting two years later in a league match with crosstown rival Everton. After enduring taunts from Everton fans who accused him of cocaine abuse, Fowler scored on a penalty kick in the fifteenth minute and celebrated by pretending to snort one of the lines marking the penalty area. Though Fowler apologized for the stunt the following day, the English F.A. was not amused and fined him $52,000.

Ill-Gotten Gains: Steaua Bucharest Rejects Romanian Cup

Steaua Bucharest has won twenty Romanian Cups, including one in 1988 in which it received all kinds of help from friends in high places.

Steaua was tied with Dinamo Bucharest, 1–1, in the ninetieth minute when the apparent winning goal, scored by Steaua forward Gavrila Balint, a Romanian international, was disallowed by the referee because of offside. Steaua's biggest fan, Valentin Ceausescu, son of Romanian President Nicolae Ceausescu, ordered the team off the field. The Minister of Sport directed the media not to report the score until the following day, when the Romanian soccer federation announced that Balint's goal indeed counted and that Steaua was the cup winner.

All video of the match was destroyed and the referee, Radu Petrescu, and the linesman who flagged Balint, George Ionescu, were fired.

In 1990, after the fall of Ceausescu, Steaua Bucharest renounced the '88 cup.

Chilean Star Retires Rather Than Serve Suspension

At age thirty-six, Iván Zamorano knew he was going to retire soon but not exactly when—until he got some help from the Chilean league.

A former star for Real Madrid and Inter Milan and coholder of the Chilean record for international goals with thirty-four, Zamorano returned to his native land in early 2003 after fourteen years in Europe and Mexico with the intention of closing out his career with Colo Colo, the Santiago club he followed as a boy.

That July, he helped Colo Colo reach the Chilean championship series, but it all came undone when Cobreloa pounded out a 4–0 second-leg victory to claim the crown. Zamorano was ejected from that game and made matters worse by shoving the referee on his way out.

That shove got him an eleven-game suspension. Rather than serve it, the man known as "Bam Bam" called it a career.

Indonesia's Self-Inflicted Loss Doesn't Pay Off

When is a loss a win?

When Indonesia intentionally scores an own goal to lose to Thailand, 3–2, in September 1999 in Ho Chi Minh City in the first round of the Tiger Cup, an eight-team competition for Southeast Asian nations.

Indonesia and Thailand were deadlocked, 2–2, in the final minute, but in a surreal scene, the Indonesians scored an own goal despite the desperate efforts of Thai players to stop the perpetrator. It capped a game in which neither side tried to win, the four previous goals notwithstanding.

The Indonesians' self-inflicted loss made them the Group A runner-up and paired them with Singapore in the semifinals, while Thailand was damned to travel to Hanoi to face the host Vietnamese in a game scheduled on their national holiday.

But crime didn't pay. Regional soccer authorities fined Indonesia and Thailand $40,000 apiece for their charade, and two days later they were punished on the field as well. Indonesia was a 2–1 upset victim to Singapore back in Ho Chi Minh City, and Thailand was humbled by Vietnam, 3–0, before the expected frenzied capacity crowd of twenty-three thousand in Hanoi.

Three days after that, Singapore took the Tiger Cup by upending Vietnam, 1–0, in Hanoi. And Indonesia and Thailand? The Indonesians prevailed in the consolation match in Ho Chi Minh City on penalty kicks, 5–4, following a 3–3 draw.

The public could trust that result because no one has yet figured out a way to score an own goal in a PK tiebreaker.

The Ultimate Protest: 149 Own Goals

If there's a record in soccer for spite, it must belong to a club from Madagascar, Stade Olympique de l'Emyrne, which in October 2002 found a particularly self-destructive way to express its displeasure with a referee's performance.

Angered at what they considered impartial officiating, SOE players proceeded to kick the ball into their own net 149 times in a season-ending match against AS Adema. Stade Olympique coach Ratsimandresy Ratsarazaka ordered his players to carry out the farce after he exchanged harsh words with the referee. At the final whistle, spectators demanded ticket refunds, and Madagascar's soccer governing body, Federation Malagasy de Football, later meted out stiff sanctions against SOE.

Ratsarazaka and his players were no doubt in a foul mood when the team took the field against Adema. SOE, the 2001 Madagascar champion, had been forced to hand over its crown to the new champion, Adema, the previous week.

Argentine Fans Threaten Own Goalkeeper with Kidnapping

They're commonly called supporters, but a knot of fans of the Buenos Aires club Lanus were anything but supportive toward their team's goalkeeper in November 2003 during an Argentine first-division match at Estadio General Arias.

Claudio Flores told the media that Lanus fans threatened to kidnap his son—and this during the second half of a scoreless draw. "They repeated my home address," said Flores, a Uruguayan, after the game against Independiente. "They said they would kidnap my family. I played a few meters further out of my goal than usual so I didn't have to hear any more. When the match was over, I called home to see if everything was OK."

Flores sent his family back to Montevideo for the final three games of the season.

England Has Its Say after Beckham's Red Card

Before he married a Spice Girl and became an international icon, David Beckham was perhaps best known for his petulant kick to the leg of midfielder Diego Simeone early in the second half of England's 1998 World Cup second-round match against Argentina at Saint-Etienne.

The kick came in retaliation for Simeone's foul on Beckham, and with the Manchester United star still sprawled on the turf, it wasn't much of a blow, not from a player already legendary for his pinpoint crosses and deadly free kicks. But he delivered it with Danish referee Kim Nielsen no more than a few feet away, and it earned Beckham a red card.

The score at the time was 2–2, and the game had been a wide-open affair to that point, a potential classic. Now shorthanded, England had to endure wave after wave of Argentine attacks for the remaining forty-three minutes of regulation and thirty minutes of overtime. Argentina ultimately won on penalty kicks.

Beckham's ill-timed ouster inspired withering criticism back home. Among the headlines: "What an Idiot" and "Dozy David Has Ruined Our Lives" (*Daily Star*); "You Let Nation Down" (*Sun*); and "10 Heroic Lions, One Stupid Boy" (*Mirror*).

Even Prince Charles weighed in: "It was very, very sad, wasn't it?"

Perhaps the worst came from a Baptist church in Nottingham, whose marquee read: "God forgives even David Beckham."

Eight months later Beckham's Manchester United and Simeone's Inter Milan would meet again in a UEFA Champions League quarterfinal.

Not averse to prematch publicity, Simeone told *Gazzetta dello Sport*, "Obviously I was clever by letting myself fall . . . and the referee fell into my trap . . . showing the red card. You can say that my falling turned a yellow card into a red card."

Manchester United won the game, 2–0, at Old Trafford as Beckham set up both goals. The English side tied Inter, 1–1, two weeks later at the San Siro in Milan to take the series on aggregate.

That proved to be the beginning of Beckham's rehabilitation. Two months later, after rallying to eliminate Juventus in the semifinals, United, in its first Euro Cup final in thirty-one years, snatched a last-gasp, 2–1 victory over Bayern Munich in Barcelona to complete a historic treble—English Premier League title, English F.A. Cup, and the Euro crown. And two years after that, Beckham, now wearing the captain's armband, scored a stunning free-kick goal in added-on time back at Old Trafford to give England a 2–2 tie with Greece in its last qualifier, allowing the English to squeeze into the 2002 World Cup.

Berlin DJs Offer Cash to Bayern Munich to Dump Game

Think the wacky radio station in your town is out of control? The zany jocks at Berlin's top-rated 104.6 RTL offered $1.23 million to any Bayern Munich player who scored an own goal in a German first-division match against Hertha Berlin in March 2004. At the time, Bayern Munich, originally the favorite to capture yet another Bundesliga championship, was nine points behind Werder Bremen with ten games left while Hertha was second to last in the eighteen-team division and in danger of relegation.

"The Bundesliga is being damaged by this offer by a network that normally doesn't even report on Hertha matches," sniffed the Deutscher Fussball-Bund (German football federation) in a statement. "We consider this to be an immoral offer and thus null and void."

As it turned out, neither of the goals in Hertha's 1–1 draw with Bayern Munich were self-inflicted. Two months later Bayern came in second, six points behind champion Werder Bremen, and the less-ambitious Hertha was safely ensconced in twelfth place, far from the relegation zone.

It's Lights Out for Soccer Gambling Scheme

Three men were given prison terms ranging from thirty months to four years in August 1999 for a scheme concocted by an Asian gambling syndicate in which they caused the stadium lights to fail at English Premier League matches.

The men, two from Malaysia and one from Hong Kong, were convicted of conspiracy to cause public nuisance for trying to end games early while the score favored the syndicate. Caught in the act during a February match between Charlton Athletic and Liverpool at Valley Stadium, they were believed to have caused the blackouts at two games in late 1997. A security guard was given an eighteen-month sentence for accepting a bribe to let the men into Valley Stadium during the Charlton game.

Coin Tossed at Referee Costs Scottish Club $72,000

A coin was thrown from the stands during a May 1999 Auld Firm match between Glasgow rivals Celtic and Rangers at Celtic's Parkhead, striking referee Hugh Dallas, who required medical attention for a head wound. Dallas finished the game.

Three months later, the Scottish F.A. fined Celtic $72,000 for failing to prevent the incident.

Gil and Gaucci: Club Owners Behaving Badly

Those who run top professional soccer clubs are a relatively dull lot, although there are the exceptions, such as Silvio Berlusconi, who rode the name recognition he gained as owner of AC Milan to election as prime minister of Italy, and Bernard Tapie, also a politician and boss of Olympique Marseille who spent a year in prison for match fixing.

Then there's Jesús Gil y Gil and Luciano Gaucci.

Gil, who died in May 2004, owned Atlético Madrid for seventeen years and seemingly spent his tenure either firing his coaches or trying to stay out of jail. He made his fortune as a property developer and first hit the headlines in 1969 after fifty-eight people were killed in the collapse of one of his buildings in Segovia, a structure that was constructed without the input of an architect. Sentenced to five years for criminal negligence, Gil was pardoned by dictator Francisco Franco and set about to rebuild his fortune.

Gil assumed control of Atlético Madrid in 1987. Four years later he ran for mayor of the jet-set resort of Marbella, where he had several holdings, and was elected in a landslide. Soon, Atlético had a new sponsor emblazoned across its jersey: Marbella.

Among the highs and lows of the Gil era at Atlético:

- Thirty-nine coaches were hired and fired, including a half dozen in a single season. The mercurial Gil also went through nearly 150 players.
- Gil and Compostela president José Maria Caneda came to blows in 1996—on live TV—when they arrived for a meeting at Spanish league headquarters.
- Gil once recommended that a certain referee seek psychiatric treatment.
- Atlético won three King's Cups, including 1995–96, when the club also took the Spanish Primera Liga championship ahead of traditional powers Real Madrid and FC Barcelona, the team's first-ever league-cup double. Gil celebrated by roaming the streets of Madrid atop an elephant.
- The Atlético supremo saw no reason to continue fielding one of the club's youth teams and dissolved it. Among the players cut loose was Raúl, who would go on to become a Spanish idol at Real Madrid and the national team's all-time scoring leader.
- Gil was forced by a judge to temporarily relinquish control of the club in 2000, and Atlético subsequently sank into the second division for the first time in sixty-six years.

Trouble followed Gil to the end. In 2002 he was jailed and later freed on nearly $1 million bail as investigators probed allegations that he lifted $35 million in municipal funds and falsified documents in Marbella. In the year before his death he was found guilty in a separate case of misappropriation of funds and fraud and handed a three-and-a-half-year sentence, which he appealed.

Scandals were all a minor concern to Gil compared to what he called his "blind love" for Atlético Madrid, which returned to the top flight in 2002. Fitted with a pacemaker in 2003 because of high blood pressure, Gil, who had stepped down as president, was ordered by doctors not to watch a match against crosstown rival Real Madrid.

Gil died at age seventy-one, six days after suffering a stroke. More than fifteen thousand, including players, politicians, and officials of rival Spanish clubs, filed past Gil's coffin in the funeral chapel erected at Atlético's Vicente Calderon Stadium.

Gil, however, was a shrinking violet compared to Gaucci, president of the modest Italian club Perugia.

Gaucci first made international headlines with his reaction to the heroics of South Korea striker Ahn Jung-Hwan, who scored the overtime goal in Daejeon that knocked heavily favored Italy out of the 2002 World Cup. The goal, giving the host Koreans a 2–1 decision and a spot in the quarterfinals, sent millions of Ahn's countrymen into a frenzy. Unfortunately, Ahn's club was Perugia, and the goal sent his boss, Gaucci, into a fury.

"I am not going to pay the salary of a guy who has been the ruin of Italian soccer," said Gaucci of Ahn, who had ridden the bench during his two years with Perugia. The comment caused the Asian Football Confederation to warn players under its jurisdiction to steer clear of Gaucci and his club.

Gaucci declared that Ahn would "never set foot in Perugia again" for scoring the goal—and he was right. After the World Cup, Ahn, still miffed by Gaucci's grandstand play, sent three faxes to Perugia saying he would not rejoin the team. Gaucci softened his stance. Perugia, which acquired the player on loan from the Korean club Pusan two years earlier and later purchased him outright for $1.6 million, exercised its option on Ahn, a move that would have kept him in the fold through 2004–5.

Ahn, however, resisted, and after failing to hook on with another European club, he landed in Japan with Shimizu S-Pulse, taking his wife, a former Miss Korea, with him.

Gaucci, meanwhile, appeared to be just warming up:

- In June 2003 the Perugia owner signed Al-Saadi Gaddafi to a two-year contract. A rather ripe thirty years old, Gaddafi was son of Libyan leader Colonel Muammar Gaddafi. He also was a Libyan international, the president of the Libyan soccer federation, and player-owner of the Libyan first-division club Al-Ittihad. The third of seven Gaddafi sons, Al-Saadi also represented Libyan Arab Foreign Investment Company, which held a 7.5 percent stake in perennial Italian champion Juventus.

Gaucci hoped the younger Gaddafi would boost Perugia's TV ratings in Libya, where 2.5 million of the country's 3.5 million residents considered themselves soccer fans. Gaddafi's Perugia debut was delayed, however, when, after three months on the bench, he was suspended for three months in November for testing positive for the performance-enhancing steroid norandrosterone. The striker claimed that the medicine he took for a bad back was probably to blame, but he didn't appeal the ban.

Gaddafi finally made his first appearance, as a substitute, in a May 2004 match against Juventus that raised eyebrows. The relegation-threatened Perugia, in a must-win situation, was clinging to a 1–0 lead at the time and could have used an extra defender. Said coach Serse Cosmi, "Gaddafi came on because he is a player and not because any one of us wanted to go into history as the one who first played the son of a head of state in the Italian championship." Not even Gaucci.

Gaddafi and Gaucci soon parted, and the Libyan didn't make his next Serie A appearance until two years later, playing the last ten minutes of Udinese's season finale.

• Not long after signing Gaddafi, Gaucci turned his attention to an even more controversial acquisition when he pursued Swedish National Women's Team strikers Hanna Ljungberg and Victoria Svensson in hopes of making them the Serie A's first female players.

The Perugia boss milked the situation for months until the women, finding Gaucci disingenuous, threw up their hands. "I find it difficult to see what I am to do in a men's team," said Svensson.

• With his club in next-to-last place in the eighteen-team Serie A, Gaucci threatened to forfeit his team's last four matches of the 2003–4 campaign in protest of calls by referees made against Perugia. "This is not a threat, but a decision," he said firmly.

Gaucci quickly backed down and Perugia picked up three wins and a draw, but the strong finish only got the club fifteenth place and a relegation playoff with Serie B's fifth-place team, Fiorentina, which it lost.

- Undaunted, the Perugia boss sought a loophole to keep his team in the top flight. Aware that Parma was in financial peril, he filed an appeal against a recent federal court ruling that any club in administration would not automatically lose its place in the league.

Gaucci had some experience in this area. A year earlier he won a legal battle against the Italian Federcalcio after he appealed against the relegation of another club he owned, Catania, from Serie B. Catania's readmission forced the Italian second division to expand from twenty teams to a bloated twenty-four.

This time, however, Gaucci's bid failed and Perugia dropped. Financial hardship followed, Gaucci's thirteen-year stewardship ended, and his beloved club soon settled into the anonymity of the Serie C.

English Hooligans Turn to Internet to Set Up Clash

Hooliganism went high-tech in August 1999 with a clash between fans of Cardiff City and Millwall over an English first-division match in Cardiff.

Authorities said an Internet bulletin board included several mentions of the match. One read, "11 o'clock Cardiff Central, where we go from there its up to u." Another: "Don't miss the tear-up of the year."

Fourteen persons were injured and police made six arrests throughout the day as hooligans battled in the middle of the Welsh capital.

The genie was out of the bottle. In Brazil an October 2005 clash between Palmeiras and Corinthians fans in a São Paulo subway station set up via the Internet resulted in a gun battle that left one dead and two critically wounded. And two months later in Rio de Janeiro, two were killed and four others injured in another Internet-arranged scrap. Botafogo and Fortaleza supporters were to brawl in nearby Niteroi, but Botafogo fans ambushed a van carrying Fortaleza fans. One of those fatally shot was the chief of the Fortaleza supporters club.

Fortunately, fans also can join forces for good.

In November 2007 some 20,000 of them from more than seventy

countries, united through the 50,000-member Web site MyFootball-Club.co.uk, purchased a controlling interest in Ebbsfleet United, a nonleague club on the outskirts of London from England's lowly fifth division. Members each paid about $72, amassing more than $1.4 million over eleven weeks, to take a 51 percent stake in the team, plus an option to buy Ebbsfleet in the future.

The deal, struck less than a year after the Web site's launch, gave the new owners one vote apiece in every matter from team lineups to player transfers. "During and after matches, Ebbsfleet supporters often give me their opinion on which players should or shouldn't start games; now they have their say," said Liam Daish, whose title was changed from team manager to head coach, which in British soccer represents a demotion.

Ebbsfleet's going truly public was the brainchild of former BBC newsman Will Brooks. Upset that his favorite English Premier League club, Fulham, had been taken over by Egyptian tycoon Mohamed Al-Fayed, Brooks came up with his idea as a protest against the commercialization of soccer in England.

MyFootballClub.co.uk was approached by nine lower division clubs and examined seven before casting its favored gaze upon Ebbsfleet.

Romanian Star Banned Until Player He Hurt Recovers

Marius Lacatus, who starred for Romania at the 1990 World Cup, paid an unusual price for a vicious tackle in April 1999. After the veteran forward, playing for Steaua Bucharest, chopped down Vasile Ardeleanu of FCM Bacau, causing a double fracture in Ardeleanu's leg, the Romanian soccer federation decided that Lacatus would be suspended until his victim could return to action.

Ardeleanu was sidelined for six months. In the meantime, Steaua Bucharest footed his hospital bill, and Lacatus, who also served as Steaua's team captain and assistant coach, paid all the bonuses Ardeleanu missed during his recovery.

First-Half Czech Walkout Gives Belgians Early Gold Medal

No team has ever walked off the field during a World Cup. No team has forfeited a World Cup match. Olympic soccer, however, hasn't been so lucky.

Belgium has been one of soccer's pioneers, the first continental European country to establish a national soccer federation and, along with France, Holland, Denmark, Sweden, and Switzerland, a founding member of FIFA.

Belgium's only major honor remains its gold medal at the 1920 Olympic Games, held, coincidentally, in the Belgian port city of Antwerp. It marked the Belgians' first appearance in a major competition, and perhaps most impressive was the fact that the Red Devils needed just 159 minutes of play to win the tournament.

World War I had canceled the 1916 Berlin Games, but the Olympics bounced back in a subdued form in Antwerp, which featured a fourteen-team soccer tournament, the biggest field to date.

Belgium, along with France, received a bye through the first round, so when the Belgians breezed past Spain, 3–1, and Holland, 3–0, the hosts found themselves a win away from the gold.

The final was played before a full house of twenty-seven thousand at the Olympisch Stadion. Belgium's opponent was the team from the newly formed country of Czechoslovakia, which had routed France in its semifinal, 4–1.

The Czechs, starring several players from the Bohemia, Sparta, and Slavia Prague clubs, had scored fifteen goals and conceded one through their first three matches. But inside left Robert Coppee, the hat-trick hero of the Belgians' semifinal win over Holland, shot his side into the lead in the sixth minute from the penalty spot after a handball violation, and inside right Henri Larnoe doubled the Belgians' advantage at the half hour.

As play became more hectic the Czech players grew increasingly unhappy with the referee. Englishman John Lewis, the man who had officiated the 1908 Olympic final without incident, was now sixty-four years old and struggling to control the match. Finally, in the thirty-ninth minute, Czech left back Karel Steiner committed a brutal foul and was sent off. Steiner's teammates protested in vain, then walked off the field.

When the Czechoslovakia team refused to come out of its dressing room, the Belgians were declared the gold medalists, having played less than two and a half matches, or about three and a half fewer than a present-day Olympic soccer champion.

By forfeiting the game the Czechs also forfeited their silver medal. The two semifinal losers, France and Holland, were the logical contenders for the silver, but the French had already gone home. As in the 1912 Stockholm Games, a consolation tournament had been held, so the organizers decided that the winner of that brief competition, Spain, would face Holland. Goalkeeper Ricardo Zamora, only nineteen years old but soon to become a legend, was, as usual, spectacular and Spain won, 3–1.

The match played behind closed doors remains one of soccer's harshest and most embarrassing punishments, but that didn't prevent FIFA from ordering just such a game during the 1936 Berlin Olympics.

Austria, 3–1 winners over Egypt in the knockout first round, was pitted in the quarterfinals against Peru, which had opened with a 7–3 rout of Finland. The Austrians held a 2–0 lead at halftime, but Peru, behind two goals by Villanueva and one each by Alcalde and Teodoro "Lolo" Fernandez, stormed back to tie and eventually win the match in overtime, 4–2. Five minutes from the end of the extra period, Peru went ahead, 3–2, and jubilant Peruvian fans poured onto the field and began to tangle with the opposing players, one of whom was kicked. Order eventually was restored and the game was completed, but not before the shaken Austrians conceded the fourth goal. Another account has the game in the final moments of overtime and Peru leading by two goals when it was abandoned because of a misunderstanding over an Austrian substitution.

Austria subsequently lodged a protest with FIFA, which nullified the result and ordered a replay in an empty stadium. Peru refused to play—or was ordered not to show up by its miffed embassy—and returned home. The Austrians defeated Poland in the semifinals, 3–1, but lost to the favored Italy, 2–1, in overtime in the final before an Olympiastadion crowd of a hundred thousand.

Hey Mister, Can We Get Our Ball Back?

Seventy-year-old retiree Juraj Výboštók got the ultimate revenge for seven years of errant balls flying into his Stozok, Slovakia, backyard from an adjacent soccer field.

Výboštók, who started it all by renting out the property for use as a playing field by the town team, ended it in October 2004. He rented a tractor and ploughed the field under, then sowed the whole spread with wild oats.

"It's my land and I'll do what I want with it," Výboštók said. "Those footballs have no place in my back garden. They need to stay on the pitch. Come the spring the pitch will be full of oats."

The team, which was forced to move its home matches to a nearby town, should have learned to improve its aim long before. Nearly forty balls landed in Výboštók's yard, and he allowed his dog to chew up every one.

TV Flies After Romanian Defeat

Look out below!

In October 2004 Radu Demerglu and his brother were on the balcony of an apartment building in Pascani, Romania, discussing the national team's just-completed 1–0 loss to the Czech Republic. Suddenly, they were nearly clobbered by a television set hurled by a neighbor from the unit above.

The Demerglu brothers did not press charges against the neighbor, forty-three-year-old Ghita Azinte. In fact, they were remarkably understanding. "At first I was shocked at my neighbor—he could have killed us," said Radu. "But when he told me he had been watching the football, I completely understood. We had also been watching it and I was furious at the Romanian team too."

Petulant Argentine Team Gives Up a Dirty Two Dozen

In November 1952 in Argentina, San Martin was leading El Fortin, 2–0, in an Olavarria league match. Believing that the referee should not have allowed San Martin's goals, the El Fortin players stopped taking the game seriously, and a San Martin striker named Orsatti took full advantage, scoring a total of twenty-four goals in a 25–0 victory.

Chilean Player Shot for Celebrating Goal

No player has to like it when the opposition celebrates a goal, but a member of a team in Chile took things a little too far in a January 2004 amateur match. The player El Rulo scored the winning goal for his team, Bandera, in the ninetieth minute and was busy celebrating when a player from La Gonzalina produced a handgun from his shorts and fired three shots at El Rulo. Two missed and one grazed his shoulder.

Irish Player Banned for Thirty Years for Attack on Referee

An amateur player from Boys' Brigade Old Boys of south Belfast was slapped with a lengthy—*very* lengthy—suspension in December 2004 for head-butting a referee. The County Antrim Football Association of Northern Ireland sanctioned the unnamed player, who kicked the referee in the groin in protest of one call, causing the match to be abandoned. Afterward, in the dressing room, the same player head-butted the ref, breaking his nose and leaving him unconscious.

The assailant will be eligible to resume playing in 2034, when he will be an Old Boy indeed.

And then there's the blue side of misbehavior . . . .

Nigeria Dogs It at the World Cup

Nigeria made its World Cup debut in 1994 and left an indelible impression by winning its first-round group over Argentina and eventual semifinalist Bulgaria, then taking eventual finalist Italy into overtime in the second round before falling, 2–1, on a pair of late goals by Roberto Baggio.

That brave run aside, the Super Eagles also supplied one of the tournament's forgettable moments during what should have been their finest hour. In their last group match, the Nigerians needed to beat Greece by two goals at Foxboro Stadium to nose out the Bulgarians for first place, and they did just that by notching a comfortable 2–0 victory.

But beating the hapless Greeks wasn't enough for Nigeria. After midfielder Finidi George scored the first goal moments before half-time, he raced to the corner and led a group of teammates, crawling on all fours, where, one by one, they simulated a dog urinating on the corner flag pole.

German Brothel Sponsors Women's Team

Every World Cup manages to inspire an early smirk as at least one of the teams' coaches orders his players to refrain from sex for the duration of the tournament. (Depending on a team's performance on the field, that's two to four weeks.)

Those coaches would no doubt have a problem with a women's

team from the east German city of Halle named Teutschenthal. The Teutschenthal women took the field for the 2003–4 season wearing jerseys sporting the name of their sponsor, a brothel named X-Carree, with the tagline, "Worth a Visit."

Coach Andreas Dittmann told the local newspaper *Mittledeutsche Zeitung* that his players weren't bothered in the least to be backed by a brothel.

When Taking a PK, Keep Your Head Down

College basketball fans are renowned for their antics behind the basket as they attempt to distract an enemy free-throw shooter. But they have nothing on a woman who apparently was a fan of Wookey FC.

Wookey and Norton Hill Rangers, both English amateur sides, were forced into a penalty-kick tiebreaker in May 2003 when their Somerset Morland Challenge Cup game ended in a draw. The Wookey fan, stationed behind the goal, lifted her top each time a Norton Hill player prepared to shoot, and Wookey went on to an infamous triumph.

How Not to Celebrate a Goal in Iran

A nineteen-year-old striker picked the worst time to lose his head when he removed his jersey and dropped his shorts in celebration of his game-winning goal during a match in Iran in April 2000.

Mohsen Rassuli, in his first appearance for Saipa of Tehran, scored late to give his side a 1–0 triumph over crosstown rival Pas in a nationally televised cup game. Although he was wearing briefs under his uniform shorts, the striptease was a violation of Islamic laws regarding public exposure.

Rassuli, who later issued an apology, had hoped that the incident would be dealt with by the national soccer federation. Unfortunately, it landed in the hands of the Iranian court, which suspended Rassuli six months and fined him $1,200.

Top That, Brandi Chastain

Two years before U.S. defender Brandi Chastain created a worldwide stir by whipping off her jersey after scoring the winning penalty kick in the 1999 Women's World Cup final, a female player in England performed an even more risqué act. Danielle Murphy of Millwall celebrated her equalizer against Everton in the English Women's League Cup final by pulling her jersey up over her face and racing around the field.

Chastain, of course, was wearing a black sports bra that was already a common sight at jogging paths and gyms around the United States. It put her on the cover of *Time*, *Newsweek*, and *Sports Illustrated*—part sweaty cheesecake and part recognition of the milestone women's sports had reached. In fact, considering that Chastain had helped design the Nike sports bra she revealed to the world, it was considered in some quarters as the ultimate in product placement. The U.S. defender merely dismissed her actions as "temporary insanity."

Murphy, on the other hand, was wearing only a conventional bra that matched her white Millwall shorts.

Chastain, who retired as an international in 2004, wrote a book entitled *It's Not About the Bra*, an examination of women's competitive sports. However, at the 2001 Major League Soccer (MLS) All-Star Game at San Jose's Spartan Stadium, it was about the bra all over again.

With the West leading, 5–4, East midfielder Jim Rooney of the Miami Fusion scored in the eighty-fourth minute and whipped off his East jersey to reveal a black sports bra à la Chastain, a San Jose native and former standout at University of California–Berkeley who had been honored by MLS the week of the game.

"It's a good thing they're comfortable," said Rooney of his extra apparel. "I was getting nervous I wasn't going to score."

The East scored again three minutes later, but two minutes into added-on time San Jose Earthquakes star Landon Donovan, then nineteen, scored his fourth goal of the match to tie things for good at 6–6, then rejoiced with a bra-revealing celebration of his own.

"You have to wonder where they got those bras," marveled East coach Ray Hudson.

Irate Brazilian Coach Performs Striptease

The coach of Itaperuna was slapped with a fourteen-month suspension for ripping off his shirt and dropping his trousers in protest of calls made against his team during a 3–2 loss to Vasco da Gama in a Rio de Janeiro state match in April 1997.

Paulo Mata exploded after Vasco scored a late goal and three of his players were ejected in quick succession. He ran onto the field and shed his shirt. When he charged at the referee and was restrained by police, down went the pants.

"I'm tired of working all week to be scandalously robbed," said Mata in announcing his retirement as a coach.

Guatemalan Tournament Gives All-Hooker Team the Boot

Organizers of a women's tournament in Guatemala held in September 2004 should have been suspicious when a team called The Stars of the Line entered their event. They didn't act, however, until after the team played its first match, booting the Stars ostensibly because of the abusive language of their supporters.

According to team captain Valeria, however, her side was disqualified after it was learned that its members were selected from among the two hundred prostitutes of the Train Line, Guatemala City's red-light district. "When they found out we were prostitutes, they tossed us out like cockroaches," Valeria said. "It's discrimination. Being prostitutes does not mean we are violent, because we are well disciplined." The well-disciplined Stars of the Line lost their lone match, 5–2, to the Blue Devils.

The Stars were only carrying on in the tradition of their soccer-savvy sisters of the past. After Brazil defeated Spain, 1–0, in its opener at the 1986 World Cup in Mexico, prostitutes in Guatemala wore the yellow of Brazil during the postmatch revelry to catch the eye of potential customers.

Business must have been good for another couple of weeks as Brazil won three more games before dropping its quarterfinal to France on penalty kicks.

Italian Linesman Could Use an Umbrella

Fans of the Italian club Taranto were quite unhappy with the work of a certain linesman on the near side during a Serie C2 match at Vigor Lamezia in November 2004, so they protested with a capital P. Make that "pee."

Fed up with the official's interpretation of the offside rule, the Taranto backers, perched not far from the touchline, urinated on the poor fellow as he ran back and forth, dousing his head and shoulders. Taranto went on to lose, 4–0, and league authorities later fined the club approximately $4,000 for the actions of its fans.

U.S. Goalkeeper Streaks to Celebrate Gold Medal

Briana Scurry, known for her clutch save of a penalty kick to help the United States beat China in the final of the 1999 Women's World Cup, is a woman of her word. Scurry promised to "run naked through the streets of Athens, Georgia," if the United States won the 1996 Atlanta Olympic tournament. The Americans topped China, 2–1, in the final before 76,489 at Athens' Sanford Stadium, and the veteran goalkeeper later made her promised sprint wearing only her gold medal.

No fool, Scurry chose a deserted suburban street late at night.

Then there is the journalist who bared it all under crowded conditions to get the attention of one Egyptian team.

A correspondent for Reuters, Eniwoke Ibagere, was having no luck in getting quotes from Zamalek players after they dropped the 1999–2000 African Champions Cup final to Shooting Stars of Nigeria.

Ibagere stripped, entered the Zamalek dressing room, and resumed his questions, and the startled players found themselves responding.

On through the halls of slaughter,
Where gallant comrades fall,
Where blood is poured like water,
They drive the trickling ball.
The fear of death before them
Is but an empty name
True to the land that bore them
The Surreys play the game.

"TOUCHSTONE," a poem that appeared
in Britain's Daily Mail, inspired by word that
East Surry Regiment, Eighth Battalion, dribbled
four soccer balls through no-man's-land in the
Somme ahead of an attack on German positions, in July 1916

5 SOCCER, WAR, AND PEACE

Most nations of the world have two major forms of conflict in common:
soccer and, unfortunately, war. International war, civil war, cold war,
militarism—all have affected soccer in modern times. Yet the game's most
notable casualty remains the twelve-year gap in World Cups caused by
the Second World War.

A Yuletide Match in No-Man's-Land

Imagine yourself an infantryman in northern France during World
War I, slogging through the trenches, tensely awaiting the whistle that
sends you over the top, then watching helplessly while buddies are
mowed down by machine-gun fire. Come Christmas Day, you and your
comrades lay down your arms . . . to play soccer with the enemy.

It happened in 1914, four months into the bloody conflict, near
the village of Laventie. Without warning, members of a German company emerged from their icy trenches to greet their Welsh counterparts in no-man's-land.

"I do remember a whole mass of us just getting up and going out
to meet them," recalled Bertie Felstead, a Royal Welsh Fusilier at the
time, in a 1999 interview. "Nothing was planned. It was spontaneous.

There was a bit of football, if you can call it that. Someone suggested it and somehow a ball was produced. It wasn't a game as such, more of a kick-around and a free-for-all. There could have been fifty on each side for all I know.

"I played because I really liked football. I don't know how long it lasted, maybe half an hour, and no one was keeping score."

The impromptu match ended abruptly when a sputtering British major came upon the astonishing sight of rival soldiers scrimmaging in the snow. He immediately ordered his Welshmen back to their trenches and angrily reminded them that they were in France to "kill the Hun, not make friends with him."

The war would drag on for another forty-seven months and claim some 15 million lives. Felstead, the oldest surviving member of the episode, died in 2001 at age 106.

So goes the tidy version of this story. But what has become known as the Christmas Truce was not an isolated incident limited to Felstead's Bedfordshire regiment and some friendly Germans. In fact, it took place in several sections along two-thirds of the Western front. Some lasted Christmas Day only; others extended through January 3.

The two sides had observed truces in the past to allow for the recovery of dead between the lines, but there were no plans for a formal Yuletide cease-fire, despite the urging of Pope Benedict XV. The Germans were willing but the Allies were not; the French, in particular, were loath to cooperate with their invaders.

Nevertheless, peace broke out unofficially along the front on Christmas Eve. Gunfire had come to an almost complete halt that night, and despondent soldiers on both sides, drenched by rain the previous few days, were well aware that the war would *not* end by Christmas as had been commonly believed.

In some areas Germans held up small Christmas trees adorned with candles. Curious Brits also heard their enemy singing "Stille Nacht, Heilige Nacht" and eventually responded with the English version, "Silent Night, Holy Night." Tensions further eased with calls of "Merry Christmas," "You no shoot, we no shoot," "Tommy, come over and talk to us," and "No, Fritz, you come over here."

On Christmas morning, soldiers gingerly began to leave their trenches, and before long no-man's-land became crowded with Tommies and Fritzes mingling, singing carols, showing off photos of loved ones, and sharing tobacco, liquor, and other luxuries. In some cases soldier-barbers from one side gave haircuts and shaves to rival soldiers. In the Sailly-Amrentiers section a Christmas Day service was conducted by a British chaplain and a German divinity student.

The sides generally agreed to warn one another of the approach of high-ranking officers, who would surely order their soldiers to get back to the business of war. (When so ordered, both sides, in the spirit of the season, were careful to aim a bit high.) After the brass left, the mingling of once and future combatants resumed.

As for Felstead's match, legend has it that the Brits were trailing the Germans, 3–2, when the ball was punctured by barbed wire. There would be no return match on Christmas 1915, however. Shaken commanders on both sides made it clear that fraternization with the enemy was treasonous and any recurrence would result in a court-martial. In fact, the last three Christmas Eves of the war were punctuated by particularly heavy shelling.

The Christmas Truce was generally applauded in Britain, where the public learned of it the following January through letters from soldiers that were published in local newspapers. The German government denied the truce ever happened, but as one of its soldiers wrote in a letter home, "It was a day of peace in war. It is only a pity that it was not a decisive peace."

The Austrian Star Who Snubbed Nazi Germany

In the early 1930s the toast of the European continent was Austria, the Wunderteam that threatened to eclipse England as Europe's leading soccer power. And the undisputed star of that team was center forward Matthias Sindelar, a ball magician nicknamed "Der Papierene" ("The Man of Paper") for his thin build and an ability to elude opponents that gave him the appearance of a sheet of paper dancing in a light breeze.

Today his legend is a distant memory and the circumstances surrounding his death in 1939 remain a mystery.

Born in 1903 in Jihlava (now part of the Czech Republic) and reared in Vienna, Sindelar rose to prominence with FK Austria Wein, leading it to the 1933 and 1936 Mitropa Cups, the predecessor of the European Champions Cup. In the '33 final his last-minute goal beat Ambrosia-Inter (later Inter Milan).

Sindelar scored in his international debut against Czechoslovakia in 1926, and while he went on to pile up twenty-seven goals in forty-three appearances, he seemed to save his best for Austria's most important games. In 1932, for example, the Paper Man struck twice in a 2–1 victory over Italy, the team that would go on to win the 1934 World Cup, 1936 Olympics, and 1938 World Cup. One of the goals was astonishing: Austria took a right-sided corner kick and Sindelar headed the ball over one defender, then another, then headed it past the goalkeeper and into the net—this from a player not known for his ability in the air. He also scored an impressive goal in a 4–3 loss to England in London that generated a host of offers from British clubs. And, in an 8–2 dismantling of archrival Hungary, the Paper Man romped to a hat trick and assisted on Austria's five other goals.

Already the darling of Viennese café society, with performances like those the high-living Sindelar was a national sensation. He endorsed products, inspired poems, and even appeared in a motion picture, *Roxi and Her Wonder Team.*

Sindelar made one star-crossed appearance in a World Cup, in 1934. A late conclusion to the Austrian league season had left the players exhausted, but Austria nevertheless reached the semifinals against host Italy in Milan. Italy won, 1–0, in a downpour on a nineteenth-minute goal by outside right Enrique Guaita that the Austrians claimed was offside. Italy's take-no-prisoners midfielder Luisito Monti and the muddy field combined to neutralize the skillful Sindelar, who was not a factor after being kicked by Monti while on the ground.

Sindelar's chance at World Cup redemption was snatched away less than three years later. In October 1937 the Austrians won their only qualifying match, a 2–1 decision over Latvia in Vienna to book passage to the 1938 World Cup in France, but in March Germany annexed Austria and, with it, the Austrian National Team.

Sindelar's greatest game may have been the following month when "Greater Germany" met the former Austria, now called "Ostmark," at Vienna's Prater Stadium. To the Germans this "reunification match" was to be a celebration of the *Anschluss* ("connection"), but to Sindelar it was a golden opportunity to show what he thought of the disappearance of his country.

As captain, Sindelar insisted that his Wunderteam wear its customary red and white one last time. There were rumors that the Nazis ordered the Austrians to lose or at least play to a low-scoring draw, and the Paper Man, now age thirty-five, appeared to comply, missing several easy chances in the goalmouth—much to the embarrassment of the German defenders. Finally, in the second half, a shot off the goalkeeper fell to his feet and Sindelar abandoned his charade and curled a shot from the left inside the base of the far post, as if to show that he could have scored at any time. The crowd of sixty thousand went wild, just as it did in the closing minutes when defender Karl Sesta, a former FK Austria teammate of Sindelar's, scored with a forty-five-yard free kick. Sindelar celebrated with a little dance in front of a VIP box filled with Nazi officials. Ostmark 2, Greater Germany 0.

Later that year, Sindelar was asked by the coach of Germany, Sepp Herberger, to play for the Greater Germany squad in the World Cup. Said Herberger, "He asked me politely to leave him out of it. . . . When I insisted again and again, I got the impression that there were also other reasons for him to refuse. I almost had the impression that it was dismay and hostility at the political developments which weighed on him and were the reason for his refusal. Finally, I gave up. I thought I understood him. He looked as if a heavy burden had been taken off his shoulders when I told him."

Germany, without Sindelar, didn't make it out of the first round. The Germans had won ten in a row in 1937, including qualifiers against Finland and Estonia, but at Francia '38 the Austria-fortified Germany couldn't stave off elimination at the hands of Switzerland at Parc des Princes through a 1–1 draw and 4–2 loss in the replay five days later.

Sindelar retired and purchased a corner café in the modest Favoriten section of Vienna. But eight months after the match against Germany he was found dead in bed next to his Italian lover, Carmilla Castagnola, who later died in a hospital.

The cause of death was listed as carbon monoxide poisoning due to fumes from a blocked chimney flue, but many believed Sindelar was murdered by the Nazis. The Paper Man, after all, had played for FK Austria, a club with a large Jewish following and Jewish directors, and while he bought his café from a dispossessed Jew, he paid full price. Sindelar also was a Social Democrat, and, of course, there was the snub of Herberger. The Gestapo had Café Sindelar under surveillance, and its famous owner welcomed all, including Jews.

Others believed Sindelar, out of despair, took his own life, although it is unlikely that he would have formed a suicide pact with Castagnola, a woman he had only recently met. Rumors that Sindelar, the son of Catholics, was actually Jewish only clouded the mystery further.

Police ended their investigation after two days, and Nazi authorities ordered the case closed six months later.

More than twenty thousand lined the streets of Vienna to watch his funeral procession. He later was chosen Austria's Sportsman of the Century. Every year on January 23, the anniversary of his death, FK Vienna officials and players past and present gather at his grave to remember their club's greatest star. And the street on which his café was located is now named Sindelar-gasse.

Not Quite a "Futbol War"

Do countries go to war over soccer?

No. But they've come close.

In the most-often cited example of soccer lending a spark to an international crisis, El Salvador and Honduras engaged in a war in June and July of 1969 in which 3,000 were killed, 12,000 were wounded, and another 150,000 were left homeless.

Soccer did not cause the conflict, which has gone down in history as the "Futbol War." Rather, a number of factors, including local resentment toward the three hundred thousand Salvadoran immigrants living in Honduras, confusion over the two nations' common border, and the limp Honduran economy deserve most of the blame. Tensions reached the breaking point at the end of April when a Honduran law was passed prohibiting Salvadorans from owning land and giving them thirty days to leave.

It just so happened that Honduras and El Salvador were scheduled to play one another June 8 and June 15 in a home-and-home qualifying series for the 1970 World Cup, which was to be held in Mexico. El Salvador was in its very first World Cup qualifying competition, Honduras in its third, and both sides were determined to qualify.

Before each game the visiting team was serenaded all night by whistles, fireworks, honking car horns, and chanting outside its hotel, and at the stadium the home fans pelted the enemy players with everything from rotten eggs to dead rats. Honduras won the first leg, 1–0, in Tegucigalpa on a goal by Roberto Cardona, but El Salvador, on three first-half goals, took the second leg, 3–0, a week later in San Salvador, setting up a tie-breaking match in neutral Mexico City two weeks later.

The second leg was particularly brutal. A cordon of Salvadoran soldiers bearing submachine guns ringed the field. Before the game, after the whistles of the Salvadoran fans drowned out the playing of the Honduran anthem, Honduras players saw a dirty rag run up the flagpole in place of their national flag. Their fans were beaten—two died and dozens were injured—as they attempted to flee back to the Honduran border. Some 150 cars belonging to Honduran supporters were burned. Said coach Mario Griffin, whose players had been transported to and from Flor Blanca Stadium in armored cars, "We're awfully lucky that we lost."

The day after the San Salvador game, paramilitary groups began to forcibly evict Salvadorans from Honduran farmland they had owned for years, triggering a mass exodus of fellow Salvadorans back to their overcrowded homeland and igniting riots on both sides of the border. Soon, many of the Salvadoran immigrants in Honduras began to recross the border. El Salvador declared a state of siege on June 24 and broke off diplomatic relations with Honduras two days later. By the time El Salvador beat Honduras in the tie-breaking match, 3–2, on June 28 before fifteen thousand, the situation was out of control. Open fighting between Salvadoran and Honduran troops erupted in the frontier, and a Honduran plane reportedly was fired upon. On July 14 the Salvadoran army swept across the border and took nearly fifty miles in one day, and El Salvador's air force won the conflict's major aerial battle with its successful attack on the Tegucigalpa airport.

The Organization of American States negotiated a cease-fire July 18, ending the war after four days. The two sides later agreed to a demilitarized zone, and an uneasy truce ensued.

Clearly, labeling the one-hundred-hour conflict the "Futbol War" may have been convenient, but it was nonetheless historically inaccurate.

While El Salvador's military savored its triumph over its neighbor, its national team was faced with one final qualifying series against Haiti, which had earlier eliminated the United States, 2–0 in Port-au-Prince and 1–0 in San Diego.

El Salvador won the opening leg, 2–1, September 21 in Port-au-Prince, but a week later, shortly before kickoff of the second leg in San Salvador, a Haitian witch doctor sprinkled a mysterious powder on the field and chanted a spell. The inspired Haiti squad, which would have been eliminated with a tie, roared to a 3–0 victory.

Again, a tie-breaker was required, and El Salvador won, 1–0, in neutral Kingston, Jamaica. Some dubbed the Salvadorans' Argentine coach, Gregorio Bundio, as the day's hero for taking out the Haiti team's witch doctor before the game with a single punch. Others cite El Salvador striker Juan Martinez, who scored the winning goal.

Safely in possession of its first World Cup berth, El Salvador's weird adventure was far from over. Bundio, who had seen El Salvador through its ten qualifying matches, was fired before the World Cup in the wake of a players' dispute over money. The players believed they deserved more for reaching the finals while the government said any money earmarked for the players would instead be used to help pay for the war.

Bundio's sacking spared the Argentine from watching from the bench as El Salvador made a quick exit from its first World Cup with losses to Group 1 opponents Belgium, 3–0, Mexico, 4–0, and Russia, 2–0.

The Mexico score was deceiving. Inexplicably, FIFA allowed the two CONCACAF rivals to be placed in the same group, so El Salvador found itself playing the World Cup hosts June 7 in front of 103,000 fans—nearly all of them hostile—at Mexico City's Aztec Stadium.

El Salvador started brightly, sending two shots off the post early, but late in the opening half the visitors fell victim to one of the worst officiating blunders in World Cup history. Egyptian referee Aly Hussain Kandil awarded a free kick to the Salvadorans, but Mexico's Mario Pérez stepped in and sent the ball the other way. The ball went to teammate Aaron Padilla, whose cross was redirected into the net by Javier Valdivia.

The infuriated Salvadoran players, after protesting to no avail, refused to fish the ball out of their net and kick off, so Kandil prudently signaled for the end of the half.

Though demoralized, El Salvador surprised many when it returned to the field for the second half, but it gave up a second goal to Valdivia in the first minute and surrendered two more before the end. The World Cup campaign that began with a very loud bang had ended with a whimper.

Among those who died as a result of the "Futbol War" was a suicide victim.

After watching Honduras' first-leg victory on television, Amelia Bolanios, eighteen, of San Salvador pulled her father's pistol from his desk drawer and shot herself in the chest. A national TV audience tuned in for her funeral, which included a military honor guard. El Salvador's president and his ministers walked behind Bolanios's flag-draped casket, as did the Salvadoran national team. It marked the end to a strange and sad day that began with those same players spat upon, jeered, and laughed at by Honduran fans at the Tegucigalpa airport while trying to catch their flight home.

Cold War Victim: "The Russian Pelé"

Seven years after his death from cancer in 1990, Russia paid tribute to perhaps its greatest player as Torpedo Moscow named its stadium for Eduard Streltsov.

Known as "The Russian Pelé," Streltsov was twice recognized as the Soviet Player of the Year, but he was denied his chance for true international greatness. At seventeen, in his USSR debut in 1955, he scored a hat trick against Sweden, and Streltsov, who went on to score thirteen more goals in some twenty national team matches, soon became a sensation behind the Iron Curtain. Yet just before the Soviet National Team left for the 1958 World Cup in Sweden, Streltsov was in a Siberian gulag.

According to one account, the handsome young player spurned the advances of the daughter of a top KGB official. The woman gained revenge when the high-living Streltsov was arrested along with two teammates on trumped-up rape charges.

While Streltsov languished for six years in a series of work camps, the USSR lost in the quarterfinals of the 1958 and 1962 World Cups. Once released, he was barred by the KGB from going to England for the 1966 World Cup, and the Soviets lost in the semifinals, their high-water mark.

Streltsov resumed his club career and led Torpedo Moscow to the 1965 USSR championship, and he returned to the national team to score eight more goals before his retirement in 1970. That same year, the Streltsov-less Soviets reached the quarterfinals in Mexico, the last time they got to the final eight of a World Cup.

Afghans' "Game of Unity" Marred by Riot

The match billed as the "Game of Unity" was anything but as a fan riot marred a friendly between British soldiers and an Afghan team in Kabul in February 2002. The game was the first played after American and British forces had routed the ruling Taliban and seized control of Afghanistan the previous year. Thousands of fans attempting to force their way into a stadium already packed with thirty thousand spectators were fought off by security personnel. Fifty fans were treated for injuries after being beaten with rifle butts and other blunt objects. Five peacekeepers were hurt by rocks thrown by the crowd.

The match eventually kicked off, and the British side prevailed, 3–1.

Warts and all, that marked a giant stride for soccer in Afghanistan, a country that joined FIFA in 1948 but whose soccer activity has been spotty at best. The country had never taken a stab at qualifying for a World Cup nor had it ever entered a team in Asian club competitions. Its most notable achievement was an appearance in the 1951 Asian Games, where it lost in the semifinals in New Delhi to host and eventual champion India, another of international soccer's minnows.

Soccer came to a halt in 1984 after the Soviet invasion, yet the USSR's eventual defeat and the 1996 takeover by the Taliban actually represented a second major step backward for the game. The Taliban first banned soccer, then relented, and the national team was allowed to re-form in May 1998. However, the Taliban decreed that "onlookers will not be permitted to clap, but will be ordered to encourage both sides equally with cheers of *Allahu Akbar* ("God is great"). Afghanistan National Team members were also directed to don uniforms with long trousers and long-sleeved jerseys and to stop for prayers during matches.

With the end of Taliban rule, Afghan soccer struggled to its feet, but it has experienced a wobbly existence. A new national team was assembled in 2002 and promptly lost its three matches at the Asian Games in South Korea by thirty-two goals. Undaunted, the Afghans the following year made a run at a berth in the 2006 World Cup but were brought back to earth quickly. In the preliminary round of the Asian qualifiers in November, they took a forty-hour bus ride to Ashkhabad and lost to host Turkmenistan, 11–0, then dropped the return leg in Kabul four days later, 2–0. Despite their swift elimination, the experience was a minor triumph for the Afghans: the second leg, played at the bullet-pocked National Stadium once used by the Taliban for public executions, was the first FIFA-sanctioned match held in Afghanistan since 1979.

The national team, composed largely of players from a loosely organized league in Kabul, took a major hit in April 2004 during a trip to Italy for a series of friendlies intended to give the players valuable experience and help raise money for Afghan orphans. Before Afghanistan could play its opener against the club Verona, nine of the players jumped the team and sought asylum.

Coach Ali Asger Akbarzola, who found himself shorthanded when he went to round up his team at its hotel on Lake Garda, said later that he received calls from some of his players, who claimed they were visiting relatives in Vicenza and Milan. Within a few days, six of the players were arrested in Germany.

"I am very, very angry," said Akbarzola. "This was supposed to be our first game in twenty-five years and an ideal opportunity to give hope to our country, and look what these players have done."

The Afghan soccer federation disbanded the team. Federation chief Halim Kohistani said a new squad would be formed, while the nine escapees would be punished "100 percent."

Soviet Stadium Built Over Jewish Cemetery

A stadium in Grodno, Belarus, stands as a grim symbol of both Soviet discrimination and Nazi atrocities against the Jews.

Nemen Stadium, now home to the club Nemen Grodno, was built in 1953—when Belarus was part of the Soviet Union—over a Jewish cemetery that held the remains of approximately 14,000 people. (A cruel irony: the stadium's original capacity was 14,000.) Some of those interred were among the 800,000 Jews killed in Belarus by the Nazis during World War II.

And Nemen Stadium's notorious origins continue to haunt Grodno. Construction crews began work on enlarging the stadium in January 2003, and they found human jawbones, gold teeth, entire skulls, and broken headstones in the soil excavated from the site. Grodno officials ordered workers to collect for reburial any remains uncovered, but they refused to stop work on the stadium. The city's Jewish community and supporters abroad asked FIFA and the UEFA to sanction any team that plays at Nemen, to no avail.

Mexican Guerrillas Play in Revolutionary Match

Javier Aguirre knew his team had won. He just wasn't sure whom it had beaten.

A former Mexican international and future coach of Mexico, Aguirre was coach of Pachuca when he organized a match in Mexico City in April 1999 between a team of over-35 stars and the Zapatista National Revolutionary Army.

The guerrillas, in town for a referendum on Indian rights, played the match wearing masks to hide their identity. Aguirre's old-timers won the forty-minute game, 5–3.

Civil War Refugees Play for Liberia

Liberia, crippled by civil war, finished last in its qualifying group in a 2004 African Nations Cup campaign that was typified by its loss to first-place Guinea in June 2003.

The match was moved from the Liberian capital of Monrovia, then under rebel siege, to neutral Accra, Ghana. Only four members of the Liberian squad could be flown to the new game site because of a lack of funds, so Liberian soccer officials went to Accra's Budumburam refugee camp, home to thousands of Liberians displaced by the fighting, and rounded up a number of top players, including ex-international Bokolo Chea and several former Liberian first-division players.

The patchwork Liberian lineup fought hard but ultimately fell to Guinea, 2–1.

Tasmania Berlin, West Germany's Hapless Cold Warriors

Big-league soccer in Germany is relatively new. The Bundesliga, and with it, full professionalism, wasn't introduced in what was West Germany until 1963. However, it took only two years for the Bundesliga to run into a major-league problem after revoking the license of its only club in Berlin, Hertha BSC, for offering money under the table to players. Not many players were keen to move to the former capital to play in the shadow of the Berlin Wall, but the cash inducements were nevertheless a violation of the league's strict salary cap.

Because of the Cold War, the Deutscher Fussball-Bund was desperate to maintain a presence in the old capital, which that year was represented on the other side of the wall by the high-flying Worwarts Berlin, on its way to its second straight East German league championship. Complicating matters were the bottom teams from the previous Bundesliga season, Karlsruher SC and Schalke 04; rather than be demoted, both demanded Hertha's spot in the top flight.

The solution was to expand the Bundesliga from sixteen clubs to eighteen and include among the new teams the unheralded Tasmania 1900 Berlin. By rights, the spot in the top tier should have gone to the defending champion of the Oberliga (regional league) Berlin, Tennis Borussia Berlin, but it lost to Bayern Munich and Borussia Moenchengladbach in the promotion playoffs. The regional league runner-up, Spandauer SV, declined an offer to move up, so, two weeks before the opening of the season, the promotion fell to Tasmania.

What followed during the 1965–66 season was a demonstration in ineptitude of epic proportions as Tasmania, a capable side in a relatively weak regional league, proved to be in over its head and then some among West Germany's elite.

After beating Karlsruher, 2–0, before eighty-one thousand at Berlin's Olympiastadion to kick off the campaign, Tasmania stumbled to a 2-28-4 record, scoring 15 goals and allowing 108, still the worst showing in the history of the Bundesliga. In an era when only two points were awarded for a win, it finished forty-two points behind Bundesliga champion 1860 Munich and sixteen behind next-to-last Borussia Neunkirchen.

The pride of Berlin also:

- lost twelve of its seventeen home games, dropping eight straight from late August to early December
- went fifteen straight home games without a win, a span of nine months

- was held scoreless for 831 minutes, a record that would last for twenty-seven years
- lost a home match to Meidericher SV, 9–0 (this mark was nearly tied in 2000 by Bayer Leverkusen, but host SSV Ulm, trailing by the same score, produced a goal in added-on time)
- dropped ten games in a row (thirty-four years later, fans of Arminia Bielefeld chanted "Tasmania Bielefeld!" when their team tied that record)
- proved, not surprisingly, to be a bust at the box office as West Berliners began to stay away in droves. Five months into this ongoing disaster, only 827 bothered to come out to see their heroes take on Borussia Moenchengladbach, yet another Bundesliga record that still stands. Fans were treated that day to a scoreless tie.

At the end of the season, the Bundesliga's laughingstock slunk back into the lower reaches of German soccer, and Berlin would be without Bundesliga soccer until Hertha's return in 1968.

In 1973 Tasmania declared bankruptcy. A new version of the club was born that same year, but with Germany since reunified and a presence in Berlin no longer an issue, the obscure team now known as SC Tasmania Gropiusstadt 73 has yet to receive another gift invitation from the Bundesliga.

Ex-Goalie Spares the World Cuban Missile Crisis II

Henry Kissinger's passion for soccer is no secret. Born in Furth, Bavaria, and reared in Manhattan after his family fled Nazi Germany, the former secretary of state, Nobel Peace Prize recipient, and boyhood goalkeeper was a New York Cosmos groupie during the height of his reign as the face of American foreign policy. When the 1994 World Cup's local organizing committee needed an honorary chairman, Kissinger was the logical choice. And every four years, at World Cup time, Kissinger's byline is likely to be found in a major newspaper or magazine above an opinion piece explaining to the average American the global significance of soccer.

There also came a time when Kissinger's understanding of the sport and the people who play it may have helped to keep the Cold War cold. In September 1970 Kissinger, then President Nixon's national security advisor, burst into the office of White House Chief of Staff H.R. "Bob" Haldeman with 8-by-10-inch photographs of soccer fields in Cienfuegos, Cuba, taken from a U.S. spy plane.

"It's a Cuban seaport, Haldeman, and these pictures show the Cubans are building soccer fields," said Kissinger, as recalled by Haldeman in his 1978 memoir, *The Ends of Power*. Haldeman imagined Nixon's agitated head of national security bursting into the Oval Office to interrupt an economic conference by hollering, "The Cubans are building soccer fields!"

"Those soccer fields could mean war, Bob," said Kissinger.

"Why?"

"Cubans play *baseball*," Kissinger replied. "*Russians* play soccer."

Kissinger's pop analysis led Haldeman to believe the Soviet Union, eight years removed from the Cuban Missile Crisis, was attempting once again to install a medium-range missile base within striking distance of key U.S. defense sites.

According to Haldeman, Kissinger then confronted the Soviet ambassador to the United States, Anatoli Dobrynin, and told him that if the USSR abandoned its base, the Americans would say nothing publicly—no nationally televised address, à la JFK eight years earlier—and detente between the two superpowers would continue.

As in 1962 the Soviets backed down. But one must wonder, given the same set of circumstances, would any member of the Kennedy administration's "Best and Brightest," certainly more familiar with touch football than soccer, have come to Kissinger's conclusion?

Government Punishes Players for Ivory Coast Defeat

When it comes to soccer, Cote D'Ivoire, or Ivory Coast, has been one of Africa's underachievers, a country that has won only one major honor, the 1992 African Nations Cup, and until 2006 had never appeared in a World Cup.

After an unsuccessful appearance at the 2000 African Nations Cup in Nigeria, the frustration apparently got to the team's higher-ups. Two days after their elimination, the players were detained for two days by their country's military government as punishment for getting knocked out in the opening round. While the surviving teams prepared for the African quarterfinals, the Ivory Coast players were hauled off to an army camp near Yamossoukro for what they were told would be "a lesson in patriotism."

Before their release, they were transported to Abidjan to be admonished by the president, Robert Guei, and the minister of sports. Guei also threatened them with military service if they did not play better in the future.

Iraq: Torture and Triumph

Soccer-mad Iraq won precious few honors from the founding of its soccer federation in 1948 through the regime of Saddam Hussein. In the region's most prestigious soccer competition, there was a fourth-place finish at the 1976 Asian Cup; at the continent's version of the Olympics, a first-place finish at the 1982 Asian Games soccer tournament, plus a sixth-place showing in 1974 and a fourth in 1978; in the Olympics, a quarterfinal appearance at Moscow '80 but three games and out at the 1984 Los Angeles and 1988 Seoul Summer Games; and on the World Cup stage, a promising debut in 1986—tough one-goal losses to Paraguay, Belgium, and host Mexico—but nothing more.

How many outsiders, however, could have guessed during the latter part of that long period of frustration and mixed results just how much pressure the Iraqi players were under? Hell for the players and other prominent Iraqi athletes began in 1984, when Hussein appointed his oldest son, Uday, as chief of both the Iraqi Football Association and the Iraqi Olympic Committee, and it lasted until the younger Hussein was killed in July 2003 in a firefight with U.S. forces in the northern Iraqi city of Mosul.

The death of Uday Hussein, age thirty-nine, alongside younger brother Qusai, ended a twenty-year reign of terror in which international athletes were systematically beaten, tortured, and jailed in the basement of Olympic Committee headquarters in eastern Baghdad and elsewhere for failing to meet Uday's expectations.

"I think the pressure in the past is the reason why Iraq didn't do well," said Husam Fawzi Naji, who made his first forty international appearances, many as captain, during Uday Hussein's tenure. "The reports of torture are true."

Not coincidentally, several of the players who ran afoul of Uday, a Sunni Muslim, were Shiite Muslims, many of them the products of the Shiite-dominated Sadr City. Among the victims was Habib Jaafer, a standout midfielder for the national team. Brought to the burned-out shell of the Olympic headquarters less than a month after Saddam Hussein's fall, he was reluctant to enter.

"Just coming to the gate fills me with fear," Jaafer said. "So often, when I came here, I knew that days of punishment lay ahead."

According to claims of recent national team members, minor blunders, such as a string of poor passes, would land a player before Uday in the dressing room, where he would be punched or slapped in the face an equal number of times. A tie, a loss, or a missed penalty kick would earn a humiliating head shaving at the Stadium of the People in Baghdad, said exiled former captain Abed Kadhim.

Players taken to the Olympic building basement were subjected to a variety of incentives to improve their play. Uday's devices of "encouragement" included a sarcophagus that featured long nails pointing inward from every surface, an airtight lid, and a metal framework designed to deliver electric shocks to its occupants.

They also could be sent to a military prison, where they might be chained to a wall; the torture there included beatings with electric cables. Others inspirations: twelve-hour sessions of push-ups, sprints, and other drills while in heavy military fatigues and boots; sleep, food, and water deprivation; and matches in which a concrete ball was kicked around in 110-degree heat. One particularly heinous punishment involved dragging players along pavement until their backs were bloodied, then dunking them in sewage to ensure the wounds became infected.

International authorities? In 1997 FIFA conducted a probe of accusations that Iraqi players were whipped with canes following a 3–1 loss at Kazakhstan that knocked the team out of the second round of Asia's qualifiers for the '98 World Cup, but it cleared the Iraqi soccer authorities of any wrongdoing. Insiders said later that players were afraid to talk to FIFA for fear of reprisal by Uday Hussein against them or their families. And the International Olympic Committee made no effort to distance itself from Uday despite years of reports by Western human rights organizations that Iraqi athletes were being punished. Finally, in December 2002, a report by the human rights group Indict prompted the IOC to suspend Iraq.

After the fall of Saddam Hussein in April 2003, what was left of the Iraqi National Team program began to turn the corner. Bernd Stange had signed a four-year contract in 2002 to coach Iraq, and he knew a thing or two about working under totalitarian conditions while coaching his native East Germany from 1983 to 1988. Stange, who waited out the U.S.-led invasion back in Germany, returned to Iraq that summer, and at the invitation of the German soccer federation practiced his squad for three weeks at Bad Woerrishofen as it prepared for the qualifiers for the 2004 Asian Cup and Athens Olympics.

Already the mood among the players had brightened considerably. Said midfielder Ali Waheb Setet, "When Saddam was there we had to play good and there was too much pressure. After every game there was pressure. But now it is a different situation. It is much better now. That is all behind us now. This is a new era. It is only football now."

And FIFA, which couldn't uncover anything untoward in the Uday era of Iraq soccer, promised to donate $70,000 to help revive the country's twenty-team national league, which had ground to a halt with twenty-nine rounds of its thirty-eight-round 2002–3 season completed. It later pledged $400,000 to rebuild the Iraqi soccer federation headquarters in Baghdad destroyed in the war. The U.S. Soccer Foundation, the body that manages the profit from the 1994 World Cup, donated sixty thousand soccer balls to help boost the country's grassroots game.

The first professional match since the invasion was played in May 2003, and a capacity crowd of ten thousand watched defending champion Police beat Al-Zawra, 2–1. In October, in its first post-Saddam appearance, Iraq routed Bahrain, 5–1, in Kuala Lumpur in its opening Asian Games match, and it went on five months later to nail down a berth in the finals in China, nosing out Bahrain on goal difference for first place in its qualifying group. In May 2004, three months after its reinstatement by the IOC, the Iraqis upset Saudi Arabia, 3–1, and, coupled with a 0–0 draw between Kuwait and Oman, qualified for Athens.

The dual qualifications over little more than two months startled the soccer-playing world because of the long line of daunting obstacles the Iraqis had vaulted along the way:

- Iraq had played all of its "home" games not in Baghdad but in neighboring Kuwait. In fact, because of war, international sanctions, and security concerns, the last time Iraq enjoyed a home-field advantage was in 1990. Training camps were held in Jordan, Japan, Bahrain, and Stange's Germany.

- Iraqi international players had been pressed into military service during the March 2003 invasion of their country. There were no casualties among the group, but all returned home suffering from poor nutrition and the effects of a lack of drinking water.
- The suspension of the national league, including its lower divisions, had forced top players to move to clubs in neighboring countries.
- The national stadium, Baghdad's Al-Sahaab Stadium, had been reduced to a parking lot for U.S. tanks and other military vehicles. Major stadiums elsewhere were damaged during the fighting, while otherwise useable playing fields had been converted to hospitals and burial grounds.
- Stange returned from Germany in June to find his office destroyed. The coach had bitterly criticized Paul Bremer, Iraq's chief U.S. administrator, for a lack of assistance for his team and what he believed was the U.S. occupiers' ignorance of soccer's unifying power in a divided nation ("Americans don't know how important soccer is"). Undaunted, for a time Stange tried to fund the national team out of his own pocket.

There would be more obstacles:

- In early July 2004, a couple of weeks before the Asian Cup, there was a major upheaval as Stange, who hadn't been paid in five months and was holed up in Jordan out of fear for his safety, resigned and was succeeded by Iraqi Olympic team coach Adnan Hamad, an Iraqi international in the 1980s. It marked the fourth time in as many years that Iraqi soccer officials turned to Hamad after the departure of a European coach.

Stange had fled Iraq for Jordan at the urging of the German Foreign Ministry and his own bodyguard because of his high profile and the attacks of insurgents on foreigners. He claimed to have been stopped in his car several times by black-masked gunmen, who recognized the coach and told him, "You're one of us," and allowed him to pass. In November 2003, however, his driver was shot. Before his resignation, Stange had written letters to Tony Blair of Great Britain and Silvio Berlusconi of Italy pleading for support; both leaders responded with invitations for the Iraqi team to train in their countries.

- The appointment of Hamad was followed by the Iraqi federation's decision to leave its veterans at home for the Asian Games and instead send its Olympic squad, in essence its youth team (the men's Olympic soccer competition since 1992 has been for teams of players age twenty-two and younger, with three exceptions). It was an admission that officials preferred to abandon any chance of winning the cup and instead blood this new generation of players—most without the emotional baggage of the Uday days—for the Olympics and beyond.
- Player pay was cut in half during the run-up to the Asian Games as funds were shifted to Iraq's more pressing problems.
- Finally, a training camp scheduled to open in South Korea two weeks before the trip to China was scuttled after a Korean hostage was beheaded in Iraq and the Korean government rolled up the welcome mat. That left Hamad with five practice sessions in Baghdad and a friendly against the Thailand Olympic squad in Bangkok in which to fine-tune his team.

Nevertheless, in late July, Iraq, propelled by a 3–2 victory over Turkmenistan and a 2–1 upset of the Saudis in the group stage, reached the Asian Games quarterfinals. Although a knockout punch—a 3–0 loss to the host Chinese in Beijing—followed, the two first-round wins ignited wild celebrations back home by euphoric Sunnis, Shiites, Kurds, and Christians. Guns were fired into the air, unnerving Allied troops who believed they were under attack.

And it was that freedom to play without looking over a shoulder that paved the way. As Husam Fawzi Naji, who captained Iraq at the Asian Cup, put it, "In the past, we were afraid. Always. All the time. We knew we must try not to lose. Now every player is free, and this is better."

There would be more jubilant gunfire, much more, in August, thanks to the team's startling run at the Athens Summer Games.

The Iraqi Olympic delegation—twenty-one officials, twenty members of the soccer team, and one athlete each in swimming, track, weightlifting, boxing, and tae kwon do—was funded by the U.S. State Department, the U.S. Olympic Committee, and several other international donors. Clad in flak jackets, delegation members were secretly flown from Baghdad to Athens by a C-130 from the Australian air force. Two days before, insurgents provided them a grim send-off, firing a mortar at National Olympic Committee offices that killed one and wounded four.

Iraq opened the soccer tournament by shocking a Portugal team led by Manchester United star Cristiano Ronaldo and six members of European Cup holders FC Porto, 4–2, in Patras. After a 2–0 victory over Costa Rica and a 2–1 loss to Morocco, the Iraqis finished atop their first-round group and marched into the quarterfinals.

There, they defeated Australia, 1–0, in the aptly named Iraklion, on the island of Crete. The hero was Mohammed Emad, who scored the only goal with a second-half bicycle kick. That surpassed Iraq's previous Olympic best, in 1980, when it reached the final eight but lost to East Germany, 4–0.

Within sight of their second-ever Olympic medal (the first was a bronze in weightlifting at the 1960 Rome Games), the Iraqis traveled to Thessaloniki and dropped their semifinal to Paraguay, 3–1, and the bronze-medal match to Italy, 1–0.

The fourth-place finish seemed to point to a bright future for Iraqi soccer. Not all was well, of course. The country remained in postwar chaos and the players at loose ends. The year concluded with a disappointing first-round exit from the Gulf Cup in Doha, Qatar. A week later Hamad, the newly crowned Asian Coach of the Year, resigned, citing, like Stange, safety worries and the difficulty of holding the team together; in fact, Hamad made his announcement following word that his home had been destroyed. Meanwhile, the sport's infrastructure was in tatters, and the man charged with leading the soccer federation was Hussain Saeed Mohamed, the federation's general secretary during the Uday era. But perhaps the greatest indication that the game had nevertheless truly progressed came early in the Olympic opener against Portugal when defender Haidar Jabar broke a 0–0 tie by scoring an own goal. Instead of thoughts of

Uday's henchmen and a postmatch beating, Jabar collected himself, as did his teammates, and a patient, methodical Iraq rallied to turn a 1–0 deficit into the two-goal triumph.

That focus paid more dividends back in Doha in December 2006 as Iraq, under new coach Yahya Manhel, fought its way to the fifteenth Asian Games soccer final before bowing to host Qatar, 1–0. Though outplayed, the Iraqis could take solace in an impressive run that included wins over Uzbekistan in the quarterfinals and South Korea in the semifinals.

Iraq's progress against all odds was hard to ignore, but in July 2007, on the eve of the fourteenth Asian Cup in Southeast Asia, no one was predicting that the Lions of Mesopotamia would be a factor. One player, Ghanim Ghudayer, age twenty-two, had been kidnapped, his whereabouts unknown. The new coach, journeyman Jorvan Vieira of Brazil, had been signed to a two-month contract in late May. And the conditions were no better than when Hamad left: at one practice in Jordan, six players showed up.

Nevertheless Iraq, based in Bangkok, got off to a bright start by winning its group with a 1–1 tie against Thailand, a 3–1 upset of Australia, and a scoreless tie with Oman. Free-kick goals by Akram and Mahmoud sank Vietnam in the quarterfinal in Bangkok, and Iraq edged South Korea on penalty kicks, 4–3, following a 0–0 deadlock, in the semifinal in Kuala Lumpur. A save by Shiite goalkeeper Noor Sabri Abbas in the fourth round of the PK duel was the difference against the Koreans.

Four days later in Jakarta a corner kick by a Kurd headed into the net by a Sunni Turkmen ultimately handed Iraq the title. Facing the three-time champion Saudi Arabians, whose attack had produced a dozen goals in their first five games, the Iraqi defense held firm, and with nineteen minutes remaining captain Younes Mahmoud drifted in at the far post and nodded home a ball from Hawar Mulla Mohammed.

At the final whistle the Iraqi players, mad with joy, celebrated wildly. But there was no mistaking which country they represented: each wore a black armband in memory of the fifty killed back home in the suicide bombings on the opposite ends of Baghdad that followed the win over South Korea. The atmosphere heading into the final was tinged by longstanding accusations by Iraq's Shiite-led government that the Saudi government was supporting the work of Sunni Arab insurgents in Iraq. Before and during the tournament, many players had received death threats or had experienced the kidnapping or murder of a loved one. Celebratory gunfire killed at least four people each after the wins over Vietnam, South Korea, and Saudi Arabia. On the day of the final, Baghdad police reported seventeen bodies dumped on the streets of their city. And Mahmoud, voted the tournament's MVP, later said he would not return home: "I don't want the Iraqi people to be angry with me, but if I go back with the team, anybody could kill me or try to hurt me." He also expressed the wish that American troops would leave his country.

Sounding the final note, Vieira announced that he was stepping down as coach.

So mere moments after the scenes of streets in Basra, Mosul, Kirkuk, and Baghdad clogged with happy, flag-waving Iraqis—chanting "One Iraq"—Iraq was back to normal, much quicker than any Iraqi had wanted. The tossing of candy, lighting of fireworks, and jubilant drumming subsided, but a band of white-clad heroes had done what Iraq's bickering politicians could not: unite, however briefly, a fractured nation of 27 million. In parting, Vieira offered some words of hope for the team he was leaving, if not for the country it represents: "We all know the problems in Iraq, but I have learned they are fantastic people. We did not have much time so we had to work quickly. We sometimes fought, we sometimes argued, but we got the work done. It was very difficult, but I am very proud of these boys."

Kiev Players Defy Order to Lose to Nazi Team

Outside Central Republican Stadium in Kiev stands a memorial to the Dynamo Kiev players who, at the height of World War II, had the temerity to humble a team made up of Nazi soldiers. The official Soviet version of the so-called Match of Death had the players, still in their uniforms, being led to a cliff, where they were shot. The truth, which was revealed by the team's last surviving member, star winger Makar Goncharenko, after the fall of the USSR, is only slightly less tragic.

In late 1941, months after the Ukrainian capital had fallen to the Germans, Josif Kordik, a soccer fanatic and manager of a Kiev bakery, had hopes of forming his own team. He saw his chance when he spotted a bedraggled man he recognized as former Dynamo goalkeeper Nikolai Trusevich, recently released from an internment camp. Kordik hired Trusevich and other top Kiev players to work at the bakery, and by June 1942 he had convinced them to play in a local league organized by the occupying Germans. Among the opponents were teams made up of military railroad workers and soldiers from the Hungarian and Romanian garrisons. Also, Flakelf, the Luftwaffe's powerful team.

The players of this bakery team, named FC Start, were malnourished and poorly equipped, but they also featured eight former members of Dynamo and three more from Lokomotiv Kiev. They rolled through their first seven matches, outscoring the opposition by a combined 47–9, then humbled Flakelf, 5–1, in early August.

To the Nazis, embarrassing non-German opposition on the soccer field was merely a harmless diversion for the locals, but this blow to the pride of the so-called Master Race would not stand, and three days later a rematch was arranged at Zenit Stadium. "Revenge Football" in large letters read the posters announcing the game.

With the referee—an ss officer—ignoring every Flakelf foul, the German side took the lead with a goal after Trusevich was left stunned by a Flakelf boot to the head. But despite the Germans' continued violent play, Start rebounded and took a 3–1 lead into halftime. The Ukrainian fans began to jeer German security, who responded by charging with their attack dogs.

During the intermission, an ss officer entered Start's dressing room and complimented the team on its play. Then he added, "You really cannot expect to win however. Just consider for a moment the consequences if you do." They might have, but this was a team, clad in Soviet red, that had refused to give the Nazi salute in pregame ceremonies. Ever defiant, Start went on to win, 5–3. Near the end, defender Oleksiy Klimenko danced through the Flakelf defense, rounded the goalkeeper, and instead of rolling in his side's sixth goal, stopped and blasted the ball back upfield. The referee ended the match before ninety minutes were up.

Later in the month, after one more rout of another league team, Start players were arrested and tortured by the Gestapo. One of the players was tortured to death, and the rest were sent just outside Kiev to the notorious Syrets labor camp, not far from Babi Yar, a ravine where one hundred thousand were murdered by the Nazis. Among the players who did not survive were Trusevich, Klimenko, and a third former Dynamo player, Ivan Kuzmenko, who all were executed in February 1943.

Founded in 1927, Dynamo Kiev had won no domestic honors to that point, its best showing a third-place finish in the 1937 Soviet first division. After the war it became the USSR's most decorated team with thirteen Soviet league titles and nine Soviet Cups. Dynamo was the first club outside Moscow to win a Soviet league title, in 1961, and it became the country's first European champion with its triumph in the 1975 Euro Cup Winners' Cup. After the breakup of the Soviet Union, which restored Ukrainian sovereignty, Dynamo won the first nine Ukrainian championships beginning in 1993.

The story of FC Start, meanwhile, inspired four motion pictures, two in the Soviet Union, a Hungarian treatment in 1961, and twenty years later the American-made *Victory*. Directed by John Huston and starring Pelé, Michael Caine, Sylvester Stallone, and Max von Sydow, *Victory* also featured cameo appearances by Osvaldo Ardilles, Bobby Moore, Kaz Deyna, and several other international soccer stars. In the film, however, there is no firing squad: a crack German team ties a team of Allied POWs, who at the final whistle escape during a pitch invasion by excited spectators.

The German Paratrooper Who Lifted the English F.A. Cup

The Second World War had been over for eleven years. London was still recovering from the seven-year conflict. And among the players lifting the English F.A. Cup, to the roars of a Wembley Stadium crowd of one hundred thousand, was a former German paratrooper.

Manchester City goalkeeper Bert Trautmann could not have imagined the moment in his wildest dreams, but then the triumph at Wembley in 1956 was just the climax of a remarkable, improbable life.

Trautmann was born in the northern German city of Bremen in 1923. He experienced the collapse of the economy under the *Wei-*

mar Republic, the rise of the Nazi party, and life in the Hitler Youth. That was only the beginning.

During the war this veteran of the battle for Arnhem was awarded the Iron Cross first class, court-martialed for sabotage, trapped in a cellar for three days after being buried by rubble, captured by the Russians (and escaped), captured by the Free French (and escaped), and captured by the Americans (and escaped).

Trautmann's luck seemed to run out when he was collared by the British, who greeted him with the cliché, "Hello, Fritz, fancy a cup of tea?" He sat out the rest of the war at a POW camp in Ashton, Makerfield, and chose to remain in England after V-E Day.

A talented left halfback as a youngster, he resumed his soccer career as an outfield player with local sides and, later, the modest St. Helens Town. Trautmann, however, was an even more talented goalkeeper, and after filling in brilliantly for the regular 'keeper he went between the posts permanently.

In 1949 he was transferred to Manchester City of the English first division to replace the popular Frank Swift, triggering an uproar. Season-ticket holders threatened a boycott, and protest letters poured into Maine Road from throughout the country. Most non-English players in the English first division were Scotsmen, Welshmen, and Irishmen; the sight of a German on an English pitch, coming hard on the heels of World War II, was too much to bear.

Trautmann responded to the anti-German atmosphere with his performances on the field. In his first appearance in London, he dazzled in a match with Fulham and at game's end was actually applauded by the opposing players.

The pinnacle of his fifteen-year, 545-game career with the club was the 1955–56 season. He not only was named England's Footballer of the Year—the second foreigner so honored—but also was dominant in the F.A. Cup final, which the Blues won, 3–1, over Birmingham City. With fifteen minutes remaining, he was knocked out in a collision with Birmingham's Peter Murphy, but he regained consciousness and made a string of big saves to preserve the victory. Prince Philip commented on the crook in Trautmann's neck while presenting the German with his winner's medal, and x-rays taken three days later revealed that the big blond had performed his heroics despite having suffered a broken neck when Murphy's right knee struck him in the head.

Trautmann was rewarded at the end of his career with a testimonial match. In a complete reversal of his original welcome to Maine Road, a crowd of sixty thousand—a record for a testimonial in England—turned out to bid the ex-German paratrooper farewell.

Anti-Communist Team Is Liquidated by Tito

Soccer clubs, even those of the first-division variety, have folded, merged with others, splintered into two. Gradjanska Zagreb can claim that it was liquidated. Not in the Josef Stalin sense but in the Tito sense.

Gradjanska (full name Prvi Hrvatski Gradanski Sportski Klub, or Croatian Citizens' Sports Club) could proudly boast that it won the Kingdom of Yugoslavia's very first national championship, in 1923, and went on to repeat the feat in 1926, 1928, 1937, and 1940. World War II interrupted soccer in Yugoslavia for the next six years, but Gradjanska took part in a Croatian league during the Nazi occupation and finished on top in 1941, 1943, and 1944.

With peace came the reconstituted Yugoslavia, and when the 1946–47 Yugoslav season kicked off, Gradjanska was no more.

The Gradjanska club, known for its opposition to the new communist regime under General Tito, himself a Croat, was disbanded in June 1945 and its archives were torched. Some of the best Gradjanska players were banished to the new army club, FK Partizan of Belgrade, and conscripted into the military, while others, led by Stejpan Bobek, were cynically combined with members of their crosstown archrival, HASK (Hrvatski Akademski Sportski Klub, or Croatian Academic Sports Club), to form NK Dinamo Zagreb, which, under the socialist model, became the electrical workers club. The new team moved into the HASK stadium, yet Dinamo adopted the blue shirts and blue shorts of the late Gradjanska and, eventually, its logo.

Dinamo went on to glory in Europe (a triumph over Leeds United of England in the 1966–67 UEFA Cup final) and at home (four Yugoslav championships and seven Yugoslav Cups). But the team's roots remained anti-communist and fiercely Croatian, and after the breakup of Yugoslavia, Dinamo changed its name twice, first to HASK-Gradjanska in 1992, then to Croatia Zagreb in 1993. HASK-Gradjanska never caught on because its name resulted in "the club of both the learned man and common man."

The team by any other name remained a domestic force if not a European power, winning nine Croatian league titles and eight Croatian Cups since 1993. The name of its rabid supporters group, the Bad Blue Boys, was inspired by the 1983 Sean Penn film, *Bad Boys.*

USSR Balks at Playing in Stadium Used for Executions

Chile doesn't come to mind when the subject is the Cold War, but the Chileans engaged in a stare-down with the Soviet Union in 1974 over a World Cup playoff. And it was the USSR that blinked.

A year earlier the pro-Marxist government of Salvador Allende had been overthrown in an army coup d'etat led by General Augusto Pinochet, who rounded up the country's communists and warehoused them at the Estadio Nacional in Santiago. Most of them were executed on the stadium floor.

Soccer then set the two nations on a collision course. The USSR won its European qualifying group over Ireland and France to advance to a playoff with the Chileans, who, after Venezuela withdrew, won its South American group by edging Peru in three games.

The Soviets played host to Chile in the first leg in Moscow and tied, 0–0, but ostensibly conscience got the better of them and they refused to play the return leg at Chile's national stadium because of its recent history.

Lengthy meetings failed to produce a solution. Even the offer of playing elsewhere in Chile failed to move the USSR, and FIFA ruled that the game should go on. On the appointed day, with no Soviet player in sight, Chile's starting eleven lined up at the national stadium, a referee whistled for kickoff, and the South Americans walked the ball into the "USSR" net to cement their forfeit victory.

The Soviets, who no doubt would have been able to present a stronger case before FIFA had they not already played the first match, could later lay claim to some sort of curse on the Chileans. Chile tuned up for the 1974 World Cup by losing a friendly with Santos of Brazil, 5–0; once in West Germany, the defensive-minded Chileans lost to the eventual champion West Germans, 1–0, in the opening match and tied East Germany, 1–1, and Australia, 0–0, to bow out quietly.

Four years later, the USSR failed to qualify for Argentina '78, but so did Chile. Needing just a tie in their last qualifier to nail down a berth, the Chileans lost to Peru, 2–0, in Lima.

Three Battles

Soccer is not war, but it has had its battles, most of them eagerly forgotten. Three of the sport's most infamous matches came during World Cup play, giving soccer two black eyes and one to spare: "the Battle of Bordeaux" at France '38, "the Battle of Berne" at Switzerland '54, and "the Battle of Santiago" at Chile '62.

Brazil, purveyor of "the Beautiful Game," was involved in two, beginning with Bordeaux at the third World Cup. The second-round match between Czechoslovakia and the South Americans opened the new Parc de Lescure, but the crowd of twenty-five thousand was treated not to a celebration but to a bloody disgrace. One fight resulted in two of the game's three ejections; Czech forward Oldrich Nejedlý left with a broken leg and goalkeeper František Plánička pressed on despite a broken arm. The result was 1–1 after overtime. Brazil won an uneventful replay, 2–1, back at Lescure two days later, but World Cup soccer had crossed a threshold, leaving behind its somewhat innocent beginnings.

Fast forward sixteen years to Berne, the 1954 World Cup, and a quarterfinal between Hungary and Brazil that was shocking mainly because the match, despite heavy rain that hindered the skillful Brazilians, was expected to be a classic involving teams that both deserved to be in the final. Instead, the crowd of forty thousand at Wankdorf Stadium witnessed a 4–2 Hungarian victory marred by three ejections, two penalties (both converted), a long string of vicious tackles, and constant stoppages (forty-two fouls total), an occasional skirmish, and the capper, a postgame free-for-all.

Hungary jumped out to a two-goal lead after seven minutes and was ahead, 2–1, early in the second half when English referee Arthur Ellis awarded the Hungarians a penalty kick for a handball violation over the vehement protests of the Brazilians. Mihaly Lantos converted.

The South Americans closed the gap to 3–2 in the sixty-sixth minute on a blast by right winger Julinho, but two of the best players on the field, captain and right halfback József Bozsik of Hungary and left back Nilton Santos of Brazil, were sent off for a punch-out in the seventieth. If Brazil had any hopes of a miracle, they evaporated in the eighty-sixth with the ejection of inside left Humberto Tozzi, who violently kicked Gyula Lóránt, then fell to his knees before referee Ellis, pleading for mercy.

With Brazil reduced to nine men, the Hungarians' insurance goal came in the final minute. Zoltan Czibor crossed from the left, and inside right Sandor Kocsis, the man known as "the Golden Head," nodded the ball into the net for one of his tournament-leading eleven goals. The strike came as revenge for Kocsis, who earlier had been comically chased around the field by his irate marker, defender Djalma Santos.

The finale to the Battle of Berne occurred underneath the grandstand. As Ellis was escorted off the field by armed guards, Hungarian star Ferenc Puskás, who watched the game from the sidelines because of injury, reportedly struck Brazil center halfback Pinheiro in the face with a bottle, opening a six-inch gash. The identity of the assailant was never determined, but the brawl was on. Brazil, wearing a chip on its shoulder from its loss to Uruguay at the 1950 World Cup final, stormed into the Hungary dressing room, smashed out the lights, and it was every man for himself as bottles and cleated shoes were swung with abandon.

This is how BBC1 host David Coleman introduced to his British audience clips of a World Cup match between Group 2 foes Chile and Italy on an early June evening in 1962: "Good evening. The game you are about to see is the most stupid, appalling, disgusting, and disgraceful exhibition of football possibly in the history of the game. Chile versus Italy. This is the first time the two countries have ever met—we hope it will be the last. . . . After seeing the film tonight, you at home may well think that teams that play in this manner ought to be expelled immediately from the competition."

The first-round match at Estadio Nacional, since dubbed "the Battle of Santiago," may have been no more violent than the battles of Bordeaux or Berne, but unlike those two games, this match, played a month ahead of the launch of Tellstar and the miracle of satellite television, was seen, sooner or later, by a growing worldwide TV audience.

Italy was already strongly resented in many parts of South America for its policy of *oriundi*, whereby over the previous three decades some of the continent's best players were lured to the Italian National Team based on the slightest of Italian ancestry. It didn't help that during the run-up to this World Cup scouts from leading Italian clubs were seen skulking about the training camps of the qualified South American sides—Uruguay, Colombia, Brazil, Argentina, and host Chile—looking for bargains.

The ill will might have been merely a pregame distraction were it not for the two Italian journalists who filed stories that criticized life in Chile—Santiago in particular—and questioned the virtue of Chilean women. The Chilean press countered with charges of drug abuse in Italian soccer, and the fuse had been lit.

Fearing for their safety, the two scribes, Corrado Pizzinelli and Antonio Ghirelli, left Chile before the big showdown, but they should have known they were playing with fire. A series of earthquakes in 1960 had killed thousands and decimated the country, placing in doubt Chile's bid to beat out Argentina and West Germany as 1962 World Cup host. (Chilean soccer federation chief Carlos Dittborn, who would die of a heart attack a month before the tournament, subsequently won sufficient sympathy from FIFA with his famous non sequitur, "We must have the World Cup *because* we have nothing.") Two fine stadiums, the Estadio Nacional in Santiago and Estadio Sausalito in Vina del Mar, were erected for the tournament, but they were overshadowed by charges of price gouging by hotels and inflated ticket prices that left many Chileans unable to attend.

On June 2 a crowd of 66,057, most of them angry Chileans, jammed the newly built national stadium. Chile-Italy would be presided over by Englishman Ken Aston, a towering referee who took the field despite being hobbled by an Achilles tendon injury. Aston was nearing the end of a distinguished officiating career and would go on to serve as director of referees for the next three World Cups. He had not been originally assigned to this game, but he was selected by FIFA based on his work during the rather placid tournament opener, Chile's 3–1 victory over Switzerland three days earlier, also in Santiago.

Chile-Italy would be an entirely different animal. The hostilities began during pregame festivities with the Chilean players' rejection of an offer of carnations by their Italian rivals. The first player, Giorgio Ferrini, was cautioned twelve seconds after kickoff. Chilean players were already spitting in the faces of their opponents when, in the eighth minute, Ferrini was kicked from behind by Chilean center forward Honorino Landa. Ferrini retaliated and was sent off, and it took Aston and police ten minutes to get the Italian inside left off the field so that play could resume. The police would appear on the field two more times before the match ended.

The physical play increased in intensity and reached a low point in the fortieth minute when an Italian *oriundi*, Argentina-born midfielder and captain Humberto Maschio, brutally tackled Chilean left winger Leonel Sanchez, who let fly with a left hook that broke Maschio's nose. Aston's back was turned and neither linesman reacted to the blow; Sanchez, the son of a boxer, remained on the field.

Sanchez helped reduce Italy to nine men in the forty-first minute, provoking Mario David into a retaliatory kick to the head (other accounts have David hauling Sanchez down by the neck) that earned the Italian right back his marching orders.

Chile didn't take advantage until the seventy-fourth minute as right winger Jaime Ramirez headed home a free kick by the ubiquitous Sanchez. Inside right Jorge Toro iced the victory with a goal from long range in the eighty-eighth.

West Germany, Chile, and Italy would finish Group 2 with three points apiece, but only two could go through to the quarterfinals. Thanks to goal difference, the Germans (+3) and Chileans (+2) advanced; the Italians (+1) were eliminated. Later, West Germany bowed to Yugoslavia, 1–0, in the final eight, but Chile rode its hometown advantage to a third-place finish as it upset the Soviet Union, 2–1, lost to eventual champion Brazil, 4–2, in the semifinals, and trimmed Yugoslavia, 1–0, in the consolation match.

As for Chile-Italy, Aston, who nearly abandoned the game at one point and had to be escorted off the field with his linesmen, later described the match as "uncontrollable."

"I wasn't reffing a football match," said Aston, a lieutenant colonel with the Royal Artillery in Asia during World War II. "I was acting as an umpire in military maneuvers." On several occasions he broke his personal rule against making physical contact with players and found himself "manhandling players left, right, and center" during the frequent skirmishes.

Aston had requested his own linesmen and was not pleased by the duo assigned to him, Fernando Buergo Elcuaz of Mexico and Leo

Goldstein of Israel, a resident of New York City. The disappointed Aston said, "I had to stick with a Mexican and a little American from New York. They weren't very good, so it became almost me against the twenty-two players."

"The little American" must have been traumatized by his afternoon in the cauldron of Santiago, not to mention the withering criticism of the Italian press and—of all people—his own referee afterward.

Then again, maybe not.

Nearly two decades earlier, Goldstein faced something much more terrifying than a hostile capacity crowd in a World Cup. In 1944 the Polish-born Jew was living day-to-day in the Nazi death camp at Auschwitz.

Eventually, Goldstein found himself among a long line of condemned, stripped naked and being herded toward the gas chamber for what they had been told would be a rare shower. Like the thousands of Jews, Gypsies, political opponents, Soviet POWs, homosexuals, and "undesirables" who had gone before him, Goldstein and the others in the queue suspected the truth.

The German guards directed the prisoners to the doorway of the gas chamber with shouts of "*Links! Links!* ["Go left!"] *Schnell!!!*" But before he entered the shower block, a guard discreetly ordered Goldstein to the right and back to his bunk. Though puzzled, Goldstein, for the moment, had been spared.

The guard, purportedly a former member of the German National Team whom Goldstein knew only as "Otto," had entered Goldstein's barracks weeks earlier and asked if anyone was familiar with the rules of soccer. There was no immediate response, but Goldstein finally murmured, "I once read the rule book."

Otto, who'd organized a team of Auschwitz guards and had lined up matches against soldiers and guards from other death camps, remembered. He needed a referee, and Goldstein, by default, was his man.

In the coming months Goldstein walked the most delicate of tightropes, refereeing matches in which he knew he could not afford to raise the ire of *any* of the twenty-two players on the field. Despite a lack of formal training as a referee, he survived his own perverse version of double jeopardy, and before his liberation he vowed to dedicate his life to officiating.

After the war Goldstein became a citizen of Israel but settled in New York City, where he drove taxicabs and refereed youth matches in the Bowery. A bachelor, he worked his way through the adult ranks to a FIFA badge, and in 1962 the U.S. Soccer Federation recommended him for that year's World Cup.

Goldstein was not selected, but he made plans to travel to Chile anyway and informed FIFA that he would be available to officiate, at no charge, if needed. Indeed he was, and he served as a linesman for one first-round match, Hungary-England in Rancagua, before getting the fateful Chile-Italy game in Santiago.

Goldstein's dates of birth and death are unknown, just as it is unknown whether he had any regrets over his offer to help in Chile. It is doubtful, however, that that wild afternoon in Santiago could compare with the day he was ordered *rechts, nicht links.*

Soccer, the Sport of the '80s.

A SOUVENIR PENNANT sold in the late '70s by the North American Soccer League, based on the hopeful public assertions of Commissioner Phil Woosnam

I recently went to the United States, where soccer is nothing. It interests no one. Their presence in Italy is frankly useless.

JOSEF HICKERSBERGER, coach of Austria, to France Football when asked about one of his team's first-round opponents at the 1990 World Cup in Italy. Austria, needing a bushel of goals in its third match to advance, was held by the United States to a 2–1 win and was eliminated.

Here, everyone's interested in baseball and American football and many people didn't even know that a soccer match was being played today. So it's easy for them, because they aren't playing under any pressure. My mother, my grandmother, or my great-grandmother could play in a team like that.

RICARDO LAVOLPE, coach of Mexico, on the U.S. National Team after it blanked his side, 2–0, in Columbus in a qualifier for the 2006 World Cup

6 AMERICA

In the world of soccer, the United States is that land through the looking glass. Not only is it the only major nation where soccer is not among the very favorite team sports, but the hostility toward the sport in some quarters of the establishment can be breathtaking. America was playing the modern game in the mid-nineteenth century, decades before other countries knew of its existence, but by the twentieth century, while soccer took the rest of the world by storm, the game here had been eclipsed by sports ranging from bowling to badminton. In many countries the spectacle of grown men playing the game well for money before large crowds made soccer wildly popular and boosted participation; in the States, the sport didn't get off its knees until the youth boom of the 1970s and '80s, which came on the heels of the collapse of a string of professional leagues. And while in most countries the women have had to play catch-up to the men, in the United States the women's national team leads the men's in world championships, 2–0.

The Greatest Upset of Them All

In terms of sheer shock value, it's bigger than the U.S. ice hockey team's gold medal triumph at the 1980 Winter Olympics. It tops the 1969 Miracle Mets, Jets quarterback Joe Namath's guaranteed win in Super Bowl III—all of them.

The U.S. National Team's 1–0 victory over England at the 1950 World Cup in Brazil was the greatest upset in the history of sports. England, the birthplace of soccer, lost to the United States, a team of semipros—plus one amateur—representing a country that was considered at the time to be on par with Antarctica on the international soccer totem pole. Imagine the 1992 U.S. Olympic basketball squad, the so-called Dream Team, tumbling to the Duchy of Grand Fenwick. So preposterous was the thought of England losing to the United States that many sports editors around the world, upon seeing the final score come over the wire from Belo Horizonte, concluded that it must have been a typographical error. Surely the actual score was England 10, United States 1.

England, at odds with FIFA from the late 1920s until just after World War II, had finally consented to play in a World Cup after skipping the first three, and it came to Brazil as a favorite. In the first round a routine victory over Chile and the expected hammering of the United States, plus a win—at worst a tie—against Spain, and the English would be through Group 2 and into the final pool for a four-team, round-robin playoff for the crown. From there England would cement its status as the game's master.

The English indeed brushed aside Chile, 2–0, June 25 at the cavernous Maracanã Stadium in Rio de Janeiro in their first-ever World Cup match. The Americans, meanwhile, had opened the cup by falling bravely to Spain in Curitiba, 3–1, giving up all three goals after the eightieth minute. Thus, the stage was set for the USA's expected elimination at the hands of England at Belo Horizonte, a mining town some three hundred miles north of Rio.

A crowd of 10,151 gathered at the intimate Mineiro Stadium on that cool, cloudy June 29, most of them curious Brazilians rooting for the United States to somehow upend England and perhaps help remove an obstacle to their own country's championship hopes. The field was bumpy—an impediment to English skill—and the dressing rooms were so cramped and foul that England chose to change beforehand at its hotel. From the opening kickoff, England set up camp on the U.S. half of the field and, early on, sailed a shot just over the crossbar. The English were laughing and joking as they sauntered back for the ensuing goal kick. Surely the slaughter would begin soon.

But, amazingly, the game remained 0–0 beyond the first half hour, and in the thirty-ninth minute (or thirty-seventh or thirty-eighth, depending on the account), the United States scored the Goal. U.S. halfback Walter Bahr, one of eight native-born Americans in the lineup, latched onto a throw-in from the right by captain Ed McIlvenny, dribbled ten yards down the wing, and rifled a twenty-five-yard shot toward the far post. English goalkeeper Bert Williams appeared to have the situation under control, but U.S. center forward Joe Gaetjens swooped in and sent a flying header into the right corner of the net.

Several English newspaper reports claimed the ball struck the unwitting Gaetjens in the head before caroming into the goal. "Williams in the England goal positioned himself perfectly to gather in Bahr's shot," wrote John Graydon of the *English Saturday Post,* "but Gaetjens, the American leader, ruined everything for him. Gaetjens jumped in, failed to connect with his forehead but the ball accidentally hit the top of his head and was deflected into the England goal." Surviving U.S. players later contended that Gaetjens was simply an unpredictable player who chose this moment to execute an unexpected diving header.

This was England's wake-up call, and the red-faced favorites—frustrated by an underdog listed at 500–1—responded with a second-half barrage that increased in intensity as the final whistle approached. But goalkeeper Frank Borghi and his back line held firm, the English marksmen were off-target, and there would be no equalizer.

At one point English defender Alf Ramsey's free kick was headed on by forward Jimmy Mullen and seemingly bound for the U.S. goal, but Borghi made a sprawling save.

England's best chance to draw level came with five minutes remaining. Inside forward Stanley Mortenson split the U.S. defense, only to be brought down just beyond the penalty area with a desperate gridiron football–style tackle by U.S. center back Charles Colombo, the team's hard man who, perhaps for reasons of intimidation, always wore gloves when he played. So vicious was the hit that their momentum carried Mortenson and Colombo to the penalty spot. Italian referee Generoso Dattilo, however, did not point to that spot to give England a penalty kick and he did not eject Colombo. True to his given name, he shook his finger at Colombo yet said, *"Bono, bono, bono!"* (in this instance, "Good job!" or "Way to go!") and awarded only a free kick that the English subsequently sent sailing over the bar.

Moments later Ramsey booted a free kick into the penalty area, where Billy Mullen's downward header got behind Borghi, but the U.S. 'keeper recovered and palmed the ball away for right back Harry Keough to clear. Dattilo rejected English claims that the ball had crossed the goal line.

Through it all, the Americans kept their cool. Late in the match, with the partisan crowd chanting *Mais um!* ("One more!"), the balding inside forward John "Clarkie" Souza dribbled around a half-dozen Englishmen to kill several seconds off the clock.

At the final whistle, Gaetjens, Borghi, and other U.S. players were paraded around the field on the shoulders of jubilant Brazilian fans, and others set newspapers ablaze in the stands in celebration. U.S. coach Bill Jeffrey, a Scotsman, danced a jig on the sidelines.

While the rest of the world buzzed, this monumental upset caused less than a ripple in the United States. Only one American reporter, Dent McSkimming, was on hand for the game, and that was only because he was on vacation and taking in the game as a tourist; his paper, the *St. Louis Post-Dispatch*, ran not a McSkimming report of the game but a wire service account. The disinterest shown the remarkable feat by the American public spoke volumes of the state of soccer in the United States in the 1950s; likewise, the shock and amazement in most quarters that greeted news of the upset said plenty about what the world thought of both English and American soccer.

Before the upset the U.S. Soccer Federation, then known as the U.S. Football Association (USFA), all but shut down its national team program following a humiliating 7–1 loss to host Italy in its only 1934 World Cup match and a respectable 1–0 loss to the eventual gold medal–winning Italians in its lone appearance at the 1936 Berlin Olympics. The United States entered the 1938 World Cup in France but withdrew after FIFA pitted the Americans against the Dutch East

Indies (now Indonesia) in a qualifying playoff. (Perhaps the USFA was influenced by a September 1937 trip to Mexico City during which the national team bowed to El Tricolores, 7–2, 7–3, and 5–1 over two weeks.)

Thanks in part to World War II, the USFA (since renamed the U.S. Soccer Football Association) didn't send a selection out onto the field again until the 1947 North American Championship in Havana, where Cuba and Mexico flattened the Americans by a combined 10–2. That was followed by the 1948 London Olympics, where the Americans—featuring future World Cup team members Bahr, Colombo, Gino Parini, Eddie Souza, and John Souza (no relation)— were humbled by Italy, 9–0, in their only match. Four days later, the squad, now appearing as the national team, was humiliated by Norway, 11–0, in Oslo, and five days after that it tumbled to Northern Ireland, 5–0, in Belfast.

Obviously, the world had changed. The United States had beaten Belgium and Paraguay to reach the 1930 World Cup semifinals with a collection of rugged characters, a smattering with pro experience from Britain but most from the hardscrabble ethnic semipro leagues of the urban United States. But over the next two decades professionalism spread to Brazil, Spain, and other soccer hotbeds, while elsewhere, from the amateurs of Scandinavia to the minnows of Central America, the game only got stronger—stronger than the likes of the Fall River FC of Massachusetts, Kearny Scots of New Jersey, Stix, Baer and Fuller of St. Louis, and other domestic powers of the era. Before long, the butchers, bakers, and candlestick makers playing in the American Soccer League and/or U.S. National Open Cup were hopelessly behind, a gap that would persist for a half-century.

U.S. failure was supposed to have continued in September 1949 with World Cup qualifiers in Mexico City, but North America was generously awarded two slots in Brazil, and the United States team, despite being beaten by Mexico, 6–0 and 6–2, punched their ticket at the expense of the Cubans, 1–1 and 5–2. Nevertheless, it was hardly a bold run-up to Brasil '50.

The venerable Home International Championship, the world's oldest international team competition (born 1883, died 1989 due to fan violence), was the annual battle for soccer supremacy among England, Scotland, Wales, and Northern Ireland. In 1949–50 it doubled as a European qualifying group for the fourth World Cup, and the English finished first by two points with a 1–0 victory over Scotland in Glasgow in their final match. A World Cup spot was also reserved for the Home's second-placed team, but the Scots deemed themselves unworthy as a runner-up and stayed home.

U.S. coach Jeffrey made his final World Cup squad selections after an April 1950 match in St. Louis between hopefuls from the East and West, which ended in a 3–3 tie. Only seven players survived from the qualifiers in Mexico City: Bahr, Borghi, Colombo, forward Nicholas DiOrio, defender Harry Keough, John Souza, and forward Francis Wallace. Jeffrey's final selection then was thumped, 5–0, by the touring Turkish club Besiktas in St. Louis; a loss to an English B team, 1–0, at New York's Randall's Island, followed, and the United States was off to Brazil.

That English B team, playing as the English F.A. XI, would become part of England's World Cup squad. It tuned up for what would be, for some players, a trip to Brazil by winning all nine of its friendlies during a tour of Canada, outscoring the opposition 66–13, including the victory over the United States.

After the U.S.-England friendly, at a banquet at the Waldorf-Astoria, English Football Association president Stanley Rous, later elected head of FIFA, was gracious in his remarks regarding the U.S. team but suggested his side was weary from the extensive travel in North America. In conclusion, he said, "When you go to Brazil and play the English National Team, then you will find out what football is all about."

After the incredible upset over England, the United States was unable to ride the victory into the tournament's final pool. The Americans lost to Chile, 5–2, three days later at Ilha do Retiro Stadium in Recife and were eliminated. Like the Spain match, the defense collapsed in the second half. After rebounding from a 2–0 deficit to tie on goals by Gino Pariani in the forty-seventh minute and Ed Souza from the penalty spot in the forty-eighth (or by Frank Wallace and Joe Maca, or by Wallace and John Souza, depending on the account), the team melted in the 110-degree heat and conceded three goals beginning in the fifty-fourth.

Nevertheless, the United States, whose squad included a postman, a school teacher, a factory worker, a knitting machine mechanic, and a hearse driver, went home tied for second in Group 2 with England and Chile, all at 1-2-0. Spain (3-0-0) took first but eventually finished last in the final pool, behind champion Uruguay, host Brazil, and third-place Sweden.

Despite disbelief over the England defeat, the United States left Brazil with a respectable all-time World Cup record of 3-4-0. Without a strong national league or public interest, however, the Americans' immediate future in international soccer was bleak, and they wouldn't make another World Cup appearance until Italia '90, where an inexperienced squad of current and former college standouts, average age twenty-three, lost all three of its games. Following USA '94 (1-2-1), France '98 (0-3-0), the Americans' encouraging quarterfinal showing at Japan/Korea '02 (2-2-1) and Germany '06 (0-2-1), the United States' all-time record in World Cup competition stood at 6-16-3.

Coach Walter Winterbottom, who had kept Stanley Matthews out of England's first two games, played the legendary winger in his team's final Group 2 match, but the English lost, 1–0, to Spain before seventy thousand at the Maracanã and trudged home. The English tumbled completely off their pedestal in 1953 when the "Magic Magyars," the invincible Hungarian National Team, routed them, 6–3, at Wembley Stadium and 7–1 six months later in Budapest.

England, of course, did not curl up and die after the losses to the United States and Hungary. Alf Ramsey, the man who played against the Yanks, was appointed coach, replacing Winterbottom, after England lost in the 1962 World Cup quarterfinals to eventual champion Brazil. The Ramsey-led English won the 1966 World Cup.

As for Belo Horizonte, England avenged that defeat four times over by humiliating the United States, 6–3, in 1953 in New York; 8–1 in 1959 in Los Angeles; 10–0 in 1964 in New York; and 5–0 in 1985 in Los Angeles. The United States came back to surprise the English, 2–0, in U.S. Cup '93 in Foxboro, Massachusetts. For now, England's advantage stands at 7-2-1, that tie coming at the 2010 World Cup.

As for Jeffrey, his tenure as U.S. coach consisted of those three games in Brazil and he returned to his day job as soccer coach at Penn State. In 1951, with the national team temporarily in mothballs, Jeffrey led his Nittany Lions on a three-game tour of Iran. The following year he closed out a successful twenty-four-year career as Penn State coach, compiling a 134-21-27 record.

McIlvenny, who like Jeffrey was born in Scotland, played for Wrexham of Wales. He moved to the United States in 1949 and played for the Philadelphia Americans, then in the midst of winning five American Soccer League titles over ten years. After the World Cup he returned to Britain and played two games with Manchester United, then closed out his career with teams in Ireland, Germany, and once again, England. Fellow defender Maca returned to his native Belgium, where he resumed his playing career as the hero who helped vanquish mighty England.

Left back Bahr followed Jeffrey to Penn State and guided the Nittany Lions to a 185-66-22 mark from 1974 to 1987. Two of Bahr's sons cut short promising professional soccer careers to pursue fame and fortune as place-kickers in the NFL. Chris, a midfielder, switched sports after scoring eleven goals and winning the 1975 NASL Rookie of the Year award with the Philadelphia Atoms. Matt, a defender, split the 1978 NASL season between the Caribous of Colorado and Tulsa Roughnecks before making the jump.

Defender Keough, later a successful coach at Saint Louis University (five NCAA titles in sixteen seasons), is the father of TV soccer commentator Ty Keough, whose playing career spanned eight appearances for the United States—ten fewer than his father—and four seasons in the NASL.

Keough, Borghi, Colombo, Wallace, and Pariani were all products of St. Louis, the latter four from the southside Italian neighborhood known as "the Hill." A reserve, Bob Annis, and Jeffrey's assistant, William "Chubby" Lyons, also were from St. Louis. As a teen, Borghi, the hearse driver who would one day become his funeral home's director, was a U.S. Army field medic in World War II. He crossed the English Channel the day after D-Day, and among the men he treated in Germany was the future voice of the St. Louis Cardinals, Jack Buck. Another army veteran, Wallace, nicknamed "Pee Wee," served in the 191st Tank Battalion and saw action on the beach at Anzio, eventually earning four Battle Stars and a Purple Heart; he was captured by the Germans and spent fifteen months in a POW camp.

Five Americans on the field at Mineiro Stadium that day were added by Jeffrey after the qualifiers in Mexico City. Of them, McIlvenny, Maca, and Gaetjens were not U.S. citizens but were allowed to play under the more lenient rules of the time. To the USSFA, a player who declared his intent to become a U.S. citizen was eligible to play for the national team. Questions were raised after the upset, but later that year FIFA declared that the United States had done nothing wrong. Of the three, however, only Maca would go on to obtain U.S. citizenship.

Before scoring the Goal, Gaetjens, the son of a Haitian mother and Belgian father, was a dishwasher in a New York restaurant, working his way through Columbia University with the help of a Haitian government scholarship. Previously his greatest claim to fame as a player had come in 1949–50 when he led the American Soccer League in scoring with eighteen goals for the last-place Brook-Hattan Galicia. After Brazil he played three years in France for Racing Club de Paris and Troyes, then returned to his native Haiti, where the rules of the day allowed him to play for the Haitians in 1953 in a World Cup qualifier against Mexico (a 4–0 loss).

Gaetjens later became a spokesman for Proctor & Gamble and owner of a string of dry-cleaning stores. Gaetjens was apolitical, but apparently some of his relatives were not, and in July 1964 he was hauled out of one of his Port-au-Prince dry-cleaning shops and taken away by "Papa Doc" Duvalier's dreaded Ton Ton Macoute secret police. Efforts to determine his whereabouts have been unsuccessful, but it is believed he died in prison in 1970, six years before he and his sixteen U.S. teammates were inducted into the National Soccer Hall of Fame.

Ironically, the Haitian government issued a commemorative stamp in Gaetjens's honor in 2000.

So just how big was this biggest of all sports upsets?

It changed nothing in the United States, and it did nothing to change English soccer's opinion of itself, nor did the rest of the world think less of England's game. An anomaly, at best.

Keough, one of the St. Louis boys, probably put it best. Years later, he told his hometown *Post-Dispatch*: "Obviously, there was no television back then and, honestly, the World Cup wasn't nearly as big a deal as it is now. We knew what we'd accomplished was something very special, but I don't think most people back home, even soccer people, had any idea how major an upset it was.

"Was it the greatest upset in history? I think so. In the [2002] World

Cup, when Senegal beat defending champion France, almost all of the players for Senegal were first-division players from top leagues all over the world. We had a team of nobodies.

"I'd say the [USA] hockey team's win [over the Soviet Union at the 1980 Olympics] was probably more significant because they went on to win that tournament. But there's no way anybody, including us, expected the U.S. to beat the English in 1950."

What If: America's First Pro Soccer League

Where would soccer in America be today if it had been driven early on by a successful professional league?

Many came and went—the first American Soccer League (1921–33), International Soccer League (1960–65), second American Soccer League (1933–82), North American Soccer League (1968–84), Major Indoor Soccer League (1978–92), and other, lesser circuits—but their club owners and administrators found themselves trapped in a catch-22: a national soccer league in the United States can't succeed without the support of grassroots participants, and few Americans will be inspired to play the game without the lure and rallying point of a successful national league.

Thus, the game at its highest level was for decades an ethnic sport tucked away in the cities of the Northeast and Midwest. Few American kids got involved, and as a result the U.S. National Team went from 1950 to 1990 without qualifying for a World Cup.

The American youth soccer boom of the 1970s, FIFA's awarding of the 1994 World Cup to the United States, the launch of Major League Soccer in 1996, and the expansion of television coverage have changed the landscape of soccer in this country. But what if the United States had formed a viable top-level soccer league around the turn of the century, as many of the reigning soccer powers of the world had?

The American League of Professional Football Clubs (ALPFC) wasn't it.

Baseball and soccer make strange bedfellows, but it was the National League's Baltimore, Boston, Brooklyn, New York, Philadelphia, and Washington clubs that banded together in 1894 to form the ALPFC as a way to keep the turnstiles at their ballparks spinning in the fall, after the baseball season ended.

A schedule running from October 5 into January was set, with each team originally slated to play ten games. Arthur I. Irwin, manager of baseball's Philadelphia Phillies, was appointed ALPFC president.

Five of the ALPFC teams were coached by the corresponding club's baseball field manager, despite the fact that they knew nothing about soccer. The squads were built around the many British and Irish players who worked in eastern factories on weekdays and played in local soccer leagues on weekends. Only the Baltimore Orioles, successful on the diamond for much of the 1890s, had the sense to import a coach from England, A.W. Stewart, who loaded his roster with eight players from England, including four from Manchester City. (Stewart also played goalkeeper for his new team.)

Baltimore drew crowds of up to eight thousand (at 25 cents a head) at a time when three thousand fans for a weekend baseball game was considered good, and the Orioles kickers averaged six goals a game while allowing fewer than one. Other clubs, however, played before sparse crowds as they struggled to keep pace with Baltimore. Bringing up the rear at the gate was Philadelphia, which played before hundreds despite being the only ALPFC team to include its star Phillies baseball players on the roster as a drawing card.

Compounding its problems, the ALPFC, in true baseball tradition, scheduled many games on weekday afternoons when the league's intended audience, immigrant working men, were on the job. ALPFC officials later claimed that the midweek matches avoided conflicts with college football games, but it's hard to believe that the blue-collar immigrants of the day would skip an ALPFC match to sit with well-scrubbed undergrads and cheer on collegiate gridders.

Shortly after the league kicked off, the club owners got cold feet and voted to suspend operations and try again the following autumn. Small crowds were only part of the reason. More pressing were rumors of the creation of a second major baseball league as well as a threat by the U.S. government to investigate Baltimore's importation of British players.

Obviously, 1895 never arrived for the ALPFC. The majority of National League club owners involved feared that the losses they incurred through soccer might jeopardize the baseball end of operations, and pro soccer as a moneymaking venture was placed on the shelf.

It is tempting to imagine what might have happened had soccer, piggybacked on the country's only pro sports organization at the time, continued—with the bugs worked out, of course. Would a successful ALPFC have inspired more grassroots participation and, eventually, become a league populated with native-born stars? Would these ALPFC stars have led the United States to victory at the first World Cup in 1930, thus giving America its first world championship in any team sport? Would the ALPFC, with a quarter-century head start, have eclipsed the fledgling NFL in the 1920s and firmly established soccer as America's preferred form of pro football?

When it pulled the plug, the Baltimore Orioles had won all six of their ALPFC matches, while the Brooklyn Bridegrooms were 5-1-0, the Boston Beaneaters 4-1-0, the New York Giants 2-4-0, the Philadelphia Phillies 2-7-0, and the Washington Nationals 1-5-0. The woeful Phillies' most notable player was Big Sam Thompson, a right fielder by trade, who is perhaps the only baseball Hall of Famer to have played professional soccer. And it was only fitting that Washington should bring up the rear in the ALPFC. The Nationals would go on to further futility in a new baseball league, where they inspired the tag, "Washington, First in War, First in Peace, and Last in the American League."

If the short-lived ALPFC can be considered the USA's first national soccer league, it predates *every* non-British national soccer league in the world, including those in Belgium (1896), Sweden (1896), Bohemia (1896), Holland (1898), Switzerland (1898), Hungary (1901), and three of today's top national leagues, Italy (1898), Germany (1903), and Spain (1929). Even soccer-mad Mexico (1903) would be behind the Americans. Only the leagues of England (1889) and Scotland and Northern Ireland (both 1891) are older. South America's pioneers, Argentina (1891) and Uruguay (1900), got underway with amateur leagues made up exclusively of teams limited to Buenos Aires and Montevideo, respectively. Uruguay, winner of the first World Cup, in 1930, didn't legalize professionalism until 1932, one year after Argentina.

NASL, MISL, MLS Invent Soccer Statistics

Record-keeping has never been of paramount importance in soccer. The great Pelé stands among the all-time leaders in international goals, scoring 97 in 111 games for Brazil. Or is it 93 goals in 97 games?

Or 77 in 92?* There is a dispute whether his approximately 1,280 goals for clubs (chiefly Santos FC, plus the New York Cosmos) and country combined are number one worldwide. Perhaps that distinction belongs to another Brazilian, Artur Friedenreich, who scored an unofficial 1,329 goals in the 1910s and 1920s for Americano FC, CA Paulistano, Sao Paulo FC, and Brazil. No one knows.

Even the British, who revel in trivia and trick questions regarding their soccer history, have, until recently, kept it largely to the basics: players' games played, goals scored, goalkeeper shutouts, and caps recorded.

So who can set this right? Exactly—the Americans.

The North American Soccer League (NASL) found itself with a public relations challenge when it was launched in 1968: how to make matches easier to cover by American reporters who may have never seen a soccer game. For decades, European and South American journalists have filed game accounts that read like theater reviews, long on nuance, impressions, and colorful interpretations, short on cold, hard numbers. What could be expected of unseasoned American journalists?

The NASL first borrowed from ice hockey, introducing statistics such as assists to give official credit to those who help set up goals and goals-against average to measure the performance of goalkeepers (multiply the number of goals allowed by 90, as in a regulation game; divide the total by total minutes played by the 'keeper).

The multiplication of numbers continued apace when the Major Indoor Soccer League (MISL) rose to prominence in the 1980s. Faced with the daunting task of making sense of the MISL's frenetic version of soccer, reporters soon were noting "blocks," "penalty minutes," and "power-play goals."

Today, the league that followed the NASL and MISL, Major League Soccer (MLS), keeps track of leaders in overall scoring by awarding two points for a goal and one for an assist, just like the NASL. Thus, the league's official scoring leader could be a playmaking midfielder with three goals and nineteen assists (good for twenty-five points)

*It's 77 goals in 92 games, putting him behind the all-time leader, Ali Daei of Iran (109 goals in 149 games) and Ferenc Puskás (83 goals in 84 games), but the 97 and 93 figures pop up frequently in newspapers, magazines, and books.

while the runner-up could be a pure striker with twelve goals and no assists (twenty-four points). But although most of those in a typical MLS press box have actually played the game, the league is far from finished in the numbers it crunches each week for the media.

Among the stat categories MLS has tracked and disseminated: goals, assists, shots, shots on goal, shot percentage, game-winning goals, game-winning assists, hat tricks, blocks, fouls committed, fouls suffered, offside, corner kicks, cautions, ejections, games played, minutes played, point streaks, goal streaks, assist streaks, and, for goalkeepers, wins and losses, minutes, saves, catches/punches, shutouts, save percentage, save average, save ratio, win streaks, and goals-against average.

If that's not enough, there's a laundry list of team statistics. And oh, yes, the MLS does keep standings.

MLS's Launch Gets at Least One Positive Review

As Major League Soccer, America's latest pro soccer league, attempts to gain a foothold in an unforgiving land, let us not forget that MLS enjoyed a pleasant, albeit brief, honeymoon.

After its inaugural season, the ten-team MLS was given the 1996 Sports Industrialist of the Year award by *The Sports Business Daily*, a publication read by the decision makers in the sports, entertainment, and television industries.

"Major League Soccer's launch and inaugural season must be considered a success on just about every measure," said Jeffrey Pollack, *The Sports Business Daily*'s president and publisher. "Armed with a sound business plan, a savvy investor and management group, and an entertainment-driven approach to marketing, MLS has laid a strong foundation for building America's fifth major professional sports league."

It also was the country's only pro league to make the United States' Hispanics a cornerstone of its marketing strategy, wooing both Latin fans and the advertisers who were seeking this fast-growing demographic.

Central to the MLS business model was a single-entity structure in which the league is not run on a one-club, one-owner basis, but by a small group of "investor-operators," the publication noted.

But by 2000 MLS admitted in federal court—during a player relations case it *won*—that it had lost more than $250 million. After the 2001 season it raised more red flags among skeptics when it jettisoned clubs in Tampa Bay and Miami, reducing membership from twelve clubs back to ten.

The roller-coaster ride eventually flattened out somewhat in 2003 after the Los Angeles Galaxy, which left the 93,000-seat Rose Bowl for its spanking new Home Depot Center (capacity a cozy 27,000), turned the first profit in MLS history, a modest $150,000. The ability to schedule matches on optimum dates and control parking, concessions, and other revenue streams made all the difference.

The jury is still out on MLS, and it will remain out long after it surpasses the seventeen-year rise and fall of the North American Soccer League. But as it marked its first fifteen years, the signs were positive:

- With the addition of an expansion team in Philadelphia, the league took the field in 2010 with sixteen clubs; the same year the number of clubs playing in new, intimate, soccer-specific stadiums reached nine.
- Despite MLS's history of red ink, in 2006 the Austrian company that makes and markets Red Bull energy drink purchased the New York MetroStars for $100 million from Anschutz Entertainment Group (AEG), which at one point owned more than half the league's teams; after AEG sold off the Chicago Fire two years later, MLS had a less embarrassing twelve owners for its then fourteen teams.
- The salary cap had been raised to $2.5 million per team (average salary, $120,000), and the purse strings had been further loosened by the so-called Beckham Rule, which allowed clubs to sign marquee players in excess of the cap and give the league some much-needed splash. English star David Beckham led the way, signing a five-year deal with Los Angeles worth at least $5.5 million a year and potentially worth $250 million in marketing and profit-sharing deals.
- While the league continued to be seen as having a level of play on a par with the second divisions of Europe, its home-grown players were nonetheless sought by European first-division clubs,

such as New York's Jozy Altidore, age eighteen, who was sold to Villarreal of Spain for $10 million.

- The novelty factor helped MLS average 17,416 in its inaugural season, but after years of flat attendance, the league appeared to be slowly pulling away from the 15,000-fans-per-game threshold. While 15,000 was a far cry from the crowds at German Bundesliga (37,000), English Premier League (34,000), and Italian Serie A (26,000) matches, it left MLS on par with the top divisions of Scotland, Holland, and even Brazil, as well as the National Basketball Association and National Hockey League. It also was better than the NASL's high-water mark in 1980, when that league's twenty-four clubs averaged 14,201.
- And on the all-important television front, in 2007 ESPN/ABC, Fox Soccer Channel, Univision, and HDNet agreed to pay $20 million a year for eight years for television rights to a league that initially had to pay to get its product on TV.

Still, Major League Soccer faced major-league questions as it wended its way through its second decade. Can it hold onto the Hispanic fans that helped give it its toehold, or, as they and their children assimilate, will pro soccer lose them to more traditional American sports? Can it figure out a way to make its regular season more meaningful, or, out of fear of seeing the attendance for losing clubs plummet, will it continue to hand out playoff berths to any team with a pulse at season's end? And can MLS lift its regular-season television ratings out of the 0.2 to 0.5 range, or will this be the first American sports league to be considered a success without having conquered the tube?

Greatest Women's Sports Moment: USA 1999

The USA's triumph at the 1999 Women's World Cup was seen in America as more significant to women's sports in general than to soccer in particular, and an e-mail poll conducted three years later backed that up.

Asked to name the greatest moment in women's sports history, 50 percent of respondents chose the U.S. penalty-kick victory over China in 1999. The signing into law of the landmark Title IX (18 percent) and Billie Jean King's win over Bobby Riggs at Houston's Astrodome in a nationally televised exhibition (8 percent) were next.

USA '94 Shatters World Cup Attendance Marks

It was supposed to be the World Cup of empty stadiums. Instead, the 1994 World Cup, awarded to the United States, proved to be the biggest box-office hit in the history of the planet's biggest single-sport event.

The FIFA Executive Committee voted in 1988 in Zurich to stage its fifteenth world championship in the United States, much to the dismay of rival bidders Brazil and Morocco. The decision, announced on the Fourth of July (fancy that), was a clear signal that a bull-headed—some would say foolhardy—committee majority was bound and determined to risk the prestige of its monster event in an effort to conquer the sport's Final Frontier and steer American dollars soccer's way.

Both soccer purists abroad and the conventional U.S. sports media agreed that a U.S.-hosted World Cup would end in disaster, but the all-time World Cup attendance list tells a different story:

1. United States 1994 (52 matches, 24 teams), 3,567,415 total attendance, 68,604 average
2. Brazil 1950 (22 matches, 13 teams), 1,337,000 total attendance, 60,772 average
3. Germany 2006 (64 matches, 32 teams), 3,359,436 total attendance, 52,491 average
4. Mexico 1970 (32 matches, 16 teams), 1,673,975 total attendance, 52,312 average
5. England 1966 (32 matches, 16 teams), 1,614,677 total attendance, 50,458 average
6. South Africa 2010 (64 matches, 32 teams), 3,178,880 total attendance, 49,670 average
7. Italy 1990 (52 matches, 24 teams), 2,514,443 total attendance, 48,354 average
8. West Germany 1974 (38 matches, 16 teams), 1,774,022 total attendance, 46,685 average
9. Mexico 1986 (52 matches, 24 teams), 2,441,731 total attendance, 43,956 average

10. France 1998 (64 matches, 32 teams), 2,770,000 total attendance, 43,000 average
11. Argentina 1978 (38 matches, 16 teams), 1,610,215 total attendance, 42,374 average
12. South Korea/Japan 2002 (64 matches, 32 teams), 2,705,197 total attendance, 42,269 average
13. Switzerland 1954 (26 matches, 16 teams), 943,000 total attendance, 36,270 average
14. Spain 1982 (52 matches, 24 teams), 1,856,277 total attendance, 35,698 average
15. France 1938 (18 matches, 15 teams), 483,000 total attendance, 26,833 average
16. Sweden 1958 (35 matches, 16 teams), 868,000 total attendance, 24,800 average
17. Chile 1962 (32 matches, 16 teams), 776,000 total attendance, 24,250 average
18. Uruguay 1930 (18 matches, 13 teams), 434,500 total attendance, 24,139 average
19. Italy 1934 (17 matches, 16 teams), 395,000 total attendance, 23,235 average

USA '94 drew a mix of U.S. soccer fans, trendy Americans in search of the next big event, expatriates who rushed to support their former country, and, of course, foreign tourists. Combine that with the nine venues—huge stadiums built primarily with major gridiron football games and other big events in mind—and the American organizers were ready to accommodate the spectators who would have been turned away from other World Cups, where stadiums with capacities in the forty thousands have been the rule. They also had the advantage of low expectations for the home team: when the United States was eliminated in the second round, tournament enthusiasm experienced barely a hiccup.

(Such was not the case at, for example, Brazil '50, where the locals showed through their turnouts for the final six games that they greatly preferred Brazilian soccer to soccer in general: 138,886 for Brazil-Sweden at Maracanã Stadium in Rio de Janeiro, 44,802 for Spain-Uruguay at Pacaembu Stadium in Sao Paulo, 152,772 for Brazil-Spain at Maracanã, 7,987 for Uruguay-Sweden at Pacaembu, 11,227 for Sweden-Spain at Pacaembu, and 199,854 [unofficially

220,000] for Brazil-Uruguay at Maracaná. The first-round match between Chile and Spain at Maracaná drew 19,790; that's 19,790 people and 179,710 no-shows.)

The global television audience for the '94 final was a reported 2 billion, and cumulative viewership hit 32.1 billion, both records at the time.

As for the bottom line, USA '94 made an unprecedented profit of $60 million, three times the profit FIFA projected before the tournament. And the biggest winner: U.S. Soccer Federation supremo Alan I. Rothenberg, who served as chief executive of World Cup USA 1994. For presiding over the most successful World Cup in history, the Los Angeles sports and entertainment attorney received a $3 million bonus and another $4 million as part of a deferred compensation deal.

Once bonuses were doled out to other World Cup USA executives, what was left—$40 million—went to the U.S. Soccer Foundation, a nonprofit body created to use the World Cup surplus to promote and support soccer in America.

The U.S. Soccer Foundation has since funded hundreds of grassroots soccer programs, from the construction of fields to outfitting leagues. And it was a substantial loan from the foundation that helped get Major League Soccer off the ground.

Not everyone in the United States, of course, was caught up in the stir caused by the 1994 World Cup. In fact, within months of the Brazil-Italy final at Pasadena's Rose Bowl, a game that was followed by an impromptu party in the city's Old Towne district attended by some ten thousand jubilant soccer fans, the tournament seemed to have no impact at ground zero at all.

Pasadena chose "Sports: Quest of Excellence" as the theme for its 1995 Tournament of Roses Parade. A chance for soccer to take one more bow, yes? But of the fifty-four float entries, *none* had anything to do with soccer.

Among the floats that rolled down Colorado Boulevard on New Year's Day were two featuring animals playing basketball. One float had a Martian playing Frisbee catch with a dog. The float from the City of Torrance, within a stone's throw of the headquarters to the six-hundred-fifty-thousand-player American Youth Soccer Organization, saluted chess.

The cup also left an underwhelming impression in other circles in America. Two examples: First, months after his administrative triumph, Rothenberg was left off *The Sporting News*' 1995 list of the 100 Most Powerful People in Sports. Rothenberg, who told his staff that he expected to top the list, was joined by FIFA President Joao Havelange as a TSN reject. Four sports agents were among the one hundred, along with ESPN sportscaster Chris Berman, known chiefly for the goofy nicknames he hangs on athletes.

And from Dave Barry, nationally syndicated humor columnist, writing apparently on behalf of an obstinate U.S. sports media establishment that hoped it had seen the last of soccer: "Elsewhere in sports, in June the World Cup came to the United States for the first time and produced hundreds of exciting games with scores of 1–1 and sometimes even 2–2, culminating in a gripping championship game between Italy and Brazil that remained 0–0 for the better part of July and was finally decided when the Italian team's visas expired."

English, Yankee Pastimes Converge at the Baseball Ground

Old Trafford. Highbury. Anfield. Elland Road. White Hart Lane. Villa Park. The names of many of England's more storied soccer stadiums are refreshingly straightforward, often drawn from the street or neighborhood in which they are located.

Not so at Derby County, which for more than a century played its home games at a stadium called the Baseball Ground. The soccer team was launched in 1884 by members of the Derbyshire County Cricket Club who believed that football played in the fall and winter would bring in money to finance the club's cricket team in the summer. Derby County, pronounced "dar-by" and nicknamed the Rams, played its first eleven soccer seasons at the Racecourse Ground, then in 1895 moved to its new home, the Baseball Ground, which featured a baseball diamond. The terraces at one end, in fact, were nicknamed Catcher's Corner. The Baseball Ground was the cornerstone of a twelve-acre complex that included cricket pitches and additional soccer fields.

The stadium's name was borne out of the efforts of club president Francis Ley, an industrialist who built the complex, to bring the American game of baseball to Britain. Ley, who discovered the sport during a trip to the United States, formed a baseball team and entered it in the National Baseball League of Great Britain and Ireland, a four-team competition that included no Irish teams, for 1890, the league's one and only season. The three other baseball teams were, like Derby County, associated with soccer clubs: Aston Villa, Preston North End, and Stoke City. The Derby County nine quickly clinched the championship, and although the team was led by second baseman and native son Steve Bloomer (also one of the era's most prolific goal scorers), the league's lone season ended in acrimony over the large number of experienced American players in the Derby lineup. Ley's nine toiled until 1898, and baseball in one form or another was played at the Baseball Ground into the 1920s. The footballing Rams continued to play at a stadium named for America's national pastime until 1997, then moved across town to the new Pride Park. The Rams' reserve team called the Baseball Ground home until 2003, when it was demolished and replaced by housing.

The Derby County footballers celebrated two English championships at the Baseball Ground, in 1971 and 1975, but the club's early years were marked by disappointment as the Rams tumbled in the 1898, 1899, and 1903 English F.A. Cup finals.

Ley, who later was knighted, could have been to blame for this drought. When he built his Baseball Ground, he also displaced a Gypsy community, which in parting placed a curse on the club. In 1946 the Rams conducted a ceremony in which captain Jack Nicholas crossed a Gypsy's palm with silver. The curse was broken and Derby County won its only F.A. Cup later that year, rolling past Charlton Athletic, 4–1, in the final.

Manchester United's First American Goalkeeper

Who was the first American to play goalkeeper for Manchester United?

No, it's not Tim Howard.

Howard made headlines in July 2003 when he left the New York/New Jersey MetroStars to sign with Man. U. for $3.6 million. A veteran of the FIFA under-17 and under-20 world championships and the 2000 Sydney Olympics, he made bigger headlines later that summer by unseating the United incumbent, French international Fabien Barthez. The brilliant but erratic Barthez, who helped France win the 1998 World Cup and 2000 European Championship, eventually slinked out of England and, early that winter, joined Olympique Marseille.

Even before the North Brunswick, New Jersey, product became United's starting 'keeper, he was already the feel-good story of American soccer, thanks to his struggle with Tourette syndrome, a neurological disorder characterized by involuntary physical and vocal tics. Some segments of the British press were more crass than sympathetic, but by January 2004 all were won over as Howard, in twenty-eight matches, allowed just eighteen goals and posted fourteen shutouts. That fairytale start with United came to an end that March with a poor parry of a shot that helped enable FC Porto of Portugal to eliminate the Red Devils from the UEFA Champions League. Though Howard was the only United player voted by the media to that season's Premier League top XI, he experienced what was described as a crisis of confidence and was replaced as the club's number one.

By May 2006 Howard had been loaned to Everton and would later sign with the Merseyside club. A month after the loan, he watched the World Cup from the USA bench as backup to veteran Kasey Keller. But with Keller's international retirement, Howard assumed the top spot and faced what appeared to be a bright international future, eventually winning the Golden Glove as the top 'keeper at the 2009 FIFA Confederations Cup over Gianluigi Buffon of Italy, Iker Casillas of Spain, and Júlio César of Brazil. A bright club future, too: he helped Everton finish fifth in the Premier League in 2008–9 and reach that season's English F.A. Cup final to earn a five-year contract extension.

So who was Manchester United's first American 'keeper?

It's Paul Rachubka, who became the answer to a trivia question three and a half years before Howard's arrival. Rachubka, born in San Luis Obispo, California, to an English mother and American father, joined Manchester United's youth system in 1997 and took advantage of his dual citizenship to play for England's under-16, under-18, and under-20 teams, including one appearance at the 1999 FIFA World Youth Championship.

Rachubka made his United debut at age nineteen in January 2000 against South Melbourne in the FIFA Club World Championship in Rio de Janeiro before a Maracanã Stadium crowd of sixty thousand. He played his first English Premier League game in March 2001 in a 2–0 victory over Leicester. His day in the Old Trafford sun was made possible after Barthez and backup Raimond van der Gouw went down with injuries.

Rachubka was soon replaced by thirty-six-year-old ex-Scotland goalkeeper Andy Goram, who was loaned to United by the Scottish club Motherwell for $142,100. After loan spells at Royal Antwerp of Belgium and back to England with Oldham Athletic, he was sold to Premier League rival Charlton Athletic in May 2002. Seven more loans to lower-tier English clubs would follow involving the likes of Burnley, Huddersfield, Milton Keynes, Northampton, Peterborough United, and, in January 2007, Blackpool, suggesting that Rachubka's chances of returning to Old Trafford in a United goalie's shirt were smaller than Howard's.

USA's Answer to the Tied Soccer Match

A tie is like kissing yer sister, goes the old American adage, so it's no surprise that it was in the United States—where no sporting event must end in a draw—that some of the longest games in professional soccer history have been played.

Nothing, it is hoped, will ever top an American prep match between the Farm Academy of Bristol, Ohio, and Erie High School in October 1965. The Farm Academy prevailed, 1–0, after twenty-eight fifteen-minute overtime periods. The game lasted nine hours and was completed with the headlights of spectators' autos trained on the darkened field. Neither team made a substitution.

Just a prelude.

Another marathon match was played in the United States in 1967, a year that could be considered the first in pro soccer's modern era in the States. Buoyed by the surprisingly high ratings drawn by the NBC telecast of the England–West Germany World Cup final (on two-hour delay, with yeoman sportscaster Jim Simpson at the mike) the previous year, two groups launched leagues on an unsuspecting American public.

One, the twelve-team United Soccer Association (USA) led by Jack Kent Cooke (then-owner of the NBA Los Angeles Lakers and future owner of the NFL Washington Redskins), imported entire teams intact and assigned them to major markets. The other, the National

Professional Soccer League (NPSL), imported a smorgasbord of players from throughout the world and formed ten teams.

Required by FIFA to recognize only one national first-division league, the U.S. Soccer Federation chose the USA, after conveniently demoting the unglamorous American Soccer League, then in its thirty-fifth year as the closest thing to big-league soccer in the United States, to regional league status. Undaunted, the NPSL pressed ahead as a pirate league, making its players personae non grata in the eyes of FIFA and subject to worldwide suspension.

For the record, the outlaw NPSL Oakland Clippers defeated the Baltimore Bays by a 4–2 aggregate in a home-and-home playoff to win the one and only championship of the league.

In the rival USA, determining a champion took only one afternoon, but it was nearly a long day's journey into night.

The Los Angeles Wolves (also known as Wolverhampton Wanderers of England) won the USA Western Division, while the Washington Whips (also known as Aberdeen of Scotland) took the East, setting up a showdown at the Los Angeles Memorial Coliseum for what proved to be the only USA championship. Both had 5-2-5 rec-ords. Something had to give. It just took a long time—an eternity for two sides of Brits not used to playing in ninety-degree temperatures in July.

With a crowd of 17,824 looking on, the two sides were tied at halftime, 1–1, on goals by the Wolves' Peter Knowles and the Whips' Jim Smith, but on the hour there was a four-minute goal explosion. Frank Munro and Jim Storrie scored for Washington, and L.A.'s David Burnside equalized after each Whips strike, leaving the score knotted at 3–3.

Smith was sent off in the eightieth minute and Burnside followed with a go-ahead goal for the Wolves, but Munro converted a last-minute penalty kick, tying the score at 4–4 and sending the match to overtime.

Derek Dougan put L.A. ahead, 5–4, and Washington appeared finished when the Wolves' Terry Wharton lined up a PK attempt. However, Whips goalkeeper Bobby Clarke, a Scottish international, made the save, and Washington was given new life on Munro's PK equalizer in the 119th minute.

The rest of the world would have gone from the thirty minutes of overtime directly to a PK tiebreaker, but this was the USA, which required unlimited fifteen-minute sudden-death overtimes after the first half-hour of extra time to determine its champion, so the teams played on. Mercifully, six minutes into the third overtime and with the Southern California sun beating down on the Coliseum floor, Los Angeles conjured up the winning goal. Defender Bobby Thomson slipped down the left wing and lifted a cross that eluded Clarke and caromed off the thigh of the Whips' Ally Shewin and into the Washington goal, giving Los Angeles a 6–5 victory and the title after a 126-minute struggle.

Wolves coach Ronnie Allen later suggested that the USA championship trophy be cut in half and a portion be awarded to each team. Allen needn't have been so generous. His club, as Wolverhampton, has to this day just three English league championships—the latest in 1959—and four English F.A. Cups since its founding in 1877. It is, however, the only English club to include an American championship trophy among its honors.

The following year, the USA and NPSL merged, creating the North American Soccer League (NASL). Just like its predecessors, the NASL eschewed the international model for settling knockout contests. And by 1971, the year in which the NASL introduced sudden-death overtime, two more marathon matches were played.

Both came in a single playoff series, the Rochester Lancers versus the Dallas Tornado in a best-of-three semifinal. Rochester finished first in the Northern Division; Dallas was the Southern Division runner-up.

In the opener September 1 in Rochester, the two sides were locked in a 1–1 struggle that didn't end until the *176th* minute, when league scoring champ and MVP Carlos Metidieri produced the winning goal for the Lancers. That was a leg-wobbling eighty-six minutes of sudden death.

Dallas took its home leg, 3–1, September 4 to set up a third game back in Rochester four days later. Fittingly, this one lasted 148 minutes before Bobby Moffat scored to give the Tornado a 2–1 decision.

In the NASL final, Dallas dropped the opener to the Southern champion Atlanta Chiefs, 2–1, September 12. This one took only

123 minutes because Atlanta's Nick Ash scored the deciding goal shortly after entering the game.

At that point, the Tornado had played 177 minutes of extra time over just four playoff matches. Apparently fed up, Dallas dispatched the Chiefs, 4–1 on September 15 at home and 2–0 on September 19, to wrap up its one and only NASL title.

It would take the NASL three more years before it would finally dump unlimited overtime periods for ties in playoff games and embrace the penalty-kick tiebreaker. And it was PKs that decided the 1974 championship game as the expansion Los Angeles Aztecs edged the host Miami Toros on penalties following a 3–3 draw.

The tie was abolished altogether in 1975. For the postseason and regular season, ties would be settled through fifteen minutes of sudden-death overtime, followed, if needed, by PKs.

In 1977 the league introduced the controversial shootout for both the regular season and the playoffs. Games deadlocked after ninety minutes went another fifteen minutes of sudden-death overtime, followed, if necessary, by a duel in which five players from each team, in alternating order, would take a ball from thirty-five yards away and be given five seconds apiece to score on the opposing team's goalkeeper.

It would be another twenty-three years before a U.S. first-division league would actually allow a regular-season match to end in a draw. After using the old NASL shootout to settle ties in its first four seasons, Major League Soccer finally gave in and, for its 2000 regular season, dumped the shootout in favor of two five-minute sudden-death overtimes to settle draws. And on March 18, the Miami Fusion and New England Revolution, unable to muster a goal in OT, recorded the league's first draw, 1–1, in Fort Lauderdale. No one in the Lockhart Stadium crowd of 8,782 threatened to riot. By 2004 MLS, in accordance with a FIFA directive, would dump overtime for regular-season games altogether.

The perfect solution to ending a match that must produce a winner has eluded even the great minds at our institutes of higher learning.

In December 1985 UCLA and American University met in the NCAA Division I men's final at Seattle's Kingdome and needed nearly three hours to determine the champion. Scoreless through regulation, the match continued with ten-minute sudden-death overtimes. Fortunately, the rules allowed limited free substitution, but the match lasted eight OTs before UCLA midfielder Andy Burke scored in the 167th minute to bring the contest to a merciful end.

Four years later, on a frigid day in New Jersey, the format for the final had changed and the result was no winner at all. The University of Virginia and Santa Clara University were tied, 1–1, after ninety minutes, then went scoreless over the maximum four fifteen-minute overtime periods and were declared national cochampions.

The NCAA now settles its playoff matches via penalty kicks.

While the concept of the tie remains largely un-American, for one year it was one thing the world's two superpowers could agree on as the Soviet soccer federation decided in 1973 that any match ending deadlocked would go to penalty kicks.

This experiment was dumped after one season. First-division champion was Ararat Yerevan of Armenia, which edged Ukraine giant Dinamo Kiev by three points, winning eighteen of its thirty games in regulation, losing five and coming out on top in three of four PK duels. The greatest beneficiary was Kairat Alma-Ata, which managed to finish ninth out of sixteen teams despite winning just eight in regulation. Had the Kazakhstan side not won ten of its eleven tiebreakers, it would have finished one point shy of relegation.

Oh, *That* Most Coveted Trophy

During ESPN's coverage of the 2002 World Cup, the cable channel ran a commercial promoting its upcoming telecasts of the National Hockey League's Stanley Cup playoffs. It can be assumed that those tuning in to ESPN to watch the battle for the FIFA World Cup trophy were mostly soccer fans who fully appreciated the global appeal of their sport and what was at stake. Nevertheless, ESPN's hockey promo began with the line, "The final battle for the most *coveted trophy in sports* begins . . ."

A TV-Friendly Sport—to a Fault

American fans with a long memory can remember the bad old days of soccer and its relationship with that mother's milk of any sport, television.

That would be Italia '90, when several World Cup matches were carried live on cable's TNT. They featured, however, not only that horror of horrors—commercial breaks during the action—but the expert commentary of British-born Atlanta Falcons place-kicker Mick Luckhurst, whose match analysis was supposed to not only satisfy soccer fans but lure NFL fans to this new and interesting sport.

If Americans wanted wall-to-wall coverage of all matches live without commercial interruption, there was the Spanish-language network Univision, which had ably covered the previous two World Cups. Some non-Spanish-speaking viewers delighted in the animated commentary of the announcers. Some tolerated it. Some turned off the sound.

Still older soccer fans can remember:

Mexico '86. NBC televised the final as well as a handful of earlier weekend matches, complete with in-game commercials. ESPN also aired games.

Spain '82. ABC showed the final, live for the first time in the United States, again with in-game commercials. PBS and ESPN also televised matches, in whole or in part.

Argentina '78. No over-the-air or cable TV coverage at all. Fans in the United States lucky enough to be living in major cities shelled out several bucks to watch the final on closed-circuit TV at a theater or arena.

West Germany '74. Week-old highlights via the BBC on CBS *Sports Spectacular.*

Mexico '70. Week-old highlights on ABC's *Wide World of Sports.*

And those with a really long memory still shudder over the very bad old days, when CBS offered the NPSL *Sunday Game of the Week* in 1967, the National Professional Soccer League's only season.

Landing a network TV contract was quite a coup for the NPSL, which the following year would merge with the year-old United Soccer Association to form the North American Soccer League. But ratings were abysmal as Americans proved they were not ready for pro soccer. CBS further exacerbated the situation with its constant advertising breaks during match telecasts, thus upsetting the flow of what is a free-flowing sport.

Under the NPSL's agreement with CBS, referees were fitted with a small radio receiver that signaled when it was time for a commercial;

officials were instructed to delay the restart of play as long as possible so viewers would miss a minimum of game action.

The ruse reached comical proportions—and briefly raised the suspicions of the Federal Communications Commission—a month into the season during a match between the Pittsburgh Phantoms and Toronto Falcons at Toronto's Varsity Stadium. English referee Peter Rhodes reportedly admitted that of the twenty-one fouls he whistled that day, eleven were made up, called so that CBS could work in its commercials. At one point, Rhodes reportedly held down fallen Pittsburgh player-coach Co Prins so a commercial could finish, despite Prins's efforts to get back to his feet.

A Ladies Team U.S. Men Couldn't Beat

Before Mia, Michelle, Carla, Kristine, and the two-time world champion U.S. National Women's Team, there was women's soccer's first glamour team, a ladies side in England organized in 1917 by a munitions factory. How good was this team? At first glance, good enough to beat some of the United States' best male professionals.

Dick, Kerr, and Company of Preston, also known as Dick, Kerr Ltd. Electric Corp., formed its team during World War I as male employees made their way to the front lines and were replaced by women. And quite a team it was. Over the forty-eight years of its existence, the Dick Kerr Ladies compiled a 758-24-46 record while pouring in some thirty-five hundred goals. At its peak in 1920, the team played a match against St. Helen's Ladies on Boxing Day at Everton's Goodison Park in Liverpool that drew fifty-three thousand; at least ten thousand were turned away. The following year, Dick, Kerr's team declined 121 invitations to play.

This wonder team began innocently enough when the Dick, Kerr's female employees began to engage in kickabouts during lunch breaks and tea time and eventually challenged the company's struggling male team to a match. From that long-forgotten showdown came the Dick Kerr Ladies, whose aim it was to raise money for war charities.

The new team debuted on Christmas Day, 1917, and thumped the Arundel Courthard Foundry, 4–0, before ten thousand at Preston North End's Deepdale ground, collecting six hundred pounds for the cause. Clad in black-and-white-striped jerseys, Dick Kerr never looked back as it rolled through the opposition, thanks in part to players like center forward Lily Parr, a fourteen-year-old who stood six feet tall and led the team in goals with forty-three in her first season.

In 1920 Dick Kerr played in Paris, where the players were greeted by a mob of enthusiastic French fans and British soldiers. Two years later the team embarked on a fall tour of Canada, but that same month the Dominion of Canada Football Association passed a resolution condemning women's soccer, so Dick Kerr left Quebec City for the United States, where it expected to play American ladies teams. There were none to be found, however, so it took on men's teams from the country's first serious attempt at professional soccer, the American Soccer League, which kicked off in 1921 just weeks before the National Football League made its debut, and prominent regional leagues. Despite facing the top American players of their day along with some highly talented imports, the Dick Kerr Ladies held their own. The results:

September 24 Paterson FC 6, DK 3, at Paterson, New Jersey
September 30 J&P Coates 4, DK 4, at Pawtucket, Rhode Island
October 1 Centro-Hispano 7, DK 5, at New York City
October 8 Washington Stars 4, DK 4, in Washington DC
October 11 New Bedford Whalers 4, DK 5, in New Bedford, Massachusetts
October 14 New York FC 4, DK 8, in New York City
October 15 Fall River Marksmen 2, DK 2, in Fall River, Massachusetts
October 22 Baltimore SC 3, DK4, in Baltimore

While the British women's 3-2-3 record was impressive (and should have been a massive blow to the Yankee ego), press reports of the games suggest that some of their opponents weren't going all out to defend their macho. According to one, from the *Fall River Globe*: "The score in no way explains how well these English lassies can play the national game of their homeland. Nor could the fans at the game tell exactly how expert are the women tourists for the opposition was from a team of the best men kickers in the country."

More telling, again from the *Globe*: "The bobbed headed and pretty Miss Redford, center forward, scored the first goal at an early stage of the game. Mr. Duncan, the Fall River goalie, deliberately let it go by him, and when Miss Redford turned up for the line up for another kick off she seemed to show that she was aware of Duncan's kindness."

Later: "During the second half Jock Lindsay twice gave Miss Redford a chance to score. The young lady passed it up however. She indicated that what she wanted to get must be earned and not received gratis."

Regardless of whether the scores against male pros and semipros were legitimate, the tour was something of a high-water mark for the Dick Kerr Ladies.

The Canadian reception was no shock to the team, whose domestic success had prompted the English Football Association to ban women's soccer the previous year on the grounds that the game was not suitable for women and ought not be encouraged. That meant no women's matches at English League grounds, no F.A.-sanctioned officials at women's matches.

Women's soccer continued under the auspices of the newly formed English Ladies F.A.—which took steps to ensure that no other team like the ambitious Dick Kerr be formed by banning any player from joining a team based more than twenty miles from her home. Soon, the novelty of women playing soccer in shorts, not bloomers, wore off, and the ladies' game in England was reduced to an afterthought in a world in which female soccer was largely unknown.

Nevertheless, Dick Kerr lasted until 1965. The English F.A.'s ban against women's matches at league grounds was dropped at long last in 1978, but the first UEFA championship for women wouldn't come until 1984. It would be another seven years before FIFA would organize a world championship for women. That competition was won by the United States, the country largely hostile to soccer in general but apparently, beginning with the visiting Dick Kerr Ladies, quite receptive to women's soccer.

Not a Domed-Good Idea

Many of Europe's great soccer stadiums have prominent roofing atop the grandstand to keep the fans dry during inclement weather (the players be damned). So why no great domed stadiums for soccer prior to the age of the retractable roof? The 1994 World Cup provided the definitive answer.

The Silverdome in Pontiac, Michigan, then home of the NFL's Detroit Lions and former home of the NASL's Detroit Express (1978–80), was one of the nine stadiums chosen for the first world championship hosted by the United States, making it the first World Cup stadium with a permanent covering. Pontiac was selected to placate a major sponsor, the Motown-based General Motors, but the stadium had an artificial turf playing surface, a FIFA no-no for World Cup finals.

The United States, of course, was the home of Astroturf and other variations of fake grass, which cause soccer balls to bounce unusually high and soccer players to suffer painful friction burns while slide tackling. Nevertheless, the United States blithely played World Cup qualifiers on synthetic surfaces in 1976 (Seattle's Kingdome, versus Canada) and 1984 (Busch Memorial Stadium in St. Louis, versus Netherlands Antilles) and won both.

Organizers quickly came up with a solution for the Silverdome and the other designated World Cup site with a rug, Giants Stadium in East Rutherford, New Jersey: large trays of natural grass measuring seven and a half feet in diameter and six inches deep would be placed over the artificial turf like a jigsaw puzzle for the World Cup matches, then removed when the circus left town.

It worked like a charm at Giants Stadium, where seven matches were played, including a memorable Bulgarian upset of Germany in the quarterfinals. But at the Silverdome, grass on a platter—1,850 of them, in fact—was less than ideal.

All had gone well twelve months earlier when the concept was tested during a U.S. Cup '93 match between England and Germany and, two days later, a U.S.-Canada women's friendly. (England captain David Platt called the Silverdome field "perfectly magnificent.") But three days shy of the summer of 1994, the World Cup's Group A opener was another matter as the United States and Switzerland staggered to a 1–1 draw. A daytime high temperature of 100 degrees, the sellout crowd of 73,425, the moisture in the imported turf, and the stagnant air combined to turn the Silverdome into the world's largest humidor. As the steamy conditions worsened, the players, despite wearing extended studs on their shoes, repeatedly slipped on a surface that Brits would kindly describe as "greasy." Adding to the surreal atmosphere was the ear-splitting crowd noise that, thanks to the stadium's plastic lid, had nowhere to go.

Things were no better at the Silverdome when it hosted Switzerland's 4–1 upset of Romania in Group A and two Group B matches, Sweden over Russia, 3–1, and Brazil-Sweden, 1–1. Those were the last matches played in Pontiac, and the remainder of the tournament was conducted exclusively in sunshine.

It took major advances in the making of artificial turf for FIFA to bow, somewhat, to synthetic grass as it allowed host Finland to hold ten matches of its 2003 FIFA World Under-17 Championship, including the final, at the home of HJK Helsinki, Töölö Stadium. Other future age-specific FIFA championships might be allowed to be played on what has become a blend of sand, ground rubber, and synthetic fibers, but, for now, the World Cup finals remain off limits.

The Bicycle-Kick Miss That Helped Create MLS

What would have been the most spectacular single moment in U.S. soccer history came and went at the 1994 World Cup when Marcelo Balboa unleashed a bicycle-kick shot late in the USA's upset of Colombia at the Rose Bowl.

The United States was already minutes away from a 2–1 victory at the time of Balboa's startling shot, which flashed just above the upper left corner of the net. Had it gone in, there's no doubt that it would have become the quintessential image of soccer in this country, a clip that would appear again and again on TV, perhaps the topper to the spectacular crash of the ski jumper in the opening of ABC's venerable *Wide World of Sports*.

There's an enormous silver lining to Balboa's unsuccessful bicycle kick, however. One of those who saw it was Denver billionaire Philip Anschutz, who was inspired by the near-miss to invest in Major League Soccer and insist that Balboa—known to Anschutz as the "player who did that funny little overhead kick"—play for his hometown Colorado Rapids. (Balboa says he was later told that Anschutz exclaimed, "*That's* the guy I want on *my* team!") Anschutz and the Kraft family became the last of the league's charter investors in June 1995, making MLS's April 1996 launch possible.

Once hooked, Anschutz increased his holdings in the fledgling league. By the time Balboa retired as a professional in 2003, Anschutz was investor-operator of not only the Rapids but also the Chicago

Fire, the New York/New Jersey MetroStars, the Los Angeles Galaxy, DC United, and the San Jose Earthquakes. That's six of ten teams. Hard to imagine what Anschutz would have done had Balboa actually scored.

As for future National Soccer Hall of Famer Balboa, in 2000 he scored on—yes—a bicycle kick for Colorado, earning MLS Goal of the Year honors.

In Two Tries, L.A. Gets Olympic Soccer Right

It's the curious hole in the otherwise successful history of Olympic soccer: "1932, tournament not held."

No soccer was played at the 1932 Summer Games in Los Angeles for a number of reasons, foremost among them the ongoing battle between FIFA and the British soccer associations over what constituted an amateur. At issue, in particular, was the concept of broken-time payments, whether a player should be compensated by his employer while away at the Olympics.

There were few tears shed by FIFA, which two years earlier had introduced its true world championship, the World Cup, open to all players, from top-priced professional to the most humble amateur, and the tournament had already begun its gradual eclipse of Olympic soccer. (It also served as a catalyst in the spread of professionalism throughout soccer.) As for the indifferent Olympic organizers of Los Angeles, they were spared the impossible task of finding suitable soccer venues for sixteen matches that they suspected would be poorly attended.

Ironically, it was back in Los Angeles fifty-two years later that soccer got its due in a U.S.-hosted Olympiad. Once again venues were problematic (several first-round matches had to be played at Harvard Stadium in Cambridge, Massachusetts; Navy-Marine Corps Memorial Stadium in Annapolis, Maryland; and Stanford Stadium in Palo Alto, California) and attendance was a concern. Moreover, the nature of the '84 tournament had been turned on its ear at the last minute: after being dominated for years by the state-supported "amateurs" of the communist bloc, the tournament was opened to professionals, with the exception of European and South American players who had appeared in a World Cup qualifier.

Despite the question marks, soccer proved to be the hottest ticket of them all in 1984. In fact, the second Los Angeles Games, the first Olympics to turn a healthy profit, might not have finished in the black had it not been for soccer. The gold medal match sold out more than a half-year in advance, and the thirty-two matches attracted 1.4 million spectators, outdrawing the twenty-two other sports, including the Olympics' traditional marquee event, track and field (1.1 million). The final turnstile count for soccer could have been much higher had twenty-one of the matches not been played hundreds (Palo Alto) and thousands (Cambridge, Annapolis) of miles away from the heart of the Olympic hoopla.

A capacity crowd of 101,799 at the Rose Bowl, still the largest in U.S. soccer history, saw France beat Brazil, 2–0, for the gold medal. More shocking was the turnout of 100,374 the night before for the *bronze* medal game between Yugoslavia and Italy, a 2–1 Yugoslav win.

(Those throngs and the other large and festive crowds weren't enough for ABC, which devoted all of twenty minutes of live airtime to the entire tournament, which ran nearly fifty hours.)

The affordable ticket prices ($7 to $12 for most games) played a part in the huge turnouts. So did the presence of the home team: the United States played Costa Rica at Stanford Stadium before 78,265 (a 3–0 win), Italy at the Rose Bowl in front of 63,624 (a 1–0 loss), and Egypt back at Stanford with 54,973 looking on (a 1–1 draw). And the allure of the Olympics, the desire of average Americans to see *something* Olympic, was undeniable. A year later, just 11,500 at a junior college stadium in the Los Angeles area saw the United States and Costa Rica meet in a critical World Cup qualifier, and most of those were rooting for the visiting team.

The next U.S.-hosted Olympics, Atlanta '96, proved that Los Angeles '84 was no fluke. Atlanta featured the first-ever women's soccer tournament, and while the combined men's and women's turnstile count—1,364,250—fell short of L.A.'s, that figure was once again more than any other Olympic sport, including male/female events like track and field, swimming and diving, gymnastics, and basketball.

A crowd of 86,117 watched Nigeria rally to edge Brazil, 3–2, in the men's gold medal game at Sanford Stadium in Athens, Georgia, two days after 76,481 turned out to see the United States beat China, 2–1, also in Athens, for the women's gold.

Without the 1984 Los Angeles Olympics there would not have been a 1994 World Cup in the United States. FIFA's decision in 1988 to award the fifteenth World Cup to the United States left soccer purists worldwide shaking their heads. But the huge crowds at the Rose Bowl and Stanford Stadium four years earlier allayed FIFA's fears that U.S. fans wouldn't show up for big-time soccer.

And the Rose Bowl's fate as site of the World Cup final might have been sealed by Dr. Kevin O'Flanagan of Ireland, a member of the International Olympic Committee, who penned the "Final Observations" section of FIFA's *Technical Report on the Football Tournament of the XXIII Olympic Games*. The good doctor called the soccer tournament perhaps the biggest success of the L.A. Games. But there was more:

> The Rose Bowl stadium itself, set in an amphitheatre with the rolling hills of Pasadena banked up behind it, was a really magnificent location, and sitting in the stand in the cool of the evening, in the midst of a 103,000 record crowd for a soccer match in the U.S.A. and the fervour and enthusiasm of this crowd as they rose in groups at half-time to send crescendoes of cheers throughout the valley [the Wave] is something all of us will remember, to say nothing of the absence of crowd violence on any occasion, and this was indeed wholly admirable, and was perhaps an example for the rest of the world.
>
> One evening well into the competition, I saw [FIFA President João] Havelange standing alone aloof with a satisfied smile on his face—it seemed to me that he was glowing with inward pride at the success he saw all around him, and I for one as an IOC member would certainly like to share with him in this moment of triumph for the FIFA organisation.

Soccer returned to the Rose Bowl in 1986 for the FIFA World All-Star Game for UNICEF, which drew sixty thousand. After that match, FIFA officials suggested that the United States bid for the 1994 World Cup. Two years later, the United States was awarded the tournament. Chief executive of World Cup USA '94, Inc., was the man who served as soccer commissioner for the Los Angeles Olympic Organizing Committee, Alan I. Rothenberg.

The USA's Remarkable World Cup Debut

It remains hard to imagine, but the U.S. National Team could have won the very first World Cup. Well, it might have, had it survived the semifinal.

The Americans, a passable 5-4-2 all-time in international play at that point, were playing their first matches after their latest squad was quickly formed through three domestic tryouts. By virtue of the nine-year-old American Soccer League, they also were one of the few World Cup participants with a professional, or at least semipro, league, and that was enough for tournament organizers to make the United States a seeded team, a distinction it has yet to earn again.

Placed in the three-team Group IV, the Americans rolled to easy 3–0 defeats of Belgium and Paraguay at Montevideo's Central Park before crowds of ten thousand and eight hundred, respectively. As group winner, they advanced to a semifinal meeting with Group I winner Argentina on July 26 across town at the massive Centenary Stadium, which had been completed only days earlier.

Featuring six starters born in Scotland or England, the United States exhibited speed, individual skill, an effective long-passing game, and an unyielding defense. It was rumored that the Americans as a whole had attained considerable professional experience in Britain, but only left back George Moorhouse had ever played in his native land (all of two games in the English third division with Tranmere, one in 1921 and one in 1923). The Americans also were big (or well-fed, or both), earning the nickname "The Shotputters" from the French team. For these reasons, the Group III–winning Uruguayans considered themselves fortunate to be facing Yugoslavia, first place in Group II, the following day in their semifinal, probably the only time the United States ever struck genuine fear in the heart of another World Cup team.

What followed for the United States, however, was a strict lesson in the ways of international soccer, as applied by Argentina, a team intent on not letting any side stand in the way of its mission, that of bringing the first world championship to the southern side of the River Plate. The Argentines had already provided a preview in their final Group I match, a 3–1 win over Chile, punctuated by a free-for-all just before halftime that had to be quelled by police. And one member of the U.S. team, halfback James Gallagher, had vivid memories of the USA's previous meeting with Argentina, an 11–2 humiliation at the 1928 Amsterdam Olympics.

A near-capacity crowd of 80,000 was on hand to see the U.S.-Argentina game, including about 250 Americans and 20,000 Argentines. Uruguayans made up the overwhelming majority, and they were rooting against their neighbors out of habit. But Argentina carried out what was later called by U.S. manager Wilfred R. Cummings "an evidently premeditated and concentrated attack . . . on our boys," and the sympathy of the crowd couldn't save them.

The South Americans probably won the foul-littered game when goalkeeper Jimmy Douglas, a veteran of the 1924 Paris Olympics, was left by the Argentines with a severely twisted knee early on, and he hobbled through the remainder of the match. (This was forty years before substitutes would be allowed in a World Cup.) The USA's problems were compounded in the nineteenth minute when center halfback Raphael Tracey sustained a serious leg injury, forcing him to move over to right wing and pushing twenty-year-old James Brown inside. But there was more. Before the intermission, halfback Andrew Auld was kicked in the face and was left with a long gash in his lip (he played the second half with his mouth stuffed with gauze). The woozy United States was in big trouble.

In addition to being reduced to eight healthy men, the Americans were trailing. Argentina had taken a 1–0 edge in the twenty-third minute on a goal by midfielder Luís Monti, who seized defender Moorhouse's poor clearance of a free kick from the right and drilled a bad-hop shot by Douglas. The U.S. team stepped up its attack late in the half, but two of its best chances fell to the limping Tracey, who missed. It wasn't discovered until after the game that his leg was broken.

Predictably, the floodgates opened in the second half. Savvy and sophisticated, Argentina scored an additional five times, including three goals in a seven-minute span. Center forward Guillermo Stàbile, on his way to leading the tournament with eight goals, and right winger Carlos Peucelle each scored two, and inside right Alejandro Scopeli one. Brown, whose son played for the United States twenty-seven years later, scored the only U.S. goal in the eighty-eighth minute, on a counterattack following a one-two with center forward Bertram Patenaude.

Provider of the lone U.S. highlight, Brown was also part of one of the game's many embarrassing moments. After Argentina's third goal, he was tackled to the ground by José Della Torre and punched the Argentine right back, touching off a brief melee. Typically, Belgian referee Jean Langenus, dressed in his coat and tie, plus fours, and cap, did not sanction either player.

Although Langenus later was assigned to officiate the final between Uruguay and Argentina, his work that day was bitterly criticized by the Americans, and their displeasure led to a bit of low comedy that has since become a part of World Cup lore. According to everyone's favorite version, during the second half U.S. trainer Jock Coll rushed onto the field to confront Langenus over a call and threw his medical bag to the ground in disgust, causing a bottle of chloroform to break. Overcome by the fumes, Coll passed out and had to be carried off the field.

Some accounts have Coll entering the field to attend to yet another injured American player; the bottle tumbled out of his bag and broke open.

Cummings's report provides a completely different story, one in which Coll was trying to treat Auld's slashed lip when an Argentine player knocked smelling salts from Coll's hand and into Auld's eyes, temporarily blinding the U.S. left halfback.

For the only time in World Cup history, there was no third-place match, so the United States concluded its trip with a friendly with Brazil in Rio de Janeiro and lost, 4–3. Two of the U.S. goals were by Patenaude, whose three goals in Uruguay tied him with five other players for fourth place on the World Cup scoring list.

Patenaude, of French-Canadian heritage, would have finished tied for third but for some questionable scorekeeping. The twenty-one-year-old scored two goals in the Paraguay match and a third was credited as an own goal by Paraguay's inside right, Aurelio Gonzales. The ruling cost the Fall River (Massachusetts) FC striker the distinction of becoming the first player to record a World Cup hat trick.

Seventy-six years on, however, the Americans, denied a consolation match, got some consolation. In November 2006 FIFA historians concluded that Patenaude should have been given credit for Gonzales's own goal, making him the World Cup's first hat trick man. That honor had previously gone to Argentine hero Stàbile, who two days after the U.S.-Paraguay game pounded home three goals in a 6–3 romp over Mexico. The correction also lifted Patenaude to a tie with Chile's Guillermo Subiabre for third place at four goals apiece. Pedro Cea of Uruguay had five and Stàbile eight.

At least the United States, thanks to Bart McGhee's goal twenty-three minutes into the tournament, left Montevideo having produced the first goal in World Cup history, yes?

The answer, eventually, is *non*.

On opening day, July 13, thirty-one-year-old left winger McGhee of the New York Nationals scored against the Belgians to send his side on its way to its first-ever World Cup victory. The native Scotsman, from a sharp angle, tucked in the rebound of a vicious shot off the crossbar by star midfielder Billy Gonsalves.

Across town in the day's only other game, however, French inside left Lucien Laurent scored against Mexico in the nineteenth minute of the official World Cup curtain-raiser at the Pocitos stadium. The times of the two games' actual kickoffs were not recorded, so for years McGhee was variously credited with having scored World Cup goal number one. But FIFA ultimately ruled that, at the very least, France-Mexico and U.S.-Belgium kicked off simultaneously, giving Laurent the honor by about 240 seconds.

Who's to say for sure? Some reports have McGhee scoring his first goal in the fortieth minute and then striking again just before halftime. Others credit the second U.S. goal to captain Thomas Florie. The United States' third goal has been variously credited to Florie and Patenaude. (FIFA has it recorded as McGhee forty-first, McGhee forty-fifth, and Patenaude eighty-eighth.)

Uruguay did avenge the United States' painful loss to Argentina, rallying for a historic 4–2 victory over its neighbor in the final before ninety-three thousand at Centenary Stadium.

Argentina, on early goals by Peucelle and Stàbile, led at halftime, 2–1. But inside left Cea got Uruguay level in the fifty-seventh minute, and left wing–half Santos "El Canario" Iriarte put Uruguay ahead for good with a twenty-five-yard bullet in the sixty-ninth. After Stàbile's would-be equalizer rang the crossbar, Uruguay inside right Hector Castro sealed the win in the final minute with a headed goal off a cross by Pablo Dorado.

The triumph, meanwhile, represented a third jewel in Uruguay's crown. Led by Cea and two other 1930 heroes, right halfback José Leandro Andrade and inside right Hector Scarone, Uruguay had dazzled Europe with its skill at two straight Olympics, defeating Switzerland at the 1924 Paris gold medal match, 3–0, and Argentina at the 1928 Amsterdam final, 2–1 (a replay after a 1–1 tie).

With the Olympics serving as the unofficial world championship up to that point, the Uruguayans could claim to have conquered the world three times in six years, and they would win a second World Cup in 1950.

As for the United States, before long the lack of a strong national league and grassroots participation transformed it from World Cup semifinalist to second-rate power in its own region.

One Man's Solution to Antisoccer Sentiment

Exasperated American soccer fans have for years tried reason and logic to defend their sport against fellow countrymen who consider soccer dull.

Perhaps the direct approach is best. In October 1999, after the Dallas Burn staged a furious second-half rally to erase a 3–1 deficit and beat the Los Angeles Galaxy, 4–3, at the Cotton Bowl in a thrilling Major League Soccer match, Burn coach David Dir told reporters: "Anyone who tells me soccer is boring, I'm going to punch them in the face."

Coach Slips Through a Loophole

Three plus one added up to a bit of embarrassment for Major League Soccer in July 2003 as an alert coach followed the league's substitution rule to the letter to solve a manpower problem.

A match between the New York/New Jersey MetroStars and DC United at RFK Stadium was in the fourth minute of overtime when midfielder Mark Lisi went down with an injury.

At the time, MLS allowed each team to substitute three field players and the goalkeeper. Metros coach Bob Bradley had already used his three field-player substitutions, so he removed Lisi, sent in rookie Eddie Gaven, a sixteen-year-old midfielder, as goalkeeper, and moved goalkeeper Tim Howard to a spot on the field.

Less than a minute later New York kicked the ball out of play, Gaven ran out of his penalty area, and on his way he tossed his goalie gloves to Howard, who positioned himself back between the posts. About five minutes after that, Gaven scored his first career goal to give the Metros a 3–2 victory.

Shortly before its 2004 season MLS reduced its substitution rule to three players per side and did away with overtime—because of a rule change ordered worldwide by FIFA, not because of Bradley's sleight of hand.

The MetroStars never won a title under Bradley, but he did get himself hired as U.S. National Team coach in 2006.

Real Football Versus *Real* Football: A War of Words and Deeds

Soccer for years has been a favorite target of gridiron football types, from prep coaches lamenting the defection of their school's better athletes for the soccer field to the likes of Representative Jack Kemp (the Republican from New York), a former NFL, CFL, and AFL quarterback.

In 1987 Kemp, prior to what should have been a routine House vote endorsing the United States' bid to host the 1994 World Cup, told his fellow congressmen, in part, "I think it is important for all those youngsters out there, who someday hope to play *real* football, where you throw it and kick it and run with it and put it in your hands, a distinction should be made that football is democratic, capitalism, whereas soccer is . . . European socialist."

Throw it, run with it, put it in your hands . . . yes, Kemp was referring to a game called "football."

Another potshot came from John Gagliardi, longtime coach of NCAA Division III power St. John's University of Minnesota, who would admonish his players with, "If you can't tackle, go play soccer."

Tackling, of course, is as important in soccer as it is in gridiron football, and in soccer you can't use your hands while doing so. Gagliardi's line is on par with a basketball coach telling his cagers, "If you can't dribble, go play soccer."

Gridiron football coaches are known for their intensity, their demand for "110 percent" effort of their players. The most-often-quoted line is attributed to legendary Green Bay Packers coach Vince Lombardi: "Winning isn't everything; it's the *only* thing." Lombardi is also said to have come up with the less memorable, "Winning isn't everything, but wanting to is." (Lombardi's famous quote was actually coined by Red Sanders, a successful grid coach at Vanderbilt University and later UCLA; in 1955 he told the year-old *Sports Illustrated* magazine, "Sure, winning isn't everything. It's the only thing.")

Many soccer coaches, however, are no less intense, like Lombardi's counterpart, the equally legendary Bill Shankly, and the Liverpool FC coach came up with an equally famous line in the 1960s about football and the will to win.

A Scottish international who played in England for Carlisle United and Preston North End in the 1930s, Shankly became a manager after World War II. He led unfashionable clubs like Carlisle, Grimsby, Workington, and Huddersfield, but his burning desire to win was never in doubt, and he achieved greatness with Liverpool, winning three English League titles, a UEFA Cup, and an F.A. Cup between 1959 and his retirement in 1974.

The exact quote by Shankly, referring to an important upcoming match: "Some people believe football is a matter of life and death. I'm very disappointed with that attitude. I can assure you that it is much, much more important than that."

Shankly also once said, "If you are first you are first. If you are second you are nothing." And, in a dig at the Merseyside's other club, hated rival Everton FC, he once said, "There are only two teams in Liverpool: Liverpool and Liverpool reserves."

Many things separate the two sports, but what happens at the end of a great player's career in each is perhaps most telling. Every summer, immortals of American football are inducted into the Pro Football Hall of Fame in Canton, Ohio; topping the festivities is the Hall of Fame Game, the first exhibition of the preseason, pitting two NFL teams. Likewise, the National Soccer Hall of Fame in Oneonta, New York, holds its annual induction ceremony, and in recent years an exhibition match follows. But while it is impossible to imagine the Canton inductees—some hobbled by the years of punishment they endured on the gridiron, some just generally out of shape—ending the day by strapping on the gear and playing one last time, Oneonta honorees do play and live to tell about it.

In August 2007, for example, U.S. National Team greats Mia Hamm and Julie Foudy accepted the plaudits of a crowd of forty-eight hundred as they were inducted, then laced up their cleats and played in a game between Hamm's former club, the Washington Freedom, and the SoccerPlus Connecticut Reds. Hamm was five months removed from having delivered twin daughters. Also taking part was ex-U.S. captain Carla Overbeck, who had been enshrined in the Hall the previous year.

As for the men, inductee Eric Wynalda played for his former club, the Chicago Fire, in the 2004 Hall match, coming on in the seventy-third minute and nearly scoring in the eighty-fourth as Chicago bowed to the New York MetroStars, 2–0. The following year's game featured a pair of inductees in action: Marcelo Balboa, late of the Colorado Rapids, and John Harkes, formerly of DC United.

Then there was the day in October 1999 when a bunch of women showed that they were just as good at one aspect of gridiron football as anyone in the NFL.

Nearly three months after winning the Women's World Cup, the U.S. National Women's Team stopped in Kansas City for a friendly against Finland at Arrowhead Stadium. According to longtime team spokesman Aaron Heifetz:

> The Chiefs were playing a preseason game the day before our game . . . so we devised a promotion whereby some of our players would kick some field goals at halftime of the game.
>
> We went out the day before [I believe] to get some practice after the Chiefs practice at their training facility. Mia [Hamm] took off her cleats . . . [and] worked her way back and hit several 40 yarders off a tee, then moved it up to 30 [yards] and hit one or two with her left foot. It was impressive. The Chiefs kickers were there to instruct, and so was a bunch of media, so we got some great shots [that appeared] in some NFL shows that week.
>
> At the game, Shannon MacMillan, Siri Mullinix, and Mia all took three kicks, one from 20, one from 30, and one from 40.

They all made their 20s and 30s, and Mac and Siri made their 40s. Mia actually overkicked her 40, and it was the only miss of the six kicks, but the place was packed and the fans loved it. The Chiefs, whose owner is innovator Lamar Hunt, gave the players authentic Chiefs jerseys with their names and numbers on the back, and after the kicks, Lamar's son came on the field with real [but of course not real] NFL contracts for the players to sign.

O.J. Simpson, Diana Ross, Oprah Winfrey, and the 1994 World Cup

Charles Cale, a prominent Los Angeles attorney, was walking his dog in the tony Los Angeles neighborhood of Brentwood the night of June 12, 1994, when he turned onto Rockingham Avenue, unwittingly stepping into what would be called the Trial of the Century.

That was the night of the murders of Nicole Brown Simpson and Ron Goldman. Nine months later Cale was a prosecution witness, telling what he saw between 9:30 and 9:45 p.m. outside the home of the accused, retired gridiron football great O.J. Simpson.

In what seemed significant at the time, what Cale, who lived a quarter-mile away, did *not* see during that quarter hour was Simpson's white Bronco. That was consistent with the testimony of Simpson houseguest Kato Kaelin and limousine driver Allan Park. Cale also testified that he spotted the vehicle the next morning at 7:00 parked on Rockingham at an odd angle.

Cale's testimony couldn't have been comforting for the defense, whose better days lay ahead. When Simpson was found not guilty in October 1995, what Cale saw and did not see were all but forgotten by a public left riveted by the courtroom drama. But that Cale was even in position to be walking his dog the night of the murders could be tied to the 1994 World Cup, which kicked off five days after the crime.

A partner in the firm Morgan, Lewis & Bockius, Cale in 1984 was group vice president for sports for the Los Angeles Olympic Organizing Committee (LAOOC). He was considered a possible candidate for the presidency of the U.S. Soccer Federation in 1990 until another attorney, Alan Rothenberg, the LAOOC's soccer commissioner, emerged and went on to win election as USSF chief.

In October 1990 Cale was appointed chief executive officer of the World Cup USA 1994 Organizing Committee, becoming its ranking full-time executive. Cale worked out of the WCUSA's Los Angeles office, while main headquarters at the time were in Washington DC. But in late 1991 he was ousted in a shake-up that left Rothenberg as WCUSA chairman and chief executive officer.

Had Cale remained at the World Cup USA helm, he would not have been walking his dog around his neighborhood the night of the murders. He would likely have been burning the midnight oil at WCUSA offices minutes away in Century City, or in Chicago, preparing for the World Cup opener at Soldier Field between Germany and Bolivia later that week. (It was Rothenberg who was introduced to the Soldier Field crowd as WCUSA '94 supremo.)

And while Cale had a role in the Simpson murder trial, Simpson had an impact on the first game of the World Cup. On June 17 Americans tuning in to the evening news saw the bizarre Simpson low-speed chase through Southern California that ended on Rockingham, preempting nightly local and network newscasts, which surely would have included shots of the World Cup's opening ceremonies, conducted on a sweltering afternoon in Chicago.

Probably to the relief of the organizers.

Though modest by Super Bowl standards, the pregame entertainment at Soldier Field was garish nonetheless, featuring fireworks, dozens of dancers, and thousands of helium-filled balloons. And the standing-room-only crowd of 63,117, including President Clinton, was treated to two major pratfalls. One was executed by mistress of ceremonies Oprah Winfrey, who rose to talk-show fame in Chicago. Winfrey managed to slip and fall on the temporary stage, twisting her right knee. The other was provided by Diana Ross. The former lead singer of the Supremes entered the field to great fanfare and was supposed to fire a penalty kick into a goal, the force of which would cause the rigged goal to collapse. Unfortunately, Ross, surrounded by photographers, toe-poked her attempt several yards wide of the left post. Everything else went to plan during Ross's shot as the goalkeeper dived the wrong way and the goal, on cue, split in half.

The tournament's opening act could do nothing to salvage the afternoon. An uninspired Germany won a yawner, 1–0, over Bolivia, which sent on star midfielder Marco Etcheverry in the seventy-ninth minute, only to see him sent off in the eighty-second for using his newly healed knee to direct a wild kick at Germany's Lothar Matthäus.

Pelé, in Praise of American Women

The U.S. National Team's progress from international laughingstock to regular World Cup participant and a power in (the relatively weak) CONCACAF is all the more remarkable in light of the fact that the Americans did it without a superstar. This was underscored in March 2004 when Pelé was asked by FIFA to commemorate its centennial year by selecting his top one hundred living players.

Predictably, the list created a minor storm of controversy. First, an unofficial version of Pelé's one hundred was leaked, and he was all but pilloried by his countrymen because his list had more Italians and Frenchmen (fourteen each) than Brazilians (twelve). Among those passed over were Roberto Rivelino and Nilton Santos.

So FIFA asked Pelé to try again, giving him twenty-five additional slots. That only drew more criticism, particularly from one of Pelé's Brazil teammates. Gérson, omitted along with two other heroes from the 1970 World Cup, Tostao and Jairzinho, was seen tearing a sheet of paper—purportedly Pelé's list of the Great 125—on TV.

"Pelé has the right to choose whoever he wants," growled Gérson, "but it's absurd to leave out teammates who carried him on their backs."

But while the experts ran down the list—alphabetized by country—and quibbled over this former star and that, what appeared at the bottom was American soccer's bottom line: United States—Michelle Akers, Mia Hamm. No American man was selected, and Akers and Hamm were the only women on the list.

Pelé's 125 greatest living players, including one each from twenty-one nations:

Argentina. Alfredo Di Stéfano, Daniel Passarella, Diego Maradona, Gabriel Batistuta, Hernán Crespo, Javier Saviola, Javier Zanetti, Juan Sebastian Veron, Mario Kempes, Omar Sivori

Belgium. Franky van der Elst, Jean-Marie Pfaff, Jan Ceulemans

Brazil. Cafu, Carlos Alberto, Djalma Santos, Roberto Falcao, Nilton Santos, Junior, Pelé, Rivaldo, Roberto Rivelino, Roberto Carlos, Romário, Ronaldinho, Ronaldo, Sócrates, Zico

Bulgaria. Hristo Stoichkov

Cameroon. Roger Milla

Chile. Elías Figueroa, Iván Zamorano

Colombia. Carlos Valderrama

Croatia. Davor Suker

Czech Republic/Czechoslovakia. Josef Masopust, Pavel Nedved

Denmark. Brian Laudrup, Michael Laudrup, Peter Schmeichel

England. Alan Shearer, Bobby Charlton, David Beckham, Gary
Lineker, Gordon Banks, Kevin Keegan, Michael Owen

France. David Trezeguet, Didier Deschamps, Eric Cantona, Jean-
Pierre Papin, Just Fontaine, Lilian Thuram, Marcel Desailly,
Marius Tresor, Michel Platini, Patrick Vieira, Raymond Kopa,
Robert Pires, Thierry Henry, Zinedine Zidane

Germany/West Germany. Franz Beckenbauer, Gerd Müller, Jürgen
Klinsmann, Karl-Heinz Rummenigge, Lothar Matthäus,
Michael Ballack, Oliver Kahn, Paul Breitner, Sepp Maier, Uwe
Seeler

Ghana. Abedi Pelé

Holland. Clarence Seedorf, Dennis Bergkamp, Edgar Davids,
Frank Rijkaard, Johan Neeskens, Johan Cruyff, Marco
van Basten, Patrick Kluivert, Rene van de Kerkhof, Rob
Rensenbrink, Ruud Gullit, Ruud van Nistlelrooy, Willie van de
Kerkhof

Hungary. Ferenc Puskás

Republic of Ireland. Roy Keane

Italy. Alessandro Del Piero, Alessandro Nesta, Christian Vieri,
Dino Zoff, Francesco Totti, Franco Baresi, Giampiero
Boniperti, Giacinto Fachetti, Gianluca Buffon, Gianni Rivera,
Giuseppe Bergomi, Paolo Rossi, Paolo Maldini, Roberto
Baggio

Japan. Hidetoshi Nakata

Liberia. George Weah

Mexico. Hugo Sanchez

Nigeria. Jay-Jay Okocha

Northern Ireland. George Best

Paraguay. Julio César Romero

Peru. Teofilo Cubillas

Poland. Zbigniew Boniek

Portugal. Eusébio, Luis Figo, Rui Costa
Romania. Gheorghe Hagi
Russia/Soviet Union. Rinat Disayev
Scotland. Kenny Dalglish
Senegal. El Hadji Diouf
South Korea. Hong Myung-Bo
Spain. Emilio Butragueño, Luis Enrique, Raúl
Turkey. Emre Belözoğlu, Rüstü Reçber
Ukraine. Andriy Shevchenko
Uruguay. Enzo Francescoli
United States. Michelle Akers, Mia Hamm

What skewed the list was the "living player" requirement. Otherwise, slots that went to some of the twenty-one one-nation, one-player selections would have instead been directed to the since-departed greats of Argentina, England, Hungary, Italy, and Uruguay. Moreover, his Russia/Soviet Union pick would have not been Disayev but FIFA's goalkeeper of the century, Lev Yashin, the savior of some 150 penalty kicks from 1953 to 1971.

Nevertheless, it was a cold day for the male side of U.S. soccer, and Pelé's picks further skewed the world's view of the game here. After all, before the 2002 World Cup, U.S. men's coach Bruce Arena was actually asked by foreign journalists whether his team could beat the U.S. women. (Arena's team answered for him, reaching the quarterfinals and generally outplaying eventual runner-up Germany before losing, 1–0.)

The United States' Biggest Rival in International Sports

Most Americans don't know it, but their country's greatest sports rivalry is the United States versus Mexico, in soccer.

The Soviet Union's basketball team is gone, as is East Germany's track-and-field squad. Team USA versus Team Canada in ice hockey? How can any American hate a Canadian, even if he's a snarling, stick-wielding cyclone on skates? Since the 1990s what has become one of the most heated rivalries anywhere in international sports concerns not the Iron Curtain but the opposite banks of the Rio Grande, Red, White, and Blue against El Tricolores, Red, White, and Green.

The passion surrounding USA versus Mexico is a three-sided square.

The Mexican and U.S. players don't like one another: the Americans are out to wipe out the memory of decades of subjugation by their southern masters; the Mexicans, who have refused to exchange jerseys with U.S. players after recent defeats, aren't about to surrender their crown as CONCACAF's de facto reigning superpower. The fans of Mexico, many of them still refusing to believe El Tri can possibly lose to those gringos from *el norte*, turn out in force no matter the game site, whether it's the cavernous Estadio Azteca of Mexico City or U.S. cities with significant Mexican and Mexican-American populations like Dallas, Houston, Phoenix, San Diego, Los Angeles, and Chicago.

The missing side of the square, of course, is the American public, which historically has demonstrated an indifference toward soccer in general and most things Mexican, Mexico's national soccer team included. But while many Americans and their media limit their global sports view to the Olympics, the Ryder Cup, and the like, they've missed out on a true and natural rivalry, each renewal a war on grass.

For example, there's the 1998 CONCACAF Gold Cup final at the Los Angeles Memorial Coliseum. While the mouths of tournament promoters watered at the thought of a championship match between Mexico and invited guest Brazil (actually a Brazilian under-23 team in training for the Olympics) the United States scuttled those hopes by shocking Brazil in the semifinals, 1–0. Mexico did its part with a harrowing 1–0 overtime decision over Jamaica to reach the final.

If promoters were disappointed that their dream final wasn't to be, they got their big payday nevertheless as a crowd of 91,255 poured into the Coliseum, most of them there to see the United States submit once again to the will of El Tri. Ten thousand fans, holding counterfeit tickets, were allowed to squeeze in as well, and another ten thousand gathered at the Los Angeles Sports Arena next door to watch a big-screen telecast of the match.

The stands were a sea of Mexican flags, and the playing of the U.S. national anthem was drowned out by the whistles and jeers of the overwhelmingly partisan Mexican crowd. American players attempting to take corner kicks were pelted with batteries, coins, and plastic bags filled with urine, and the match was littered with skirmishes among the players. If that didn't make the U.S. players believe they were hardly playing a home match, the deafening roar of the crowd two minutes before halftime—when Mexico's Luis Hernandez headed in the game's only goal—convinced them.

For Mexico, it was yet another defeat of the United States, giving it an overwhelming 29-5-9 record. But what put a charge in the huge partisan Mexican crowd and turned what happened on the field into a pitched battle was the realization by all that a corner already had been turned.

The about-face in the series began back at the Coliseum, seven years earlier at the inaugural Gold Cup, as the United States, eleven months removed from its three-and-out performance at the 1990 World Cup, upset Mexico, 2–0, in the semifinals en route to the title. This was still the Mexico-beats-America-like-a-drum era, so embattled El Tri coach Manuel Lapuente did the only logical thing and resigned on the spot.

Mexico avenged that upset by thumping the United States, 4–0, in its next meeting, the 1993 Gold Cup final in Mexico City. But a 1–0 U.S. victory in a 1994 World Cup tune-up before a full house at Pasadena's Rose Bowl was followed by an astonishing 4–0 USA rout at RFK Stadium in Washington DC, at U.S. Cup '95. A month after that, the Americans trimmed the Mexicans on penalty kicks, 4–1, in Paysandu in the Copa America quarterfinals in Uruguay. The 180 was completed in Jeonju, South Korea, at the second round of the 2002 World Cup, a comprehensive 2–0 U.S. victory.

One of the goal scorers in Jeonju, Landon Donovan, managed to dump a drum of petrol on the flames two years later by getting caught by TV crews urinating on the periphery of the field at Guadalajara's Estadio Jalisco during a practice session two days before a qualifier for the 2004 Athens Olympics. The next evening, with some in the crowd of sixty thousand chanting "Osama! Osama!"—a taunt in reference to al-Qaeda leader Osama bin Laden—El Tri then roared to a comprehensive 4–0 victory, knocking the Americans out of the Olympics for the first time since 1976 and ending their streak of a world-best nineteen consecutive qualifications for the men's under-17, under-20, under-23 (Olympics), and World Cup finals.

Donovan's lack of manners only made the impish speedster, winner of the Golden Ball as the top player at the 1997 World Under-17 Tournament in New Zealand, the unofficial lightning rod for Mexican revulsion. Frequently the U.S. captain, Donovan scored in his first appearance with the full national team, coincidentally a 2–0 victory over Mexico, in 2000. He went on to become a member of the 2002 All-World Cup Honorable Mention Team, an annual winner of the Honda Player of the Year award (top male U.S. player), and, in 2008, both the United States' all-time scoring leader and the fourth youngest American to reach one hundred caps. Donovan was, clearly to Mexico, the first individual gringo to pose a real danger on the field, and after several meetings he could barely conceal his contempt for his Mexican opponents. Following a 2–0 victory over Mexico in September 2005 that qualified the United States for the 2006 World Cup, Donovan expressed his feelings to the media with the crude but succinct, "They suck."

By the time the United States edged their neighbors in the 2007 Gold Cup final at Chicago's Soldier Field before sixty thousand—a majority of them Mexico fans—the Americans had gone unbeaten at home against Mexico for nine games (8-0-1). That increased to eleven in February 2009 after the United States beat Mexico, 2–0, in a World Cup qualifier in Columbus, an evening capped by a postmatch incident in which Mexico assistant coach Francisco Ramirez slapped U.S. defender Frankie Hejduk in the stadium tunnel and was suspended by FIFA. Over sixteen meetings from 2000 through 2009, the Americans lost only four games, three of them in the thin air of Mexico City, where smog, heat, altitude (7,260 feet above sea level), and the din created by 105,000 Mexican fanatics turn the Azteca into a cauldron. It's a place where Mexico has lost only a handful of matches since the stadium opened in 1966 and where the United States has gone 0-9-1 overall.

Of course, this recent run by the United States merely improved its all-time record against Mexico to 15-31-11 (0-23-1 on Mexican soil, 2-1-1 at neutral sites), with 65 goals for and 125 against. The United States won the two countries' first-ever meeting, a 4–2 decision in Rome in a qualifier held on the eve of the 1934 World Cup, but El Tri went unbeaten over the next two dozen games (21-0-3), a run that didn't end until the United States prevailed, 2–1, in Fort Lauderdale in 1980 in a 1982 World Cup qualifier played after the United States had already been eliminated.

So why was the early history of this now boiling rivalry so one-sided? Mexico deserves all the credit, and the Stars and Stripes all the blame.

The Mexicans have the strongest and oldest national league in the region, one founded in 1903 that has since become among the wealthiest in the western hemisphere, and the sport itself is by far the nation's most popular pastime. The United States, in contrast, has neither that same passion for soccer nor, until recently, a comparable professional league structure. In fact, until the creation of Major League Soccer, America's best opportunity to develop native talent and close the gap was the North American Soccer League, but the NASL had little interest in the fate of the U.S. National Team; when the league folded in March 1985, it still allowed the majority of the players on the field to be non–North Americans.

Compounding the United States' shortcomings was a lack of organization that plagued its national teams from the 1930s through the 1980s, a period when Mexico played in nine World Cups to the United States' three. Squads were selected through hastily arranged tryouts, at times one covering each half of the country, and the players were chosen not by the coach but by a selection committee formed by the U.S. Soccer Federation. Players went into major international matches with few practices or none at all; often, those representing the USA met for the first time on the ship or plane bringing them to a match or tournament. When there were practices, sometimes those who had taken part were replaced before games by new players.

This was never better illustrated than in September 1972, during the United States' final qualifier for the 1974 World Cup, against Mexico. Once again, the Americans had already been eliminated, this time in a 3–1 loss in Mexico City. For the home game a week later in Los Angeles, injuries and general mismanagement by the USSF left coach Bob Kehoe with ten men. As the hours ticked away, Fred Kovacs was recruited to make his international debut on the back line, and forward Dieter Ficken arrived from New York. Finally, two hours before kickoff, Slodubian "Barney" Djordjevic was spotted by Ficken sitting in the stands. Djordjevic, a former player for Intergiuliana of the semipro German-American League in New York, was given a uniform, signed the necessary paperwork, met his new coach and teammates, and played the entire game at left wing.

Djordjevic did not score and the United States, despite taking the lead in the eighth minute, came from ahead to lose, 2–1.

7 REFEREES

*They're only human. That's probably the nicest thing you'll ever hear
many players, coaches, and fans say about referees. For all their dedication,
sense of fairness, and knowledge of the Laws of the Game, they still can't
be everywhere on the field at once, see everything, and get every one of their
couple hundred calls (or noncalls) right. Still, they continue to pursue that
elusive, perfectly officiated match, and as only their colleagues will point
out, some occasionally come mighty close.*

Hand of God

It was one of the greatest—if not *the* greatest goal—in World Cup history. A long, breathtaking solo run and a brilliant finish, the kind
of goal that prompts those unfamiliar with soccer to wonder, "Why
can't they just do that all the time?" and leaves those who know better shaking their heads in awe.

Of course, soccer players can't score at will, but for about ten seconds during the 1986 World Cup quarterfinals Argentine idol Diego
Maradona made it look possible as he shredded the English defense
over seventy yards before slipping a left-footed shot from short range
past goalkeeper Peter Shilton.

In the fifty-fifth minute Maradona collected a ball in his own half
and roared down the right wing. He sped past Peter Reid, cut left to
beat Gary Stevens, sent Terry Butcher the wrong way, fought off Terry

Fenwick, and invaded the right side of the penalty area, all the while in complete control of his special delivery package.

As Maradona homed in on Shilton, Butcher sprinted up from behind and attempted a slide tackle. A split second ahead, the Argentine shifted the ball from his right foot to his left and deposited his package into the net.

Maradona had an option. Running down the middle of the field was Jorge Valdano. He never received the square pass that would have set up an easy goal, and the midfielder understood.

"Only when Diego got past the last defender and was bearing down on Shilton did it occur to him that he could score himself," said Valdano.

The tally, which gave Argentina a two-goal lead en route to its 2–1 victory, should have been the defining moment of the 1986 World Cup, one that Argentina went on to win.

Far from it.

All the attention was focused on Maradona's other strike, the so-called Hand of God goal scored just four minutes earlier.

Maradona, on an attack, passed to the right for Valdano, who lost the ball to Steve Hodge, who in turn shanked his attempted clearance. The lurking Maradona beat Shilton to the ball and, at five and a half feet tall, lacking the height for a header, leaped and extended a fist just above his head, punching the ball over the outstretched arms of the goalkeeper and into the net.

Many of the players on the field did not see the intentional handball—certainly Tunisian referee Ali Bennaceur and his linesman, the Bulgarian Bogdan Dotschev, missed it. But most in the sellout crowd of one hundred fourteen thousand at Mexico City's Estadio Azteca saw it, as did the onsite journalists. Butcher asked Maradona later in the game if he handled the ball, and "he just smiled and pointed to his head," said the big Englishman.

Maradona came up with his coy "Hand of God" response during the postmatch press conference, and he maintained that stance until the furor died down. But in August 2000, ahead of the release of his autobiography, he fessed up in an interview aired on British television.

"I was and always will be happy with the goal I scored with my hand," Maradona said. "I offer the English a thousand apologies, but I'd still do it again.

"That's what I did to the English: I stole their wallets without them realizing. Argentines are proud because no one saw me. They identify with that."

The interview took place in Cuba, where Maradona was being treated for heart problems caused in part by cocaine abuse. It was a final stop of sorts for El Pibe de Oro, "the Golden Kid," who had derailed his career by the 1990s with not one but two fifteen-month suspensions for failing drug tests. Had FIFA introduced its World Player of the Year award earlier than 1991, he might have won it at least three times in the 1980s.

Then came the release of *I Am Diego*.

"I don't know how I jumped so high," he—or someone—wrote. "I raised my left fist and moved my head backwards [as if preparing to head the ball]. Shilton had no idea what was happening, and it was defender Fenwick, who was heading back towards the goal, who was the first to call for a hand ball."

Maradona then spotted Dotschev running to the halfway line for the ensuing kickoff and realized that the goal had been allowed.

"All the English were protesting to the referee, and Valdano, who had passed me the ball, put his finger on his mouth, saying, 'Ssshhh,' as if he were a nurse in a hospital," Maradona wrote.

Maradona also made note of the short but bitter battle between Argentina and Britain over the Falkland Islands—or La Guerra de Las Malvinas—fought in 1982.

"Although we said that the match had nothing to do with the Falklands War, we knew that many young Argentines had died there, and that they had been killed like flies."

Maradona added to the "Hand of God" legend four years after at Italia '90. In a first-round match in Naples, the Soviet Union should have taken a 1–0 lead through a header by midfielder Oleg Kuznetsov off a corner kick, but Maradona batted down Kuznetsov's goal-bound shot with his hand. Standing ten yards from the play was referee Erik Fredriksson, who was working his third World Cup. The Swede made no call, the Argentines went on to a 2–0 win, and the Soviets failed to advance out of the opening round by a single point.

"What an all-around player Maradona is," marveled Brazil coach Sebastião Lazaroni later. "He can score goals with his left hand, and save them with his right."

Maradona seemingly had the last laugh on Lazaroni. Brazil met Argentina in the second round in Turin, and after eighty scoreless minutes, against the run of play, Maradona split the Brazilian defense with a perfect pass and striker Claudio Canniggia scored for a 1–0 victory. But two weeks after, it was Lazaroni and his Brazilians, back home and no doubt watching on TV, who at least could share a smirk as Maradona's Argentina bowed to West Germany on an eighty-fifth-minute penalty kick by Andreas Brehme, 1–0, in the final in Rome.

Years later, the "Hand of God" fallout still hadn't ended, thanks in part to linesman Dotschev. He broke his silence in January 2007 to explain to the world that he thought Maradona had handled the ball . . . but did nothing to assist Bennaceur in coming to the correct decision to award England a free kick at the point of the infraction and show Maradona a yellow card, at the very least.

Dotschev told the London tabloid *Sun*, "With the ref having said the goal was valid, I couldn't have waved my flag and told him the goal wasn't good—the rules were different back then."

(They weren't, of course. Then as now, Law VI calls for linesmen to "draw the referee's attention to any breach of the Laws of the Game of which they become aware if they consider that the referee may not have seen it, but the referee shall always be the judge of the decision to be taken." In fact, in 1930, soccer's rule-making body, the International Football Association Board, declared that "if a linesman notices an incident on the pitch that is liable to discredit the sport, he shall immediately notify the referee." Maradona's outrageous act would seem to apply.)

By running to the halfway line, Dotschev not only failed to do his duty but helped remove any doubt Bennaceur may have had as to the legitimacy of Maradona's goal.

Dotschev also had one final word for his boss that day, telling the *Sun* that Bennaceur was "an idiot more fit to herd camels in the desert than take charge of a World Cup game."

Referee Takes Pity, Scores for Losing Side

Wimpole was trailing Earls Colne, 18–1, late in an English amateur cup match in 2001 when it got a helping foot from an unlikely source. With ten minutes remaining, referee Brian Savill, apparently touched by the plight of the deflated Wimpole players, took action. During one of Wimpole's rare forays into the opposition half, Savill, age forty-seven, stunned everyone by volleying a loose ball past the Earls Colne goalkeeper.

"When the ball went in, I turned around in celebration, blew my whistle, and indicated that the goal would stand," Savill said. "Twenty or thirty people were just staring at me—half of them were stunned, the other half were applauding and laughing.

"After the match, an Earls Colne player came up to me, shook my hand, and said, 'Well done.' I think I saw the funny side of it all."

Final score, with the help of the charitable referee: Earls Colne 20, Wimpole 2.

Weeks later, Savill was handed a lengthy suspension by the English Football Association. Rather than serve it, he turned in his whistle.

Brazilian Player Penalized for Being Too Creative

Brazil is renowned for its five World Cup championships and the ball artists who made those titles possible. So it was no surprise when a referee was showered with criticism for penalizing a player during a September 2002 national championship match for putting on a show.

With Coritiba beating Santos, 4–2, late in the game, Coritiba forward Jaba collected a ball near the touchline and, with a Santos defender planted in his path, lifted his foot over it several times as if he would set off on a dribble at any moment. Referee Leonardo Gaciba Junior apparently had enough of Jaba's feints and awarded a free kick to Santos.

"The rule says that a player cannot endanger an opponent or himself," said Gaciba. "He wasn't being objective, so I awarded a free kick to protect him. If somebody had broken his leg, they will say that I was not clamping down on violence."

His explanation, however, triggered a torrent of derision from both the media and prominent referees. "What Leonardo Gaciba did was absurd; it can't happen," said ex-FIFA referee José Roberto Wright. "What he did in fact was to stamp out the skill of the player and not the violence of the opponents."

Wrote Fernando Calazans of the Rio de Janeiro-based daily *O Globo,* "Where on earth have you seen a player be protected by having a free kick awarded against him? Mr. Gaciba has to allow Jaba to play. His Highness has a duty to protect football, punishing the bully boys with their perverse sliding tackles, their flying scissors kicks, and their repetitive fouling carried out on the orders of bully-boy coaches."

Roberto Assaf of *Jornal do Brasil* was more succinct: "There is no fun left in football."

Referee Gaciba, however, knew what he was talking about. In June 1999 a bit of hot-doggery by Edilson triggered a brawl among players that brought the second leg of the São Paulo state championship final between Palmeiras and Corinthians to a halt.

Corinthians had taken the first leg, 3–0, and was tied, 2–2, seventy-five minutes into the second leg when the Brazilian international striker, left unmarked in the midfield, received a ball, juggled it, then flipped it over his head, and let it roll down his back.

Incensed not only by Edilson's impertinence but his time-wasting as well, Palmeiras' Zinho, Junior, and Paulo Nunes attacked Edilson, who got in one kick before scampering to the dressing room. Corinthian players rushed to Edilson's aid, and TV and radio reporters invaded the field, attempting to interview the battling players. The match was abandoned and Corinthians were immediately declared São Paulo state champs by a 5–2 aggregate.

Edilson may have gotten his team the title a quarter hour early, but it came at a price. Brazilian National Team coach Wanderley Luxemburgo blamed the striker for inciting the brawl and dropped him from his roster for the following month's Copa America, South America's biennial championship. However, three years later, with Luiz Felipe Scolari in charge, Edilson was part of the Brazil team that won the 2002 World Cup.

Dutch Player Shares the Love with Official

Had enough when it comes to players who show a bit too much affection toward teammates following a goal? Tell it to the Dutch.

An unidentified amateur player in the eastern town of Hengelo was suspended in November 2002 by Holland's soccer federation for eight games after kissing the referee who had ejected him from a match. The player, shown a yellow card, directed some choice words at the referee and was issued a second. But before he left the field he grabbed the official's head and kissed him on the mouth.

Norwegian Referee Too Embarrassed to Book Players

Players in the amateur Norwegian fourth division in the 1990s knew they could get away with plenty whenever Per Arne Brataas was the referee. It wasn't until after his retirement as an official, however, that they found out why.

Brataas, it turned out, suffered from dyslexia and was too embarrassed to write down the names of offending players during a match.

"I was reluctant to give red cards," he told an Oslo daily in 2003. "I didn't give yellow cards either, so then I avoided having to write the reports."

Surprise! Study Says Fans *Do* Get to Officials

Researchers at an Austrian university have concluded that referees in the German Bundesliga favor the home team. Matthias Sutter and Martin Kocher of the University of Innsbruck studied every game of the 2000–2001 German first-division season and found that referees gave more added-on time when the home team trailed, awarded more penalty kicks to the hosts, and sent off more visiting players.

They blamed pressure from the home crowd and recommended that video replays be used to help officials in making calls.

Entire Team Gets a Red Card in Brazilian Match

Eleven red cards? It happened in the eightieth minute of a Rio de Janeiro state championship match in March 2003. Host Bangu and Olaria were scoreless when Bangu was awarded a controversial penalty kick and the Olaria team bench, led by coach Sergio Cosme, ran onto the field and stood around the penalty spot in protest to prevent Bangu from taking its kick.

After a twenty-minute melee, referee José Ezequiel summoned the Olaria captain and told him that his entire team had been ejected.

World Cup Match Is Ended Just a Bit Too Early

Argentina was leading France, 1–0, late in a 1930 World Cup match in Montevideo, Uruguay, when French forward Marcel Langiller dribbled the length of the field and closed in on Argentine goalkeeper Angel Bossio.

Just then, referee Almeida Rego of Brazil blew his whistle to end the match. While French players protested, Argentina fans raced onto the field to congratulate the winning players.

One problem: Rego had ended the game six minutes early.

Realizing his error, the red-faced ref rounded up the scattered players while mounted police cleared the field. The match was resumed, but the shaken French couldn't produce the equalizer and lost.

Demoralized, France, which had started the tournament brightly with a 4–1 romp over Mexico, followed its controversial loss to eventual finalist Argentina with another defeat, 1–0, to Chile and was eliminated.

If the referee can taketh away, he can also giveth.

Liverpool met Thailand's national team in a July 2003 friendly in Bangkok, and before kickoff Gerard Houllier, coach of the English club, informed the referee that he intended to make wholesale substitutions in the sixtieth minute.

The referee, however, thought that Houllier asked that the first half last an hour. Although he found it a highly unusual request, the referee complied. By the fiftieth minute, with both sides wondering what happened to the halftime break, Thailand coach Peter Withe, an ex-England international, was shouting in vain from the sidelines, "Stop the game! Stop the game!"

The sixty-minute first half was followed by a conventional forty-five-minute second half, and Liverpool went on to win, 3–1, in 105 minutes.

German Technology Produces Computerized Officials

Will linesmen one day be replaced by machines? They will, if a team of German researchers has its way.

The researchers in 2002 introduced a computer system intended to detect offside violations, determine whether a shot has entered the goal, and measure the distance from a defensive wall to the spot of a free kick.

The Cairos System, developed jointly by the Frauenhofer Institute in Erlangen and Munich's Technical University, features small sensors inside the ball and the players' shin guards that beam information about their location and movement to a half dozen relay stations on the field. The information is fed into a computer, which signals to a receiver worn by the referee whether an attacker is behind a defender when a pass is made or if a goal has been scored.

More testing was planned, but the system was to have the bargain price of just $245,000 per unit.

The German team was not alone. Two years earlier Belgian inventor Antoon Soetens claimed to have come up with an electronic device that can determine with 100 percent accuracy whether a player is offside.

In the Soetens device, an electronic emitter sends a signal to a central receiver whenever a pass is made to an attacking player, and a second emitter sends a signal every time a player moves into an offside position. If the receiver gets a signal from the second emitter before the first, a device held by each linesman vibrates.

Soetens tested it out during a match between two Brussels amateur sides, FC Escanafles and FC Molenbaix, and claimed the gadget passed with a perfect score.

Soetens presented his invention to the Belgian soccer federation's referees committee but apparently was unsuccessful in gaining the blessing of FIFA, which has repeatedly rejected technical solutions to officiating challenges.

Too Late the Linesman at Center of World Cup Error

The linesman whose flag helped disallow what would have been Spain's winning goal in its 2002 World Cup quarterfinal against co-host South Korea acknowledged a month after the fact that he may have erred.

Spain (a 13-2 pick to lift its first World Cup) and South Korea (a 150-1 long shot) were locked in a 0–0 overtime battle in Gwangju when winger Joaquin dribbled along the end line right of the goal and crossed to Fernando Morientes, who nodded the ball into the net.

Before the Spaniards could begin to celebrate their golden goal and passage to the semifinals, referee Wagih Farag of Egypt spotted the upraised flag of linesman Ali Tomusange of Uganda and whistled for a goal kick for South Korea.

TV replays clearly showed that Joaquin had kept the ball in play before crossing. No matter. The Koreans held on through the rest of overtime and won the game on penalty kicks, 5–3.

"I could have made a mistake when I raised my flag and disallowed the goal," Tomusange later commented.

He made this admission after being honored by the Ugandan parliament for his performance at the World Cup.

World Cup Game Ended with Ball En Route to Goal

You won't find a mention of it in the Laws of the Game, but it is customary—at least at the professional level—for a referee to end things when the ball is a safe distance from either goal. If there's a corner kick, a dangerous free kick, a goalmouth scramble, or a promising breakaway in progress when time expires, he generally allows the situation to play itself out before whistling for the conclusion of the half or the game.

Imagine the surprise caused by referee Clive Thomas of Wales, then, when he signaled the end of a 1978 World Cup first-round match between Brazil and Sweden in Mar del Plata, Argentina. Brazil had caught the Swedes at 1–1 with a goal by Reinaldo deep in first-half added-on time, and it had an apparent last-gasp winner when midfield star Zico redirected a corner kick into the net at the end of the second half. But to everyone's amazement, Thomas whistled the end of the game a split-second before the ball crossed the goal line.

The Swedish players claimed they relaxed with the corner kick still airborne when they heard Thomas's whistle. The Brazilian players protested vehemently and their fans pelted Thomas with coins, but the 1–1 score stood.

Two decades later, the name Clive Thomas was back in the headlines. In December 1998 an English F.A. Cup third-round match between Wimbledon of the Premier League and Welsh upstart Wrexham, a second-division side, was tied in added-on time at Selhurst Park in London. Wimbledon's Neil Ardley swung a corner kick toward the Wrexham goal and before Marcus Gayle could head it into the net, referee Steve Dunn blew his whistle to end the game.

"I've been waiting twenty years for someone else to do that," said Thomas, who always vigorously defended his Brazil-Sweden decision. "Twenty years I have been praying, every cup tie. The law is there.

The amount of time is at the discretion of the referee. Time should only be extended for a penalty kick."

Thomas added that he had long advocated soccer's adoption of the rugby rule that requires that there be a stoppage before the final whistle can be blown.

Wimbledon coach Joe Kinnear demanded that Dunn be replaced for the replay to no avail, but Dunn proved to be his greatest ally at Wrexham's Racecourse Ground. In the thirty-fifth minute Gayle, ironically, scored on a glancing header from an Ardley corner, and Dunn allowed the goal despite whistling moments earlier for a foul, giving the Dons a 3–1 lead. The referee also ignored three appeals for penalty kicks by Wrexham in the second half, and Wimbledon went on to win, 3–2.

There was more of the same in the Honduran league in November 1997. Vida of La Ceiba was leading Victoria, 1–0, at home in the closing moments when the visitors were awarded a penalty kick. With the twelve-yard shot by Victoria's Alejandro Naif on its blink-of-an-eye journey into the net, referee Benigno Pinedo whistled the match over.

Enraged Victoria players attempted to attack Pinedo, and outside Nilmo Edwards Stadium, Victoria fans fired guns and hurled missiles at parked cars until they were routed in a police tear-gas attack.

Witches' Curse Can't Stop Romanian Ref

Romanian witches placed a curse on Swiss referee Urs Meier for his work during Romania's 2–2 draw with Denmark in a European Championship qualifier in Copenhagen in September 2003. Meier awarded what Romanian supporters considered a questionable penalty to Denmark in the first half and added five minutes of stoppage time at the end of the game, long enough for the Danes' Martin Laursen to score the tying goal. The result left Romania, which needed a win to earn a playoff berth, in danger of being eliminated entirely.

In response, seven witches from Craiova cursed Meier to lose his ability to blow his whistle, and for good measure their hex aimed to make him lame in the legs and to feel pain in his soul.

It was in his personal computer, however, where Meier felt immediate pain. Romanian newspapers published his e-mail address, and the referee later complained of having received approximately fourteen thousand angry messages from Romania.

The witches evidently were satisfied that they had set things right. They were quoted by the media as saying, "Romania will never feel pain and injustice from referees again after they see what happened to Urs Meier."

Wrong. That draw was the Romanians' last qualifier and left them with fourteen points from eight games while Denmark had fourteen with a game in hand. The Danes then held on for a 1–1 draw at Bosnia-Herzegovina in their final qualifier for the point that punched their ticket to the 2004 European Championship in Portugal.

Meier? He was among the elite dozen selected by the UEFA to referee at the Euro Championship.

Shot Caroms off Referee and into Goal

Virtually everything on a soccer field—the players, the corner flags, the framework of the goals—is part of the game. That includes the officials, and one, referee Ivan Robinson, demonstrated that concept in embarrassing fashion during a November 1968 match between English third-division rivals Plymouth Argyle and host Barrow.

The game was scoreless through seventy-seven minutes when Barrow was awarded a corner kick. The ball was cleared by the Plymouth defense, and Barrow's George McLean pounced on the loose ball and unleashed a shot from outside the penalty area that was wide of the mark. That was unfortunate for Robinson and Plymouth, because as the referee, fifteen yards from the goal, leaped to elude the errant shot, the ball struck the inside of his left foot and bounded past the astonished goalkeeper, Pat Dunne, and into the net.

Knowing that the goal counted, a red-faced Robinson pointed to the center circle. The goal was charitably, but correctly, credited to McLean. Plymouth failed to muster an equalizer, and after blowing the final whistle Robinson did his best to avoid Barrow fans who were eager to slap him on the back.

At least Robinson could leave his worst moment on the field. One Argentine referee had to take it home with him.

In an August 1907 match between Porteño and San Martín, a San

Martín shot caromed off referee Mario Balerdi, past the Porteño goalkeeper, and into the goal.

The Porteño 'keeper was Balerdi's brother, Escipion.

Fed-up Youth Ref Red-Cards the Whole Crowd

A referee can red-card anyone he chooses. He also can red-card everyone.

In an English boys under-11 match played in November 1995, parents of players from Gillway and Bedworth were jaw to jaw, shouting and swearing at one another, when referee Dave Warwick took action: he sent off the entire crowd of fifty.

Warwick warned the parents that he would abandon the match if they did not leave. The parents retired to the parking lot, the game resumed, and Gillway completed its 4–3 victory.

Belgian Referee Pantsed by Spectator

The referee of a Belgian amateur match in February 2004 was attacked by a fan and escaped with his pride mortally wounded. While FC Zelzate and Young Stars Eeklo did battle, a spectator ran at referee Jacky Temmerman and, rather than throwing a punch, pulled down the official's shorts and underwear, then fled. The assailant, identified as a twenty-year-old player from another amateur club, KFC Eeklo, and coach of a youth team, later said he didn't know what came over him.

"I looked very nice in front of a few hundred supporters," Temmerman grumbled. "That man made a fool of me.

"I will never dare to show up for another match. They can look for another idiot who is prepared to stand with his ass naked for 20 euros [$30] a game."

Bludgeon the Referee?

The president of Como, Enrico Preziosi, watched with dismay as his club tumbled from Italy's Serie A to Serie B in 2002, and he criticized the referees all the way down.

Fed up, he directed his toy company, Giochi Preziosi, to produce and market a computer game in which soccer players attack the referee with hammers. The game, called "Catch the Ref," provoked yet another fine against Preziosi from the Italian soccer federation.

John Gregory, coach of England's Aston Villa, was more direct. Said Gregory in October 1999: "Referees should be wired up to a couple of electrodes and they should be allowed to make three mistakes before you run fifty thousand volts through their genitals."

Maybe the Long View Is Best

The U.S. Soccer Federation requires its referees to be fit. A referee sanctioned to work a top-division professional match, for example, must be able to run 2,700 meters in twelve minutes, 50 meters in seven and a half seconds, and 200 meters in thirty-two seconds.

Apparently, however, it is the softer, slower referee—the one who lags behind play—who may be doing the better job. A 1998 study by the Free University of Amsterdam of the top referees in Holland concluded that most officiating mistakes are made when the referee is fifteen yards or closer to the action. Conversely, errors are fewest when the distance from ref to perceived infraction is twenty-two yards or more.

The conclusion by the author of the study, Raymond Verheijen: FIFA should reconsider its mandatory retirement age for international referees, which was once fifty and presently stands at forty-five.

No Advantage to This Advantage Call

Should a referee celebrate when he nails a critical call?

No.

Leeds United had just tied host Liverpool, 1–1, in a January 2000 English Premier League match when referee Mike Reed invoked the advantage clause—soccer's version of "no harm, no foul"—during a sequence involving Liverpool's Vladimir Šmicer in the sixty-ninth minute.

The ref waved play on, allowing Smicer to continue on his way and set up the go-ahead goal by teammate Patrik Berger. At the moment the ball entered the goal, Reed—either exultant or just relieved that he made the correct call—was seen punching the air by the Anfield crowd of 44,783, raising the ire of the Leeds fans on hand.

Leeds lost, 3–1, but the big loser was the referee, who was in the last four months of a distinguished fifteen-year career in England's top division. Reed was reprimanded by league officials, and six weeks later he was replaced as referee of a match at Everton that was to be nationally televised.

Angry Italian Amateur Makes Meal of Red Card

Shown a red card during an Italian amateur league game against Arpax in 1989, Fernando D'Ercoli of Pianta grabbed the card out of the referee's hand and ate it.

Referee Ejects His Power-mad Linesman

In England, during an Andover and District Sunday League game in November 1998 between Lardicake Pub and Over Wallop Reserves, linesman Phil Cooper signaled for a foul against Over Wallop. Referee Terry Gilligan overruled him, but Cooper, landlord of the Lardicake Pub, continued to wave his flag. So, Gilligan red-carded his own linesman.

When Cooper refused to leave, Gilligan picked up the ball and abandoned the match.

Cooper was later fined some $125 and suspended ninety-one days by the Hampshire Football Association (ninety days apparently not being a stiff enough punishment).

What, then, should be done when it's the referee who misbehaves? Thirty-year-old ref Andy Wain demonstrated during another English amateur match, this one played in January 2005.

Royal Mail AYL had just taken a 2–1 lead over Peterborough North End FC, and Peterborough goalkeeper Richard McGaffin let Wain know that he did not believe the go-ahead goal should have counted. McGaffin must have said the wrong thing, because Wain, a truck driver by trade, attacked the 'keeper. When order was restored, Wain red-carded himself.

"It was totally unprofessional," Wain said later. "If a player did that I would send him off, so I had to go."

Intimidated, Uruguayan Ref Hides for Forty Minutes

Long, drawn-out halftimes are usually the domain of gridiron football, but a Uruguayan first-division match in Montevideo in May 2004 had a forty-minute intermission, and there were no marching bands or paragliders to alleviate the fans' boredom.

Nelson Canarte of Wanderers was yellow-carded in the sixteenth minute and sent off in the nineteenth by referee Oliver Veira for wasting time while taking a free kick. At the half, angry Wanderers directors surrounded Veira as he made his way to the officials' dressing room. Concerned for his safety, the referee locked himself in the dressing room, and seven police officers assembled to stand guard.

Veira didn't emerge until the Wanderers directors had been driven from the area and TV camera crews agreed to film his return to the field.

The long rest apparently reinvigorated the Wanderers' opponent, defending champion Penarol, which broke down the Wanderers' packed defense and got an eighty-second-minute goal from Carlos Bueno to win, 1–0.

Aussie Shown Three Yellow Cards

No sporting event is more closely scrutinized than a World Cup match. If the hundreds of millions of viewers, via a dozen or so TV cameras, aren't enough, there are the hundreds of eyewitnesses on press row and enough FIFA functionaries prying into every nook and cranny in the stadium to put the old KGB to shame. The game won't kick off until everything is just so, right down to the length of the grass on the field, which must meet FIFA specifications to the millimeter.

But things do go wrong. For example, the Germany '06 showdown between Group F rivals Australia and Croatia in Stuttgart.

The Aussies twice rallied to tie the Croats in a 2–2 draw in Stuttgart that put them into the second round as group runner-up behind Brazil; Croatia finished third and was eliminated. However, had the Croats won—and the game was a chaotic affair whose outcome was in doubt to the bitter end—Australia had grounds for a protest thanks to an astonishing blunder by referee Graham Poll, one of the most highly regarded officials in the English Premier League and an early favorite to work the World Cup final in Berlin.

In the worst of several missteps by Poll, defender Josip Simunic was allowed to remain on the field after being shown a second yellow card and wasn't red-carded until being cautioned a third time moments after the final whistle. The official FIFA match report lists Poll as cautioning Croats Dario Simic (thirty-second minute), Igor Tudor (thirty-eighth), Simunic (sixty-first), Stipe Pletikosa (seventieth), Simic again (eighty-fifth), and Simunic yet again (ninety-third), as well as the Socceroos' Brett Emerton twice (eighty-first and eighty-seventh). A messy match indeed.

Simic and Emerton were sent off, of course, but Poll apparently forgot that he had yellow-carded Simunic in the ninetieth minute for collaring an Aussie attacker and dragging him down in the midfield, so the yellow he pulled out on Simunic for dissent at the end of injury time came one card too late.

The triple yellows would have been enough to bring about an unprecedented replay had Croatia won and eliminated Australia.

It was clear that Poll was in for a forgettable evening at Gottlieb-Daimler-Stadion in the thirty-eighth minute, when he awarded Australia a penalty kick for a blatant handball in the box by Stjepan Tomas. Croatia had taken a lead in the second minute on a brilliant free-kick strike by Darijo Srna, so Craig Moore's PK conversion leveled the score at 1–1. Lost amidst the Aussie celebration was Poll's failure to caution Tomas.

Croat captain Niko Kovac, thanks to a bumbling save attempt by Socceroo goalkeeper Zeljko Kalac, scored in the fifty-sixth minute to put Croatia ahead, and Poll was back in the unwanted spotlight minutes later for missing a second clear handball in the area by Tomas. But Poll got off the hook, ultimately, in the seventy-ninth minute after 'Roos star Harry Kewell blasted a volley into the net for the 2–2 tie.

The ejections of Simic and Emerton followed in the dying minutes, seemingly closing out a madcap evening. But Poll evidently wasn't satisfied to go quietly into that good night. Aussie Tim Cahill booted a shot into the net to put Croatia's elimination beyond doubt, only for Poll to whistle the end of the game a split second before, nullifying the goal.

In the end FIFA sent Poll home early, along with several other World Cup referees, including Valentin Ivanov, who handed out sixteen cautions and four ejections, both World Cup records, in Portugal's ugly 1–0 win over Holland in Nuremberg in another second-round match. Ivanov's performance prompted a stinging rebuke from FIFA president Sepp Blatter, who told a TV interviewer that the Russian should have given himself a yellow card. Which begs the question, if Ivanov had done so, would Poll have noticed?

And as for the Socceroos, four days later in Kaiserslautern they were involved in another refereeing error, but this time it hurt. In the second round Australia played eventual champion Italy to a scoreless deadlock for ninety minutes and on into added-on time. In the ninety-fourth, Italian defender Fabio Grosso dribbled into the left side of the Australian penalty area; 'Roos defender Lucas Neill executed a slide tackle and Grosso did his very best to tangle himself in Neill's legs before tumbling. Referee Luis Medina Cantalejo of Spain amazingly pointed to the spot, and Francesco Totti drilled home the resulting penalty kick. The Aussies went home, Cantalejo was rewarded with an assignment to work the glamour quarterfinal between France and Brazil, and Italy went on to win the championship.

Perhaps Poll's error was actually a makeup call for a similar gaffe involving Australia more than thirty years earlier. Back in Germany—West Germany '74, that is—the Socceroos, in their World Cup debut, played Chile in a first-round game in Berlin. Australia was already eliminated, and the 0–0 result that day would knock out the Chileans as well. No wonder only 14,681 showed up at the Olympiastadion, capacity 83,000. Nevertheless, the Aussies got a late boost from Iranian referee Jafar Namdar, who yellow-carded midfielder Raymond Richards—his second—in the eighty-third minute for time-wasting, but didn't send him off until the eighty-eighth. Those were the only cautions issued in the match, and linesman Vital Loraux of Belgium alerted Namdar that he had made a mistake . . . which is more than Poll's linesmen and fourth official did for him.

Hush, Hush, Sweet Referee

The 1936 Berlin Olympics had it all, from the heroic exploits of Jesse Owens to the low comedy of the opening match of the soccer competition.

The United States was expected to lose that first-round game to Italy. The Italians had hosted and won the 1934 World Cup, and this latest crop—listed officially as "students" to comply with the Olympics' amateur ideals—came from many of Italy's leading first-division clubs.

A crowd of nine thousand at Post Stadion saw the physically superior Americans hold the match scoreless through the first half, and in the fifty-third minute fullback Pietro Rava was ejected by German referee Carl Weingartner for a harsh tackle. But they couldn't capitalize on their one-man advantage, and Italy took the lead in the fifty-eighth when a high ball skidded on the wet turf past U.S. left back Ferdinand Zbikowski, and right winger Annibale Frossi, wearing his customary spectacles and headband, swooped in to score.

With no substitutes allowed, Italy was taking no prisoners that day. While chest-trapping a ball, George Nemchik, the USA's inside right, took a hit to the groin that briefly left him unconscious. Inside left William Fiedler was struck in the mouth and later suffered torn knee ligaments when shoved by Achille Piccini. That blow prompted Weingartner to send off Piccini, who refused to leave. Three times the referee tried to get the Italian halfback off the field. At one point, six Italian players surrounded Weingartner, pinned his arms to his sides, and placed their hands over his mouth.

The German ref gave up, Piccini finished the game, and the United States lost, 1–0, and was eliminated. Italy, with Frossi leading all scorers with seven goals, went on to win the gold medal.

The Curious Officiating of Byron Moreno

Soccer is the most international of games. In what other sport could an Ecuadoran cause nationwide joy in South Korea and despair throughout Italy on a single day?

Byron Moreno is the Ecuadoran, a referee whose questionable work during South Korea's 2–1 victory over the favored Italians in Daejeon in the second round of the 2002 World Cup arguably altered the outcome of the tournament.

The then–three time champions were ahead, 1–0, on a headed goal by striker Christian Vieri in the eighteenth minute and doing what they do best, protecting a slim lead. The only bump in Italy's road came back in the fourth minute when a debatable penalty kick was awarded to Korea, but goalkeeper Gianluigi Buffon saved off the foot of striker Ahn Jung-Hwan. In the eighty-eighth, however, Seol Ki-Hyeon slipped in, pounced on a misplay by defender Christian Panucci, and beat Buffon with a low shot to level the score.

Thirteen minutes into overtime, it all began to unravel for Italy as playmaker Francesco Totti dived in the penalty area and was shown a second yellow card by Moreno for attempting to draw a penalty kick. The shorthanded Italians then had a seemingly valid goal by midfielder Damiano Tommasi nullified by Moreno for offside. Given new life, the Koreans finally produced the winner three minutes from the end of extra time when Lee Young-Pyo floated a cross onto the head of Ahn, who nodded in the golden goal.

More than a million Koreans flooded downtown Seoul in the biggest of the impromptu celebrations staged throughout a country where seemingly everyone was wearing a bright crimson "Be the Reds" T-shirt. Many of the revelers linked the South Korean triumph of 2002 to the North Korea upset of Italy in the 1966 World Cup.

In Italy, the reaction was quite different. "Shame!" and "Thieves" read the headlines in Italy's leading sports dailies, *La Gazzetta dello Sport* and *Corriere dello Sport*, and Italian commentators suggested that Moreno was part of a plot by FIFA to prevent a fourth Italian world championship and/or to deliver South Korea, the tournament co-host, into the quarterfinals. One Italian town named a row of toilets after Moreno.

Italians were already in a snit over the officiating during their team's earlier 2–1 loss to Croatia, a result that left Italy second to Mexico in its group. A first-place finish would have pitted Italy against what was believed to be a soft touch, the United States, in the second round.

"Italy has been thrown out of a dirty World Cup, where referees and linesmen are used as hitmen," read a commentary in the normally reserved *Corriere della Sera*.

FIFA, which selected Moreno to work the match, received approximately four hundred thousand e-mails from fans of Italy regarding the state of the officiating at the Korea-Italy game, causing the world soccer governing body's system server to crash. A FIFA spokesman described the e-mails as "virulent, some quite abusive, some of them very threatening, some of them quite disturbing."

Even FIFA president Sepp Blatter seemed to believe that Moreno and his brother referees had it out for the Azzurri. "Unfortunately, through exceptional circumstances and coincidences, numerous and consecutive errors were concentrated on the Italian team," Blatter said.

So the thirty-two-year-old Moreno went home in disgrace. He wasn't quite done, however. That September, Moreno was still refereeing— and running for a seat on the Quito city council. While working an Ecuadoran league match between Liga Quito and Barcelona of Guayaquil in Quito, he awarded a hotly disputed PK to each team, ejected two players, and disallowed a goal he originally okayed.

The topper: With ninety minutes gone, Barcelona was leading, 3–2, and Moreno signaled for six minutes of stoppage time. Unfortunately for the visitors, Moreno extended stoppage time for a total of thirteen minutes, and Liga scored in the 99th and 101st minutes to pull out a 4–3 win.

Exasperated by the performance of its supposed top referee—and by the perception that he was trying to capitalize on his exposure as a ref to win public office—the Ecuadoran soccer federation suspended Moreno for twenty games.

Within weeks FIFA began an investigation "as a result of a number of controversies regarding referee Byron Moreno in Japan, Italy, and South America over the past few months." At the new year, he was dropped from FIFA's list of international referees.

In May 2003, three matches after his twenty-game suspension ended, Moreno was at it again, ejecting three Deportivo Quito players during a league match at Deportivo Cuenca. All three were sent off for being cautioned twice. Quito somehow survived, holding Cuenca to a 1–1 draw.

The Ecuadoran referees' association finally had enough and booted Moreno out in 2004 when it was discovered that he was officiating regional tournaments without authorization.

South African Ref Shoots Knife-wielding Player

A South African referee acted out a man-bites-dog scenario to tragic effect in February 1999 when he shot and killed a knife-wielding player who disagreed with his call on a disputed goal during a match in the black township of Hartbeesfontein. Isaac Mkhwetha's Wallabies were leading the Try Agains, 2–0, in a local match before six hundred spectators when referee Lebogang Mokgethi, age thirty-four, allowed a Try Agains goal. Angry Wallabies fans invaded the field to protest, and the referee retrieved his licensed 9 mm handgun, which he had given to a friend to hold during the match.

Mkhwetha also left the field to fetch his knife and returned to confront Mokgethi. Mokgethi shot Mkhwetha in the chest. Mkhwetha, age twenty, died later at a police station.

Moldovan Club President Tries to Run Down Referee

The president of AC Roso Floreni was suspended for the remainder of the 2004–5 Moldova second-division season for what could only be described as reckless driving during a match with AC Politechnica Chisinau.

After fifteen minutes, with the score 1–1, referee Vitalie Onica awarded Chisinau a penalty kick that was converted, causing Roso boss Mihal Macovei to blow his top. Macovei jumped into his Jeep, drove onto to the field, and chased Onica, who proved to be quite nimble.

Muttered Chisinau coach Ion Caras later, "It was a miracle nobody died."

Spanish Fans Sue over Calls against Team

A group of Valencia fans, believing themselves the victims of incompetence, took legal steps in February 2004 after a late decision that favored Real Madrid turned a 1–0 Valencia lead into a 1–1 draw in a key Spanish Primera Liga match. Referee Pedro Tristante Oliva awarded Madrid a questionable penalty kick for Carlos Marchena's tackle of Real star Raúl with just seconds remaining, and teammate Luis Figo converted.

Outraged, some 130 Valencia season-ticket holders pursued an unsuccessful suit against Oliva, seeking a public apology and about $1.20 each in damages.

"We want the error to be publicly acknowledged and compensation paid as professional negligence has been committed," said the group's attorney, Andres Sanchis.

The Valencia fans had to know that their chances of getting a voluntary apology from Oliva were slim after learning of a Spanish referees training course held not long after. Course instructors selected a film clip of the Marchena challenge of Raúl to illustrate what in their opinion was a crystal-clear penalty call.

Gazza Cautions a Referee

Just one Paul "Gazza" Gascoigne story.

Gazza was one of the most talented and eccentric players in English history, leading England to the 1990 World Cup semifinals while earning fifty-seven caps over ten years. He also starred for Newcastle, Tottenham, Lazio, Glasgow Rangers, and Middlesbrough, all the while making headlines for drinking, injuries, domestic abuse, a battle with the waistline, and bouts of depression.

Gazza was at his mischievous best in December 1995 as Rangers pounded Hibernian, 7–0. Referee Dougie Smith had dropped his yellow card as he and the players retreated for a goal kick, and the fastidious Gazza retrieved it. But as he returned it to Smith he first held it up, as if to caution the referee. Smith nodded, as if to say, "Okay, you've had your fun," accepted the card, then beckoned Gascoigne and showed *him* the yellow.

A costly joke for Gascoigne: that caution from Smith took Gazza over the limit for accumulated yellows, earning him a two-match suspension.

Reverse Angle Saves the Day for U.S. Ref

Never has a referee received so strange an exoneration after making a controversial call. Esse Baharmast, the lone American among the referees appointed to work the 1998 World Cup in France, was in the middle for Norway's 2–1 upset of eventual finalist Brazil in Marseilles, awarding an eighty-ninth-minute penalty kick to the Norwegians that Kjetil Rekdal converted for the winning margin.

TV replays appeared to show that Norway forward Tore André Flo took a dive in the penalty area following incidental contact with Brazil defender Junior Baiano during a corner kick. Baharmast was roasted by the press, and he became public enemy number one in Morocco, which would have advanced out of Group A with a Brazilian victory. It appeared that Baharmast had only reinforced the international view that U.S. referees were as clueless as their national team was weak.

But three days later, independent film crews and photographers stationed at field level and opposite the TV cameras provided proof that Baiano grabbed Flo's jersey and pulled him backward moments before the corner kick. Baharmast had no choice but to point to the penalty spot.

The video tape and photos of the incident probably spared Baharmast from being sent packing early by FIFA, which as a World Cup progresses dumps referees who receive poor marks. Instead, he went on to work the entertaining Group D match between Nigeria and Spain, becoming the first American to referee two World Cup games in the same tournament. He later served as fourth official for the Spain-Paraguay (Group D) and France-Paraguay (second round) matches.

A month after France '98, Baharmast, once expected to return home to Golden, Colorado, in disgrace, began his ride into the refereeing sunset with his appointment as the U.S. Soccer Federation's director of officials.

8 COACHES

*Players win games, coaches lose games, and referees ruin games, goes the
saying that undoubtedly was coined by a player. And it is true—at least
the part about coaches losing games. A soccer coach cannot call a time-out
or make unlimited substitutions, and some of the most brilliant plays executed by the players come not from a coach's tactics but from their creativity
and improvisation. Nevertheless, the coach is a lightning rod for criticism,
a nonmoving target for fans and journalists alike, and rare is the coach,
manager, or technical director who stays in one place for long. Hence, one
of the shortest chapters in this book.*

Nine Coaches in One Season

If you were coach of Esperance Zarzis, a club in southern Tunisia, at
any time during the 2002–3 season, you were also an ex-coach before long. Zarzis went through *nine* coaches—a rate of one a month—
including former Tunisian National Team boss Mrad Mahjoubi. Also
walking the plank during a midseason tailspin were the club president
and several board members.

Nearly as unforgiving was Olympique Beja, which hired and fired
seven coaches.

Thanks to those two clubs and the likes of Stade Tunisien (four coaches), the twelve-team Tunisian first division chewed up and spit out thirty-three coaches that season.

One Italian club owner so enjoyed sacking one coach in particular that he did it twice in a season. Luciano Spalletti, formerly coach of Empoli and Sampdoria, was hired by Venezia owner Maurizio Zamparini to coach his team for the 1999–2000 Serie A campaign, but he lasted only until November when Zamparini fired Spalletti and replaced him with Giuseppe Materazzi.

Three games later, however, the mercurial Zamparini changed his mind and replaced Materazzi with Spalletti.

Two months after that, Zamparini reversed course yet again and sacked Spalletti a second time.

Francesco Oddo was the Venezia boss's choice this time, but he was not up to the task as the team finished third to last and was relegated to Serie B.

Brazilian Club Hands the Reins to a Scribe

The love-hate relationship between coaches and journalists got turned on its head in September 1995 with the announcement by Brazilian powerhouse Flamengo, in the throes of a three-match losing skid, that it had replaced Coach Edinho with Washington Rodrigues, the dean of Rio radio commentators and a columnist for the daily *Jornal dos Sports*.

Even Flamengo president Kléber Leite, a former radio reporter and colleague of Rodrigues, called it "a crazy idea," and the media wasn't about to dispute it. "Flamengo Makes a Grandstand Play," sniffed Rodrigues's own paper, and the Rio daily *O Dia* dismissed the appointment as "Another Shot in the Dark." Perhaps the criticism was a bit restrained because Rodrigues took a three-month sabbatical to accept Leite's offer and intended to return to the microphone and keyboard when it was up.

Leite, of course, was only following the advice of Rodrigues, who suggested in print that Edinho be fired. (Rodrigues also had had little positive to write about Flamengo's star striker, mercurial 1994 World Cup hero Romário: With Romário, "no coach will fix Flamengo.")

The Brazilian soccer coaches association immediately filed suit in an attempt to bar the paunchy fifty-nine-year-old from taking the Flamengo helm, finding it absurd that Brazil's most popular and accomplished club, set to celebrate its centennial later that year, was in the hands of a man whose playing career had been limited to weekend pickup games.

Said ex-Brazilian National Team coach Sebastião Lazaroni, who had preceded Edinho as Flamengo boss, "I think that to be a soccer coach, you have to study and live the profession. I wouldn't dare be a journalist. How can Rodrigues dare be a coach?"

Countered Rodrigues, "Maybe I'm not a soccer coach, but I've been in the window for thirty-five years and I'm not dumb. I know how the band plays."

Another former Brazil coach, Telê Santana, found it amusing that the hunter was now the hunted. "He went from slingshot to plate glass window," quipped Santana, who was roasted by the Brazilian media for failing to guide the national team to glory at the 1982 and 1986 World Cups. "Now he will feel in his own skin how hard it is to be a soccer coach."

Rodrigues found out. Flamengo was 1-3-1 in the Brazilian national championship under Edinho and 4-6-8 with Rodrigues at the helm to finish twenty-first out of twenty-four teams. The following year, his successor, the well-traveled Joel Santana, guided the club to the Rio de Janeiro state title. As for Rodrigues, he eventually was elevated to Flamengo's director of soccer.

Rodrigues's stint was not unprecedented. In April 1922 Spain, prepped by a trio of journalists, dismantled France, 4–0, in a friendly in Bordeaux; three years later, one of them, José María Mateos, became the team's official manager. And BBC sportscaster and newspaperman George Allison, handed the reins of defending English champion Arsenal in 1934, promptly steered the Gunners to a second consecutive first-division title. Arsenal would win two more before Allison stepped down in 1947.

Guy Roux: Forty-four Years, Zero Pink Slips

The poster boy for coaching stability is Guy Roux, whose club, AJ Auxerre, represents the smallest market by far in the French first division, a city of fifty thousand souls situated on the banks of the Yonne River in Burgundy.

Roux, known as much for his uncanny eye for young talent as his quirky sense of humor, assumed the helm of the club—then mired in the fourth division—in 1961 at age twenty-three as player-coach and was still in charge more than two thousand matches later. It took the crusty Roux nineteen years to get Auxerre into the first division, and an additional thirteen years would pass before the club, founded in 1905, would earn its first honor, but team officials were as loyal to Roux as Roux was to Auxerre. After Auxerre hoisted the 1994 French Cup, a league-cup double followed in 1996, and the club took another French Cup in 2003. During this run, Auxerre made an appearance in the UEFA Champions League quarterfinals and one in the UEFA Cup semifinals.

Roux suffered a heart attack during an Auxerre training session in November 2001. He was rushed to a Paris hospital for bypass surgery and recovered to complete his thirty-ninth year in charge.

At the end of the 2004–5 season—his forty-fourth as boss—Roux announced he was stepping down, one day after leading Auxerre to its fourth French Cup. He couldn't leave well enough alone, however. In 2007, though beyond the mandatory retirement age for coaches in France, Roux, then sixty-eight, was offered the reins of RC Lens. With the backing of French president Nicolas Sarkozy, the league gave Roux special dispensation to return, but Lens stumbled and he retired for good two months into the season.

"If I had a striker who was nearly as good as the questions I was asked by journalists, we'd have won more games," said Roux.

Rudi Gutendorf: Seventeen National Teams, Zero Honors

The vagabond of all vagabonds among soccer coaches is Rudi Gutendorf, a German with an undistinguished playing career who set some sort of record by coaching seventeen different national teams—none of them Germany, West Germany, or East Germany.

Gutendorf hung up his shoes in 1953 while with TuS Neuendorf, took a coaching course under West German National Team boss Sepp Herberger the following year, and started coaching, beginning with Blue Stars Zurich (Switzerland) in 1955. He lasted a year there, then coached US Monastir (Tunisia) in 1961, VfB Stuttgart (West Germany) in 1965–66, and the St. Louis Stars (United States) in 1968.

Gutendorf was only getting warmed up. He began his international coaching career, first with Bermuda (1968) and followed by Chile

(1972–73), Bolivia (1974), Venezuela (1974), Trinidad and Tobago (1976), Grenada (1976), Antigua and Barbuda (1976), Botswana (1976), Australia (1979–81), New Caledonia (1981), Fiji (1981), Nepal (1981), Tonga (1981), Tanzania (1981), São Tomé and Principe (1984), Ghana (1985–86), Nepal again (1986), Fiji again (1987), China (1988), Iran under-23s (1988), China again (1991–92), Zimbabwe (1995–96), Mauritius (1997), and Rwanda (1999).

Between his hirings, firings, and resignations on the international level, Gutendorf coached a few other clubs, including Schalke 04 (West Germany) in 1968–70, Kickers Offenbach (West Germany) in 1970–71, Sporting Cristal (Peru) in 1971, 1860 Munich (West Germany) in 1974, Real Valladolid (Spain) in 1975, Fortuna Cologne (West Germany) in 1975–76, Hamburger sv (West Germany) in 1977, and Hertha Berlin (West Germany) in 1984.

Continents: six. Nations: twenty-seven. Longest stay: two years. Major honors won: none.

No Sympathy for Coach's Shorthanded Team

There is no such thing as a sick-out in soccer. During the 1997–98 English Premier League season, Bryan Robson, coach of Middlesbrough following a stellar career that included captaining England and Manchester United, unilaterally called off a December match against Blackburn Rovers, claiming that injuries and a flu bug had sidelined twenty-three of his players.

League officials were unimpressed and not only deducted three points from Middlesbrough in the standings but rescheduled the 'Boro-Blackburn match. Robson's team lost that game and, sure enough, at season's end Middlesbrough was relegated to the second tier by a single point.

The drop ended a bittersweet year for 'Boro, which had never won an honor since its founding in 1876. In March the club reached the English League Cup final and lost to Leicester City in a replay, and a week after the season ended, Robson's side lost to Chelsea, 2–0, in the English F.A. Cup final.

Despite the topsy-turvy campaign, Robson, handed a high-priced squad and under pressure to produce results, kept his job. Next season 'Boro won promotion back to the Premier League. It also nearly picked up its first trophy, losing to Chelsea in the English League Cup final.

German Coach Gets the Hook at Halftime

"Wait, I'm not finished!" could have been the cry of former West German National Team goalkeeper Harald "Toni" Schumacher, who was fired as coach of Fortuna Cologne in December 1999 during halftime of the team's German second-division match against Waldhof Mannheim.

After the Cologne squad trudged into the dressing room at halftime, down 2–0, Fortuna club president Jean Loering poked his head inside and told Schumacher to leave—now.

"I had hesitated from firing him for quite some time," Loering said later, "but I had to do it then. I idolized Schumacher as a player, but I am not going to sit on my hands while he takes my club to the grave."

Schumacher, perhaps best known for his brutal collision with (make that assault on) France's Patrick Battiston in a 1982 World Cup semifinal (Battiston nearly died and was hospitalized for months), stormed out of the stadium. Assistant coach Ralf Minge took over on the spot, but he couldn't prevent Mannheim from rolling to a 5–1 victory.

And while Fortuna Cologna didn't go to the grave, as Loering had feared, at season's end it did slide into the third division.

Sometimes, however, this sort of thing works.

During a Swiss Cup match played in October 2006, FC Sion, which had recently been eliminated from the UEFA Cup, was losing, 1–0, at FC La Chaux-de-Fonds. So at halftime, coach Nestor Clausen quit. Thus energized, Sion stormed back to win, 3–1.

If it was intended to be a ploy to inspire his side, it blew up in the former Argentine star's face. Club president Christian Constantin officially accepted the coach's resignation after the match. Marco Schaellibaum was named Clausen's successor, marking the twenty-second coaching change in Constantin's first eight years as Sion chief executive. Clausen had lasted four months at the Sion helm; Schaellibaum would survive for forty-six days.

Real Madrid Coach Can't Get Substitutions Right

Jorge Valdano was an outstanding player. Once a graceful midfielder, he is perhaps best known for the goal he scored in Argentina's 3–2 triumph over West Germany in the 1986 World Cup final. Later, Valdano proved himself a sharp administrator: as Real Madrid sports director he engineered the $41 million deal that brought Manchester United star David Beckham to Real in 2003.

But as a coach . . .

Valdano was coach of Real Madrid early in the 1994–95 Spanish first-division season when he found himself in a bit of trouble during a match against lowly Compostela. He already had Michael Laudrup of Denmark, Fernando Redondo of Argentina, and Ivan Zamorano of Chile on the field when he substituted in Petr Dubovský of Slovakia in the eightieth minute. At the time, however, Spanish league rules allowed only three foreigners on the field per side. Valdano discovered the error and pulled Dubovský off the field. Real Madrid played with ten men for the last eight minutes and survived with a 1–1 tie.

Valdano later was suspended for a month for the gaffe, but he won an appeal and was instead ordered to pay an $800 fine.

His arithmetic hadn't improved three years later, however. At that time, as coach of another major Spanish club, Valencia, Valdano again lost track of his players. League rules this time allowed four foreigners, but Valdano inserted a fifth, Brazilian international Marcelinho Carioca, in the sixty-second minute of a match against Racing Santander. It took the referee two minutes to spot the error, and he ordered Valdano to remove one of the five imports. The ten-man Valencia went on to lose, 2–1.

Brazilian Coach Honored for Not Quitting

In 2003 the Brazilian national championship was in fine form, averaging one coaching change a week, thus maintaining a tradition long ago dubbed "the Dance of the Coaches." In June, however, one man bucked the trend.

Abel Braga was presented by his club with a silver plaque for deciding to see out the season with Ponte Preta, which was next to last in the twenty-four-club Brazilian national championship. Braga, who at that point had coached eighteen different clubs (never staying more than two seasons with any of them) was honored after turning down an offer to coach the more prestigious Gremio.

Ironically, Ponte Preta went on to finish tied with Gremio for twentieth place, and Braga's club would have ended up tied for eighteenth had it not used an ineligible player in two matches. Braga then left for greener pastures, coaching Flamengo to the Rio state crown in 2004 and doing the same for crosstown rival Fluminense the following season.

Braga certainly showed more commitment than Marius Lacatus. In February 2004 the former Romanian National Team forward agreed one evening to a two-and-a-half-year contract to replace the fired Nicolo Napoli as coach of Universitatea Craiova. But when Lacatus arrived the next morning at the site of the press conference called to officially announce his hiring, he was headed off by about thirty Universitatea fans, enraged that their club would hire as coach a man who made his name as a player for bitter crosstown rival Steaua Bucharest.

Not only did the fans decorate the building with anti-Lacatus slogans but they also jostled and spat on their team's would-be field boss. Lacatus got the message and beat a hasty retreat without signing on the dotted line.

Weeks later, Lacatus signed a six-month deal to coach Ceahlaul Piatra Neamt, a club at the bottom of the first division with no apparent rivals.

As for the luckless Universitatea brass, they quickly hired ex-Romania goalkeeper Silviu Lung as coach and appointed Nicolo Napoli as assistant. Napoli had been dismissed earlier as Universitatea's top man when the club learned that his training failed to meet minimum coaching standards.

Mystery Motorist Revealed

Portsmouth was playing Havant and Waterlooville in a friendly prior to the 2003–4 English season when the public address announcer informed the crowd that a car parked illegally outside the stadium would be towed if it wasn't promptly moved.

The crowd of three thousand roared as the culprit dashed out of the stadium: Portsmouth coach Harry Redknapp.

Redknapp was just slightly less red-faced than a certain local radio personality who in October 2007 was serving as public address announcer for the Irish League Cup final between host Derry City and Bohemians FC. During the match Mark Patterson was given a note about a car blocking an entrance, and for a half hour the P.A. man read the notice repeatedly without a response from the Brandywell Road crowd . . . until he realized that the car registration number in the note belonged to his own vehicle.

Coach Wolf Wolf of Wolf

The unofficial title of World's Most Appropriately Named Coach was held from 1998 to 2003 by Wolfgang Wolf.

His club, of course, was VfL Wolfsburg of Germany.

Coach Gets Midseason Bonus for Winning Romanian Title

Just how confident are you that your team will cross the finish line first after opening a big lead at midseason?

In December 2006, to the board of FC Dinamo 1948 Bucharest, it was elementary: reward coach Mircea Rednic now for winning the Romanian championship, six months before the season's end. After all, Dinamo's record was 17-1-1, good for a robust thirteen-point lead over second-place Steaua Bucharest.

Rednic was given an early Christmas present—$50,000 of the $100,000 bonus promised him for steering Dinamo to its eighteenth Romanian crown.

The coach was not nearly as cocksure as the board. "I've told the major shareholders that I'm investing it all as soon as I can. It won't be possible to return it."

No need. The following May, Dinamo tied host Politehnica Iasi, 1–1, to take an insurmountable thirteen-point lead over runner-up CFR Cluj with four rounds remaining. And Dinamo did it without much charity from the referees: Romanian scoring champ Claudiu Niculescu produced the Dinamo goal after his side was awarded a penalty kick—its very first PK of the season.

Spanish Boss Takes a Hike in Honor of Big Win

Many is the time a player has wished he could tell his coach to take a hike. Rare is the coach who has volunteered to do so. Javier Irureta is one such man.

Irureta's Deportivo La Coruña was in a deep hole in late March 2004 after losing at AC Milan, 4–1, in the first leg of the UEFA Champions League quarterfinals.

"If we beat Milan . . . I will do the Pilgrims Walk between La Coruña and Santiago de Compostela, on my knees if I have to," vowed the coach before the second leg.

Deportivo not only won the match but did so by a 4–0 margin, allowing the Spanish club to advance to the semifinals via a 5–4 aggregate.

La Coruña was eliminated in the semifinals by eventual champ FC Porto, 0–0 and 1–0, but in May, Irureta made good on his promise. Accompanied by his assistant coaches and team trainer, he covered the forty-three and a half miles—on his feet—in eight hours.

"Five or six of our players wouldn't have been able to stomach this walk," the coach quipped, "but I won't let on who they are."

German Study: Don't Bother Firing the Coach

The team is in a dreadful skid and there is no evidence that it will pull out of it anytime soon, so the coach is fired. Only one problem with that perceived panacea, however: according to a German study, it usually doesn't improve things.

A research team from the University of Münster's Institute of Sports Science analyzed the aftermath of 206 coaching changes in the German Bundesliga from its first season in 1963 through 1998 and found that the good times usually last for no more than three to four matches. The study, presented at a September 2003 congress of sports scientists in Münster, plotted the fortunes of clubs twelve games before and twelve games after a coaching change. It also examined whether sacking a coach helped a struggling team escape relegation. Nearly 60 percent of those teams with new coaches ended the season with a drop to the second division. Of the clubs one notch below in the standings that stood by their man at the time of their rival's coaching change, about 52 percent ultimately went down; of the clubs a spot above that remained loyal, just 37 percent dropped.

The study was close to the heart of one of its two authors. Alexandra Tippenhauer is the daughter of Hans-Dieter Tippenhauer, who was fired as coach of Arminia Bielefeld in November 1980 with the club in the Bundesliga cellar. Under Tippenhauer's replacement, Horst Franz, Arminia finished fourth from the bottom to avoid relegation.

Dutch Fans Happy to Pay for Coach to Go Away

Hit the road, Dick.

Dutch fans from Amsterdam to the Hague burned the national flag and hurled bottles and stones at police after Holland turned an early 2–0 lead over the Czech Republic into a 3–2 defeat in Aveiro, Portugal, in the opening round of the 2004 European Championship.

Many blamed the result on coach Dick Advocaat, who removed star forward Arjen Robben with his side leading, 2–1, and replaced him with defensive midfielder Paul Bosvelt. The daily *De Telegraaf* laid the loss at the feet of Advocaat with the headline, "Wrong Substitution Cost Victory," and many of his own players agreed.

Some Dutchmen flailed away blindly. In Veenendaal, fans burned team memorabilia in a bonfire in the town square. An Apeldoorn man uprooted traffic signs. A Web site devoted to "the worst substitution of all time" was created.

But a group of disappointed Holland supporters following the team in Portugal took concrete action. In all of three minutes they pooled the $197 necessary to book a Virgin Express flight for Advocaat from Faro to Brussels in the hopes that the embattled coach would leave Portugal the day before Holland's final group match against Latvia.

"We will give him the ticket through room service at his hotel," said ringleader Johan de Laat. "All he needs is his passport. He doesn't have to come back to the Netherlands."

Much to the dismay of de Laat and his compatriots, the ticket went unclaimed. And the 5'7" Advocaat, known unaffectionately back home as "the Little General," briefly turned Dutch frowns upside down as his team recovered and reached the semifinals. The Dutch, however, lost to Portugal, 2–1, and Advocaat quit two days later, blaming the criticism heaped on him throughout the tournament.

Advocaat later admitted his controversial substitution was a mistake.

Press Ignores New President to Interview New Coach

Coaches may be a punching bag for fans and media, but in soccer-mad countries it's clear that the head of the team is more important than the mere head of the government.

In April 1973 Istanbul giant Fenerbahçe caused a minor sensation when it signed Didí, considered by many the finest player at the 1958 World Cup, as its technical advisor. When the Brazilian arrived at Istanbul's airport, he was engulfed by a mob of local journalists. That allowed Turkey's newly elected president, Fahri Koruturk, to disembark the same plane virtually unnoticed.

During Didí's two-season tenure as Fenerbahçe boss, the club won its tenth and eleventh Turkish league championships. Koruturk, Turkey's sixth president, served his seven-year term with considerably fewer highlights.

Koruturk took his snub much better than did another chief executive. In September 2007 Santana Lopes, the former prime minister of Portugal, was being interviewed live in a Portuguese television studio when the station cut away to the arrival at the Lisbon airport of high-profile coach José Mourinho, who was returning home after being dismissed by English power Chelsea.

"This country is going crazy," fumed Lopes after he stalked out of the studio. "With all due respect, I am not going ahead with the interview. People have to learn."

God created me to delight
people with my goals.
Brazilian striker **ROMÁRIO**

9 SUPERLATIVES

*Of the many criticisms leveled at soccer by American pundits is the indif-
ference shown by those in the sport to statistics. Numbers are all well
and good, but numbers cannot tell the story of such a free-flowing sport.
Still, sometimes, when a remarkable thing happens in a match, someone
with a calculator or measuring stick records it.*

Fast Goals and Other Feats

Little did the International Football Association Board, soccer's official rule-making body, know in 1997 when it tinkered with Law
VIII ("The Start and Restart of Play") that it would allow one of the
game's quirkier records to be shaved to the nub.

The board, made up of four FIFA representatives and one each
from England, Scotland, Wales, and Northern Ireland (in recognition of Britain as the home of modern soccer), decided at its annual meeting to allow a goal to be scored directly from the kickoff.
No longer was an anxious player required to first have a teammate
touch the ball forward before it could be blasted toward the net. It
also declared the ball in play when it was kicked and moved forward,
dumping the stipulation that it be touched one complete revolution
before it could be played by another player.

Until then, one of the fastest goals scored was by Adelaide City's
Damian Mori—3.69 seconds—in an Australian league match in
December 1994.

Not quite so fast—unofficially—was the strike by 1970 World Cup hero Roberto Rivelino. In August 1974 Rivelino, preparing to kick off the second half for Corinthians in a São Paulo state championship game at Parque São Jorge against lowly Rio Preto EC, spied the opposing goalkeeper, Pirangi, on his knees in his goalmouth, engaged in his customary prewhistle prayer. The ball was touched to Rivelino, who used his vaunted left foot to blast a shot from the halfway line past the bowed head of the devout-but-oblivious Pirangi and into the Rio Preto net.

A year after the 1997 rule change, the Guinness World Record for fastest goal was chopped to 2.8 seconds by Ricardo Olivera in a match in Argentina. That mark survived the efforts of rapid-fire challengers worldwide until May 2004, when an amateur player in England scored in just 2.5 seconds.

Marc Burrows of Cowes Sports took advantage of a fortuitous tail wind to score the first of his three goals that day. "The wind was so strong I thought it was worth a go," said Burrows, whose lightning strike was confirmed by the English F.A. based on the match report by referee John Sorrell. "The ball just sailed over their poor 'keeper. I was so stunned I didn't really celebrate. I just put my hands in the air and burst out laughing."

The fastest hat trick ever scored is believed to have been produced by center forward Eduardo Andres Maglioni, who in March 1973 exploded for three goals in just one minute, fifty-one seconds in Independiente's 4–0 rout of Gimnasia y Esgrima in an Argentine match. Independiente was leading, 1–0, on a goal by Uruguayan defender Ricardo Pavoni when Maglioni humbled Gimnasia goalkeeper Gurruciaga early in the second half.

The fastest hat trick not witnessed by the scorer's two biggest fans was scored in February 2004 by Bournemouth's James Hayter in an English second-division game against visiting Wrexham. Hayter's parents patiently waited through the first eighty minutes of the match in hopes of seeing their son play. The twenty-four-year-old striker, however, remained affixed to the Cherries' bench and with Bournemouth sitting on a 3–0 lead, the Hayters made their way out of Dean Court Ground.

Three minutes later Hayter entered the match and scored in the eighty-fifth, eighty-sixth, and eighty-eighth minutes—three goals in two minutes, twenty seconds for the fastest hat trick in English history.

Hayter's explosion topped the record for fastest international treble shared by a trio of players who each accomplished their feat in about four minutes. Abdel Hamid was the latest, helping Egypt crush Namibia, 8–2, in July 2001 in a World Cup qualifier. Japan striker Masashi Nakayama (versus Brunei in 2000) and Mexico's Dionisio Mejia (versus Cuba in 1934) also bagged three in four minutes.

Just who has scored the longest goal in soccer history is unknown, but goalkeeper Yuri Zhevnov of the Belarus club FC BATE Borisov would be a good candidate.

BATE was playing host to Dinamo Tbilisi of Georgia in the first leg of the 2004–5 UEFA Cup's first qualifying round when, in the fifteenth minute, Zhevnov rushed off his line to boot a ball out of danger. Zhevnov's thunderous clearance landed in front of Dinamo 'keeper Irakli Zoidze, took a wicked hop over his head, and landed in the Tbilisi net, in all a journey of some eighty-four yards.

Despite the miraculous strike from its most unlikely source, BATE lost, 3–2, then dropped the Tbilisi leg, 1–0, and was eliminated. Zhevnov, however, had his goal, which was the first—and most certainly the last—of his career.

Zhevnov was only following in the footsteps of fellow goalkeeper Pat Jennings. In August 1967 the Northern Ireland legend scored the opening goal of Tottenham's 3–3 draw with Manchester United in the Charity Shield, the traditional curtain-raiser to the English season. With eight minutes gone, Jennings boomed a punt out of his area and watched as the ball bounced over United 'keeper Alex Stepney before nestling in the net. Estimated distance: ninety yards.

Juggling the Length of a Marathon Course

Cuba isn't known for its soccer, but one Cuban holds a record that isn't likely to be broken any time soon—at least not by anyone sane.

In 1999 Eric Hernandez completed a marathon in seven hours, twelve minutes, but he had an excuse for his rather pokey time: Hernandez was juggling a soccer ball the whole way.

That's just more than twenty-six miles while keeping a ball in the air with feet, thighs, chest, and head, and he didn't let the ball hit the ground once.

Perhaps as amazing as Hernandez's feat was the fact that he broke a record in pulling it off. The previous best in juggling through a marathon course was set in July 1990 in Prague by Dr. Jan Skorkovský of Czechoslovakia, who did so in seven hours . . . eighteen minutes.

At last count, the high exalted master of soccer jugglers was Nikolai Kutsenko of Ukraine, who in December 1995 kept a ball aloft for twenty-four hours, thirty minutes. The greatest challenge to Kutsenko's mark came eight years later from a Brazilian, Martinho Eduardo Orige, who lasted nineteen and a half hours. A mere piker by comparison was perhaps the first juggler of note, the Swiss Kurt Rothenfluh and his 1983 record, a paltry six hours, forty minutes (105,400 consecutive touches).

And don't assume that juggling insanity afflicts just the odd individual. In April 2002 Juan Carlos and Jose Antonio Figueroa Wong of Peru both caught the bug and set a bizarre record by heading a ball back and forth over nineteen kilometers—nearly twelve miles—without a single miscue. A year and a half later, Agim Agushi and Bujar Ajeti of Serbia exchanged headers for four hours, two minutes (11,111 touches), in Germany.

In this business, however, two heads aren't better than one. In May 1996 Goderdzi Makharadze, a twenty-eight-year-old student who was living in a Tbilisi box car because he had lost his dormitory room, headed a ball for eight hours, twelve minutes. Ultimately, all it got Makharadze was second place in the world of heading to Tomas Lundman of Sweden and his 2004 milestone of eight hours, thirty-two minutes.

Other juggling milestones:

- Ricardo Silva Neves of Brazil juggled a ball while walking 448 miles over twelve days, ending his trek in the capital, Brasilia, in June 1992.
- Manfred Wagner of Switzerland combined the one-hundred-meter dash and juggling and was clocked at 15.9 seconds, in July 1996.
- Abraham Munoz of the United States was juggling when he cov-

ered two hundred meters in 40.26 seconds, in October 2000. Munoz also juggled for one hour, nineteen minutes while running up and down stairs, covering 2,754 steps, in December 2002.

• And the ultimate in juggling insanity: the Serbian Agushi drove a car for more than four miles while heading a ball through the sunroof, in August 2004.

Thirteen-year-old Professionals

No official records exist, so it's difficult to determine the youngest pro player in soccer history. But thirteen seems to be the threshold.

One candidate is Fernando Garcia Lopez, only thirteen and a secondary school student who was believed by FIFA to be the youngest pro ever, making his debut for Juan Aurich de Chiclayo in a Peruvian league match against Estudiantes de Medicina in May 2001.

Another is Dmitry Kudryashov, age thirteen, who in May 1997 nearly became the youngest player to score in a Russian Cup match when his goal was disallowed.

Kudryashov, a member of the Russian national under-15 team, came on as a substitute with his second-division club, Zenit Izhevsk, trailing the third division's Elektron Vyatskiye, 1–0. Kudryashov got off a last-minute shot but the referee ruled that the ball did not go into the goal. His coach later claimed that the referee did not want the match to go into overtime.

In dispute is the feat of Souleymane Mamam, who was listed as thirteen when he played for Togo against Zambia in May 2001, thus becoming the youngest player ever in a World Cup qualifier. While FIFA recognized the teenage midfielder's birth date as June 30, 1987, his Belgian club, Royal Antwerp, listed it as June 20, 1985.

Lopez, Kudryashov, and Mamam were indeed early bloomers, but none burst onto the scene quite like Freddy Adu, the Ghana-born, U.S.-reared prodigy who at age thirteen signed a $1 million endorsement deal with Nike in 2003 even though he would not play his first professional match for more than a year. The Nike agreement came shortly after a series of dazzling performances by Adu for the United States at the FIFA Under-17 World Championship in Finland. Three months later he was a late call-up to the U.S. National Under-20 Team and played in the FIFA World Youth Championship in the United

Arab Emirates, becoming the youngest player ever to appear in that competition.

Still, Adu the professional had no pro club. That finally changed in December 2003 when Major League Soccer signed him to a multiyear contract that paid him a league-record $500,000 a year and assigned him to DC United so he could play close to his Potomac, Maryland, home. Adu made his pro debut that April in United's '04 season opener against the San Jose Earthquakes before a national TV audience, becoming—at fourteen years, ten months, and one day—the youngest person to play for a major U.S. professional team since a kid named Fred Chapman pitched for the Philadelphia Athletics of the American Association in 1887.

MLS was counting on Adu to outdo Chapman, who, at fourteen years, seven months, and twenty-nine days, saw his pro baseball career begin and end with one abbreviated start in which he gave up six runs and eight hits for a lifetime ERA of 7.20. Adu did indeed outdo Chapman as he contributed a respectable five goals and three assists while appearing, mostly as a substitute, in all thirty of his team's games. And he was on the field when DC United defeated the Kansas City Wizards, 3–2, in Los Angeles in the 2004 MLS final to capture its fourth league championship in the league's nine-year history. But at the all-important turnstile, Adu proved to be a bargain for MLS as "Freddy Mania" helped United lead the league in road attendance, averaging 23,686 fans for fifteen games, more than 8,000 better than the league-wide average.

Showing a level of maturity that prompted some to wonder just how old this kid was, Adu handled his newfound celebrity with aplomb. Adu appeared on *60 Minutes* and *Late Night with David Letterman*, filmed a soft-drink commercial with Pelé, and rubbed shoulders with the likes of David Bowie, Robert Duvall, Shaquille O'Neal, and U.S. Attorney General John Ashcroft. He also signed several other endorsement deals and still had time to finish high school through an accelerated program at a sports academy in Florida.

Adu's signing proved to be a double-edged sword for MLS, which reaped a publicity bonanza but was accused in some quarters of exploiting a child. That knock faded and after Adu was traded to Real Salt Lake prior to the 2007 season, he was sold that summer to Portuguese power Benfica for $2 million.

For uproar over child exploitation, however, nothing concerning Adu approached the storm created by the nine-minute appearance of striker Mauricio Baldivieso, age twelve years, eleven months, and twenty-eight days, in a July 2009 Bolivian match between Aurora of Cochabamba and host La Paz FC.

Aurora coach Julio César Baldivieso, who played for Bolivia at the 1994 World Cup, sent his son on despite a 1-0 deficit. Within minutes Mauricio was chopped down from behind by La Paz defender Henry Alaca; after writhing in pain, the youngster received medical treatment, dried his tears, and finished the match.

The elder Baldivieso wasn't as fortunate: two days after Mauricio's thirteenth birthday, Julio César, who had guided Aurora to a league title the previous year, was forced out by club directors.

Iceland's Father-Son International Duo

History was made in April 1996 when Arnor Gudjohnsen, age thirty-five, and his son, Eldur-Smari Gudjohnsen, age seventeen, played in Iceland's 3–0 victory over Estonia in a friendly in Tallinn.

The Gudjohnsens, however, did not become the first father and son to play together in an international: Eldur-Smari came on as a substitute for his father in the sixty-second minute.

A Red, White, and Blue Bro/Sis

The United States boasts the most-capped brother-sister combo in international soccer history. It recalls, however, the baseball record for career home runs hit by two brothers held by the Aarons (Tommie, 13; Hank, 755).

Eric Biefeld, a standout defender at UCLA from Huntington Beach, California, made two appearances for the U.S. National Team in 1986, in a 0–0 tie with Canada and a 1–1 draw with Uruguay, both in Miami.

Younger sister Joy, also a defender, made her debut with the U.S. National Women's Team the following year, playing in seven international matches as a UC–Berkeley freshman.

But that was only the beginning for Joy. Better known by her married name, Fawcett, Eric's little sister went on to help the United States win the 1991 and 1999 Women's World Cups and the 1996 and 2004 women's Olympic gold medals. The mother of three (making her the ultimate soccer mom) earned her two hundredth cap in 2002 at age thirty-four, becoming the fourth player in the world to reach that milestone. Now a member of the National Soccer Hall of Fame, she retired at age thirty-six after the 2004 Athens Olympics with 239 caps.

That left the Biefeld family at a combined 241 international appearances . . . and counting?

Perfection from the Penalty Spot

A penalty kick is said to be a 90 percent proposition in favor of the shooter, but two English amateur teams turned the shot into a 100 percenter when they converted all thirty-four of their PK attempts during a December 2002 tiebreaker.

Storthes Hall and host Littletown had to abandon their West Riding Amateur League Cup match because of darkness with the PK duel tied at 17–17.

Littletown was leading, 1–0, in the eighty-ninth minute when the visitors equalized, sending the game to overtime and, ultimately, penalties. With darkness falling, spectators trained their car headlights on the field to keep the match going.

In the replay January 26, Storthes Hall brought the struggle to a merciful end with a 2–1 victory.

According to the *Guinness Book of Records*, the previous mark for a PK tiebreaker—in Britain, at least—was twenty-eight tries, set in 1987 in a Freight Rover Trophy Southern Section quarterfinal between Fulham and Aldershot.

The rest of the world is another matter. In January 2005 KK Palace and Civics needed forty-eight penalty kicks to decide their Namibian Cup match in Tsumeb. KK Palace prevailed, 17–16, to move to the second round. Fortunately for the two sides, which were tied, 2–2, after ninety minutes, no overtime was played and they went straight to penalties.

That broke the record set in Buenos Aires in November 1988, during a season in which the Argentine Primera Division experimented with PKs as a way to eliminate draws, awarding a winner in regulation the customary three points but giving a PK winner two points and a PK loser one. Argentinos Juniors and Racing Club deadlocked, 2–2, and then shot forty-four times from the spot before Argentinos won, 20–19. The crowd at Estadio Ricardo Etcheverry was on pins and needles for the first few kicks, but before long tension turned to boredom, and only a smattering of fans were on hand to see Argentinos Juniors claim their extra point.

The European record for longest tiebreaker among top-level clubs is the thirty-four PKS it took to separate Turkish rivals Genclerbirligi and Istanbul power Galatasaray following a 1–1 draw in a November 1996 cup match. Thirty-three attempts found the net as Genclerbirligi won, 17–16.

A dozen years later, Genclerbirligi was at it again, this time in the Turkish Cup final. The Ankara side played Kayserispor to a scoreless tie, then lost a twenty-eight-round tiebreaker, 11–10.

Northern Ireland's Long National Team Nightmare

Northern Ireland is the birthplace of George Best, the Manchester United genius who spent the 1960s and early '70s tormenting opposing defenders and goalkeepers with his skill and imagination.

Four decades later, the Northern Irish probably would have been keen to pull Best—then fifty-seven years old and still engaged in his losing battle with John Barleycorn—out of retirement if it would have helped end a nightmare.

A 1,298-minute goal-less nightmare.

By the time Northern Ireland completed its dismal 0-5-3 run through the qualifiers for the 2004 European Championship with a 1–0 upset loss to Armenia, it had gone twelve games without scoring, a European record. That's 1,152 minutes, or about nineteen hours, of offensive futility.

The goal-scoring drought claimed coach Sammy McIllroy, who was replaced by Lawrie Sanchez with the skid at 1,242 minutes. But Sanchez broke the spell in his very first game, a friendly against Norway in February 2004 in Belfast. In the fifty-sixth minute, striker David Healy—the last player to score for the Northern Irish, back in October 2001—headed Keith Gillespie's cross into the net, leaving the twelve thousand brave souls at Windsor Park in euphoria.

It was not an entirely successful day for the Northern Irish, however. By going the first half hour without a goal they set what was believed to be a new world record for futility at 1,272 minutes, or about twenty-one hours. Norway won the match easily, 4–1, leaving the hosts winless in sixteen straight games. And Gillespie helped seal the Norwegian victory by scoring an own goal less than a minute after Healy's strike.

Six weeks later, Northern Ireland defeated Estonia, 1–0, in Tallinn. And no, it wasn't through an own goal. Healy, on what by Northern Irish standards would be a hot streak, scored the winner from the penalty spot.

The Smallest of Minnows

On June 30, 2002, while Brazil was beating Germany, 2–0, in the World Cup final in Yokohama, Japan, a match of quite another sort was being played hundreds of miles away in Thimphu, Bhutan. There, at Changlimithang Stadium, the two worst national teams on the planet, according to the monthly FIFA World Rankings, squared off in a friendly.

The pairing of Bhutan, ranked No. 202, and Montserrat, ranked No. 203, was the brainchild of two Dutch filmmakers, who shot the Himalayan showdown for a documentary they called *The Other Final.*

Fittingly, Bhutan, the world's next-to-worst team, routed Montserrat, 4–0.

The Montserratian team, a collection of office clerks, police officers, and construction workers, could be excused for their defeat, however. The tiny Caribbean island nation, population 7,600, had joined FIFA only six years earlier. The Montserrat Football Association had only 150 registered adult players, four clubs, and two referees.

And as if the British protectorate had nothing to worry about but its standing in world soccer, Montserrat was still recovering from the 1995 eruption of the Soufriere Hills volcano. One of seven active volcanoes on Montserrat, Soufriere wiped out a third of the island, displacing thousands, several national team members among them. Years later, team practices were still interrupted frequently so that players could wipe the volcanic ash from their eyes.

Law's Double Hat Trick Is All for Naught

The most productive day of your soccer-playing life, and it counts for nothing. So it went for Scottish legend Denis Law after his Manchester City side fell behind to Luton Town, 2–0, after seventeen rainy minutes in the fourth round of the 1960–61 English F.A. Cup.

Law, who would go on to greater fame across town with Manchester United, took matters into his own hands and fired home *six* goals—a double hat trick—over the next fifty minutes. But the field became impossibly muddy, and in the sixty-ninth minute referee Ken Tuck brought the slipping and sliding to a halt by abandoning the match. That wiped out Law's half-dozen explosion and forced a replay, which Luton won, 3–1, to advance to the fifth round. The Manchester City goal that day was scored, of course, by Law.

Most players would rather have a hat trick that counts, so Law might have been jealous of the tear Masashi Nakayama of Jubilo Iwata went on in April 1998. The veteran Japanese international striker scored a hat trick—at least—in four consecutive J-League matches: five goals at Cerezo Osaka, four versus Sanfrecce Hiroshima, four at Avispa Kukuoka, and a paltry three versus Consadole Sapporo.

Twins, Times Two

Fans at a Women's United Soccer Association match in 2002 were seeing double-double as twin sisters Jacqui and Skylar Little and the Washington Freedom defeated twins Nancy and Julie Augustyniak and the Atlanta Beat, 1–0.

The league, founded in 2000 and shut down after its 2003 season, boasted clubs in eight major U.S. markets. It also boasted two other sets of twins: U.S. international Lorrie Fair (Philadelphia Charge) and sister Ronnie (New York Power) and the duo of Margaret Tietjen (San Diego Spirit) and Jennifer Tietjen (Philadelphia Charge).

Deux Own Goals

The stars appeared to be perfectly aligned for South Africa defender Pierre Issa in June 1998. Not only was his nation playing the first World Cup game in its history but it also was scheduled to face host and eventual champion France at the Stade Velodrome, the home of Issa's club, Olympique Marseille.

But the stars lied. Issa deflected a shot by France's Youri Djorkaeff past South Africa goalkeeper Hans Vonk and into his own net in the seventy-seventh minute and did it again on Thierry Henry's shot in the closing moments. The matching set of own goals turned a 1–0 South African deficit into a comfortable 3–0 French victory.

Some small consolation for Issa: rather than leave the South African as the only player to score twice into his own net in a World Cup match, officials later credited the second goal to Henry.

Five Games, One Result

Here's why tied games in single-elimination competitions are decided by penalty kicks.

In the original format of the English Football Association Cup, the world's oldest knockout team competition, a drawn match was settled by a replay. Ninety minutes and no winner? Play another ninety. Still tied? Play another ninety. And so on.

Under this system, the loser couldn't complain that it was robbed in overtime or was unlucky during a penalty-kick tiebreaker.

Sometimes, however, the notion of the replay doesn't seem so quaint. In the fourth round of the 1971 English F.A. Cup, Alvechurch and Oxford City played five draws—2–2, 1–1, 1–1, 0–0, and 0–0—before Alvechurch prevailed, 1–0. That's nine hours of soccer to get one result.

The F.A. Cup format has since been modified. If the first replay ends in a tie, the contest is settled through thirty minutes of overtime and, if necessary, mercifully, PKs.

The Veteran and the Rookie, Side by Side

During the 1994 World Cup one could only wonder what teammates Rigobert Song and Roger Milla possibly had in common, except that they both wore the Cameroon jersey. When the Indomitable Lions faced Russia in the first round at Stanford Stadium, Song was just seventeen years old while Milla was forty-two, having appeared in his first World Cup when Song was five.

The match, a 6–1 Russian rout, was forgettable for Cameroon except for Milla's goal two minutes into the second half, making him the oldest player to score in a World Cup.

The biggest age difference among world champion players involved Italy, whose lineup ranged from forty-year-old captain, goalkeeper Dino Zoff, to eighteen-year-old defender Giuseppe Bergomi. Man and boy both accepted winner's medals after helping the Azzurri beat West Germany, 3–1, in the 1982 World Cup final in Madrid.

On the other hand, the coach of Argentina's 1930 World Cup

squad, Juan José Tramutola, could no doubt easily relate with his charges. At twenty-seven, Tramutola, the youngest World Cup team boss ever, was younger than seven of his twenty-two players. The oldest was thirty.

Australia 31 (or was it 32?), American Samoa 0

Soccer's Oceania confederation has long been regarded as Australia, New Zealand, and the ten Dwarves, an awkwardly drawn region in which the Socceroos and Kiwis regularly beat up on Fiji, Tahiti, Papua New Guinea, Samoa, American Samoa, Tonga, Vanuatu, New Caledonia, the Cook Islands, and the Solomon Islands.

The Australians were at their most Goliath-like, relatively speaking, at Coffs Harbour in April 2001 in the Oceania Group I qualifiers for the 2002 World Cup.

The first victim was Tonga, which was dismantled 22–0, but the Socceroos were only getting warmed up. Two days later they crushed American Samoa by an amazing 31–0, giving Australia fifty-three goals in two games.

Or was it fifty-four goals? So overwhelming was the victory over American Samoa that the fellow running the scoreboard lost count. The final result wasn't confirmed until FIFA received the referee's official report (it was indeed 31–0).

Aussie striker Archie Thompson set a world record for goals in an international game with thirteen, and David Zdrillic added eight. The previous mark for goals in an international was first established by Denmark's Spohus Nielson, who scored ten against France in a 17–1 rout in the 1908 London Olympics; Gottfried Fuchs of Germany equaled that feat in the 1912 Stockholm Games as Czarist Russia was humbled, 16–0, in a consolation match.

Eight of Thompson's goals came before halftime, helping Australia, ranked No. 77 in the world at the time, to take a 16–0 lead over a country that was No. 203 and dead last.

The squad sent to Coffs Harbour by American Samoa probably deserved a much lower rating, if that was possible. All but a couple members of American Samoa's original roster were ruled ineligible on the eve of the qualifying tournament because they did not have proper passports. As a result, coach Tunoa Lui was forced to scrape together a squad whose average age was nineteen. His youngest player was fifteen. In addition to the Aussie debacle, Lui's selection was forced to endure losses of 13–0 to Fiji, 8–0 to Samoa, and 5–0 to Tonga. That's no goals scored and fifty-seven allowed in four games.

The Australian romp over American Samoa shattered the record for winning margin in a World Cup qualifier, which had been established in the Socceroos' twenty-two-goal rout of Tonga. The previous mark had been set just five months earlier by Iran, which had flattened Guam, 19–0, in Tabriz. It also topped an unconfirmed 1966 match between Libya and Oman won by the Libyans, 21–0, and a qualifier for the 2000 Asian Cup in which Kuwait stomped Bhutan, 20–0, as well as China's 19–0 romp over Guam a month earlier in the same competition.

Against Tonga, Socceroo marksman Thompson, inserted in the seventy-fourth minute, scored only once—his first as an international. He replaced John Aloisi, who was no doubt exhausted after pouring in six goals. Damian Mori scored four, as did Kevin Muscat, who produced three of them from the penalty spot.

If Tonga needed an excuse, it could use two: first, it went into the match ranked 178th in the world, and second, many of its players weren't accustomed to wearing shoes.

Australia finished Group I play with a 4-0-0 record and a goals-for, goals-against ledger of 66–0. The Socceroos then proceeded to polish off the only other nation in Oceania that could give them a game, Group II winner New Zealand, in a home-and-home playoff, 2–0 and 4–1.

But that was Oceania. Dispatching New Zealand only gave Australia another opportunity to add to its long history of World Cup disappointment. The Socceroos advanced to a home-and-home playoff that November with South America's fifth-place finisher, Uruguay, for a berth in Japan/South Korea '02 and lost, 1–0 in Sydney and 3–0 in Montevideo, continuing the heartbreak.

Although British coal miners introduced the game Down Under in the 1870s, Australia did not formally become a full member of FIFA until 1963 and thus was not eligible for the first seven World Cups. By that time the tremendous popularity of rugby and Australian Rules football, coupled with the Aussies' isolation, left the country anything but soccer crazed. A national soccer team that beat up on its tiny neighbors but struggled against the rest of the world wasn't about to lift the sport's image.

After spearheading the creation of the Oceania Football Federation (four charter members, two provisional members) in 1965, Australia embarked on its first bid to play for a world championship and began a tradition in which it got beyond the World Cup doorstep but three times, as of South Africa '10:

1966. Every African, Asian, and Oceania nation but Australia and North Korea withdrew from the qualifiers in protest over the FIFA decision to allocate those combined regions just one berth in the sixteen-nation finals in England. Needing to step over only one opponent, the Australians dropped their playoff with the North Koreans, 6–1 and 3–1, in neutral Phnom Penh, Cambodia.

1970. The Aussies knocked off Japan, South Korea, and Rhodesia to reach the final of an Asia-Oceania competition but tripped at the last hurdle, bowing to Israel, 1–0 and 1–1.

1974. Believing it was going nowhere in the backwater of Oceania, the Australian Soccer Federation quit and attempted to align itself with the Asian Football Confederation; FIFA objected, leaving the Aussies in limbo. The Socceroos nevertheless won an Asia-Oceania qualifying competition to secure its first World Cup berth, slipping past South Korea in the final, 0–0 in Sydney, 2–2 in Seoul, and, in a tiebreaking third match played in Hong Kong, 1–0. It was a hollow triumph, however, as Australia celebrated its World Cup debut with a 2–0 loss to East Germany, a 3–0 loss to host West Germany, and a scoreless tie with Chile.

1978. Back in Oceania after an offer by the Asia-based Taiwan to trade places fizzled, Australia began a fruitless quest for a second World Cup appearance, finishing behind qualifier Iran, South Korea, and Kuwait in a combined Asia-Oceania qualifying series.

1982. New Zealand became the first nation to qualify for a World Cup as an Oceania member, winning the Asia-Oceania qualifiers; Australia crashed out in the first round. At España '82, the Kiwis predictably tumbled in the group stage.

1986. With the World Cup having been expanded from sixteen to twenty-four nations four years earlier, the Asia-Oceania qualifying format was dropped and the Asians were awarded two outright berths while Oceania got a so-called half-berth. The Australians won

Oceania over New Zealand and two Asia exiles, Israel and Taiwan, but that only earned them a home-and-home interregional playoff against Europe's fifteenth-place finisher, Scotland. Australia lost, 2–0 and 0–0.

1990. Another frustrating exit with a World Cup within sight. Needing a win in its final Oceania group match to advance to a playoff with Colombia, Australia was held to a 1–1 tie by Israel in Sydney and finished second by a single point. The Israelis, still shunned by Asia, lost to Colombia, 1–0 and 0–0.

1994. Australia beat New Zealand, 3–0 and 1–0, in the Oceania final to set up a playoff against Canada, which it won in dramatic fashion— a 2–1 victory in Edmonton and a 2–1 loss in Sydney, followed by a tiebreaking 4–1 penalty-kick decision. But under that year's format it only got Australia to a second playoff, against Argentina, which it lost, 1–1 in Sydney and 1–0 in Buenos Aires. The margin was a major embarrassment for the Argentines, while being required to go through two interregional playoffs after conquering its own part of the world only further frustrated the Australians.

1998. Another victory over New Zealand in the Oceania final and another interregional playoff, this time against Iran. Once again, an unhappy ending, perhaps the bitterest in Socceroo history. Australia eked out a 1–1 tie in the opening leg in Tehran and was leading the second leg in Melbourne a week later, 2–0, with fifteen minutes remaining. But Iran rallied to tie, 2–2. With the aggregate knotted at 3–3, the Iranians took the series on away goals, 2–1.

2002. This time, Oceania winner Australia came from ahead to lose in its home-and-home interregional playoff against Uruguay on aggregate, 3–1.

2006. Angered that Oceania was still on the outside looking in, Australia successfully lobbied FIFA to award the region an outright berth for Germany '06. But there was subsequent pressure from South America, which stood to lose one of its spots as a result; FIFA backed down and assigned Oceania a half-berth yet again. Unfazed, Oceania winner Australia, featuring more than a dozen players from top European clubs, faced Uruguay in a playoff. After a 1–0 loss in Montevideo, the Socceroos beat the Uruguayans in Sydney, 1–0, and took the penalty-kick tiebreaker that followed overtime, 4–2—the first time PKs had determined a World Cup berth. With its ticket punched to Germany '06, Australia announced days later that it would quit Oceania and rejoin Asia.

To the chagrin of South Korea, Japan, Saudi Arabia, Iran, and other Asian powers, the Australians then served notice that they would be a force on the earth's largest continent by making it to the second round—thanks in part to an opening-game 3–1 win over the Japanese—before losing controversially to eventual champion Italy, 1–0, on a stoppage-time goal.

With the Oceania Football Confederation left to New Zealand, Australia moved on to Asia having scored 267 goals in ninety-one World Cup qualifiers. Only Mexico (340 goals in 123 games through the '06 World Cup qualifiers), frequently pitted against another set of island nations—these from the Caribbean—has scored more.

More Severe Beatings

One country's champion is another's doormat.

A 19–0 victory by Deportivo Arabe Unido of Panama over FC Deportivo Jalapa of Nicaragua in October 2002 in a CONCACAF Champions Cup qualifying match was declared by the International Federation of Football History and Statistics as the biggest blowout in international club competition.

That lopsided score surpassed the 18–0 beating Suwon Bluewings of South Korea inflicted on Saunders SC of Sri Lanka in the 2001 Asian Cup Winners Cup.

Arabe Unido's Alfredo Barrera scored five goals against Jalapa, and Blas Perez and Alfredo Anderson both notched hat tricks.

Humbling losses were nothing new to the hapless Nicaraguan club. Two days earlier Jalapa lost in another qualifier to CD FAS of El Salvador, 17–0.

For solace, Jalapa and Saunders could turn to the world of futsal, a five-a-side version of soccer usually played on a court with a smaller ball. In an October 2006 tournament in Macau, Timor Leste lost to Portugal, 56–0, before losing to Brazil, 76–0. The Brazilians scored a goal on average every thirty-one seconds.

World's Smallest League

This Sunday, the Garrison Gunners and Woolpack Wanderers will meet at Garrison Field on the island of St. Mary's, some twenty-eight miles southwest of the English mainland. They'll do it again next Sunday, and the next Sunday, and the Sunday after that.

The Gunners and Wanderers comprise the world's smallest soccer league, a two-team circuit actually affiliated with the English Football Association. Two teams, playing one another over and over, with nothing at stake but the championship of the Isles of Scilly (pronounced—yes—"silly"), an archipelago of 150 dots of land, of which only five are populated.

Soccer has been played on the Isles of Scilly, settled by visitors from Cornwall four thousand years ago, since World War I. But by the 1950s the competition was reduced to the fifteen hundred residents of St. Mary's (six square kilometers large, or small) and their two teams. No matter. The Gunners and Wanderers carry on, playing one another over a sixteen-game schedule, plus various cups, including Youngsters versus Old Men each Boxing Day. The level of play is, ahem, modest, but no player can be accused of being fooled by a move he's never seen before.

Ronaldo's Juggling Bride

What kind of woman would make the perfect wife of a soccer superstar?

Great cook and homemaker? Best-looking bride in the players' wives section at the stadium? Knows when to make herself invisible at home after the big guy has scored an own goal in an important match?

In the case of Brazil scoring ace Ronaldo, how about a former fashion model who sets juggling records?

Milene Domingues, who was wed to the future Real Madrid star after the 1998 World Cup, has played soccer since age twelve. In 1995 she set a women's world mark by keeping a ball from touching the ground for nine hours, six minutes, recording 55,187 touches.

Domingues graced many a catwalk during her modeling career, but her biggest public appearance came in 2003 when she entertained a crowd of sixty thousand at Zayed Sports City Stadium in Abu Dhabi, United Arab Emirates, juggling a ball during halftime of the farewell match for UAE favorite Adnan Al Tayani that featured Juventus of Italy against an all-world selection. It wasn't until later that the crowd learned that the petite blonde down on the field was the woman sometimes known as "Ronaldinha."

Domingues also made headlines on the eve of the 2003 Women's World Cup when she was included in Brazil's twenty-member squad. Coach Paulo Goncalves selected eighteen of the players; Ronaldinha, listed simply as "Milene," was one of two players chosen by the team's delegation chief, Luiz Miguel de Oliveira.

"She's made the women's national team more visible, and that's very important," said De Oliveira of Ronaldo's wife, who had yet to actually play a game for Brazil.

And she was still waiting after the World Cup. Milene, wearing No. 20, never moved from the bench, and Brazil was eliminated in the quarterfinals.

A couple of months later, Ronaldo and Ronaldinha, the parents of one child, divorced.

A Goal-Poor Swedish Champion

When AIK Stockholm claimed its tenth Swedish league championship in 1998, its fans were probably too drowsy to stage much of a celebration. That year, AIK (11-2-13, forty-six points), outlasted Helsingborg IF (12-6-8, 44 points). The Stockholm side also conceded just fifteen goals in its twenty-six matches, an average of 0.57 a game. However, AIK also scored less than a goal a game, twenty-five, the lowest in the entire fourteen-team Allsvenskan. Even last-place Östers IF, which won just five matches in earning a demotion to the second division, scored twenty-six.

Six of AIK's victories were by 1–0. Ten of its games ended 1–1, and the three others were scoreless. Twice, the Stockholm side ran wild to post 2–0 wins. In all, spectators at AIK games that season saw an average of 1.53 goals (that's home team and opponent combined).

Coming in a close second was 1993–94 European Cup champion AC Milan. Boasting a defense of Italian stars Franco Baresi, Alessandro Costacurta, and Paolo Maldini playing behind French standout Marcel Desailly, the Rossoneri suffered fifteen goals against in winning its third straight Italian Serie A crown. However, Milan, minus injured marksman Marco Van Basten, scored only thirty-six in its thirty-four league matches. That's a robust 1.2 goals in Milan's league games. This from a side that unsheathed its scoring touch during that season's European Cup, rolling past AS Monaco, 3–0, in the semifinal and hammering FC Barcelona, 4–0, in the final.

Uruguay's National Team Is *Nacional*

Most national teams today are a mix of top citizen players from the country's leading clubs and those playing for clubs abroad. But in September 1903 the Uruguayan National Team lined up for a friendly against Argentina in Buenos Aires with an eleven composed entirely of players from the Montevideo club Nacional. The National team, or Nacional team, won, 3–2.

Actually, Nacional got its name in 1899 when the merger of Montevideo FC and Defensor FC created the first club in the South American country formed not by foreigners but by Uruguayan nationals.

Such was the state of the sport in South America in the late nineteenth and early twentieth centuries, when futbol, introduced by Brits, was not yet the game of the common man.

In 1891, the first season of the Argentine Amateur League, the forerunner of Argentina's national pro league, Saint Andrews AC and Old Caledonians FC finished their five-team season with identical 6-1-1 records. Although Saint Andrews won at Old Caledonians, 4–0, and tied in the return leg, 3–3, a playoff was ordered, which Saint Andrews won in overtime, 3–1.

What was notable was that there was not a single Argentine on the field in the final battle for the first Argentine national championship. As the team names would suggest, all twenty-two players were Scottish.

Robert Maxwell has just bought
Brighton & Hove Albion, and he's
furious to find it is only one club.
TOMMY DOCHERTY, Scottish coach,
on the new owner of the modest English club

John Harkes Going to Sheffield,
Wednesday
NEW YORK POST headline over a
report on the U.S. National Team midfielder's
move to the English Premier League club
Sheffield Wednesday

10 SNAFUS

*The English call a dreadful mistake by a player a "howler." Here is a
kaleidoscope of howlers.*

Good Intentions Gone Wrong

Despite the violence and corruption that stain the sport, soccer remains a game in which the players enter the field walking side by
side and concludes, on special occasions, with the combatants exchanging jerseys.

And there's one other shining example of sportsmanship that's a
soccer staple: when Team A purposely kicks a ball over the touchline
to stop play and allow an injured player to receive medical treatment,
a Team B player will then toss the ball back to a Team A player on
the ensuing throw-in.

Sometimes, however, that sporting gesture goes awry.

In February 1999 Arsenal and Sheffield United were tied, 1–1, in
the fifth round of the English F.A. Cup in London when United's
Lee Morris was tackled inside the Arsenal area. No penalty kick was
awarded and play continued on the other side of the field before a

United teammate spotted the injured Morris and kicked the ball into the stands so Morris could be tended to.

But when Arsenal's Ray Parlour, according to soccer etiquette, tried to send his throw-in back upfield to United goalkeeper Alan Kelly, Nigerian star Nwankwo Kanu—in his first appearance for the Gunners—intercepted the ball. With the Sheffield defense frozen, Kanu crossed to unmarked teammate Marc Overmars, who ran into the United area and scored easily. Referee Peter Jones could do nothing but allow the goal.

Sheffield coach Steve Bruce called his stunned players off the field in protest, but he later decided to allow them to finish the match, which they lost, 2–1.

At game's end Arsenal coach Arsene Wenger amazed all with an unprecedented offer to have the game replayed because of the breach of sportsmanship—a first in the 127-year history of the F.A. Cup, the oldest knockout team competition in sports.

Kanu and Overmars, Dutch internationals and former teammates at Ajax Amsterdam, both admitted they erred and agreed with the decision, which was praised in the *Daily Telegraph* the next day under the headline, "Beau Geste." FIFA also extended its support of the replay decision.

While most of the nation's fans and critics applauded Wenger's offer, a spokesman for English Premier League referees said a Pandora's box may have been opened.

"Whatever one may think about the rights and wrongs of what happened, no laws were broken when the goal was scored, and it should stand," said Philip Don.

The F.A. initially applauded Wenger's gesture but did not greenlight the replay until a couple of days later. Wenger had already threatened to pull Arsenal from the tournament if the F.A. rejected his offer.

The episode didn't have an entirely happy ending. Arsenal ignored calls to donate profits from the first match to charity and instead cut ticket prices in half for the replay. England's bookmakers, who paid out rather than voiding bets on Arsenal to win, lost millions because of the replay decision. And, as expected, underdog Sheffield dropped the replay, 2–1, ten days later. Scoring the first Arsenal goal was Overmars.

Was a Pandora's box opened? Not in the way some referees feared, but the Arsenal–Sheffield United incident would be repeated nearly five years later a few hundred miles to the south in another fifth-round national cup match in another country.

Host Lierse and fourth-division upstart KS Millen were tied, 2–2, late in a Belgian Cup game when the Millen goalkeeper booted a ball out because one of his defenders went down with an apparent injury. With the disabled player still on the field, Lierse quickly threw the ball in to one of its own, Archie Thompson, an Australian, who pounced on it and scored the winner.

Millen claimed that referee Yves Marchand should have stopped play and either ordered treatment for the injured player on the field or have him carried off. Countered Marchand, "I cannot ask a player to give a ball that has just been kicked out back to his opponents, and if I let the injured player lay on the ground it was because I was sure he was faking an injury."

Millen officially protested to the Belgian soccer federation, invoking FIFA's fair play code, which asks players to respect opponents, teammates, referees, officials, and spectators, in requesting a replay.

Lierse supported Millen's replay request. Said Lierse coach Emilio Ferrera, "We want to win without discussion."

Belgian officials okayed the replay and the second game was played. As in the English example, the underdog lost: Lierse 5, Millen 0. Lierse went on to tumble in the sixth round to Germinal Beerschot on penalty kicks, 3–1, after a 1–1 draw.

What if your good intentions are undone by a lousy return pass? Lee Johnson, a forward for Yeovil FC found out in August 2004 during an English League Cup match with Plymouth Argyle.

Plymouth played a ball out so its central defender, Graham Coughlan, could be treated for a bloody nose. A Yeovil player threw the ball in to Johnson, expecting him to kick it back to Plymouth goalkeeper Luke McCormick, but Johnson put too much on his charity pass and the ball sailed past McCormick and into the net.

Not only did it make the score 3–1 for Yeovil but it also gave Johnson a hat trick.

How to fix this mess? Johnson's father, Yeovil coach Gary Johnson, had the answer. He instructed his players to allow Plymouth to score on the ensuing kickoff, and they stepped aside as Plymouth's Steve Crawford deposited the ball into the Yeovil net.

"I have never seen a goal like our equalizer in my life," said Plymouth coach Bobby Williamson.

Said a charitable Johnson, "I think most managers would have done the same. Bobby's a much bigger chap than me, after all."

Despite the good intentions, it was too little, too late. Yeovil, a second-division side, defeated its first-division visitors, 3–2.

More good intentions all for naught, this time in September 2007 during an English League Cup second-round match between Nottingham Forest and Leicester City.

Fans at the City Ground were treated to a most unusual goal twenty-three seconds into the game as Forest goalkeeper Paul Smith dribbled the length of the field through a motionless Leicester team and sent the ball into the Foxes' net. The visitors were so accommodating that not only did Leicester goalkeeper Marton Fulop do nothing to stop Smith, but he high-fived his counterpart as Smith completed his tally.

A little background: The two sides originally met three weeks earlier, but after Leicester defender Clive Clarke collapsed in the dressing room at halftime with a heart attack and had to be treated with a defibrillator, Nottingham, which led, 1–0, agreed to the visitors' request that the match be abandoned and postponed. In an effort to make things completely right, appreciative Leicester manager Gary Megson instructed his side before the second meeting to allow Forest to score. Hence the first goal of Smith's career, and the Reds' 1–0 lead had been restored.

It wouldn't last. Defender Alan Sheehan equalized for Leicester on a free kick in the thirty-first minute, and after Nathan Tyson put Forest back on top, 2–1, in the sixty-fourth, the Foxes got goals from substitute Richard Stearman and Stephen Clemence in the final three minutes to win, 3–2, and advance to the third round.

Said Megson, "We felt it was morally right for us to come here and start 1–0 behind in reacting to what went on three weeks ago. As a football club we felt it was the right way to behave and it was a gesture meant in the spirit of the game."

Forest manager Colin Calderwood had a different view: "Football has a habit of biting your backside."

Megson came to his decision at the urging of his players. After consulting with Leicester owner Milan Mandaric, he notified Calderwood of his plan twenty minutes before the match. And Calderwood, mindful that bookmakers had taken bets on who would be the game's first scorer, selected the longest of long shots, goalkeeper Smith, to do the honors. Two major bookmakers later honored bets made on both a 3–1 and 3–2 final score; they also paid out on those who chose Sheehan as the game's first goal scorer.

Despite his magnanimous gesture, before the second game Megson was booed lustily by Forest fans who remembered Megson's recent one-year stint as Reds manager, one that ended with the team plunging into the second division. As for his current employer, Megson was hardly a Leicester institution with the carte blanche to extend such an offer to an opponent without concern for his own situation. In fact, he had been hired only after the impatient Mandaric fired Martin Allen a mere four games into the season.

Eight days after the Foxes and Reds settled matters, Leicester bowed at Aston Villa, 1–0, in the third round.

As for Clarke, the twenty-seven-year-old was hospitalized and survived, but his playing career was effectively over.

Czech Club Orders Players to Pay for Fans' Tickets

When it comes to professional team sports, it's the fans, to a certain extent, who pay the players' salaries. But in November 2002 a struggling Czech Republic club turned that concept upside down while punishing its players for their poor play.

Sigma Olomouc, muddling along in thirteenth place in the Czech first division with a 2-5-5 record, ordered its players to pay for the tickets of fans who showed up for their match against perennial power Sparta Prague.

Sigma's Andruv Stadium seats 12,119. Tickets sell for $1.70. Sparta's annual trip to Olomouc ordinarily results in a full house, and a sellout would cost the players roughly $20,000—in a country where the average salary at the time was $5,900.

"We were wondering how best to punish players who are paid royally but play lousily," said Sigma chairman Jiří Kubíček. "Then a club official came up with this idea."

The players were remarkably contrite. "None of us even thought about grumbling," allowed captain Martin Vaniak. "We hope the stadium will be packed. We want to get the fans back on our side."

Unfortunately for the club—and fortunately for the players—only seventy-four hundred bothered to show up free of charge to see Sigma lose to Sparta.

While the players were suitably chastised, a second-division team from Harstad, Norway, did Sigma one better four months earlier.

Harstad Idrettslag, based in a city of twenty-three thousand located 155 miles above the Artic Circle, got fed up with its average attendance of fewer than a hundred spectators and decided to pay those who showed up for its match against Staalkameratene ten kroners—a whopping $1.39—apiece.

Local sponsors, including a furniture store run by club board member Gunnar Berg, footed the bill. "The five sponsors are really hoping that this will cost them as much as possible," said Berg. He was no doubt disappointed when the match attracted 333. But in typical Norwegian fashion, 139 of the spectators put their buck-39 in a box as a donation to help the team.

That day, the two sides played to a 2–2 tie. At the end of 2002 Harstad, marking its ninety-ninth year, finished in twelfth place in second-division Group 4; Staalkameratene was two places lower and dead last. Both were relegated to the third division.

And the reason this sort of thing is rare:

In 1999 Kléber Leite, owner of Flamengo and frustrated by his team's seven-game winless skid, promised fans a money-back guarantee if his Rio de Janeiro club defeated lowly Portuguesa.

Only 791 watched Flamengo's previous match, but a throng of 52,340 turned out for this one. They saw 1994 World Cup hero Romário score two goals and Flamengo appeared headed for a 2–1 victory, but the home team collapsed after two of its players were ejected for reckless tackles, and Portuguesa rallied for a 3–2 win.

Leite, who had never fully explained his refund policy, found himself in the midst of a public relations nightmare. Some Flamengo fans saved him the trouble: disgusted, they tore up their tickets when the match ended. As for Flamengo coach Toninho Barroso, he resigned on the spot, three weeks after he was hired.

Full-Page Ad Apologizes for Swiss Club's Tailspin

Extra! Extra! Read all about our crummy team.

Just when the players of the Swiss Nationalliga club St. Gallen hoped that they could limp through a dreadful 2002–3 season in obscurity, they were dismantled, 11–3, by local rival FC Wil.

Not only did the margin of defeat set a Swiss record, but the loss left St. Gallen in eleventh place in the twelve-team division with little chance of reaching the league's eight-team second stage.

But rather than hide, coach Thomas Staub and his players took out a full-page advertisement in the daily newspaper *St Galler Tag-Blatt*. "We, the players of FC St. Gallen, made fools of ourselves," the ad declared. "We know you are the best fans in Switzerland, and we've let you down. We are sorry. Unfortunately we cannot turn back the clock."

A team photo accompanied the apology. Among those pictured was U.S. National Team midfielder Frankie Hejduk, a veteran of the 1998 and 2002 World Cups.

Creative Scheduling Slashes the Gate in Argentina

Oriente Petrolero and Wilstermann were to meet in March 2003 in the final of the Copa Aerosur, the opening competition of the Bolivian season. The match was moved out of the country to Estadio España in Buenos Aires to attract the Argentine capital's large Bolivian population, and a crowd of twenty-five thousand was expected.

All was well until the night before the match, when Buenos Aires police ordered the match moved from afternoon to morning to avoid a conflict with an Argentine league game between San Lorenzo and Boca Juniors at nearby Estadio San Lorenzo. No one thought to publicize the time change, however, and only three hundred arrived early enough to watch Oriente Petrolero beat Wilstermann, 1–0.

"People were arriving to watch the game as we were leaving the stadium," said an incredulous Nestor Clausen, coach of Oriente. "It was madness."

As winner of the competition, Clausen's club won free travel on the Aerosur airline for the rest of the year. It is presumed that none of Oriente's Aerosur flights depart early.

The flip side to the Bolivian snafu comes from Brazil, where in December 1999 a court ruling made a mess of the national championship.

Atlético Mineiro beat Corinthians, 3–2, at home in the opening leg of the final, but Corinthians prevailed in the second leg, 2–0. Because it was not a total goals series, that left the two sides deadlocked at a win apiece.

A tiebreaking match was set to be played in São Paulo, where the city council, expecting traffic snarls around the stadium, won a court order to move kickoff from 4:00 p.m. to 9:40 that night. Unfortunately, the ruling wasn't handed down until 1:15 p.m. on the day of the match, leaving many of the eighty thousand ticket holders, unaware of the switch, milling outside a locked stadium for hours.

Most of them went home happy: Corinthians held on for a 0–0 tie and claimed the title based on its better record during the national championship's opening stage.

Romanian Club Can't Afford Promotion to Top Division

How not to celebrate your team's promotion from the second division to the first, as demonstrated in Romania:

Barely a month after Petrolul Ploiesti earned promotion to Romania's top flight for the 2003–4 season, its officials determined that life in the first division would be beyond its means and promptly arranged a merger with Petrolul's longtime rival, Astra Ploiesti. Despite the pleas of hundreds of Petrolul supporters at Ploiesti city hall for the municipal government to intercede, the merger creating Petrolul-Astra became official, leaving truly die-hard Petrolul fans without a team.

Three years earlier Baia Mare had also won promotion to the first division, but because of a financial crisis it sold its spot to a club that had been relegated, FCM Bacau, for an undisclosed sum.

The Kids Aren't All Right in Bolivia

Blooming found out in October 2002 what its youth players were made of when it rounded up its kids for a Bolivian first-division match after its first-team players refused to suit up because of a pay dispute.

Blooming youth team coach Cesar Soto rousted the youngsters, ages fifteen to seventeen, from their homes less than twenty-four hours before the game, and the nightmare was on.

First, several players became ill during the plane ride from Santa Cruz de la Sierra to La Paz because they had never flown before.

Once off the plane, the teens, who live in the tropical lowlands of Bolivia, found themselves struggling with the thin air of La Paz, which is more than two miles above sea level.

Finally, the Blooming kids, who hadn't played in two weeks after being kicked out of a tournament for failing to pay their fees, absorbed a 10–1 pounding at the hands of Bolivar, the first-division leader.

Unfortunately, resorting to youth players is not uncommon in South America.

Union Central of Tarija in southernmost Bolivia, for example, did so in 2003 as a way to cut costs while fulfilling its first-division schedule. Rather than flying its first-team players to away games, financially strapped Union got through the 2003 season by sending its youth team by bus, forcing its boys to endure hours on the road. The results were predictable: in one two-week span, the Union youngsters lost 6–1 at Oriente Petrolero and 12–0 at Wilstermann.

Mexican P.A. Announcer Speaks out of Turn

An award for jumping the gun could have gone in May 2003 to the public address announcer at the home stadium of Cuernavaca, whose fans were led to believe that their club had succeeded in its last-ditch effort to avoid relegation from the Mexican first division.

Cuernavaca played Cruz Azul to a 0–0 tie at home to conclude the Mexican summer season with a fourth-place finish in Group 1. The players, coaches, and fans thought that Cuernavaca had done enough to remain in the top flight under Mexico's complicated promotion-relegation system after the announcer informed them that Puebla, seven points behind, had lost to Pachuca and that Jaguares de Chiapas, last in Group 3, had tied UAG Tecos. (Promotion/relegation in Mexico is determined by a club's performance over three seasons. Cuernavaca's record was only seventh worst in the twenty-club first division during the 2003 summer season, but it had fared far worse in the previous two campaigns.) Relieved Cuernavaca players took a victory lap and captain Jorge Jerez was carried to the middle of the field on the shoulders of delighted supporters.

But journalists at the match learned minutes later that Puebla had in fact tied Pachuca, 1–1, and Chiapas had beaten UAG, 1–0. Some of them chased the players to deliver the bad news, and word quickly spread throughout the stands. As jubilation turned to sorrow and Cuernavaca officially sank into the second division, the P.A. announcer no doubt found a good place to hide.

German Goalkeeper's Teams Are Relegated Five Times

Bad luck, thy name is Jürgen Rynio.

In Rynio's native Germany, the league set-up is simple: The eighteen clubs of the Bundesliga No. 1 play for the national championship; below that are another eighteen in Bundesliga No. 2, and below that are a third division and regional leagues. At season's end, the top three clubs from Bundesliga No. 2 are promoted, and the bottom three clubs from No. 1 are relegated.

Rynio, a goalkeeper, set some sort of record by going down with the ship five times. Sinking from Bundesliga No. 1 to No. 2 with the Jonah of soccer, Rynio, on board were Karlsruhe SC in 1968, FC Nürnberg in 1969, Borussia Dortmund in 1972, FC St. Pauli in 1978, and Hannover 96 in 1986.

McDonald's Finds Sponsoring Soccer a Challenge

One of international soccer's major sponsors, McDonald's, added Besiktas to its empire in 2001 when it agreed to sponsor the popular Turkish club, and to mark the occasion the fast-food behemoth opened a restaurant near Besiktas's Inonu Stadium in Istanbul.

One problem: the restaurant's sign, those golden arches with red trim, resemble the colors of Besiktas's hated rival, Galatasaray.

The solution: Besiktas's colors are black and white, so Istanbul became home to the world's only McDonald's with a black and white sign.

He Ain't Dead Yet

The City of Verona decided in 1996 to name one of its soccer venues the Aldo Olivieri Memorial Stadium in honor of the goalkeeper of the 1938 World Cup–winning Italian National Team.

Then officials discovered that Olivieri wasn't dead.

Verona had made all the necessary preparations to dedicate the stadium in Olivieri's memory when the oversight was discovered. Olivieri, then eighty-six, thanked the city fathers but said he preferred to remain alive and unhonored for the time being.

Olivieri, known during his playing career as "Always-Standing Little Hercules," died in 2001 in Lido di Camaiore. He was ninety.

Austrian Goalkeeper Beaned Twice

A Spanish first-division goalkeeper, struck two years earlier by a bottle thrown from the stands during a game in Italy, was hit in the head by fireworks tossed at him during a March 1997 match between his club, Real Zaragoza, and host Athletic Bilbao at San Mames Stadium.

Otto Konrad was released from a local hospital after being treated for first-degree burns near his eye suffered during the Spanish first-division game.

Two days later, the Spanish soccer federation ordered Athletic Bilbao to play its next two home games behind closed doors as punishment for the incident.

Konrad was playing for Casino Salzburg in his native Austria during a 1994–95 UEFA Champions League match against AC Milan at San Siro stadium when he was felled by a bottle thrown from the stands. Like Bilbao, Milan was ordered to play two home games in an empty stadium. Though also docked two points by the UEFA, Milan survived the group stage and reached the final in Vienna, where it lost to Ajax Amsterdam, 1–0.

Argentine Clubs Do Double Duty on Same Day

Two games in two countries in one day for two clubs.

That was the assignment as Velez Sarsfield and Racing Club were scheduled in March 1997 to not only face one another in an Argentine first-division game but play matches in the Copa Libertadores—South America's annual club championship—as well.

The results? In the league match, Racing's first team beat the Velez Sarsfield reserve team, 2–1, in Buenos Aires. Velez's first team was defeated by Emelec, 3–2, in Guayaquil, Ecuador, in its Copa Libertadores game. Racing's reserves were blanked, 2–0, by Nacional in Quito, Ecuador, in their Copa Libertadores game.

Schedule congestion of ridiculous proportions is, unfortunately, common in South America, although sometimes a club emerges unscathed.

Like São Paulo FC. One day in 1994 it was scheduled to play at home—twice. Its reserve side beat Peru's Sporting Cristal, 3–1, in a CONMEBOL Cup quarterfinal, then its full team defeated Grêmio in the nightcap by the same score in a Brazilian national championship match. The diminutive midfielder Juninho Paulista, who would earn sixty-eight caps for Brazil, appeared as a substitute in both games. São Paulo held Sporting to a scoreless tie in the road leg and went on to win the CONMEBOL Cup by beating Uruguay's Penarol in the final on aggregate, 6–4.

Sometimes, however, it doesn't work.

In May 2005 Independiente Medellin lost a Libertadores Cup match in Buenos Aires to Banfield, 3–0, on the same day that its reserve side tumbled to Tolima, 3–1, in Ibague in the semifinal round of a Colombian championship playoff.

Chivas Guadalajara repeated the fate of Racing and Velez in August 2006 when it tried to play both at home and at its home away from home on the same day.

Scheduled to open the Mexican *torneo apertura*, or "opening season," a team of Chivas reserves lost at Toluca, 1–0.

Early that evening, a fully loaded Guadalajara squad took on defending European Cup champion FC Barcelona in a friendly in Los Angeles and tied the star-studded Spanish side, 1–1.

Scheduling a mere exhibition on opening day was somewhat understandable for the Chivas brass: there are almost as many Chivas fans in L.A. as there are in Guadalajara, and indeed a sellout crowd of 92,650—most of them sporting the red-and-white stripes of Chivas—showed up at the Coliseum. Not a bad payday.

Torn by it all was Guadalajara coach José Manuel de la Torre. The man known as "Chepo" guided his reserves to defeat in Mexico, then hopped on a northbound private jet chartered by Chivas owner Jorge Vergara and arrived at the Los Angeles Memorial Coliseum fifteen minutes into the Barcelona match.

"The ideal situation," de la Torre deadpanned, "would have been to have a full team for both matches."

The Romanian Olympic Team in Disguise

The Egyptian Olympic Team believed that it was playing the Romanian Olympic Team in a pair of friendlies in July 2002. Instead, the Egyptians were up against Tractorul Brasov, a Romanian second-division club that apparently was posing as its nation's Olympic squad, clad in Romania's traditional yellow jerseys and blue shorts.

The ruse might have come off had not Romanian journalists spotted an Egyptian telecast of one of the matches, which were played in Romania.

The Romanian soccer federation suspended the club from international play for two years and imposed a $1,500 fine. Tractorul claimed that it was all a misunderstanding, that match organizers—Tractorul officials and an Egyptian businessman—instructed the club to play in Romanian uniforms because the club's green jerseys too closely resembled Egypt's.

Perhaps most embarrassing to the Egyptian Olympic Team was that it had split its two games with such an obscure side, losing the first match 2–1 before recovering two days later for a 3–0 win.

"Neverkusen" Blows Three Titles in Twelve Days

Call Bayer Leverkusen the Sisyphus of German soccer. Like the mythical Greek figure who was doomed to roll an enormous boulder almost—almost—to the peak of a mountain in Hades, only to see it roll to the bottom ad nauseam, Leverkusen let three boulders roll down its mountainside over a maddening twelve-day period in the spring of 2002.

Boulder One. Leverkusen was edged out for the German Bundesliga championship on May 4 when it finished the regular season one point behind Borussia Dortmund. Leverkusen, which squandered leads in losing its third- and second-to-last matches, beat Hertha Berlin, 2–1, in its final game but could only watch helplessly as Dortmund edged Werder Bremen at home by the same score. The second-place finish was the fourth in six years for Leverkusen, which had never won a German league title in its ninety-eight-year history.

Boulder Two. The misery continued May 11 when Leverkusen dropped a 4–2 decision to Schalke in the German Cup final before an Olympic Stadium crowd of seventy thousand in Berlin.

Boulder Three. Leverkusen completed its hat trick of futility May 15 by bowing to Real Madrid, 2–1, in the UEFA Champions League final at Hampden Park in Glasgow, Scotland.

Three bitter disappointments in less than a fortnight. No wonder the German press dubbed the team "Neverkusen."

The year 2002 was especially troubling for Bayer Leverkusen's rising star, midfielder Michael Ballack. Named the German Footballer of the Year for getting his club within touching distance of three major honors, Ballack capped that season as a member of the German team that lost the World Cup final to Brazil, 2–0. In fact, Ballack had to watch the game in street clothes because of a suspension earned while helping Germany beat South Korea, 1–0, in the semifinals.

Six years later Ballack was playing for Chelsea, but he apparently brought to his London club the Neverkusen curse. In February Chelsea lost the English League Cup final to crosstown rivals Tottenham, 2–1. In May Chelsea lost out on the English Premier League title to Manchester United by two points, and later in the month the Blues fell to United again, this time in the UEFA Champions League final, on penalty kicks. Ballack then repeated his four-peat of disappointment, captaining Germany to the final of the 2008 European Championship in Vienna, where it lost to Spain, 1–0.

There is indeed gold in the Ballack trophy case: Bundesliga championships with Kaiserslautern (1997–98) and Bayern Munich (2002–3, 2004–5, 2005–6), German Cups with Bayern Munich (2003 through 2006), and English F.A. Cups with Chelsea (2007 and 2009).

But those eight near-misses in 2002 and 2008, plus second-place finishes with Leverkusen during the 1999–2000 Bundesliga season, Bayern Munich in the German Cup (2004) and Chelsea during the 2007 Premier League season, made Ballack soccer's Sisyphus eleven times over.

Mexico's Amazing Penalty-kick Futility

Mexico has a proud history in soccer, thoroughly dominating—until recently—the North/Central American and Caribbean region. The Mexicans have appeared in fourteen of the first nineteen World Cups, captured seven CONCACAF championships, and for decades fielded the region's strongest and richest national league.

For all their success, however, what Mexicans seemingly cannot do is win penalty-kick tiebreakers.

In forty-three significant competitions involving its national team or clubs, the Mexican ledger read 13–29 from the penalty spot after El Tricolores' 4–2 defeat at the hands of South Korea at the Rose Bowl in the semifinals of the 2002 CONCACAF Gold Cup.

The curse continued three years later in Germany at the FIFA Confederations Cup. In their semifinal in Hannover the Mexicans snapped a scoreless draw with Argentina with a goal early in overtime, only to give up an equalizer that sent the contest to—gulp—penalties. Mexico fans covering their eyes didn't see Argentine goalkeeper German Lux save defender Ricardo Osorio's shot, the only miss over the six-round drama.

That defeat left the Mexican National Team with a 36 percent success rate in PK tiebreakers—the worst among nations with ten or more trips to the penalty spot in regional or world championships on the senior level. According to www.penaltyshootouts.co.uk, the sad tale of the tape read: thirty-nine PK attempts, twenty-five converted, fourteen not converted (64 percent success rate), and an overall record of 4-7. In comparison Argentina (73 percent success rate) was the world leader; it nailed forty of fifty tries to post an 8-3 mark. Second was Brazil (64 percent, thirty-nine of forty-seven, 7-4 record), followed by Thailand (55 percent, eighteen of twenty-four, 6-5), Iran (46 percent, twenty-six of thirty-six, 5-6), Zambia (45 percent, thirty-one of forty-five, 5-6), and Uganda (40 percent, eleven of seventeen, 4-6).

Mexico's northern neighbor, the United States, has been put to the test only six times, but the Americans have netted twenty-one of thirty tries in winning five (83 percent). Others include Germany (71 percent, twenty-eight of thirty-three, 5-2) and England (a dismal 17 percent, twenty-one of thirty-one, 1-5).

Mexico's most heartbreaking loss in a tiebreaker took place at the 1986 World Cup it hosted. El Tri lost meekly on PKs in Monterrey in the quarterfinals to West Germany after tenaciously holding the eventual runners-up scoreless through 120 minutes of regulation and overtime. More than 70 million Mexicans hoped against hope and were rewarded with one PK goal to the Germans' four. It was the first scoreless World Cup match to be decided by penalties, and

Mexico's lone goal was the worst performance by a losing side in a World Cup tiebreaker.

(Incidentally, Mexico's biggest single failure from the penalty spot occurred in a first-round game against underdog Paraguay two weeks earlier in Mexico City. With the score 1–1, a sellout crowd of one hundred and fourteen thousand roared when Mexico was awarded a last-minute penalty kick, but the shot by ace marksman Hugo Sanchez was turned outside the post by Paraguay goalkeeper Roberto Fernandez.)

Other notable Mexican PK disappointments:

- 1977 World Youth Championship final (9–8 PK loss to the Soviet Union, following a 2–2 tie. Mexico had triumphed over Brazil on penalties in the semifinals, 5–3)
- 1993 FIFA World Youth Championship quarterfinals (4–3 to eventual third-place finisher England, after a scoreless draw)
- 1994 World Cup second round (3–1 to eventual fourth-place finisher Bulgaria, after a 1–1 tie. Alberto García Aspe, who converted a penalty kick in the eighteenth minute to give Mexico a 1–0 lead, opened the tiebreaker by ripping his shot high over the crossbar)
- 1995 Copa America quarterfinals (4–1 to eventual fourth-place finisher United States, after a 0–0 draw)
- 2000 Sydney Olympic Games qualifiers (5–4 to eventual qualifier Honduras after a scoreless tie)

The Mexicans also were shot down from the penalty spot at the 1987 and 1995 Pan American Games soccer tournaments.

Mexico's lone shining PK moment came at the 1995 Intercontinental Cup in Riyadh, Saudi Arabia, known as the King Fahd V Cup and the precursor to the FIFA Confederations Cup. The Mexicans battled Nigeria to a 1–1 stalemate, then took the PK duel, 5–4.

The curious Mexican penalty-kick curse has extended to club competitions. Cruz Azul was ousted from the 2001 Copa Libertadores, and Santos Laguna and Necaxa met the same fate in the 2000 and 2001 Copa Merconorte, respectively.

If anyone can come up with a better tiebreaker than alternating spot kicks from twelve paces, contact Mexico first.

23 Minus 10 Doesn't Add Up for Argentina

Numerous clubs worldwide have retired jerseys, some worn by all-time greats, some by players notable for their local popularity. But no country had ever retired a national team shirt until the Argentine Football Association (AFA) announced in November 2001 that none of its national team players would ever wear the No. 10 made famous by Diego Maradona.

And that created a problem in the eyes of FIFA, which requires a national team taking part in a World Cup to number its twenty-three players 1 through 23. If Argentina wanted to retire No. 10, it would be forced to go to the 2002 World Cup with one less player. In other words, to FIFA, Maradona may have been good, but he was not immortal.

Said a somewhat disingenuous Maradona, then forty-one, before a farewell match at Boca Juniors' Bombonera Stadium in Buenos Aires, "It was a wonderful idea . . . but it seems other people didn't like it. It's the law of FIFA—they give the orders and we have to accept it."

The AFA ultimately backed down and Argentina showed up at the 2002 World Cup with twenty-three players, including No. 10, Ariel Ortega.

Barcelona Engages in Some Midnight Madness

FC Barcelona tied Sevilla, 1–1, at Nou Camp Stadium in its 2003–4 Spanish first-division opener. The match drew eighty thousand and would have attracted Barcelona's customary capacity crowd of ninety-eight thousand had it not kicked off at five minutes past midnight.

The game had been scheduled for a Wednesday evening, but five Barcelona starters had been recalled by their respective national teams and were expected to report Tuesday. When Sevilla refused a request to move the match to Tuesday, a spiteful Barca moved it to the middle of the night and hoped that the national team coaches would allow the players to squeeze in the Sevilla match in the wee hours of Wednesday and then report a few hours late.

As it turned out, only Portugal winger Ricardo Quaresma was given an OK to be tardy, but Barca went ahead with its midnight madness anyway, dubbing it "Football for Insomniacs."

The club offered its supporters a free picnic and a variety show to ensure that the game wouldn't be a box-office bomb, although there was little chance of that happening. There are some one hundred fifty thousand card-carrying FC Barcelona club members, and Spaniards in general are known for their late hours.

Still, despite picking up a valuable road point with the tie, Sevilla coach Joaquin Caparros was not amused. "It's a complete farce," he said. "It also creates a really dangerous precedent and now every team will want to change the time of a kickoff to suit their own interests."

A neutral observer, Deportivo La Coruña coach Javier Irureta, found the humorous side to it all. "How are you going to expect your wife to believe that you are off to see the football at midnight?" he asked. "She's just going to think you are cheating on her."

English Jersey Exposes Frenchman's Ruse

Whoever wants to know the heart and mind of a passport forger had better learn football. Such was the lesson offered by police in Cyprus after they apprehended a Senegalese man attempting to pass a checkpoint on the Mediterranean island in July 2006. The authorities became suspicious when the twenty-two-year-old man, wearing a replica English National Team shirt, presented a French passport on the border between the Turkish Cypriot north and Greek Cypriot south.

"Being a football fan, the officer found it highly unlikely that a Frenchman would want to wear an England football jersey," said a police spokesman.

Upon further examination, the passport proved to be a fake, and the man was jailed for six days.

Stadium Girder Gets in the Way of a World Cup Entrance

Here is perhaps the oddest instance of the so-called home-field advantage. In its last first-round match of the 1950 World Cup, Brazil needed a win over Yugoslavia in Rio de Janeiro to advance to the final four-team playoff pool that would determine the world champion. A tie would put Yugoslavia through and plunge the country of Brazil into a state of mourning.

To the rescue came the match site, full name Estádio Municipal, o Maracaña, Mário Filho, a massive structure newly built and named for both a nearby stream and the founder of the influential daily *Jor-*

nal dos Sport. Make that *barely* built. Work on this graceful stadium was begun in 1948 and wouldn't be officially completed until 1965. Though its sweeping oval design inspired other, smaller stadiums in São Paulo, Belo Horizonte, and elsewhere in Brazil, come the World Cup the Maracanã was more a construction site than a gleaming soccer palace.

So, minutes ahead of kickoff, before a crowd of 142,409, out of the bowels of this bowl came the Yugoslavian National Team . . . minus Rajko Mitic. The star inside right had struck his head on a steel girder as he followed his teammates through the players' tunnel and went down with a deep laceration to his forehead.

In this era of no substitutes, the Yugoslavs chose to start with ten men. Minus Mitic, the legendary captain of Yugoslav power Red Star Belgrade, the visitors gave up a fourth-minute goal to Ademir and never recovered. The heavily bandaged Mitic wasn't ready to enter the field until the twentieth minute; he missed Ademir's goal while being treated and didn't learn of it until halftime. Still shaken from his accidental rendezvous with the stadium beam, Mitic was hardly a factor in the game and the Brazilians went on to seal their victory with a brilliant solo goal by Zizinho in the sixty-ninth.

Mitic and Yugoslavia went home; the Brazilians' home-field edge ultimately deserted them in the match that determined the championship, a 2–1 loss to Uruguay back at the Maracanã.

Palermo's Three P K Misses in the Copa America

Some players—many of them defenders—go years without scoring. Not even a half-chance at glory. Martin Palermo's performance during a 1999 Copa America match in Paraguay between Argentina and Colombia, then, is the stuff of legend.

Palermo's Argentina, which allowed several stars to skip the tournament, lost, 3–0, but it could have forged at least a tie with the Colombians if the Boca Juniors star had converted the three penalty-kick attempts he had taken. The burly forward with the blond crew cut sent his first try off the top of the Colombian crossbar, his second sailed high into the stands, and his third was pounced on by goalkeeper Miguel Calero. Colombia won the group and Argentina finished second.

Why didn't somebody do something during this train wreck? Argentina coach Marcelo Bielsa had been red-carded by the time his side had been awarded its third penalty kick; he tried furiously via mobile phone to get word to the Argentine bench to have anyone but Palermo take it, but to no avail.

That lack of performance cost Palermo his job as PK marksman, and his bad karma around the penalty spot seemed to carry over into the quarterfinals, where Argentina bowed to archrival Brazil, 2–1, in Ciudad del Este. Argentina's chance to tie the match with twelve minutes left was squandered by captain Roberto Ayala, whose PK attempt was saved brilliantly by goalkeeper Dida.

Palermo's international career never recovered, and he subsequently left Boca Juniors for Spain, where he played for Villarreal, Real Betis, and Alaves. While with Villarreal he celebrated one goal by leaping onto a small concrete wall; the wall collapsed under the weight of jubilant fans and Palermo suffered a broken leg. Once healed, he returned to Boca and eclipsed the club record of 180 career goals scored in the 1930s by Francisco Varallo. One of Palermo's goals was a bomb from inside his own half, a shot of some sixty yards—odd for a fellow who in one game in Paraguay had so much trouble from one-fifth that distance.

If Palermo needed company in the penalty-kick doghouse, he would have had to wait until August 2006 when Drogheda United defender Graham Gartland's two misses in a PK tiebreaker against IK Start of Norway sent the Irish side tumbling out of the second qualifying round of the UEFA Cup.

Drogheda had dropped the first leg in Kristiansand, 1–0, and two weeks later at Dalymount Park appeared on its way out until substitute Eamon Zayed scored on a header in the eighty-fourth minute to level the aggregate at 1–1. After thirty scoreless minutes of overtime, the two sides squared off in a duel from the penalty spot.

Gartland began matters with a miss, his shot stopped by Start goalkeeper Rune Nilssen. But if the Drogs' defender was craving a chance at redemption, he got it as the two sides found themselves deadlocked, 10–10, after eleven rounds.

So Gartland stepped up a second time and watched in dismay as Nilssen saved again. Stefan Barlin drilled his chance into the net, and Start was on its way to the opening round of the UEFA Cup (where, no doubt exhausted, it lost to Dutch power Ajax Amsterdam).

And from Moldova comes Vladimir Taranu, who in May 2007 became a one-man Gang That Couldn't Shoot Straight.

In a Divizia Nationala match between FC Olimpia Balti and host FC Nistru Otaci, Nistru was awarded a penalty kick and leading scorer Taranu stepped to the spot. Olimpia goalkeeper Eugeni Bahurinsky knocked down Taranu's shot, but when Taranu pounced on the rebound he was tripped by the 'keeper and awarded a second PK. Bahurinsky parried this shot as well, and again Taranu was first to the loose ball. The Nistru marksman's follow-up shot struck the post and caromed back to Taranu, who sent yet another shot against the post, and Olimpia gained possession.

Nistru won, two goals to one, despite Taranu's four rapid-fire chances to make it three.

English Player Exposes Dangers of Watching TV

Couch potatoes of the world, beware.

England international Rio Ferdinand proved in January 2001 that watching TV can be dangerous when he strained a tendon behind his knee while at home, glued to the telly. Ferdinand, then with Leeds United, suffered the injury as the result of leaving his foot propped on a coffee table for several hours.

Ferdinand, who became the world's most expensive defender two months earlier when he was purchased from English rival West Ham for $25.3 million, was lost to Leeds for two games. It is not known how much TV he watched during his layoff.

FIFA Makes a Mess of Its Top Player Poll

So who's the best player of the twentieth century, O Rey or El Pibe de Oro?

In a mess of worldwide proportions, FIFA in December 1999 found itself naming both "The King," Pelé, and "The Golden Kid," Diego Maradona, as the greatest player of the century during its annual awards gala in Rome.

FIFA sponsored a fan vote for the Player of the Century via the Internet, apparently expecting Pelé to be the runaway winner. When the October-to-November voting window closed, however, Maradona had won in a landslide.

At the time of the balloting, the fallen Argentine idol was a recovering cocaine addict. He'd twice been suspended late in his playing career, each time for fifteen months, for drug use. Nevertheless, he attracted 53.6 percent of the vote, leaving Brazilian legend Pelé far behind at 18.5 percent.

Eusébio (6.2 percent), Roberto Baggio (5.4 percent), Romário (1.7 percent), Marco van Basten (1.57 percent), Ronaldo (1.55 percent), Franz Beckenbauer (1.5 percent), Zinedine Zidane (1.3 percent), and Rivaldo (1.2 percent) rounded out the top ten.

Far back in the pack were Johan Cruyff in thirteenth place (0.8 percent); Alfredo Di Stéfano, fourteenth (0.6 percent); Michel Platini, fifteenth (0.5 percent); Bobby Charlton, sixteenth (0.4 percent); Ferenc Puskás, seventeenth, (0.37 percent); and George Best, twentieth (0.32 percent).

That was only the beginning of FIFA's problems.

Not long after balloting closed but before the results were to be revealed, a Spanish newspaper broke the news of Maradona's overwhelming Internet triumph. Early in December, the FIFA Web site curiously announced that the Internet vote would determine a "Player of the Decade." (Interesting, because Maradona's heyday was the mid- to late 1980s.) Three days later a FIFA spokesman clumsily said a typing error caused the title to read "decade" rather than "decades."

Back-pedaling quickly, FIFA quietly formed a "football family" committee of unnamed FIFA officials, national team coaches, and journalists to take part in another vote for the century's greatest—and Pelé won.

In that poll, Pelé drew 72.7 percent of the vote, followed by Di Stéfano (9.7 percent), Maradona (6.0 percent), Beckenbauer (2.5 percent), Cruyff (2.0 percent), Best (2.0 percent), Platini (1.0 percent), Gerd Müller (1.0 percent), and Baggio (1.0).

How to reconcile these two results? FIFA President Joseph Blatter announced days later that there would be two awards, the FIFA Player of the Century, to Pelé, and the "FIFA Internet Award, Men," to Maradona.

By then, the two ex-players had been drawn into the flap. Maradona, calling Pelé overrated, said that he proved himself in the tougher leagues of Spain and Italy, citing the tight marking he had to endure, while Pelé spent most of his career far from Europe, in Brazil. Pelé countered that he considered Maradona behind several Brazilian and Argentine greats, including Di Stéfano, Sócrates, Rivelino, Romário, Tostao, and José Manuel Moreno.

It didn't get any better at the gala in Rome. Maradona dedicated his award to all Argentines, his (soon-to-be-ex) wife, Cuban leader Fidel Castro, and the world's soccer players—then left the building in a snub of Pelé, who had yet to be presented his award.

"I would have liked to have had Maradona up here on stage with me," Pelé told the audience, "but it looks like he's already gone."

The controversy was only the latest entry in the long and stormy soccer rivalry between the two South American neighbors. While delighted Argentines crowed, outraged Brazilians claimed that the Argentine Football Association had spearheaded a campaign to get out the Internet vote for Maradona, who benefited from the support of younger adults who were computer savvy but had not seen Pelé at the peak of his career.

On the distaff side, Chinese striker Sun Wen won the "FIFA Internet Award, Women" despite coming from a country not known for its Internet freedom, while a FIFA favorite, U.S. midfielder Michelle Akers, received the Woman Player of the Century nod.

American Goalkeeper Gives a Stand-up Effort

Juergen Sommer, a member of the United States' 1994 and 1998 World Cup teams, is perhaps best known as the first American goalkeeper to play in England's top division. A towering 6'5", he went directly from Indiana University to Luton Town in 1991, then joined Queens Park Rangers in 1995 before returning to the United States in 1998 to play for the Columbus Crew and, later, the New England Revolution.

Sommer, however, returned to England in February 2001 and, for one day at least, probably wished he had stayed home.

Bolton Wanderers, which had lost its number one goalkeeper to injury and his backup to suspension, picked up Sommer as a free agent on a noncontract basis to get the team through a F.A. Cup fifth-round match with Blackburn Rovers. Sommer's Blackburn counterpart was another American, U.S. international Brad Friedel, formerly of Bay Village, Ohio; UCLA; IF Brondby of Denmark; Galatasaray of Turkey; and Liverpool. Friedel and Sommer had been teammates on the 1994 U.S. World Cup team, and Friedel had preceded Sommer at Columbus in 1996 and 1997.

Sommer pulled a muscle in his right thigh in the fifth minute of the Blackburn match while kicking away a low ball. With no other 'keeper on the bench (Bolton's number three was on loan to another team), he was forced to hobble through the rest of the game, and Bolton ultimately paid the price.

In the fortieth minute Blackburn's David Dunn ripped a twenty-five-yard free kick into the net that sailed over Sommer, who was unable to leap to palm the ball over the crossbar. But Michael Ricketts of Bolton beat Friedel for the equalizer in the sixty-second minute, and Sommer managed to hold on. He let defender Colin Hendry take Bolton's goal kicks, and twice he denied Rovers' Matt Jansen from point-blank range, gimpy leg and all.

That cameo was Sommer's only appearance for Bolton, which had its top two goalkeepers back by the time it met Blackburn the following month in the replay.

Friedel came out a 3–0 winner in that game, but Rovers bowed three days later to eventual F.A. Cup runner-up Arsenal, 3–0.

Mum Washes Autographs off Son's Special Jersey

Leigh Walker, a goalkeeper for a nonleague team, Scarborough, played the game of his life in January 2004 in limiting Premier League power Chelsea to a 1–0 victory in an English F.A. Cup fourth-round match. The impressed Chelsea players autographed Walker's jersey, and his Chelsea counterpart, Italian Carlo Cudicini, added a personal note of praise. But before he could frame the shirt, Walker's mum got hold of it and gave it a good scrubbing, wiping out the Chelsea signatures. Or so said the initial press reports.

Actually, she said she tried to wash only the sleeves and leave the autographs alone, "but the water spread and washed off all the writing."

Not good enough for Walker.

"I'm gutted," he said. "It was a special souvenir of the biggest match I've ever played. Now it's ruined."

Players of Cash-Strapped Colombian Club Go Hungry

Most coaches want their players to take the field hungry—for victory, of course. One coach in the Colombian first division quit his post because his players were hungry for nothing more than something edible.

Diego Umana resigned as boss of Quindio in April 2004 after the cash-strapped club stopped paying the players, leaving them without the means to buy food.

"I arrived at training and four players turned up who had not eaten on Monday and who did not have breakfast on Tuesday," Umana told reporters. "They won't give [the players] any more food in the house where they're staying because they haven't been paid. It's not easy to play Sunday-Wednesday-Sunday without eating. They want to evict them because the rent hasn't been paid."

Umana agreed to remain at the helm through Quindio's next game. Predictably, the famished team lost at Bucaramanga, 1–0, to remain next-to-last in the eighteen-team first division.

Two Balls in One Game Doesn't Quite Work

Hmmm, two balls in one game.

Perhaps that idea had already occurred to those who find soccer too low scoring by the time LDU and Deportivo Quito met in an Ecuadoran league match in October 2006. It indeed produced an unexpected goal, enabling LDU to win, 2–1.

In the eighty-ninth minute, with the score tied, 1–1, Deportivo goalkeeper Daniel Viteri bundled an LDU shot over his goal line. Viteri briefly protested referee Daniel Salazar's corner kick call, then bent down to pick up the out-of-bounds ball. At that moment LDU's Elkin Murillo, given another ball by a nearby ball boy, got off a harried corner kick. Caught out of position, Viteri threw his ball at Murillo's corner kick. He missed, and LDU's Agustin Delgado headed Murillo's ball into the empty net for the winner.

The real loser was referee Salazar, who was suspended for three matches by the Ecuadoran football federation for allowing this bit of slapstick. The linesman running the Deportivo half was likewise banned for three games; the other linesman was suspended for one.

Two balls in play was actually proved to be a bad idea back in November 1895, during the inaugural Belgian league season.

Racing Club de Bruxelles, which would win five championships over the next eight seasons, took on the winless Laglasts Union FC d'Ixelles and were so dominating their visitors that at one point goalkeeper Gustave Pelgrims began to knock a spare ball back and forth with one of his defenders, much to the amusement of the home crowd.

Just then, a Union player, riding a strong tail wind, hoofed a shot from his own half into Pelgrims's net.

Union won, 1–0, its only victory that season. The cheeky Racing Club was knocked into a fourth-place tie in the seven-team league, one point away from relegation.

Russian Club Pays the Price for Traveling Light

A Russian second-division team, Spartak-Chukotka Moscow, folded in August 2000 with more than two months left in the season following a 7–0 hammering at the hands of Lokomotiv Chita.

The club was so cash-strapped it could afford to fly only its starting lineup to Chita for the match. Eleven players, no substitutes.

Chukotka president and coach Anatoly Shelest said the club had ambitions of winning promotion to the first division, but with the team's demise, his goal was to find jobs for the players, who hadn't been paid all summer.

Brazilian Learns "Play the Whistle" the Hard Way

Youth players are always admonished to "play the whistle"—that is, keep playing and assume that no call has been made unless the referee signals otherwise.

Pia, a midfielder for Ponte Preta, was no kid in November 1999, but he could have used a refresher when his side met São Paulo FC in a Brazilian championship quarterfinal.

Pia claimed he was fouled in his own penalty area and picked up the ball. The referee made no such call, however, and was forced to award São Paulo a penalty kick for a handball violation in the box. Former Brazil captain Rai converted and São Paulo went on to win, 3–2.

São Paulo in fact needed the charity that day. Midfielder Vagner gave a ball boy a halftime tongue lashing that earned the player a red card, thus forcing São Paulo to play the second half shorthanded.

Goal-scoring Goalkeeper Is Brought Back to Earth

Latin America is known for its flamboyant goalkeepers, so it's no surprise that the top four goal-scoring 'keepers hail from that part of the world.

Rogerio Ceni of São Paulo FC and Brazil became number one in August 2006 when he scored on a free kick in a league match against Cruzeiro, eclipsing the mark of sixty-two career goals set by José Luis Chilavert. A longtime Paraguay captain, Chilavert drilled home twenty-two penalty kicks and forty free kicks during his colorful career. Ceni also celebrated the day by saving a Cruzeiro penalty kick.

Number three on the list was René Higuita of Colombia (thirty-seven PKs, four free kicks, forty-one total goals), followed by Jorge Campos of Mexico (nine PKs, thirty-one free kicks, forty total).

Number five was Hans-Jorg Butt of Bayer Leverkusen with twenty-seven goals, all from the penalty spot. Butt led his previous club, Hamburg SV, in scoring with nine goals in 1999–2000; that same season he almost single-handedly beat Schalke, scoring and saving a penalty in a 3–1 win.

The big German, however, once demonstrated that he should stick to saving goals and leave the scoring to the Latin Americans. In April 2004 Butt converted a penalty kick in a German first-division game against Schalke, and after returning to his own half for the ensuing kickoff he continued his own minicelebration.

Alert Schalke forward Mike Hanke spotted the jubilant Butt waving to the fans and got revenge, blasting the ball direct from the kickoff into the Leverkusen net.

That's all Schalke got as Leverkusen prevailed, 3–2, thus sparing Butt further embarrassment.

Nearly four years later it took half a team to outdo Butt, and this time it was costly.

Real Madrid had been held to a scoreless tie into the second half of a Spanish league match by lightly regarded Getafe when Arjen Robben appeared to put the hosts ahead. Ruud van Nistelrooy's shot was parried to the left by Getafe goalkeeper Pato Abbondanzieri, but Raúl collected the loose ball and centered for Robben, who beat Abbondanzieri.

While Robben and five of his teammates celebrated in the right corner of Getafe's half, they failed to notice that the linesman had lifted his flag for offside and the referee signaled for a Getafe free kick. The alert visitors quickly restarted play and, led by Francisco Casquero, charged down the field on a four-on-two counterattack. Casquero passed to Pablo Hernandez on the right, and he played the ball back across to striker Uche, who drilled his shot past Madrid goalkeeper Iker Casillas.

Getafe made that goal stand up for a 1–0 victory that cut Madrid's lead in the Spanish championship to two points over archrival FC Barcelona.

Brazilian Team Is Given Time Enough to Lose

Be careful what you ask for.

Volta Redondo scored in the fifth minute of a Rio de Janeiro state championship match in May 1997 against Vasco da Gama and was still clinging to its 1–0 lead in the fourth minute of added-on time when Vasco equalized.

Already reduced to nine men because of a couple of questionable ejections early in the second half, the irate Volta players surrounded the referee and argued that the game had been extended so that Vasco could get even.

The ref, in a peacemaking move, said he would add another two minutes and play was resumed. Vasco promptly scored again for a 2–1 win.

Uruguayan Hero Smothered by Teammates

Uruguay nearly staged its own version of the killing of the Golden Goose after center forward Juan Eduardo Hohberg scored two goals in the final fifteen minutes of regulation to give his side a 2–2 tie with Hungary in a 1954 World Cup semifinal in Lausanne, Switzerland, and force overtime.

On the equalizer Hohberg took a pass from Juan Schiaffino, nearly lost it, won it back, and beat Hungary goalkeeper Gyula Grosics with four minutes left. It capped one of the most dramatic comebacks in World Cup history, and his exultant teammates mobbed him and executed such an airtight group hug that Hohberg passed out.

Hohberg was revived and later sent a shot off the post in the first overtime, but Hungary went on to win, 4–2. It was the first loss suffered by the two-time champion Uruguay in World Cup play.

A Paraguayan Fashion Faux Pas

In the world of Paraguayan soccer, there are few teams perennial power Olimpia of Asunción would rather beat than its crosstown rival, Cerro Porteño. So Olimpia players and officials were more than incensed in November 1999 when Velez Sarsfield of Argentina showed up for a Copa Mercosur quarterfinal match at Olimpia's Manuel Ferreira Stadium wearing the blue-and-maroon stripes of . . . Cerro Porteño.

Velez borrowed the Cerro uniforms after it arrived in Asuncion having failed to bring its alternate uniforms. The Argentine side claimed that before leaving Buenos Aires it agreed with Olimpia that it could wear its traditional white and blue. Olimpia's primary jersey is white with a black hoop.

If Velez indeed meant to rile up its opponent, the ploy backfired. It lost to Olimpia, 2–1, to drop the series by a 6–4 aggregate, and the South American soccer confederation later reprimanded the Argentine side.

Physicist Bohr a Bust as a Goalkeeper

Goalkeepers are expected to concentrate regardless of the position of the ball or what's being said by the spectators situated behind the net. No wonder, then, that Niels Henrik David Bohr was a washout as a 'keeper.

One of the most important physicists of the twentieth century and Denmark's only Nobel Prize winner, Bohr worked in atomic structure and quantum mechanics, making him a vital member of the Manhattan Project team.

His work as a member of another team, Akademisk Boldklub (Academic Ball Club), was another matter. He was described as being less than vocal and a little too reluctant to come off his line. And in Bohr's only season with AB, in 1905, he demonstrated beyond a doubt that as a goalkeeper he was a brilliant physicist.

AB was playing a German side, Mittweidaer BC, when a player from the opposition launched a long shot that Bohr should have handled easily. As the story goes, the ball sailed into the AB net unmolested.

Bohr apologized to his teammates after the match, admitting that he'd been caught daydreaming about the solution to a mathematical problem.

Bohr's brother proved to be more adept at balancing science and soccer. Harald Bohr, who went on to become a groundbreaking mathematician, made his AB debut as a sixteen-year-old halfback and later scored two goals for the Danish team that won a silver medal in soccer at the 1908 London Olympics.

Albania Can't Afford to Swap Jerseys

Albania wears red jerseys, red shorts, and red socks at home, and its players would have been red-faced to match in September 1993 had they swapped shirts with Spain after a World Cup qualifying loss in Tirana.

Spain pounded the Albanians, 5–1, to close out qualifying play in first place in European Group 3, while Albania, fifteen points behind, brought up the rear. But if the Spaniards wanted to celebrate their official passage to World Cup USA '94 by swapping jerseys, they were rebuffed by the poverty-stricken Albanians, who were on orders from their coach not to trade shirts—lest they play their next qualifier on a "shirts versus skins" basis.

It seems the Albanian soccer federation, Federata Shqiptarë e Futbollit, had no money for replacement jerseys. In fact, it had a hard time rounding up enough uniforms for the Spain match. As for the players, they had to make their way to the game, at the modest twenty-thousand-seat national stadium, Qemal Stafa, at their own expense.

As it turned out, it didn't matter what Albania wore or did not wear nearly eight months later in its next match. The Albanians lost, again 5–1, to Macedonia in Tetovo.

The Albanians were no less embarrassed than the players from APOP/ Kinyras Peyias FC, who played host to Cypriot league rival Alki Larnaca FC in October 2007.

Both sides donned similar blue-and-yellow uniforms, so, as is custom, the home team was ordered to change. But into what? Having no alternate uniform, APOP took the field in generic white shirts with numbers written on the back with a marking pen.

Crowd of Twenty-nine Watches Twenty-two Scotsmen Open the Season

A total of twenty-nine spectators—seven more than the number of players on the field—were on hand to watch East Stirling beat host Clydebank, 2–1, to open the 1999–2000 Scottish first-division season. The turnout was the smallest ever for a senior match in Britain.

Clydebank had sold its stadium, Kilbowie Park, to pay its bills and was forced to play its home games forty-five miles away in Greenock, apparently a trek too long for most Clydebank supporters.

The only thing worse than twenty-nine watching twenty-two was played out in Alajuela, where in August 2005 just nineteen fans turned up at Carmelita's 2,200-capacity stadium for a Costa Rican first-division match with Santos.

Not only did Carmelita lose, 2–1, but fifteen of those paying customers were backing Santos. Gate receipts totaled $78—not even enough to pay stadium security guards.

Ball Bursts on Way to Goal in Belgian Match

It's the odd question that pops up on referee tests: What should be done if a ball bursts or becomes deflated during play?

Farfetched, but the situation landed in the lap of referee Serge Gumienny in November 2004 during a Belgian first-division match in Brussels between RSC Anderlecht and RAA Louvieroise.

In the sixty-fourth minute, with the visitors leading, 1–0, Anderlecht's Walter Baseggio unleashed a vicious shot from the fringe of the penalty area. The ball exploded on impact with Baseggio's foot, but it made like a dying quail and twisted its way into the goal nevertheless.

Gumienny, unaware that the ball had gone flat, allowed the goal, despite the vehement protests of La Louviere players. Anderlecht went on to win, 2–1.

Had the referee seen what TV viewers saw, he would have noted that the ball's rubber lining had come loose from the leather casing and burst on its way to La Louviere's net.

Perhaps he would then have taken the proper action, according to the Laws of the Game: "The game shall be stopped and restarted by dropping the new ball at the place where the first ball became defective, unless it was within the goal-area at that time, in which case it shall be dropped on that part of the goal-area line which runs parallel to the goal-line, at the point nearest to where the ball was when play was stopped."

Six-man Pachuca Won't Do

It took Puebla only eighty minutes to defeat host Pachuca, 4–1, in a Mexican first-division match in February 2001, thanks to Pachuca's inability to keep enough players on the field.

Four Pachuca players—Omar Arellano, Francisco Ferreira, Adao Martinez, and Pedro Pineda—had already been ejected and the Tuzos ("Gophers") had made all three of their substitutions when, with ten minutes remaining, Raymundo Gonzalez collapsed and had to be carried from the field.

Left with six players, one below the minimum, Pachuca forfeited. The most disappointed player on the field was Puebla and Mexico midfielder Alberto García Aspe, who had scored all four of his side's goals to wipe out a 1–0 deficit and was gunning for a fifth.

Goalkeepers Are Their Own Worst Enemies

Goalkeepers are, well, different.

Two examples from February 2004:

Goalkeeper Gabor Kiraly was watching from the sidelines as his club, Hertha Berlin, played host Hannover 96 in a German second-division match, when Hertha scored. Kiraly, a Hungarian international, leaped off the bench in celebration and landed awkwardly, sustaining a calf injury that kept him out of action for two months.

That same weekend in Istanbul, Fenerbahçe 'keeper Volkan Demirel decided to celebrate a Turkish first-division victory over crosstown rival Galatasaray by tossing his jersey into the crowd. Demirel apparently hurled the shirt with too much vigor because he dislocated his shoulder and missed Fenerbahçe's next two games.

And here's one from February 2007:

Bayern Munich thought it was in a bit of trouble heading into its UEFA Cup match at Aberdeen after German international goalkeeper Oliver Kahn was sent home with the flu. Then his backup, Michael Rensing, injured his back . . . while tying his shoes.

"In an emergency we'll find someone to tie his laces for him," Bayern coach Ottmar Hitzfeld told reporters.

It was not exactly a laughing matter for Hitzfeld. If Rensing couldn't play, he'd have to turn to his number three, forty-one-year-old Bernd Dreher, who had played only three matches for the German giant over the previous three seasons.

Rensing, however, recovered in time—in time to start the first leg and give up two first-half goals that put Bayern in a 2–1 hole. Fortunately for Rensing, Bayern later equalized to escape with a 2–2 draw, and in the second leg two weeks later in Munich, the Germans rolled to a 5–1 win to stride into the round of sixteen. In goal for Bayern that night was Kahn, while Rensing was safe and sound on the bench.

Player Loses Finger in Fence-climbing Celebration

Here's a story for every girl who's complained that the referee wouldn't allow her to play while wearing a bracelet, for every boy denied his wristwatch or lucky necklace, for every GQ type ordered to put tape over his stud earrings.

In December 2004 Paolo Diogo scored in a Swiss first-division match to give his struggling club, Servette, an insurmountable 4–1 lead over Schaffhausen. To celebrate, Diogo ran to the grandstand and scaled a perimeter fence, but when he came down he was missing a finger.

"When I jumped down from the fence, I didn't feel anything at all," Diogo, age twenty-nine, told the daily *Blick*. "The first thing that I noticed that [indicated] something was missing from my hand was when it started to hurt. And it hurt tremendously."

Half of the Portuguese player's finger was snapped off after his wedding band caught on the fence as he leaped to the ground. Club officials recovered the digit, but surgeons were unable to reattach it.

Incidentally, during Diogo's climb up the fence, referee Florian Etter gave him a yellow card for excessive celebration.

An ankle injury can't compare with losing a digit, but it can be just as embarrassing, as Fabian Espindola demonstrated in September 2008 during a Major League Soccer match between Real Salt Lake and the host Los Angeles Galaxy.

Six minutes into the game, Espindola scored for Salt Lake. As the

Galaxy defense pulled out of its own penalty area, leaving the Argentine striker offside, Real's Kyle Beckerman pounded a volley off a poor L.A. clearance that Espindola head-flicked past Galaxy goalkeeper Josh Wicks, who was making his MLS debut.

While Espindola was celebrating with his customary backflip, referee Michael Kennedy mulled over the situation, eventually ruling Espindola offside on the play. Bad enough, but Espindola also failed to stick his landing at the end of his backflip: landing awkwardly, he injured his right ankle and was sidelined for two months.

With Espindola watching the second half on crutches, Salt Lake scratched out a 2–2 draw. His replacement, Yura Movsisyan, scored one goal and assisted on a second.

A Painful Testimonial Match

It was the soccer equivalent of the birthday boy getting sick at his own party: the August 2000 testimonial match for Manchester United favorite Denis Irwin, pitting United against crosstown rival Manchester City at Old Trafford.

Just eight minutes into the match, Irwin was cut down by a clumsy challenge by City's George Weah and had to be stretchered off. Weah put his arm around Irwin's shoulder by way of apology, but the Irishman angrily brushed it aside. Irwin returned and hobbled about the field on his swollen ankle until he was substituted in the thirty-seventh minute.

Weah, the Liberian legend who later was named African Player of the Century, later caused Phil Neville to suffer a head laceration in an aerial clash, and he brought down Danny Tiatto with a harsh tackle. Irwin, noting those and other challenges by the newly promoted City, called the evening "the toughest testimonial I have ever played in."

If Irwin, capped fifty-six times by Ireland and winner of fifteen major honors during his ten years with United, needed any consolation, he got it: United won, 2–0. Oh, and the match netted Irwin a cool million.

11 TRAGEDIES

*In the United States, soccer is associated with fan riots and similar may-
hem. But the dark side of the sport is darker than that. This chapter
opens with accounts of air crashes involving top teams; later, accounts of
player deaths, as well as stories of stadium disasters. Imagine the New
York Yankees' plane going down in the midst of a pennant race, or a star
Green Bay Packer collapsing and dying on the fifty-yard line during a
nationally televised game. Soccer has suffered that and much more.*

Death of a Team

It's the unthinkable that haunts the world of sports: a plane plum-
mets, claiming a star athlete or an entire team. Such a dreadful tragedy has happened several times since the emergence of commercial
flight, and the worst of all involved defending Italian first-division
champion Torino Calcio in 1949.

On May 4 the plane carrying the entire Torino team plunged into
the Basilica di Superga that overlooks Turin, killing all thirty-one
aboard, including every first-team and reserve-team player, the manager, the coach, and the trainer. Torino was returning from Lisbon,

where it had played a benefit match against Benfica the day before; a thick fog was blanketing Turin at 5:05 p.m., when the three-engine aircraft went down west of the city.

The crash devastated Italian soccer as the country lost not only its best club but also ten members of its national team. The entire nation closed down for a week, and the Italian League temporarily suspended play. An estimated half million, said to be the largest such turnout in Italy, attended a state funeral given for the team. The grief in Turin was acute because Il Grande Torino had won the last four Italian Serie A championships and was well on its way to a fifth.

Torino was left with only its youth team. Torino's last four games that season were contested by the Torino boys and, out of fairness, the youth teams of the originally scheduled opponents. The inspired Torino boys won all four to leave their club on top, five points ahead of Inter Milan.

Torino, known as the people's team in Turin, would not win another championship until 1976, by which time Juventus, its aristocratic crosstown rival, had won fourteen, a haul it has since doubled.

There was, however, a silver lining to the tragedy in the form of Sandor Mazzola. Mazzola was the son of Valentino Mazzola, the Torino and Italy captain who had scored 109 goals in just 220 league matches. Sandor was only six years old when his father died in the Torino crash, but in the 1960s he became one of the most popular players ever in Italy. A gifted goal scorer, the younger Mazzola made seventy appearances for the national team and scored 115 goals in 405 games for Inter Milan, helping that club to European Cup triumphs in 1964 and 1965.

A lesser-known silver lining to the disaster was provided by the young son of another star player. Striker Ladislao Kubala, after fleeing his native Hungary in the wake of the communist takeover of that country, settled in with the Italian club Pro Patria in 1949. That May he agreed to join Torino as a guest player in Lisbon but bowed out at the last minute because his son fell ill. Thus spared, Kubala moved to Spain and, despite seven knee injuries, would go on to score 256 goals in 329 matches for FC Barcelona (1951–61) and coach the Spanish National Team for nearly a dozen years.

Other soccer-related air disasters:
1958. Twenty-three were killed in early February when an Elizabe-

than airliner carrying Manchester United home from a European Cup quarterfinal at Red Star Belgrade crashed in Munich. The plane stopped to refuel, then went down in a snowstorm during its third take-off attempt. Among the dead were England right halfback Duncan Edwards as well as Roger Byrne, Geoff Bent, Eddie Colman, David Pegg, Mark Jones, Tommy Taylor, and Liam "Billy" Whelan, plus three United officials and eight journalists. Two other players were so severely injured that they never played again.

Coach Matt Busby was badly hurt in the crash—he was twice read his last rites—but soon recovered and quickly set about rebuilding his team. His centerpiece was star center forward Bobby Charlton, who in the crash was thrown sixty yards from the plane and later was found near the wreckage, still strapped to his seat and suffering from deep shock. The club eventually allowed him to return to his home in Ashington for a two-week break, and the twenty-one-year-old Charlton, still despondent over the tragedy, found himself on the brink of walking away from soccer. But one day he received a pep talk from his physician and later watched children in a kickabout in a local park, and he was inspired to carry on.

Weeks after the crash, a decimated Manchester United lost in the Euro Cup semifinals to AC Milan by a 7–1 aggregate, but in May United fell gallantly in the English F.A. Cup final to Bolton Wanderers, 2–0. Soon the team, known as "Busby's Babes," hit its stride. Featuring Charlton and newcomers George Best and Denis Law, United won the F.A. Cup in 1963; English league championships in 1965, 1967, and 1968; and the ultimate prize, the European Cup, in 1968.

In addition to his heroics for Man U., Charlton and his brother Jackie, a towering center halfback for Leeds United, would help England win the 1966 World Cup.

1961. A plane crash claimed the lives of twenty-four members of Green Cross, which was on its way to a Chilean Cup match.

1969. All seventy-four aboard, including twenty-five players, coaches, and officials from one of Bolivia's most popular teams, The Strongest, died when their plane crashed into a mountain in the Andes, 15,500 feet above sea level and seventy-two miles from its destination, La Paz.

A twenty-sixth Strongest player, Rolando Vargas, did not make the trip because he had been ejected from the team's previous match and was sitting out a suspension.

1979. Pakhtakor Tashkent of the Soviet first division lost seventeen players and coaches when the plane carrying the team to a match in Minsk collided with another aircraft above Donetsk.

The division's seventeen other clubs each gave several players to the crippled Uzbekistan-based team. Although league officials also granted Pakhtakor an amnesty from relegation, it didn't need it as it went on to finish the 1979 campaign in ninth place.

1987. Twenty Alianza Lima players were killed when their flight from Pacullpa plunged into the Pacific near Lima, Peru, shortly before Christmas.

1989. Fourteen Holland-based Surinamese players were among the 174 killed in a crash at Paramaribo airport. The players were returning to Surinam to take part in a postseason tour.

1993. Zambia lost eighteen members of its national team when a military plane carrying the squad to a World Cup qualifier in Senegal crashed into the Atlantic near Libreville, Gabon. All thirty people on board, including five team officials, perished.

The Zambians carried on with a team of inexperienced replacements and went into their final qualifying match needing only a tie with Morocco—second in the group and two points behind Zambia—to advance to their first World Cup. The Moroccans, however, won, 1–0, to edge Zambia by a single point and deny the 1994 World Cup of what would have been the tournament's overwhelming sentimental favorite.

Player Deaths

Soccer is the contact sport without a reputation among soccer moms for being overly dangerous, but the game has had its share of on-field fatalities, some because of congenital health problems, some the result of freak accidents, some due to the contact nature of the sport.

The most prominent player to die on-field was Cameroon's Marc-Vivien Foe, whose life ended in France during a FIFA Confederations Cup semifinal against Colombia in Lyon in June 2003. The twenty-eight-year-old Foe, who as a teen played every minute of Cameroon's three matches at the 1994 World Cup, collapsed in the center circle in the seventy-second minute.

Foe died of a heart attack; in technical terms, a hereditary cardiac hypertrophia of the left and right ventricles and a hypoplasia of the apex of the heart. But whatever the wording of the cause, what happened to the popular Foe sent shock waves throughout the sport and cast a pall over the remainder of the tournament, which ended with France's victory over a despondent Cameroon in the final.

There have been several other notable soccer deaths over the years. In December 2007, thirty-five-year-old Motherwell captain Phil O'Donnell suffered an apparent seizure and collapsed late in a Scottish Premier League match with Dundee United. He died later that day at a hospital, the victim of a heart attack.

O'Donnell went down as he was about to leave the field for a substitute. Medical staff from both Motherwell and Dundee United treated the veteran midfielder on the field at Fir Park for five minutes before he was stretchered off.

The match was resumed with his substitute, Marc Fitzpatrick, officially entering the game in the seventy-eighth minute. Moments later, however, O'Donnell's nephew, David Clarkson, was substituted because he was too upset to continue playing. Motherwell won, 5–3, thanks in part to Clarkson's two goals.

O'Donnell, who made one appearance for Scotland in a once-bright career dimmed by injury, was married with four children.

Spanish international Antonio Puerta, age twenty-two, died in a Seville hospital in August 2007, three days after he suffered an apparent heart attack in a league match. Puerta was near his team's goal in the thirty-first minute of a Spanish first-division game between host Sevilla and Getafe when he lost consciousness and crumpled to the turf. The young Sevilla midfielder left the field under his own power minutes later but collapsed again in the dressing room, and his condition worsened at the hospital.

At the time of his death, Puerta was six weeks away from becoming a father for the first time.

Hard-nosed defender Serginho of São Caetano, told during a physical exam nine months earlier that he would be lucky not to drop dead because of cardiac problems, did just that in November 2004 in a Brazilian league match with host São Paulo FC at Morumbi Stadium. Serginho, age thirty, fell to the turf during a goal kick in the fifty-ninth minute of a scoreless game. One player tripped over him before physicians realized what happened and sprinted onto the field to perform CPR. He was rushed to São Luiz Hospital, where he died hours later, leaving a wife and four-year-old son.

Though São Caetano's medical staff said the player had been receiving treatment for his heart, three weeks later authorities charged club president Nairo Ferreira de Souza and team doctor Paulo Fortes with murder for allowing Serginho to play despite the risk. Club attorney Luiz Fernando Pacheco expressed surprise over the charges; he maintained that the prestigious Incor Heart Institute, where Serginho underwent his exam earlier in the year, did not inform São Caetano of the defender's life-threatening condition. Said Pacheco, "There was just a note saying he wasn't fit to practice."

The derby between Guatemala City rivals Municipal and Comunicaciones took a deadly turn in February 2004 when a player suffered fatal injuries in a collision during a league match.

Municipal goalkeeper Danny Ortiz, age twenty-seven, was the victim, absorbing a blow to the chest from Comunicaciones forward Mario Rodriguez.

Ortiz, formerly a member of Comunicaciones and the Guatemalan National Team, was knocked unconscious and taken to a hospital, where he initially was listed in stable condition. But hours later he died of internal bleeding and heart complications.

Hungarian international striker Miklós Fehér collapsed and died of a heart attack in the final moments of a Portuguese league match between his club, Benfica, and host Vitoria Guimaraes in January 2004. Fehér, due to be married later in the year, was buried in Györ following a funeral attended by thousands.

The twenty-four-year-old had entered the game in the sixtieth minute and, in added-on time, was shown a yellow card. Fehér smiled at the referee and then, with his hands on his thighs, leaned forward before pitching backward.

As team medics attempted to revive the former Hungarian Youth Player of the Year, some Benfica teammates kneeled to pray while coach José Antonio Camacho and other players wept.

Brazilian forward Marcio Dos Santos, twenty-eight years old, died of a heart attack hours after scoring for Deportivo Wanka in an October 2002 Peruvian league match. Also that month, a lightning bolt killed striker Geovanny Cordoba and former Colombian international Hermann Gaviria during a Deportivo Cali training session held in a downpour. Three months earlier, a player in Ukraine was struck by lightning and died.

Youssef Belkhoja, a defender for Wydad Casablanca, dropped dead on the field in the twenty-second minute of a September 2001 Moroccan Cup semifinal game against Raja Casablanca. Cause of death was a heart attack. Belkhoja was buried in his hometown of Kenitra, on a Sunday, one day before he was to have joined the Moroccan National Team's training camp in Rabat.

Two players, one of them sixteen years old, were killed and ten others severely burned in August 2001 when a bolt of lightning struck a stadium in Chiquimulilla, Guatemala, during a third-division match. The bolt hit a metal guard rail, creating a ring of electricity that burned players, coaches, and officials. Remarkably, no spectators were hurt.

In fifteen months over 1999–2000 four Romanian league players collapsed and died, including Astra Ploiesti's Stefan Vrabioru, who succumbed en route to the hospital after making his first-division debut at Rapid Bucharest in his team's season opener.

Eleven players were killed and more than thirty spectators injured by a lightning strike at an October 1999 match in Congo between village teams from Bena Tshadi and Basangana. All eleven players were from the host Bena Tshadi team, prompting investigators to blame the fateful bolt on witchcraft. None of the Basangana players were hurt.

Wahib Jbara of Hapoel Taiba collapsed and later died during an Israeli first-division match with Tel Aviv's Bnei Yehuda in May 1997. Spectators and TV viewers watched the frantic efforts of doctors and paramedics to save the twenty-three-year-old, who died while being transported to a hospital.

Jbara, it was later learned, had been diagnosed two years earlier with a genetic heart condition. His club announced that the team would be known as Hapoel Wahib Taiba in the player's memory. A week later, galvanized by the death of Jbara, Hapoel defeated Zafririm Holon, 1–0, its first win in six months.

The 1995 Arab Player of the Year died of a heart attack in January 1997 after playing in a friendly at Louiten Stadium in Tunis. Tunisian international defender Medi Ben Rekhissa, age twenty-six, collapsed and efforts to revive him at the stadium and later at a local hospital were unsuccessful.

York City striker Dave Longhurst, twenty-five years old, collapsed and died from a rare heart condition during a September 1990 English league match against Lincoln City.

Nigeria's Samuel Okwarji, age twenty-four, collapsed and died of a heart attack in the eightieth minute of a 1–0 victory over Angola in August 1989. Okwarji might have been saved had someone been able to locate the key to the stadium locker containing CPR equipment. (Compounding the tragedy that day were the deaths of seven fans who suffocated because one hundred thousand spectators were allowed to jam a stadium built to hold eighty thousand.)

With his father, former Holland goalkeeper Jan Jongbloed, looking on, DWS 'keeper Erik Jongbloed was struck by lightning and killed during a September 1984 Dutch league match.

In the thirteenth minute of the thirteenth game of the 1973–74 Portuguese season, FC Porto's Fernando Pascoal "Pavao" das Neves collapsed and died, an apparent heart attack victim.

Oliver Petit, age twenty, collapsed during a French amateur match and died of a blood clot in the brain in 1987. His younger brother, Arsenal midfielder Emmanuel Petit, would go on to help France win its first World Cup, in 1998.

One player was killed and four others were seriously injured in February 1967 when lightning struck during an English Amateur Cup quarterfinal between Highgate United and Enfield.

Wanderers of Montevideo won the Uruguayan championship in December 1931, but the excitement of the moment caused Uruguayan international René Borjas to suffer a fatal heart attack, a week before his thirty-fourth birthday.

In September 1931 goalkeeper John Thompson of Glasgow Celtic dived at the feet of Rangers forward Sam English and suffered a fractured skull. A Scottish international, Thompson, age twenty-three, died in a hospital five hours later without regaining consciousness. It was the first known death of a player resulting from an on-field injury in the history of high-level soccer.

Oscar Lopez de Filippis of Olimpia collided with another player in a February 1923 match in Paraguay with Sastre Sport in Asunción and died of internal injuries.

The Lancet reported in 1899 that nearly one hundred men in Britain had lost their lives over the previous eight years while playing soccer or rugby. One 1896 incident claimed the life of Joseph Powell of Arsenal. In a match with Kettering Town, Powell caught his foot on the shoulder of an opponent while attempting to kick a high ball; he fell and suffered a compound fracture of the arm. (One man who rushed to his aid fainted at the sight of the protruding bone.) The arm was amputated above the elbow, but infection set in and Powell died days later at age twenty-six.

And off the field:

The goalkeeper of Benin's under-20 team was beaten to death in January 2005 by an angry mob that blamed the eighteen-year-old for his side's defeat in its opening match of the eight-nation African Youth Championship. Benin, hosting the tournament in Cotonou, lost to neighboring Nigeria, 3–0. That night, Samiou Yessoufou, nicknamed "Campos" after the acrobatic Mexican goalkeeping star Jorge Campos, was kicked and beaten at a nightclub near the team's hotel. He died of a brain hemorrhage the following morning. Later, authorities arrested six men believed to have attacked Yessoufou in a botched attempt to steal his mobile phone.

The grief-stricken Benin players upset Ivory Coast, 4–1, in their next match and went on to qualify for the 2005 FIFA World Youth Championship as one of Africa's top four teams. In Africa's third-place game Benin played Morocco to a 1–1 draw, then won on penalty kicks, 5–3, as Yessoufou's successor, Djidonou, saved the Moroccans' final attempt.

The most infamous death in soccer history might not have happened the way many Americans were led to believe. Defender Andrés Escobar, who scored the own goal that contributed to Colombia's 2–1 loss to the United States at the Rose Bowl in the first round of the 1994 World Cup, was shot dead ten days later outside El Indio, an exclusive Medellin nightclub. His fiancée, who witnessed the shooting, was not hurt.

The gunman was said to have sneered, "This is for the autogoal" (own goal) while firing the fatal shots. Other accounts have him barking "Goal!" before each of the six shots he fired into Escobar.

Thousands attended the funeral for Escobar, including Colombian President César Gaviria.

Early reports described the man behind the gun as a disappointed fan who'd let his emotions boil over. For Americans whose limited knowledge of soccer was shaped in part by reports of crazed soccer fans abroad, Escobar's death only reinforced their image of the sport's supporters.

Later accounts, however, described the shooter as a hit man from a gambling syndicate that lost hundreds of thousands of dollars as the result of Escobar's miscue. Indeed, Colombia had been predicted by Pelé and several other experts to be the tournament's giant-killer. After the team's unexpectedly quick exit, some members of the Colombian delegation received death threats, and several players decided to lay low, extending their stays in the United States. Escobar, unfortunately, returned home immediately.

Police ultimately concluded that the shooting was the result of an argument over Escobar's poor job of parking his car at the nightclub. Those who support that version ask that if the shooting was a classic hit by a professional, why was the shooter accompanied at the time by several other men and a woman? Escobar's family, meanwhile, maintained that authorities had no interest in getting to the bottom of what they believe was a contract killing.

The supposed hit man, Humberto Muñoz Castro, was caught with the Llama .38 used in the shooting and confessed, but he claimed that he did not know his victim was Escobar.

And there are those who believe this scenario: brothers Pedro Gallon Henao and Santiago Gallon Henao, gangsters whose interests included drugs, money laundering, and professional Colombian soccer clubs, taunted Escobar outside the Medellin nightclub; Escobar maintained that the own goal was a mistake, but the brothers disagreed and ordered a bodyguard, Muñoz, to bump off the player.

Muñoz's forty-three-year prison term was confirmed by the Colombian Supreme Court in March 2000, but he was released in October 2005 after serving eleven years. (The judge, whose name was not revealed for security reasons, cited Muñoz's good behavior.) This is yet another curious twist in a country where fifteen professional players, including other Colombian internationals, have been murdered in the years since Escobar's slaying. Most of those killings remain unsolved.

Goal Topples, Man Is Killed

A man in Decatur, Tennessee, was killed in August 1995 when a goal fell on him, making him one of more than two dozen victims of fatal soccer goal accidents in the United States since 1979.

Juan Santa Rosa, age thirty-two, was swinging from the crossbar of a goal at Athens Regional Park, causing the goal to topple. Santa Rosa died of severe chest trauma.

Signs posted in English and Spanish warning park visitors not to climb on the goals had been torn down by vandals.

Heading Balls Takes Fatal Toll on English Star

A playing career spent heading heavy leather balls was a major factor in the January 2002 death of a former English international. Jeff Astle, who collapsed and died at age fifty-nine, was found to have been suffering from a degenerative brain disease, a coroner said.

The former West Bromwich Albion striker scored 137 goals in 292 games—many of them with his head.

South Staffordshire coroner Andrew Haigh said the cause of death was a buildup of protein in blood vessels in the brain, a condition exacerbated in his younger days by heading. One consultant neurological pathologist told a coroner's inquest that the damage to Astle's brain was at the front of the head and consistent with "repeated minor trauma" such as that found in boxers. With the ruling, the death was officially attributed to "industrial disease."

The conclusion would appear to back up recent studies that suggest a link between damage to the brain and an excessive number of headers. However, the ball used in Astle's era was made of leather and was not waterproof. On wet days—the norm in England during the soccer season—the ball would quickly pick up moisture and significantly gain weight beyond the accepted maximum of sixteen ounces. Beginning in the mid-1970s, balls have been made of synthetic material that maintains the proper weight throughout a match.

Soviets Keep Fatal Stadium Crush a Secret

In January 1971 Celtic was leading its bitter Glasgow rival, Rangers, by a goal late in a Scottish first-division match at Ibrox Park when Rangers scored an equalizer. Disappointed Rangers fans who had been exiting the stadium heard the crowd roar and attempted to rush back inside, but the crush caused a steel barrier to collapse, killing 66 and injuring 140.

Eleven years later Spartak Moscow was leading Haarlem of Holland, 1–0, in the second round of the UEFA Cup at the Grand Arena of the Central Lenin Stadium before a crowd of fifteen thousand when the Soviet side scored a late clincher. Spartak fans who had been leaving via icy steps tried to force their way back in and created a crush in which possibly 340 people died.

The whole world had learned of the Ibrox disaster almost immediately. The extent of the Soviet tragedy, however, was kept a secret by the government until 1989.

In 1992, after the fall of the communist bloc, a memorial was created at what is now known as the Luzhniki Stadium for the victims of the Spartak-Haarlem disaster. In 2007, on the twenty-fifth anniversary of the tragedy, Spartak and Haarlem players met again in a charity match for the families of those who died. Said former Spartak forward Sergei Shvetsov, whose strike set off the stampede, "I wish I hadn't scored that goal."

The Worst of the Stadium Disasters

Americans who consider soccer synonymous with fan violence have good reason: it has been estimated that as many as thirteen hundred spectators have been killed at soccer matches since 1955, usually the result of high emotions, antiquated stadium design, or incompetent crowd control that bordered on the criminal.

Here is the disaster that, in the minds of many Americans, first helped tie the words *soccer* and *fan violence* together.

In May 1964 Argentina was leading Peru, 1–0, late in an Olympic qualifying match before a crowd of forty-five thousand at the National Stadium in Lima. Although Peru had three games remaining, its chances of reaching the final sixteen at the Tokyo Olympics soccer tournament were thin. When an apparent equalizer by Peru in the eighty-fourth minute was disallowed by Uruguayan referee Angel Eduardo Pazos, two fans attacked the referee, whose decision to abandon the match triggered a mass invasion of the field.

Security guards, in an effort to scatter the marauding fans, fired tear gas grenades and bullets, but that only touched off a stampede. At the stadium's north end, three of five steel gates were left locked by stadium personnel who apparently had wandered off to watch the game, and some two hundred perished in the resulting crush. According to one report, a police officer in the upper stands, seized and dangled by fans, was dropped to the concrete fifty feet below and was killed. Later, many others died or were hurt in the rioting that raged outside the stadium.

In all, 318 were killed and more than 500 injured. Peruvian President Fernando Belaúnde Terry declared a week of national mourning and a monthlong suspension of constitutional rights.

Other stadium disasters:

Abidjan. Pushing and shoving outside Felix Houphouet-Boigny stadium prior to a March 2009 match turned into a deadly stampede that claimed 22 lives and injured 132. Forty minutes prior to kickoff of a World Cup qualifier between Malawi and host Ivory Coast, fans began to force their way forward and police, in a misguided attempt to control the situation, fired tear gas canisters. The weight of the surging crowd caused a wall to collapse, and several fans fell to their death.

The match was played nevertheless; Ivory Coast won, 5–0.

FIFA later fined Ivory Coast's soccer federation $46,800 and ordered capacity at Houphouet-Boigny stadium cut from 34,600 to 20,000 for the next World Cup qualifier.

Accra. A total of 126 fans were killed in May 2001 in a stadium stampede during a match between two of Ghana's top clubs. Hearts of Oak were leading the visiting Asante Kotoko, 2–1, in the eighty-fifth minute when Asante supporters began hurling seats, bottles, and other missiles onto the field. Police fired tear gas, and that set off a stampede.

The injured were rushed to local hospitals, and appeals for help from all available doctors were broadcast by radio stations.

The disaster was the worst in a spate of similar incidents in Africa. Two weeks earlier, eight fans were killed and another fifty were hurt in a stampede during a match in Lubumbashi between two of Congo's leading clubs, Mazembe and Lupopo. Spectators began hurling bottles after Mazembe tied the score at 1–1 in the eightieth minute, and police responded with tear gas, causing a panic. Packed beyond the stadium's capacity of twenty thousand, fans knocked over barriers in their attempts to escape the crush.

Nearly three weeks before that, forty-three were killed in a stampede during a league match between archrivals Kaizer Chiefs and Orlando Pirates at Ellis Park in Johannesburg, South Africa. And in July 2000, thirteen died in a stampede during a World Cup qualifier in Harare between host Zimbabwe and South Africa after police fired tear gas to control unruly fans with ten minutes remaining.

The string of disasters in Africa led to action, at least in Accra. Six months after the Hearts of Oak–Asante Kotoko match, a half dozen high-ranking police officers were charged with manslaughter by a commission that concluded that the use of tear gas turned the situation deadly.

Guatemala City. Eighty-two fans were killed and another 150 were injured in a stadium stampede in October 1996 before a World Cup qualifier between Guatemala and Costa Rica. Dozens of bodies were laid along the stadium track as order was restored.

Capacity at Mateo Flores National Stadium is forty-five thousand, but approximately sixty thousand fans, many holding counterfeit tickets, tried to force their way in, creating a deadly crush along the perimeter fence at the base of the grandstand.

At the time of the disaster both Guatemalan President Alvaro Arzu and his Costa Rican counterpart were inside the stadium. In fact, it was Arzu who announced that the match had been postponed.

Ten months later, the families of each of the dead were presented with a $6,500 check from FIFA. The money was drawn from fines imposed on FIFA member-nations for infractions and misconduct.

Bastia, Corsica. The UEFA banned the practice of adding temporary stands for high-profile matches in Europe after eighteen fans were killed and more than two thousand injured in the collapse of seating at Armand-Césari de Furiani Stadium before a May 1992 French Cup semifinal between host Bastia and Olympique Marseille.

Furiani's official capacity was eight thousand, but ten thousand seats were added to accommodate the demand for tickets.

Orkney. At least forty were killed and fifty injured in a panic sparked by brawls in the stands during a January 1991 game between South Africa's Orlando Pirates and Kaizer Chiefs attended by thirty thousand. Many of the dead were pinned against a fence separating the stands from the field.

Sheffield. Ninety-six fans were crushed to death at Hillsborough

Stadium in April 1989 prior to an English F.A. Cup semifinal between Liverpool and Nottingham Forest. Liverpool fans without tickets massed outside a stadium gate and security guards, believing they were defusing a dangerous situation, made the fatal mistake of allowing two thousand of them to enter. The surge overwhelmed two sections and ultimately created a crush at the bottom of the standing-room-only terrace, which was separated from the field by a tall perimeter fence.

The dead—all Liverpool supporters—ranged in age from ten to sixty-seven, but most were teenagers. Some of the survivors were saved when they were hauled out of the crush by spectators sitting in an upper section.

This tragedy prompted FIFA to embark on a long-overdue campaign to eliminate standing-room sections from major stadiums throughout the world.

As an epilogue to this tragedy, in May 2004 goalkeeper Paul Harrison, age nineteen, made his debut for Liverpool as a substitute in a season-ending match with visiting Newcastle. Fifteen years and one month earlier, Harrison's father, Gary, and his uncle, Stephen, were killed in the Hillsborough disaster.

Katmandu. Ninety-three were trampled to death or suffocated and more than one hundred were injured in March 1988 after a fierce hailstorm scattered a crowd of thirty thousand watching a match between a team from host Nepal and one from Bangladesh. Seven of the stadium's eight exits were locked.

Bradford. In May 1985, as host Bradford City and Lincoln City closed out the English third-division campaign, the roof at Valley Parade Ground caught fire just before halftime and the stadium was reduced to ashes in four minutes.

The blaze, officially blamed on a discarded cigarette, killed fifty-six, many of them children and elderly, among them Bradford's former club chairman, Samuel Firth, age eighty-six. Another 265 were injured, including those who suffered burns.

Several were trapped when they found exits locked. As one spectator described it, panicked fans rushed to a padlocked exit and were saved only after a couple of burly men lowered their shoulders and broke open the gate. A total of twenty-two fans and police officers later were awarded commendations for their bravery during the blaze.

Strong winds and Valley Parade Ground's wooden roof were later listed as contributing factors. The club had already made plans to replace the roof with one made of steel after the season.

A crowd of eleven thousand had turned out for what was supposed to be a celebration: before the game Bradford captain Peter Jackson was presented with the third division championship trophy, and Bradford fans were looking forward to a 1985–86 season in the second division.

Brussels. In the second disaster involving Liverpool in four years, thirty-nine people were killed at Heysel Stadium as the result of fan violence prior to the 1985 European Cup final. The carnage was seen by a worldwide television audience that had tuned in for pre-match coverage.

The violence began an hour before kickoff of the Juventus-Liverpool match as opposing fans hurled missiles at one another over a chicken-wire fence meant to keep the two sides apart. (In fact, the Juventus fans occupied a section where so-called neutral spectators were supposed to be seated.) Eventually, enraged Liverpool fans charged; fleeing Juventus fans were crushed when a wall blocking their escape collapsed. The death toll: thirty-eight Italians, one Belgian.

Remarkably, the game was played. France and Juventus star (and future UEFA president) Michel Platini, who scored the only goal of the evening, later called the tragedy "a deep wound that cannot be healed."

The disaster came to symbolize the hooliganism that had been building throughout Europe—particularly in England—since the 1970s. English clubs were initially barred by FIFA from international play; that ban was eventually lifted but the UEFA's ban within Europe lasted five years.

A Brussels court found fourteen British fans guilty of manslaughter and slapped them with fines and partly suspended jail sentences; another ten were acquitted.

Cairo. Forty-eight were trampled to death in February 1974 when fans broke down barriers and scrambled for seats at an Egyptian club match.

Buenos Aires. During a showdown of crosstown rivals at Estadio Monumental in June 1968, Boca Juniors fans ignited torches and dropped them onto River Plate supporters. Seventy-four were killed in the panic.

Kayseri, Turkey. A rock-throwing melee between warring fans of Kayserispor and Sivasspor during a Turkish second-division match at Kayseri Ataturk Stadium in September 1967 caused a stampede that left forty-four dead and approximately three hundred injured. Fan violence continued for days in Kayseri and Sivas.

Manchester. Thirty-three were killed and more than four hundred injured in March 1946 during an English F.A. Cup game between host Bolton and Stoke City. Some sixty-five thousand were inside Burnden Park, but some fans in a throng of twenty thousand left outside broke through gates, causing a wall to collapse and touching off a stampede.

Glasgow. More than one hundred people, many of them police and firefighters, were injured in 1909 after crosstown rivals Celtic and Rangers tied in a replay of the Scottish Cup final at Hampden Park (the first match ended 2–2). Spectators tore down barricades and ignited a bonfire, which was kept ablaze by whiskey. A second replay was not staged, and the cup was withheld.

Glasgow was the scene for another, earlier catastrophe as well. Though not the result of violence, the first instance of large-scale death in the stands was the 1902 collapse of a portion of the grandstand at Ibrox Park during a Scotland-England match. Twenty-five were killed and 517 were injured. Some fell as much as forty feet. The newly built stand had been undermined by heavy rainfall the night before.

An Innocuous Challenge Turns Deadly

In contact sports it's often the routine collision—not the spectacular crash of bodies—that leaves one or both of the players involved with serious injuries. Such was the case in March 2001 in Macoya, Trinidad and Tobago, where a clean clash of heads in a CONCACAF qualifier for that year's FIFA World Youth Championship ended the career, and ultimately the life, of a promising teen player.

In the fifth minute of a match between host Trinidad and Tobago and the United States, T&T under-20 captain Marvin Lee and the USA's Landon Donovan banged heads over a loose ball, leaving both players crumpled on the turf. Lee and Donovan were stretchered off the field. While the 5'8", 145-pound Donovan quickly returned to score a goal and set up two others in a 5–1 U.S. rout, the 6'2", 225-pound Lee was fitted with a neck brace and taken out of the stadium by ambulance. He never walked again.

In November that year, Donovan returned to Trinidad and Tobago as a member of the U.S. National Team and, prior to a World Cup qualifier against T&T at Port-of-Spain, presented a wheelchair-bound Lee with a U.S. jersey. Nearly two years to the day after suffering the injuries that left him paralyzed, Lee, twenty-one years old, died of pneumonia in a hospital near his home. A capacity crowd attended the memorial service for Lee at the site of his injury, the Dr. Joao Havelange Centre of Excellence, which was renamed in the player's honor.

A year before his death Lee told an interviewer: "Being the person that I am, I never really think the injury is as bad as people see it. For me, it's just like an off season—football done and [you're] doing other things now."

Tragedy revisited the T&T National Under-20 Team five months after Lee's death. Eighteen-year-old prodigy Dwight Lewis accidentally jostled a twenty-eight-year-old patron while leaving a store in Arima, Trinidad, causing the man to spill his beer. The two exchanged words, triggering a fight in which bottles were thrown. The man and two companions then chased down Lewis and repeatedly stabbed him in the head and back.

The youngster died at a local hospital. With the assailants still at large, Lewis's father, Clarence, suffered a near-fatal heart attack while identifying his son's body.

The Black Cloud over San Lorenzo

San Lorenzo, founded in 1908, has never won a Copa Libertadores, the annual South American club championship, and from 1933 it has produced just eight national titles. But if there's a curse on the club, it's directed at the players, not the team trophy case.

In 1981 San Lorenzo defender Hugo Peña was bathing an injured foot in a basin when he turned on his television and was fatally electrocuted.

Four years later, midfielder Jorge Coufanes was shot dead in a botched mugging.

The bad luck got worse for San Lorenzo in 1999–2000. Forward Ruben Bernuncio slammed his car into a bus and later died at a hospital. Winger Jose Casas was accidentally shot in the upper arm while walking near a military base; the arm was subsequently amputated, forcing him to retire. A hooligan tossed a bomb into the San Lorenzo dressing room after a match in Cordoba, injuring defender Zacarias and ending his career.

The worst blow came in April 2000 with the suicide of Mirco Saric. The twenty-one-year-old had suffered an injury and was despondent over the likelihood that his career was over.

Though San Lorenzo managed to survive its first seven decades without a player fatality, the inspiration for its founding was telling. In 1908 a priest, Lorenzo Massa, watched as a boy was seriously injured by a tram while he and other gang members played soccer in the Buenos Aires neighborhood of Almagro. Massa invited the children to move their game to his church's grounds as long as they attended mass. This collection of immigrants and Creoles grew in strength, and eventually the new club San Lorenzo de Almagro became a force in Buenos Aires.

Double Tragedy in Syria

In many cases the violence at a soccer match has more to do with ancient feuds, cultural differences, politics, or religion than anything that happens on the field. Indeed, it was a combination of all four that was at the heart of a bizarre and tragic double riot in Syria in March 2004.

Ba'thists, in control in Syria, had kept a tight lid on their Kurdish minority—some 2 million people—for years, but next door, the recent unseating of the ruling Ba'thist party in Iraq by invading U.S. forces had emboldened discontented Kurds throughout the region.

The flashpoint came in the predominantly Kurdish town of Qameshli, near the Turkish border, as a crowd estimated at up to seven thousand awaited the kickoff of a Syrian league match between Al-Jihad, a club backed by Kurds, and Al-Fatwa, supported by Arabs. While Al-Fatwa fans taunted their Al-Jihad counterparts by brandishing portraits of Iraqi leader Sadam Hussein, Al-Jihad fans waved a Kurdish flag and signs praising U.S. President George W. Bush. Stones were hurled at both Al-Jihad players and supporters. Riot police fired into the air in an effort to disperse the warring fans, but it only set off a stampede among fleeing Al-Jihad supporters. Outside the stadium, Al-Jihad fans who learned of the crush surrounded Al-Fatwa backers and attacked them.

Police reportedly shot six people to death, and another three, believed to be children, died in the stampede. One hundred were injured. But that was only Act I.

The next day, hundreds of Al-Fatwa supporters rioted at a funeral for victims of the stampede. Before it was over, one more person had died, another seventeen were hurt, and a string of shops and government offices in the area had been vandalized.

Two days after the aborted match, violence spread throughout Syria, including Damascus, 450 miles to the south, and reached as far as Belgium, where Kurds there stormed the Syrian embassy in Brussels, causing minor damage.

Illinois Youth Referee Killed by Lightning Strike

The referee of a 1996 youth match in Park Ridge, Illinois, halted play because of a passing rainstorm. Although the storm brought no thunder, John Scott Wade, age twenty, made sure that all the youngsters had safely exited the field, and despite criticism from spectators for stopping the match, he waited until skies cleared before calling the players back.

After play resumed, Wade was struck by lightning and killed.

Park Ridge subsequently installed a state-of-the-art lightning prediction system throughout the town.

Bolivian City Burns during Soccer Celebration

A portion of the jungle city of Ixiamas in northwest Bolivia was burned to the ground in August 1993 during an impromptu celebration of the national team's 3–1 upset of Uruguay in La Paz in a World Cup qualifying match.

The fire, touched off when a firework was accidentally tossed onto a thatched roof, went unnoticed as the residents made merry. Forty homes were destroyed before the blaze was extinguished.

Bolivia went on to qualify for its first World Cup in forty-four years, but it, too, went down in flames at the finals in the United States (1–0 against Germany, 0–0 versus South Korea, and 3–1 facing Spain).

Fading Uruguayan Star Commits Suicide

Nacional, the Montevideo club that for decades virtually co-owned the Uruguayan championship with crosstown rival Peñarol, began its first golden era in the 1910s, a decade in which it won the title five times.

One of that team's many stars was stalwart defensive midfielder Abdón Porte, who played 207 matches beginning in 1911 and helped Uruguay win the inaugural Copa America in 1916. Seven years after his Nacional debut, however, he lost his form and ultimately his spot in the starting lineup. Given another chance, Porte's performances drew jeers from the once-adoring Nacional fans, and the man known as El Indio was replaced by Alfredo Zibecchi.

In March 1918 Nacional celebrated yet another victory with its customary postmatch dinner at club headquarters. Shortly after midnight Porte slipped outside and returned to the team's home stadium, the Parque Central. Standing in the center circle he pulled out a revolver and fired a bullet into his heart.

Porte was twenty-seven. Tucked into his straw hat was one letter to the chairman of Nacional and one to his fiancée, whom he was to wed the following month.

Honduran Players Fight Over Pen to Sign Contract

In April 2004 the twenty-three-year-old goalkeeper for a Honduran club was convicted of murder and sentenced to ten years in prison for the slaying of a teammate following a struggle over a pen.

Robinson Tomas Melendez and Jorge Alberto Espinoza were signing their contracts at the office of Club Platense in Puerto Cortés when Espinoza asked to borrow Melendez's ballpoint pen. The goalkeeper declined and Espinoza complained to club officials. Miffed, Melendez punched his teammate in the face.

That ignited a brawl that spilled onto the street. Before it could be broken up, Espinoza had suffered massive head injuries. He later died of internal bleeding.

Garrincha

Several players over the years have worn the unofficial title of world's greatest dribbler, but there was no more unlikely holder than Manoel Francisco dos Santos, the man known as Garrincha, Portuguese slang for "Little Bird."

Garrincha became the most spellbinding dribbler of the late 1950s and early 1960s despite having one leg that was distorted and shorter than the other, the result of childhood polio.

His dazzling runs down the right wing inspired a more appropriate nickname, "The Force of Nature," but he also was known as O Torto ("The Deformed One") and Mané ("The Fool") and, worse still, Mané Garrincha. That latter tag stemmed as much from Garrincha's simple-mindedness as from his tendency to put showmanship ahead of the scoreboard. For instance: Garrincha was once in front of an open net with the ball at his feet, but he continued to dribble, eluding three defenders and the goalkeeper. Rather than score this time, he waited for one of the beaten defenders to challenge him again, then made a cut that forced the defender to grab the post to keep from falling. Garrincha walked the ball into the goal and nonchalantly strolled back to the center circle for the ensuing kickoff, the ball under one arm.

In another instance the Little Bird, playing for his club, Botafogo of Rio de Janeiro, was in a duel with a defender when the ball went across the touchline. So consumed were the two men that they ignored the whistle and continued their one-on-one war on the running track adjoining the field.

Later, while touring with Botafogo in Argentina, Garrincha repeatedly teased bull-like defender Vairo with his mesmerizing runs, inspiring shouts of "Olé!" from the amused spectators. Finally, Garrincha set off again but at one point left the ball behind; the desperate Vairo continued to run alongside his tormentor, unaware that he no longer had the ball. (It is believed to be the first time a Latin American crowd saluted a player or team for a successful move or pass with the now-common cry of "Olé!")

Born in 1933 in Pau Grande, Garrincha hit the big time at age twenty with Botafogo. He made his Brazilian National Team debut at the

1957 Copa America but was dropped after Brazil finished second. According to some accounts the veteran players, led by Nilton Santos, successfully lobbied coach Vicente Feola for Garrincha's inclusion in the 1958 World Cup squad, and his reinstatement paid dividends. He and the seventeen-year-old Pelé impressed in a 2–0 first-round win over the Soviet Union, and in the final Garrincha's breathtaking runs set up two of Brazil's goals in its 5–2 victory over host Sweden in Stockholm.

Four years later at the World Cup in Chile, Garrincha was even more devastating. He scored two goals to help beat England, 3–1, in the quarterfinals, and in the semifinal against Chile he scored twice more and assisted on a third goal in a 4–2 win to help Brazil become the first repeat world champion since Italy (1934 and 1938).

Garrincha, playing despite a fever, was kept quiet during Brazil's 3–1 triumph over Czechoslovakia in the final in Santiago, but he was lucky to play at all. After being ejected from the semifinal with six minutes remaining for kneeing Chilean midfielder Eladio Rojas in the seat of his pants, he should have served a one-match suspension like the five other players who had been sent off during the tournament. But Brazilian officials pleaded for mercy, pointing out that they had already lost Pelé to an injury sustained in Brazil's second game. Unable to contact the linesman who spotted the blow (he'd left Chile the next day) and holding a less-than-damning game report by Peruvian referee Arturo Maldonado Yamasaki (he'd been pressured by the president of Peru to go easy on Garrincha), FIFA backed down and gave Garrincha only a reprimand.

That 1962 world championship would be the Little Bird's last day at the top of the tree. He was diagnosed with degenerative knee problems and in 1963 underwent the ligament surgery he had long resisted. Already hounded by the tax man, he became embroiled in a pay dispute with Botafogo, which had taken advantage of its star's lack of sophistication by having him sign a series of blank contracts on which a figure lower than that paid his teammates would be filled in later. Despite having led Botafogo to three Rio state titles, he was unceremoniously sold off to Corinthians.

Noticeably slowed, his last hurrah in a Brazil shirt was an inspiring performance against Bulgaria at the 1966 World Cup, capped by one of his signature bending free-kick goals in a 2–0 win. Brazil lost its next game, 3–1, to Hungary, marking the only time it lost with Garrincha in the lineup. That was his fifty-first and final international appearance, and he bowed out with twelve goals and dozens of assists.

Garrincha drifted from Flamengo to Bangu to Portuguesa Santista, then played briefly in Italy and France. All the while his popularity never waned. In fact, he survived the biggest scandal of his career—leaving his wife and eight children for samba-singing star Elza Soares—virtually unscathed. He had a son, Garrinchinha ("Little Garrincha"), with Elza, giving the notorious ladies' man thirteen children with four women.

Once he retired in 1972 following a brief comeback with the modest Brazilian club Olaria, the illiterate Garrincha found that he was virtually unemployable and turned his attention to drink. Garrincha's downward spiral was hastened by a traffic accident in which the car he was driving struck a truck, killing his passenger, Elza's mother. That incident prompted several suicide attempts.

In 1983 he died a pauper at age forty-nine. Two years later, Garrinchinha, then nine years old, was being driven back from a youth match on the same road that had claimed his grandmother. The car in which he was riding overturned into a river and the boy drowned.

And two near tragedies:

First, the luckiest man on the field during the 1982 World Cup first-round match between Belgium and El Salvador in Elche, Spain, was Belgian goalkeeper Jean-Marie Pfaff, and not because he was given little to do in a 1–0 victory. The popular Pfaff nearly drowned in the team's hotel pool shortly before the match but recovered sufficiently to play.

And second, there was the promising young Spanish goalkeeper whose near-death experience forced him to give up soccer for good. A law student, he was a member of Real Madrid's youth team until a 1963 car crash the night before his twentieth birthday left him with a form of paralysis for more than two years.

But during his long recuperation, Julio Iglesias was given a guitar by a nurse to help him regain the dexterity in his hands. He recovered fully and turned to singing, eventually becoming an international star whose hits include "To All the Girls I've Loved Before" and "Begin the Beguine."

That's great. Tell him he's Pelé and
get him back on.

JOHN LAMBIE, coach of Partick Thistle,
during a 1993 Scottish match after being informed
that striker Colin McGlashan had suffered a
concussion and didn't know who he was

I don't believe in God. In Spain, all twenty-
two players cross themselves. If it works, the
game is always going to be a tie.

Dutch legend and former FC Barcelona star
JOHAN CRUYFF

12 ONLY IN SOCCER

The game's colorful, humorous, unusual side.

A Rather Pedestrian Match

The slowest matches on earth were played in England in the 1930s when teams representing the Crewe and Derby railway veterans associations strolled their way to glory in an annual series of games in which running was strictly prohibited.

The players, however, had an excuse: every one of them was at least sixty-five years old.

In the sixth annual match, played in May 1937 at Derby County's Baseball Ground, a crowd of fifteen hundred turned out to see a scintillating contest that ended in a 0–0 draw. According to one account: "Crewe started well on top and looked set for a walkaway victory. By comparison, Derby looked pedestrian, which, of course, they were. But once Derby discovered their wing men, the pattern of play changed. Their left-wing pair of Collier and Briddon walked rings around the Crewe right flank, while Radford, only 67, put in some good walks and centres on the Derby right. Radford had the best chance of the match, only the goalkeeper to beat, but shot five yards wide. The crowd groaned. They felt he could have walked the ball in."

It also was noted that referee Arthur Kingscott, a veteran of two English F.A. Cup finals, had no trouble keeping up with play, which at times reached six miles an hour.

Sir Elton John: Pianist, Composer, Watford Fan

There was a brief period in the 1970s when the North American Soccer League got a shot of rock 'n' roll glamour. Elton John became part owner of the Los Angeles Aztecs in 1976, and two years later he was outdone by the expansion Philadelphia Fury, whose ownership group included Paul Simon, Peter Frampton, Rick Wakeman, the owners of A&M and Chrysalis records, and the Rolling Stones' tour manager. (Mick Jagger was rumored to be part of the Fury group, but his advisors persuaded him to stay on the sidelines.)

John, Simon, and the rest cut their ties with the NASL long before their respective clubs folded, but for John, his best days as a soccer club owner were ahead of him.

John, born Reginald Dwight, had soccer in his blood, or bloodline: an uncle, Roy Dwight, scored the opening goal in Nottingham Forest's 2–1 victory over Luton in the 1959 English F.A. Cup final—twenty-four minutes before breaking his leg. In 1972 the piano-pounding pop star purchased a controlling interest in Watford, then part of the English third division. With John assuming an active role as club chairman, Watford slid from the second division into the fourth by 1976, thus setting the stage for a breathtaking run.

The Hornets took the 1977–78 fourth division championship to win promotion and finished as runner-up in the third division the following season, earning a spot in the second division. In 1981–82 Watford completed its ascent to the top flight by taking second place.

John's club wasn't through, however. Watford moved from nearly worst to nearly first in its first-ever season in the first division (now known as the Premier League), finishing a distant second but second nonetheless to the glamorous Liverpool. That's a climb of more than *sixty places* in the league standings—a truly meteoric rise in a sport where improvement by a few places from one season to the next would have been hailed as a major achievement for coach Graham Taylor and his Golden Boys.

The club and John had their ups and downs thereafter. The Hornets made it to the 1984 English F.A. Cup final, which they lost to Everton, 2–0. The pop icon eventually lost interest and stepped down temporarily as chairman in 1990, three years after Taylor left for Aston Villa, and Watford slid back into the second division, only to return in the Premier League in 1995.

The Watford roller coaster never stopped as the Hornets found themselves in the third tier in 1997, but with Taylor back at the helm they shot back to the top, earning promotions in successive seasons.

In 2002 John resigned yet again as chairman but was dubbed the club's "president for life." Watford later was forced to sell off Vicarage Road, its home since 1922, but John resurfaced to stage a fundraising concert at the stadium in 2005 that helped the team buy back its home ground for some $15 million.

Lesson in Sportsmanship from an Unlikely Source

Leave it to a pair of players known for their fierce competitiveness to give the world of soccer lessons in sportsmanship.

One was Paolo di Canio, whose startling act in a match in January 2001 earned him the year's FIFA Fair Play Award.

Di Canio, a fiery Italian striker winding up his career in the English Premier League, was playing for West Ham against Everton in a 1–1 deadlock when a ball was crossed to him with the goal at his mercy. The goal was open, however, because Everton goalkeeper Paul Gerrard lay in a heap at the top of the penalty area with a knee injury. Di Canio spotted the fallen Gerrard and caught the ball to halt play, giving possession over to Everton because of the deliberate handball.

The game ended in a 1–1 tie.

Di Canio's startling catch won praise from all quarters, including FIFA President Sepp Blatter, who wrote to the player three days later: "Gestures like this are all too rare in football, especially at the professional level. Your spontaneous action in the game against Everton thus deserves our special recognition and respect. I would like to congratulate and thank you on behalf of FIFA and all fair-minded football fans for this splendid gesture made in the true spirit of fair play, and encourage you to continue to set such positive examples for others to follow."

This was the same Di Canio who, just fourteen months earlier while playing for Sheffield Wednesday, was slapped with an eleven-game suspension and fined $17,000 for pushing a referee to the turf.

The other true sportsman was defender Sinisa Mihajlovic of Lazio.

Mihajlovic's side was leading Como, 2–0, in an Italian Serie A match in Rome in April 2003 when forward Bernardo Corradi scored an apparent third goal. But Mihajlovic, a Serbia and Montenegro international, approached referee Daniele Tombolini and told him that Lazio's Giuseppe Pancaro had committed a handball violation just prior to the goal.

Tombolini agreed and disallowed the goal. Lazio later got a legitimate third goal and went on to win, 3–0.

"It was a very sporting gesture from Sinisa," said Corradi. "Maybe it is one we should see more often on the field."

Lazio coach Eugenio Fascetti was unaware of what Mihajlovic had done at the time, but he praised his player after the game: "If that is true, then that is an extraordinary gesture which merits congratulations."

Sportsmanship aside, there was the East German striker who recognized that discretion is the better part of a good brother-in-law.

In 1981 Emil Gerhardt was playing in a match in Dresden when he tumbled near the enemy goal and the referee awarded a penalty kick. Gerhardt, however, leaped to his feet and ran to the official to argue that he had simply fallen and hadn't been tripped by an opposing defender. The startled referee reversed his call.

Afterward Gerhardt told reporters, "I'm marrying [that defender's] sister, Hildegard, next Saturday. I didn't want to get off on the wrong foot with the family, did I?"

The Fall and Rise of Fiorentina

It seemingly was the end of an era in Florence when Associazione Calcio Fiorentina, founded in 1926 through the merger of two local clubs, winner of two Serie A titles and later the springboard to fame for a young Roberto Baggio, was relegated to the Italian Serie B after the 2001–2 season and then kicked out of the league altogether because it was $50 million in the red and unable to pay its players.

To those in this city of six hundred fifty thousand and site of four 1990 World Cup matches, this was unacceptable. Local leaders quickly formed a new team, known as Fiorentia Viola (for the distinctive purple jerseys of the original Fiorentina), and secured a place for it in the lowly Serie C2.

The newly created club, under owner Diego Della Valle, a shoe manufacturer, quickly became a rallying point for the fans of Florence. Nearly fifteen thousand season tickets were sold, dwarfing the support Fiorentina had received in its final years, and a crowd of twenty-five thousand—an astounding figure for a fourth-division match in Italy—turned up at Fiorentina's original home, Artemio Franchi Stadium, to see Fiorentia Viola crush Castel di Sangro, 5–1, in its opener.

It was Castel di Sangro's modest climb through the lower reaches of the Italian league in the latter 1990s that was chronicled in the book *The Miracle of Castel di Sangro* by Joe McGinniss. But that feat would be trumped by Fiorentia Viola, which would require just two years to lift Florence from the bottom of the league to the top.

Halfway into Fiorentia Viola's first season, the club was mired in the middle of the standings and coach Pietro Vierchowod, a popular ex-Italian international and former Fiorentina player, was fired. But it rallied to win the C2 title, then gained a place in Serie B when the second division was expanded.

Fiorentia bought back its original name in the summer of 2003 and finished sixth in Serie B in 2003–4, earning a playoff with the Serie A's fifteenth-place club, Perugia. After a 1–0 road win, the new Fiorentina sealed its return to Serie A with a 1–1 tie in front of forty-five thousand ecstatic supporters.

Among those in the jam-packed stands was former Argentine international Gabriel Batistuta. The player known as "Batigol" was beloved in Florence for his goal-scoring exploits but perhaps more so for loyally remaining with the club after it dropped briefly to Serie B in the early 1990s.

Of greater significance was the presence on the field of ex-Italy midfielder Angelo Di Livio, who continued to play for the team after its death and rebirth.

"I want to thank all the boys that played this year and last," said the thirty-seven-year-old. "They've done a great job and never gave up on the hope of Serie A.

"Personally, I didn't want to turn my back on this city."

There's something about Fiorentina and player loyalty.

In 1990 the club, with then-owner Flavio Pontello in serious financial straits, sold Baggio to Juventus for a then–world record $19 million on the very day the two teams were to meet in the deciding leg of the UEFA Cup final. (Juve held Fiorentina to a scoreless tie that day and claimed the cup thanks to a 3–1 first-leg victory.) The defeat was bad enough, but the loss of the man who would later be regarded as one of the greatest players of the twentieth century pushed some Fiorentina fans over the edge as more than fifty were injured over two days of street riots.

Baggio never endeared himself to Juventus fans, and no wonder after the drama that played out during the first meeting of his new club and former club during the 1990–91 Serie A season. Juventus was awarded a penalty kick, but Baggio, the obvious choice to take it, refused. His stand-in missed the PK, and Baggio was substituted shortly thereafter. On his way to the dressing room Baggio picked up a Fiorentina scarf that had been tossed his way and kissed it.

Peñarol and Nacional See Eye-to-Eye for a Day

With more than eighty Uruguayan championships and a century of ill will between them, bitter Montevideo rivals Nacional and Peñarol hardly have sportsmanship on their minds whenever they meet. But in September 1948 a Nacional-Peñarol match was the scene of a remarkable gesture.

Peñarol players were quite upset when teammate Walter Gomez was sent off by referee Juan Castaldi for a foul that gave Nacional a penalty kick. Their Nacional counterparts were in full agreement, and right winger Schubert Gambetta—already disgusted with Castaldi's poor performance—demonstrated his outrage over the unjust call by purposely blasting the ensuing PK wide of the mark. Nacional went on to win, 2–0.

Gambetta's gesture became part of Uruguayan soccer lore, and no referee dared call a penalty kick against Nacional in a Peñarol derby for the next eighteen years.

A Star Player by Any Other Name . . .

Glasgow Rangers proudly reported on its club Web site in 2003 that it had purchased the great Turkish striker Yardis Alpolfo from Istanbul giant Galatasaray for $15 million. Wire services Reuters and Teletext, along with other media outlets, duly reported the big acquisition. Then wiser heads spotted the date of the announcement—April 1—and realized that "Yardis Alpolfo" was an anagram for April Fool's Day.

If it worked on one side of the world, why not the other?

That same day, a Japanese newspaper reported that David Beckham was headed from Manchester United to the J-League. The England captain was said to be outraged by United coach Alex Ferguson's criticism of the singing ability of Mrs. Beckham, the former Spice Girl Victoria, and wanted a change of scenery.

Beckham's supposed move was announced by the midfielder's supposed agent, Shigatsu Baka, whose name is Japanese for "April Fool."

(Beckham left Manchester United—honest—two months later, sold to Real Madrid for $41.3 million.)

Julie Foudy's Greatest Honor

The trophy case of U.S. National Women's Team midfielder Julie Foudy is filled with impressive honors, including winner's medals from the 1991 and 1999 Women's World Cups and a gold medal from the 1996 Atlanta Olympics.

Also on the shelf is perhaps her most impressive piece of hardware, the FIFA Fair Play Award. Known by her teammates as "Loudy Foudy" for her outgoing personality, the former Stanford University standout was given the award not for what she said but for what she saw.

In March 1997, with child labor across the globe a hot issue and Foudy in talks with potential sponsor Reebok, the U.S. captain asked to accompany Reebok executives to the Punjab city of Sialkot, the center of Pakistan's sporting goods industry, to see how the company's soccer balls were made. The lion's share of the world's soccer balls are stitched together in Pakistan; annual retail sales of those balls total $1 billion.

"A lot of athletes, myself included, had tended not to think about how the equipment we use is made," said Foudy, a Mission Viejo, California, product. "I strongly felt that, in order to speak publicly about the issue of child labor in soccer, I needed to see the situation for myself."

Reebok had sent out its balls to so-called stitching centers common in Pakistan, where an estimated 20 percent of the balls were assembled by children. As a result of Foudy's well-publicized trip, Reebok promptly halted that practice, and other companies soon followed suit.

Foudy remains active off the field. In October 1999 she was elected to a two-year term as president of the Women's Sports Foundation's board of trustees. Twelve months later—and a month after she helped the U.S. women claim the soccer silver at the Sydney Olympics—Foudy reached the $64,000 level of a special Olympics-themed version of the quiz show *Who Wants to Be a Millionaire?* Foudy donated her winnings to Uniroyal Tire TopSoccer, an outreach program that gives children with mental and physical disabilities the opportunity to play soccer. In February 2004 she was appointed to the U.S. Olympic Committee's influential nominating and governing committee.

And in August 2004, back on the field, Foudy captained the United States to its second Olympic gold medal, at the Athens Games, retiring three months later with 271 international appearances over sixteen years.

U.S. Goalkeeper Nervous about Not Being Nervous

Are players jittery when they make their first appearance for their national team? Don't ask Kristin Luckenbill.

The 2002 Women's United Soccer Association's Goalkeeper of the Year while with the Carolina Courage, Luckenbill entered the U.S. National Women's Team's friendly against Brazil in April 2004 in Birmingham, Alabama, in the sixty-sixth minute and helped the United States close out a 5–1 victory.

Said Dartmouth grad Luckenbill later, "You know, I was so not nervous that I started getting nervous about why I wasn't more nervous."

Club Owner Does It All in Kalamazoo Triumph

There are hands-on club owners, and then there is Chris Keenan.

In May 2000 the Kalamazoo Kingdom was trailing the Mid Michigan Bucks, 2–1, in the eightieth minute of a Premier Development League match. This was upsetting to Keenan, owner of the fourth-division Kingdom, who was watching his team's home opener be spoiled. It was even more upsetting to the coach, who also happened to be Keenan.

To Coach Keenan, the solution was obvious: send in Chris Keenan.

Minutes later the thirty-four-year-old owner-coach-player took a length-of-the-field pass from goalkeeper Carl Whitehouse and slipped the ball through the legs of Bucks 'keeper Alan Placek to force overtime.

In the second OT period, Keenan's corner kick was flicked into the net by teammate David Prahl for the winning goal.

José Manuel Moreno was merely a player-coach when he accomplished a similar feat in 1960 in South America, but he did so at a higher level.

Moreno, a star for River Plate in the late 1930s and early 1940s, was considered along with Alfredo Di Stéfano and Adolfo Pedernera to be one of the greatest of pre-Maradona Argentines.

In 1954 he began a six-year stint as player-coach of Independiente Medellin of Colombia. In his final season Medellin was trailing Argentina's Boca Juniors, 1–0, with time running out when Moreno, irritated with his players' performance, put himself into the game. The forty-five-year-old scored twice and Independiente escaped with a 2–1 victory.

Faeroe Islands: The Minnow That Roared

Beginner's luck is fickle. In international soccer it ignored future five-time world champion Brazil, which was humbled by Argentina, 3–0, in Buenos Aires in 1914 in its first-ever match. It also skipped three-time champ Germany, a 5–3 loser to Switzerland in Basle in 1908 in its debut.

Instead, beginner's luck smiled on the Faeroe Islands, a collection of specks in the North Sea surrounded by Scotland, Iceland, and, to the east, Norway.

Covering 540 square miles and with a population (forty-five thousand) that wouldn't fill many of the major stadiums of Europe, the Faeroe Islands, an autonomous part of Denmark, joined FIFA along with fellow minnow San Marino in 1988. The country took part in a series of friendlies against the likes of Greenland, the Shetland Islands, Canada, Iceland, and Anglesy before playing its first competitive match, a European Championship qualifier against Austria, in 1990 in Landskrona.

Austria, a faded power in Europe since appearing in the 1954 World Cup semifinals, was coming off a respectable showing at the World Cup in Italy three months earlier, losing to the host Italians and Czechoslovakia by 1–0 scores before beating the United States, 2–1.

Faeroe Islands, meanwhile, fielded a collection of amateurs whose most experienced members had played in the Norwegian second division. The locals also suffered a setback shortly before the match when the UEFA ruled that Faeroe Islands couldn't play Austria on one of the artificial surfaces that had become common in a country where a constant breeze and frequent rainstorms make growing grass impossible.

With the odds stacked firmly against the hosts, the Faeroese upended the Austrians, 1–0. In the sixty-third minute Torkil Nielsen beat a disorganized Austria defense and fired past goalkeeper Michael Konsel to give the underdogs a famous victory.

"Of course I'm delighted," said Faeroe Islands Prime Minister Jogvan Sunstein of the stunning upset. "We expected to lose by seven or eight goals—it was our first match in the competition.

"I think there'll be great celebrations in Törshavn tonight."

Hardly. There are no bars in Faeroe Islands, and alcohol is rationed. The streets of Törshavn, the capital, are known to be deserted by 7:00 p.m.

Austria coach Josef Hickersberger resigned in disgrace shortly after, and his team went on to finish next-to-last in its Euro 1992 qualifying group. The Faeroe Islands, of course, took up the rear in that group and hasn't come close to making a dent in international soccer since. But for a country whose name in its ancient Viking tongue means "Sheep Island," it could cherish its stunning competitive debut.

Fourth-Division Calais Reaches French Cup Final

The open cup competition is the great tease of sports, a false promise to downtrodden teams everywhere of a shot at glory. Year after year, no one beats the odds and the final involves the usual giants.

But every once in a while . . .

There's nowhere to go but up if you're in the French fourth division, and that's exactly where little Calais Racing Union FC went during its breathtaking run to the 1999–2000 French Cup final. Calais became the unofficial darling of amateur teams worldwide as its collection of shopkeepers and bureaucrats reeled off seven consecutive victories against the mighty and the not so mighty.

The campaign began modestly enough with a 1–0 win over Boune of the fifth division, followed by a 4–0 rout of a fourth-division rival, US Dunkerque. If Calais began to get stars in its eyes, it would have come after the third match, when it tied the second division's Lille, 1–1, and survived on penalty kicks, 7–6.

A 3–0 blanking of Langon-Castets-en-Dorthe, a fifth-division club, put Calais into the round of sixteen, where it tied AS Cannes Foot of the second division, 1–1, and won on PKs, 4–1. All of France then took notice as Calais upset two first-division teams, RC Strasbourg, 2–1, in the quarterfinals and 1999 French champion Girondins Bordeaux, 3–1, in the semifinals.

The team's six-month quest reached its climax in May in Saint-Denis outside Paris, where the wide-eyed Calais players walked into the cavernous Stade de France to face one last first-division side, Nantes, before a crowd of 78,717.

Alas, the story had a disappointing ending for minnows everywhere. After taking a shocking 1–0 lead on a thirty-fourth-minute goal by Jerome Dutitre (a physical education teacher), Calais conceded an equalizer by Nantes' Antoine Sibierski five minutes after halftime. And just seconds from overtime, Nantes substitute Alain Caveglia went down in the penalty area during a struggle with Calais defender Fabrice Baron, earning a penalty kick that Sibierski converted.

With the 2–1 defeat, Calais players collected their runner-up medals and returned to their full-time jobs, and the amateur teams of the world went back to dreams of uniforms that match and unlocked stadium restrooms.

Rare Happy Ending to a Kidnapping in Colombia

Kidnapping and worse are a part of life in Colombia, but despite the mayhem, soccer goes on. Usually.

In April 2000 a game in the opening phase of the Colombian championship between host Nacional Medellin and Deportivo Cali was delayed because the players from both sides refused to kick off until Nacional midfielder Andrés Estrada, kidnapped two days earlier, was released.

Pleas by the referee and television executives fell on deaf ears. Finally, over the stadium public address system came the voice of Estrada, who said by phone that he was safe and at his mother's home.

The match got under way and the two sides played to a 2–2 tie.

The terrorists who snatched Estrada later claimed that they kidnapped the player by mistake and had to await orders from superiors before releasing him.

Depression-Era Goalkeeper Still Kicking at Ninety-two

If it's true that goalkeepers get better with age, Srdjan Mrkušić must have been a coach's dream.

Mrkušić, a former Red Star Belgrade favorite whose career began in 1935, went on to play for the Red Star veterans team. What made him special was that he was still there in May 2007, when he turned ninety-two.

The native of Sinj, in present-day Croatia, was so old he could boast that he began his career with Hajduk Split in the midst of the Depression, and, after a stretch with Belgrade power BSK, became one of the founding members of the venerable Crvena Zvezda Beograd, or Red Star, in 1945.

As a standout goalkeeper by his midtwenties, Mrkušić made his international debut with the Kingdom of Yugoslavia in 1941, two weeks before the Nazi invasion. He earned the last of his eleven caps as a member of the national team of the communist Federal People's Republic of Yugoslavia, at the 1950 World Cup, a 2–0 loss to Brazil before one hundred forty-two thousand at Maracanã Stadium in Rio de Janeiro. After retiring from Red Star in 1955 at the tender age of thirty-nine with four Yugoslav league titles and three Yugoslav Cups to his credit, Mrkušić went on to make use of the forestry degree he had earned at the University of Belgrade.

As his years with the Red Star veterans team rolled by, Mrkušić gave new meaning to the word *ageless*. During a routine physical examination, a doctor, unaware that his subject was already ninety, gave Mrkušić the happy news that he had a good chance to live to be eighty.

Mrkušić said his goal was to live to be one hundred, but he died five months after his ninety-second birthday following a short illness.

Brazilian, Norwegian Wed at Brazil-Norway Game

A pair of soccer fans couldn't have chosen a more appropriate setting for their wedding than the playing field at the Stade de Velodrome in Marseilles. There, in June 1998, with bridesmaids, ushers, and sixty thousand witnesses looking on, Oivind Ekeland of Norway exchanged vows with Rosangela de Souza of Brazil. A World Cup match between Norway and Brazil immediately followed.

The Ekelands' day then came to a perfect end as Norway upset Brazil, 2–1, enabling both sides to advance to the second round.

Real Madrid Is Unmentionable to Bayern Munich

Wink, wink, nod, nod.

Bayern Munich officials, weary of hearing about Real Madrid, its upcoming opponent in a 2003–4 UEFA Champions League round of sixteen series, threatened its players with a $6,500 fine if they dared to utter the team's name around the media.

The players were obedient.

Said Bayern's Dutch international striker, Roy Makaay: "Yes, I'm really looking forward to playing against that Spanish team who wear white shirts."

And Bayern's German international goalkeeper, Oliver Kahn: "We can't wait to meet that side coached by Carlos Queiroz whose stadium is called the Santiago Bernabeu."

As it were, that Spanish team in white eliminated the red-and-blue-clad team from southern Germany, 1–1 and 1–0.

One Close Family

Maybe it's a Liverpool thing.

In a scene early in the movie *Help!* the four Beatles each walk to the front door of their homes—four flats side by side—and walk inside in unison. Another famous Liverpudlian, England striker Michael Owen, then the reigning European Footballer of the Year, went two steps further.

In 2001 Owen, obviously a family man, bought six houses in a row on the same street for himself; his father, Terry, and mother, Janette; his brothers, Terry and Andrew; and his sisters, Lesley and Karen.

Denmark the Stand-in Wins European Championship

After decades as one of Europe's minnows, Denmark appeared to have hit its high-water mark in 1986. Two years removed from their impressive appearance in the European Championship in France, the Danes were in Mexico, playing in their first World Cup. They were led by a host of stars playing for top clubs abroad, including Allan Simonsen, Michael Laudrup, Preben Elkjaer-Larsen, Soren Lerby, Jan Molby, and Jesper Olsen. They humiliated Uruguay, 6–1, en route to winning the so-called first-round Group of Death, and some pegged them to capture the world championship.

It all came apart in a matter of minutes, however, in a second-round match against Spain in Queretaro. Holding a 1–0 lead two minutes from halftime, Olsen made a dreadful back pass that led to the first of four goals by Spanish striker Emilio Butragueño, and Denmark was out.

Before long Denmark, with its festive, well-behaved followers known not as hooligans but Roligans (Danish slang for "Peaceful Fans"), was all but forgotten. Old age claimed the stars of Euro '84 and Mexico '86, and Denmark was unimpressive at the 1988 Euro Championship in West Germany. Two years later the Danes failed to qualify for the World Cup. In the qualifiers for the 1992 European Championship that followed the Danes lost their most prominent player, Michael Laudrup, to a falling-out with new coach Richard Möller Nielsen, and they finished second in their group by a point to Yugoslavia. A generation of stars gone, and with the team once hailed as Danish Dynamite for its invention and flair transformed by Nielsen's conservative, defensive approach, an era in Denmark apparently had come to a close.

Shortly before kickoff of Euro '92 in Sweden, however, war-torn Yugoslavia withdrew, and the UEFA invited Denmark to replace the Yugoslavs in the eight-nation finals. The players, many on seaside vacations, were hastily recalled and assembled under very low expectations.

After tying England, 0–0, in Malmö and losing to Sweden, 1–0, in Stockholm, the Danes edged France, 2–1, in Malmö on a goal by forward Lars Elstrup with eleven minutes left to finish second to the Swedes in Group 1 and advance to the semifinals. There they nipped Holland on penalty kicks, 5–4, in Gothenburg following a 2–2 draw. In the final Denmark completed its remarkable run, blanking defending world champion Germany, 2–0, in Gothenburg on goals by midfielders John Jensen and Kim Vilfort.

That has been Denmark's one and only major honor. And though Danish teams that were more talented, in better shape, and better prepared went on to impress at the 1998 and 2002 World Cups, neither could produce the brass ring like their nothing-to-lose predecessors of 1992.

The Terrifying Tiny Joyce

Back in the days when a goalkeeper who stood six feet tall and weighed two hundred pounds was considered highly imposing, one of the most frightening 'keepers in England was John "Tiny" Joyce, who began his career in 1893 and went on to play for Tottenham Hotspur and Millwall. He played nearly three hundred games for Millwall before retiring just after World War I.

Joyce was the first goalkeeper to score a goal for Spurs, converting a penalty kick in April 1914 in a win against Bolton. He had scored other PKS, but it was how the colorful Joyce went about it that made him doubly imposing.

No two- or three-step run-up for Tiny. With the ball resting on the penalty spot, Joyce routinely backed into his own goalmouth, then took off on a run of about ninety yards that ended with a thunderous blast from twelve yards against the enemy goal. He never missed one.

The piece de resistance came when Spurs was playing a team in France and was awarded a penalty kick. Joyce, in full flight, got to the halfway line before the terrified French 'keeper fled, leaving Tiny with an open net and an easy poke into the goal.

A great idea, that long run up. Or maybe not.

Years later, Manchester City featured one Franny Lee, known for drawing penalty kicks, then converting them after building up a head of steam with a long, long approach. One season, the Blues scored fifteen penalty kicks and Lee accounted for all of them. No wonder his nickname was "Lee Won Pen" because the newspaper scoring summary for City games frequently included the line, "Lee, 1 pen."

In the third round of the 1967–68 English F.A. Cup, host Manchester City won a penalty kick against Reading. Lee placed the ball on the spot and made his long customary walk beyond the penalty area. With his back still turned, however, teammate Tony Coleman stepped up instead and . . . drilled the ball far into the grandstand.

The game ended in a 0–0 tie; City took the replay four days later at Reading, 7–0.

In Paraguay, December 8 Comes before October 12

The club known as 8 de Diciembre ended the second stage of the 1994 Paraguayan Torneo Nacional in sixteenth place, one notch ahead of the club known as 12 de Octubre. Diciembre finished with a 3-7-9 record; Octubre was 3-8-8.

The Master Gets to Mingle with the Help

A middle-aged club director became the oldest man to appear in an English League match when John Ryan played the last minute of Doncaster Rovers' victory over Hereford in a fourth-division game in April 2003.

At fifty-two years, eleven months, Ryan beat out Neil McBain, fifty-two years, four months, the manager of the now defunct New Brighton who came on as an emergency substitute during a 1947 third-division game against Hartlepool.

"It was wonderful," Ryan told the BBC later. "We won, 4–2, as well, so I'm over the moon. I have also made it into the *Guinness Book of Records*.

"I came on when the ref put his board up for an extra three minutes of injury time. I didn't actually get a kick of the ball, but I had a good run around."

None of the Doncaster players were likely to complain about one of their bosses romping among them. Ryan, whose cosmetic surgery business made him a multimillionaire, had sunk $6.4 million into the club, saving it from extinction.

Four months after his appearance, Ryan's record came under threat when a second-division club, Plymouth Argyle, signed one of its directors, former politician Michael Foot. Best known in Britain for his battles with Margaret Thatcher's Conservatives during three stormy years as Labor Party leader, the aptly named Foot wasn't likely to see much playing time with Plymouth: he was ninety when he inked his Plymouth contract. The signing was in recognition of Foot's recent birthday and his lifelong support of the club. He was issued jersey No. 90.

Brazilian Goalkeeping Hero Lands on Church Team

Maybe winning a World Cup isn't all that it's cracked up to be.

Claudio Taffarel should have been one of international soccer's most coveted goalkeepers after playing a key role in Brazil's championship at the 1994 World Cup. He gave up only three goals in his team's first six matches, then capped that run by holding Italy scoreless for 120 minutes in the final as Brazil won on penalty kicks, with Taffarel saving Daniele Massaro's attempt in a nail-biting 3–2 decision.

Less than a year later Taffarel, then twenty-nine, was in northern Italy, playing for a church team based in Reggio Emilia.

What happened?

Taffarel began his career in 1985 with Internacional Porto Alegre and made his national team debut two years later. In 1988, at the Olympic semifinals in Seoul, he became a hero with his three saves in Brazil's 3–2 penalty-kick decision over West Germany following a 1–1 tie. After the 1990 World Cup, where he started in all four of Brazil's games, Taffarel was sold to Parma, an Italian club on the rise. Parma continued to add non-Italians, and eventually, because of foreign player quotas, there was no room for the Brazilian. He was loaned to newly promoted Reggina before USA '94, but upon his return from the United States he learned there was no place for him there, either.

"I was unemployed for seven months," said Taffarel. "Imagine, a world champion without a club! It's unbelievable. I ended up playing for my church team, just for fun. I even played center forward for a while and scored fifteen goals in seven games."

Before the end of 1994 he returned home to play for Atlético Mineiro. Ups and downs followed. He was blamed for Brazil's shootout loss to Uruguay in the 1995 Copa America, but he was a hero again after helping Brazil win the 1997 Copa. He saved two shots in a shootout win over Holland in the 1998 World Cup semifinal but days later was on the losing end as France won the final, 3–0. After that World Cup, Taffarel moved to Turkey, where he helped Galatasaray to the 2000 UEFA Cup title, then returned to Parma for two more years.

Taffarel ended his Brazil career with 106 appearances, including 18 in three World Cups, tying the international mark for goalkeepers set by West Germany's Sepp Maier. His club career came to a close in 2003. He was on his way to sign a contract with Empoli when his BMW conked out on the Italian A1 autostrada.

"This was no mechanical coincidence," said the longtime member of the Fellowship of Christian Athletes. "God was telling me it was time to call it a day."

The last people who would have been shocked by Taffarel's premature fall off the soccer map in the middle of his career would be Brazilians, who consider goalkeepers one of the game's necessary evils, like referees.

But not a field player, and especially not a midfield artiste like Rivaldo, who hit an amazing series of highs and lows in December 1999.

The day after the Brazil and FC Barcelona star was named European Player of the Year, he was benched by Barcelona coach Louis van Gaal for refusing to move from the center of the midfield to the left side.

Two days later Rivaldo was named a finalist for the FIFA World Player of the Year award (he won over England's David Beckham and Argentina's Gabriel Batistuta). In addition, it was reported that Lazio of Rome had offered a world-record $65 million for him. And finally, Barcelona tied Rayo Vallecano, 1–1, in a Spanish league match. In the final minute, Luis Figo missed a penalty kick. Said a pious Van Gaal, "That was a real shame. Rivaldo always scores from the penalty spot."

Rivaldo and Van Gaal never made up, and the Dutch boss was fired at the end of that season. Rivaldo enjoyed a stellar 2002 World Cup as he scored in Brazil's first five games and set up both of Ronaldo's goals in the Brazilians' 2–0 win over Germany in the final. Van Gaal, however, returned to the Barcelona helm that same month and Rivaldo was released. He spent one injury-plagued season with

AC Milan, playing largely the part of spectator as the team won the 2002–3 UEFA Champions League, then returned home to play briefly for Cruzeiro before winding down his career in Greece with Olympiakos and AEK Athens.

With No Cash, Brazilian Club Pays Players in Cattle

Strapped for cash, Londrina of the Brazilian second division paid its players in cattle in lieu of cash bonuses in 1996.

Seventy head were divided among the players based on their performances on the field (the players', not the cattle's), helping Londrina cut its debts from $5 million to $2 million.

Manchester United Fan Names Son after Entire Team

Graham Alex Jimmy Stewart Gerry Brian Martin Steve Sammy Stuart Lou Gordon David Tommy Matt Cross was born in 1976. The boy was named by his parents after members of that year's Manchester United team and, fittingly, he was offered a contract by United fifteen years later.

The fairy-tale story ends there, however. Young Cross, who once scored every goal in leading his central English boys team, Walsall, to an 8–0 rout, turned down United and instead signed with Leeds.

As for the 1976 Manchester United squad that inspired Cross's parents, it won the English F.A. Cup the next year and wouldn't win another honor for fifteen years.

Cameroon Star Backs Apology with Ticket Refund

Samuel Eto'o of Mallorca was sorry. Really sorry.

The Cameroon international announced that he would foot the bill for $31,000 in tickets paid by his team's fans as a way to apologize for being sent off thirty minutes into a December 2002 Spanish Primera Liga match for kicking at FC Barcelona's Thiago Motta.

Eto'o's ejection left host Mallorca with nine men in a game Barcelona would win, 4–0.

Betting on Junior and England Glory

A very proud father placed a $30 bet in 1996—at 50,000-to-1 odds—with London bookmakers that his son, then fourteen months old, would score a goal for England at the twenty-first World Cup.

Steve Caldicott of Birmingham will win nearly $1.7 million if his son, Jack, scores the big goal in 2018.

We'll see.

Meanwhile, the elder Caldicott was no different from another English dad, Eddie Kirkland. In 1991 when his son, Chris, was ten, Kirkland convinced nine relatives, friends, and fellow workers to put down a 100-pound bet with bookmaker William Hill at 100-to-1 odds that the boy would play for England before his thirtieth birthday.

Chris became a standout goalkeeper for Liverpool and was called up by England coach Sven-Goran Eriksson for an August 2003 friendly against Croatia. With Eddie poised to share a $158,500 payout with his buddies, Eriksson played his number one 'keeper David James in the first half and . . . Paul Robinson of Leeds United, the goalie considered number three, in the second.

The near-miss may have caused a near-swoon for Eddie, but Pop finally got his payoff in August 2006 after Eriksson's successor, Steve McClaren, sent Chris on the field for the second half of a friendly with Greece in Manchester. The twenty-five-year-old Chris, since acquired by Wigan Athletic, kept his net clean in England's 4–0 victory, and Eddie and his colleagues pocketed approximately $19,000.

The Caldicott and Kirkland sagas, however, are only two examples of the Brits' sick romance between bookmakers and imaginative punters. One of the players on the field for that 2003 England-Croatia match was English superstar David Beckham, whose toddler son, Brooklyn, has been established as a 100-to-1 shot to one day play for the national team. London bookmakers had started Brooklyn out at 1,000-to-1 not long after his birth, but they slashed the odds in August 2001 when Beckham was quoted as saying his son was a better soccer player than he was at the same age.

Watch What You Eat at the Soccer Training Table

Poppy seeds in a bread roll eaten as part of a pregame meal nearly got a Brazilian international a hefty suspension in December 1997.

Midfielder Anderson of Internacional Porto Alegre ate the roll the morning of a 4–0 loss to Santos in a Brazilian national championship match, and he later tested positive for morphine. He was let off the hook after physicians for Anderson's club gave students similar rolls and they, too, failed their drug tests.

Not so lucky was Kazuki Ganaha. A striker for the J-League's Kawasaki Frontale, Ganaha was suspended for six games and fined more than $100,000 for receiving an intravenous injection from the club doctor in July 2007.

Ganaha was suffering from the flu, and what was injected was garlic. Nevertheless, the Japanese league prohibited such injections regardless of the substance.

Ecuadoran Teams Need Twenty-five Days to Finish Game

It took twenty-five days, but an Ecuadoran league match between Deportivo Quito and Barcelona of Guayaquil was finally completed in 2003 with Deportivo the winner, 4–1.

The two sides kicked off March 2 in Quito and got to the thirty-seventh minute when the referee was struck by a chunk of ice hurled from the stands, forcing the match to be abandoned.

The Ecuadoran soccer federation later ordered the remaining fifty-three minutes to be played March 27 behind closed doors—with the same twenty-two players on the field.

Deportivo's Carlos Bertola had suffered an injury since appearing in the first part of the match and was unfit to play, so he was dutifully trotted onto the field, then substituted by Wellington Paredes immediately after the game was resumed.

Mariano Campodonico scored twice during the latter portion of the match to lead Deportivo to the win and knock the previously unbeaten and untied Barcelona out of first place.

Coming in a close second to Deportivo-Barcelona was an Argentine second-division game between Atlanta and Defensores de Cambaceres in April 2003. This game took a mere twenty-four days.

The match kicked off the first Sunday of the month and reached the eighty-fifth minute when a controversial penalty call against Defensores ignited a riot, prematurely ending the game. On the last Wednesday of April, play resumed at a neutral site behind closed doors with the taking of the penalty kick. Striker Lucas Ferreiro converted it and Atlanta held on for a 1–0 win.

Manchester United Fan Impersonates Radio Reporter

The "Fletch" of soccer would have to be forty-four-year-old Manchester United fan Jamie Mardon, whose boldness landed him a brief encounter with one of his heroes at Cardiff's Millennium Stadium after the 2003 Charity Shield match.

United had just beaten Arsenal on penalty kicks when spectator Mardon spotted an unattended microphone and set of headphones on a desk in the press section. Mardon snatched the electronic gear, made his way down to the field, and quickly engaged United winger Ryan Giggs in an impromptu interview. As soon as Giggs could say, "A win's a win," the Welsh star noticed that his interviewer's mike wasn't plugged in.

While Giggs called over teammate Rio Ferdinand to tell him about the bogus interview (Ferdinand doubled over in laughter), Mardon was led away by the authorities and later charged with "invading the pitch."

Movie Studio Turns Spanish Team into Marquee Players

Eleven cinema marquees running around a soccer field. That was the intended result in September 2003 when Atlético Madrid took the field to open the Spanish first-division season. Emblazoned across the players' jerseys was *Hollywood Homicide*, the title of the new release by the club's latest sponsor, Columbia Tri-Star Pictures, starring Harrison Ford.

Atlético players sported the names of other Columbia Tri-Star releases on their shirts during the season, including movies starring Samuel L. Jackson and Halle Berry.

El Presidente Scores from the Spot

Care to take the penalty, Señor Presidente?

An unusual question, indeed, and it was directed at Argentina's chief executive, die-hard soccer fan Carlos Menem, during an April 1997 charity match in Mar del Plata.

The flamboyant Menem, then sixty-three years old, took the field for the Argentine National Team against a team of veteran stars and was given two chances to score from the penalty spot. He converted one.

Argentina and Menem defeated the stars, which included Ubaldo Fillol, Hector Enrique, Tapia, and Giusti, by a comfortable 6–1.

Real Stand-up Fans

Standing room—large sections of stadiums with no seating—has been a part of soccer as long as fans have been charged admission. The prime nonseater locations were the concrete or wooden terraces behind the goals, where the most loyal and vociferous fans stood and sang, chanted, and generally did their best to lift their heroes and unnerve the opposition. Prompted by safety concerns, however, FIFA launched a campaign in the 1990s to do away with standing room.

Manchester United's Old Trafford was one such stadium that became a so-called all-seater during a major facelift in 1997. Capacity was increased from 56,385 to 67,000 as the stomping, chanting regulars on the terraces were given seats.

The fans, however, barely noticed. With a modern, clean plastic seat at their backside, many simply stood during matches as they always had.

The problem became so acute by March 2001 that United officials threatened to close down sections of Old Trafford for a UEFA Champions League match against Sturm Graz of Austria. The fans sat, and Manchester United won, 3–0.

Settlement Gives Brazilian Player a Stadium

Gremio striker Luizão found himself in possession of a São Paulo stadium in October 2003 as part of a settlement in a dispute with his former club, Corinthians, over $2 million in back pay.

"I never wanted it to come to this," said the new owner of the fifteen-thousand-capacity Alfredo Schuring Stadium, also known as Parque São Jorge.

In better times Luizão helped Corinthians win the inaugural FIFA Club World Championship, in 2000. He also was a member of Brazil's 2002 World Cup championship team, coming off the bench in two matches.

Ajax Can Grow Players but Not Turf

Ajax Amsterdam, a four-time champion of the European Cup, is renowned for its youth development system, one that has produced a long string of great players headed by Johan Cruyff. But while Ajax has a knack for growing new stars, it seemingly cannot grow grass.

The Dutch powerhouse moved in 1996 from the homely De Meer Stadium to a new state-of-the-art facility, the AmsterdamArena, whose crowning glory is a retractable roof that allows sunlight in. But for a variety of reasons the playing surface had to be replaced twenty-four times in its first five years.

Ajax fans became so frustrated—and embarrassed—by the situation that in January 2001 a group of them expressed their opinion by letting two cows loose on the field. One of the cows made a much-needed contribution of manure before being led away by stadium personnel.

Atlético Madrid had a problem of a different kind eleven months earlier at its Vicente Calderon Stadium as flocks of pigeons pecked away at the turf and left large areas around the goalmouths barren. Atlético groundskeepers scattered pigeon carcasses on the field and enlisted the help of cats, to no avail.

It was a much more modest club, v v Cercle Oedelem of Belgium, that figured out how to outsmart Mother Nature. In the summer of 2004 Cercle players showed up for preseason training and found their training ground overrun by rabbits. With his players turning ankles as they stepped in the rabbit holes, club chairman Eddy Sypre appealed to the team's fans for donations of their old, smelly sneakers. The shoes were scattered about the playing field, and the rabbits, overwhelmed by the stench, withdrew.

Sypre got the idea while visiting a friend's house in Limburg—yes, the home of Limburger cheese. The friend ran off local rabbits by placing fragrant footwear throughout his vegetable garden.

Universe Resembles a Soccer Ball, Say Scientists

"And all the world is football shaped, it's just for me to kick its face," sang the 1980s rock group x t c. According to a handful of scientists, the band didn't go far enough.

A study led by Jean-Pierre Luminet of the Paris Observatory proposed that all of outer space resembles the surface of a soccer ball, with cosmic patches stitched together to form a decidedly finite universe, the journal Nature reported in October 2003. The concept involves blocks of space "with opposite faces abstractly glued together. An object sliding off an edge of one block will instantly slide into view at the edge of its opposing block." Think of it this way: you move a cursor off the right side of a screen and it reappears on the left.

Luminet suggested that the universe is a dodecahedron, a complex pattern of twelve pentagonal shapes, with opposite faces connected in pairs. For the record, a soccer ball is commonly made up of twelve pentagonal and twenty hexagonal panels.

But before FIFA considers changing its world-as-a-soccer-ball logo to something larger in scope, those behind the study acknowledged that more research is needed.

Bobby Moore Doubles as Referee

Bobby Moore, captain of England's 1966 World Cup–winning side, was renowned for his hard, clean play. He was awarded with an OBE (Order of the British Empire) medal in 1967, and a fair play honor bears his name. A tackle he made on Jairzinho in the 1970 World Cup during a 1–0 loss to Brazil, a match regarded as a classic for many other reasons, has often been cited as the most perfect challenge ever.

But Moore was sportsmanship personified in November 1970 during an English league match between his club, West Ham United, and Wolverhampton at Upton Park in London. Moore, who had already scored, sent a clearance away from the Hammers' goal that caught referee J. Lewis in the back of the head, knocking him unconscious. Moore rushed over, picked up the fallen Lewis's whistle, and blew it to halt play.

Such was Moore's reputation for fair play that the players immediately stopped, and Lewis was attended to.

Final score: West Ham 3, Wolves 3.

Romanian Player Sold for Sausages

In a sport in which lower-tier players have been sold by one club to another for everything from candy bars to firewood, Regal Hornia of the Romanian fourth division was just carrying on a proud soccer tradition during the 2005–6 season when it purchased defender Marius Cioara for fifteen kilograms of sausages.

Cioara put up with the jokes (e.g., he would've brought in more sausages from a German club) for just a day before he ended his soccer career and left Romania to work on a farm in Spain.

"We are upset because we lost twice," said a Regal Hornia spokesman. "Firstly, because we lost a good player, and secondly, because we lost our team's food for a whole week."

For the record, soccer clubs usually pay in cash. Top price, as of 2009, was the $132 million Real Madrid of Spain paid Manchester United that year for Portuguese superstar Cristiano Ronaldo.

Romanian Fan Walks to England to See Team Lose

Romania's most dedicated fan and most disappointed fan of 1996 was the same person, the dogged and ultimately dejected Constantin Ciuca.

Ciuca set off on foot from his hometown of Brasov in March, bound for England, site of that year's European Championship. With only a ferry across the English Channel to interrupt his trek, he made it to Newcastle's St. James' Park three months later to watch Romania drop its Group B opener to France, 1–0. Ciuca then saw his countrymen tumble to Bulgaria by the same score three days later.

With his team eliminated, he skipped Romania's last group match, a 2–1 loss to Spain at Leeds' Elland Road. Instead, he flew to New York to begin his walk to Atlanta for the 1996 Summer Olympics.

Seagull Gets Assist on English Lad's Goal

A bank shot for the ages. The Stalybridge Celtic Colts were on their way to a 7–1 thrashing of Hollingworth Juniors in an English youth match in Manchester in October 1999, so fans weren't holding their breath as thirteen-year-old Colts forward Danny Worthington unleashed a hopeful thirty-yard shot. The effort appeared to be far off the mark, and Worthington turned away in disgust.

What he missed was the sight of the ball striking a passing seagull in the head and caroming into the net.

The English F.A. later gave the goal its official sanction. As for the bird, it fell to the turf, then recovered quickly and flew off without celebrating with its temporary Stalybridge teammates.

Dogs are smarter than birds, so leave it to a dog to actually score a goal, also in England.

In November 1985, fourteen years before the Stalybridge gull, Knave of Clubs was playing Newcastle Town at Monks Neil Park in the Staffordshire Sunday Cup. Newcastle led, 2–0, when a Knave player, on a breakaway, was left with only the goalkeeper to beat. He shot wide from fifteen yards, but at that moment a dog ran onto the field, jumped up, and headed the ball into the net. Air Bud, indeed.

As in Manchester, the referee allowed the goal, but even man's best friend couldn't prevent Knave's 3–2 defeat.

It's easier in soccer to destroy than create, as any defender will grudgingly admit and as a certain dog demonstrated during a 1991 match in Venezuela. An Estudiantes de Merida player got off a shot against Atlético Zamora, only to see a dog race onto the field and intercept the ball, stopping a certain goal.

The game ended 0–0.

High Winds Halt Israeli Cup Shootout

Finally, a match that can truly be called a blow-out.

Howling winds forced the end of an Israeli Cup match in January 2000 in Haifa as Hapoel Haifa and Ironi Rishon Lezion were unable to carry out their penalty-kick tiebreaker.

Following a 1–1 draw, Rishon converted its first PK attempt, but the wind picked up and Haifa's Giovanni Rosso was unable to keep the ball on the penalty spot and get off his kick.

Referee Eran Frost eventually picked up the ball, called for a ten-minute break, and retreated to the dressing room. His plans to resume the PK duel were scuttled, however, when the winds grew so strong that the team benches were blown onto the field.

Spanish Club Buys Relegation Insurance

Any club that is relegated from its national league's top division stands to lose a lot. Gone are the big TV paydays and healthy gate receipts, and in anticipation the team usually jettisons its marquee players, thus making a return to the top flight that much more difficult.

Fearing the worst late in the 1997–98 Spanish Primera Liga season, Real Racing Club Santander, languishing near the bottom, took precautions, purchasing insurance against a plunge into the second division.

Racing Santander never collected on what was a $12 million premium—but its fears were well founded. The club, which has never won a Spanish league or cup title since its founding in 1913, finished that season tied at forty-five points with Tenerife and Salamanca and averted a trip to the relegation playoffs by a single point.

Scottish Club Happy to Go Downhill

Good-bye, Easter Road Slope. Hibernian defeated Aberdeen, 1–0, in April 2000 in Edinburgh to bid a fond farewell to a home ground with one of the biggest quirks in professional soccer, a tilted playing surface that fell more than two yards from goal line to goal line.

Bulldozers arrived shortly after that Scottish Premier League match as part of an overhaul of Easter Road Stadium, Hibs' home since 1892.

During its glory days, Hibernian won the Scottish championship in 1948, 1951, and 1952. Said a member of those teams, onetime Scotland forward Lawrie Reilly: "If we won the [coin] toss, we would always kick up the hill in the first half, and shooting downhill in the second half was just like a war cry to our fans."

Vicar Appeals to Higher Source to Help Local Club

With Bolton Wanderers in danger of relegation from the English Premier League to the first division in May 2003, a British clergyman conducted a special service at St. Peter's Church in Manchester to pull in some divine help for coach Sam Allardyce and the boys.

The Reverend Roger Oldfield delivered a sermon entitled, "What Would Jesus Say to Sam Allardyce?" The church was decorated to resemble Bolton's Reebok Stadium and an Allardyce look-alike shouted out instructions from a dugout in front of the pews.

At halftime—make that midway through the service—orange slices were doled out to the congregation.

It worked. Wanderers edged Middlesbrough, 2–1, in their final match and finished seventeenth in the twenty-team Premier League, two points ahead of West Ham and one place away from a drop.

Northern Irish Player Scores All Goals in 2–2 Tie

As a Northern Ireland international who played more than six hundred matches in the English league, Chris Nicholl possessed credentials that were solid but hardly of superstar caliber. But in an English first division match in March 1976 against Leicester City, the Aston Villa central defender was positively dominating as he took care of all the scoring—for both sides.

Fifteen minutes after the opening kickoff, Leicester's Brian Alderson got off a shot that was seemingly wide of the mark, but Nicholl inadvertently headed the ball past Villa goalkeeper John Burridge and into his own net.

Nicholl got his chance to make amends five minutes before half-time. A header by Villa's Brian Little created a goalmouth scramble and Nicholl hooked the loose ball home for a 1–1 tie.

In the fifty-third minute, Nicholl struck again. For Leicester. Frank Worthington of Leicester chipped a ball into the penalty area and the Villa center back outleaped Leicester's Bob Lee and nodded the ball the wrong way to put Leicester on top, 2–1. (The own goal was the third for Nicholl in two games. The previous week he inadvertently scored for Tottenham.)

One more goal would be scored, and of course Nicholl was responsible. With four minutes remaining, Chico Hamilton of Villa swung a corner kick into the goalmouth and Nicholl, capping his one-man show, scored.

Final score: Leicester 2, Aston Villa 2, Chris Nicholl 4.

On a much larger stage two years later, Holland's Ernie Brandts made like Nicholl and caused all of Italy to leap for joy and, ultimately, weep.

In a second-round group match that would determine which team would go to the 1978 World Cup semifinals in Argentina, the Dutch faced the Italians at Estadio Antonio Liberti, "The Monumental," in Buenos Aires. In the nineteenth minute, defender Brandts, attempting to stop an Italian breakaway led by strikers Paolo Rossi and Roberto Bettega, redirected the ball into his own net. In giving Italy a 1–0 lead, Brandts also slammed into goalkeeper Piet Schrijvers and sent him off the field on a stretcher. Schrijvers was replaced by Jan Jongbloed, who had been benched after giving up three goals to Scotland in the opening round.

Italy's new best friend, however, turned on the Azzurri five minutes after halftime, equalizing on a twenty-yard shot. That allowed

Brandts a sigh of relief—Holland had gone into the match needing only a tie to clinch the group—and midfielder Arie Haan got Brandts completely off the hook by scoring the game winner from thirty yards in the seventy-fifth minute.

Well, Brandts wasn't off the hook completely. Schrijvers, his knee injured in his collision with Brandts, missed the final. And Jongbloed, with Brandts playing in front of him, allowed two goals in overtime as Argentina defeated the Dutch, 3–1, back at the Monumental.

And one from the mid-1970s:

John Burridge, who went on to play in the English first division for Crystal Palace, recalled a dreadful day while a teenager with the fourth division's Workington.

"We were hammering Southend United, 4–0. A cameraman behind my goal told me we were playing injury time.

"Just then a Workington teammate hit a back pass to me. As I clutched the ball I heard the referee blow his whistle. I turned towards my goal, let out a victorious cheer, and blasted the ball into the net as I ran to collect my gloves and cap.

"My teammates were staggered. The whistle had been blown by a supporter. The ref had to award a goal.

"I felt an absolute idiot."

Italian Club Picks Up a Deadly Sponsor

An obscure Italian team outside Naples, Stella Azzurra of San Felice Castello, turned to the Grim Reaper in picking up a new sponsor in October 2001, the Lettieri Last Travel funeral parlor. Players were issued black uniforms as a nod to the sponsor, and they were given jewelry boxes resembling a miniature coffin to hand out to fans as gifts.

Stella Azzurra president Franco Maiulo and his friend, funeral parlor director Antonio Lettieri, decided to join hands in an effort to attract attention to the team.

While Stella's publicity stunt went unchallenged, a 1990 effort by an English fourth-division club wasn't as fortunate. Cash-strapped Scarborough was ordered by league officials to drop its sponsor, a Luxembourg-based vodka and schnapps libation named "Black Death," after it took the field with jerseys reading, "Black Death Vodka—Drink in Peace."

Player Won't Sign Extension Because the End Is Near

No mere negotiating ploy, this.

After Real Mallorca won the 1998–99 European Cup Winners' Cup, the grateful Spanish club offered star goalkeeper Carlos Roa a contract extension. However, Roa, Argentina's starting 'keeper at the 1998 World Cup, told Mallorca that he was reluctant to sign because he believed the world would end in 2000.

"There's no point in having a new one," shrugged Roa, a Seventh Day Adventist.

Roa's religious beliefs had previously become an issue when a proposed transfer from Mallorca to Manchester United fizzled because his faith prohibits him from playing or training on Saturdays before sunset. The English Premier League schedules most of its matches for Saturday afternoons; the Spanish Primera Liga plays most of its games on Sundays, and its handful of Saturday matches are after dark.

Roa, in fact, left soccer altogether and spent the 1999–2000 season engaged in religious and charity work. He returned to action with Mallorca for 2000–2001 after the world failed to end.

Precursor to the Bicycle Kick: The Somersault

Fiery Mexico striker Cuauhtemoc Blanco has embarrassed defenders for years with his signature move: when confronted by two opponents, he wedges the ball between his feet and leaps between them.

He has never come close to matching Patsy Gallagher of Glasgow Celtic, however. In the 1925 Scottish Cup final, with Dundee FC ahead, 1–0, Gallagher latched onto the ball in Blanco fashion at the Dundee goal line and turned a somersault, depositing the equalizer into the net.

Celtic won, 2–1.

Juventus' Pink Jerseys

Juventus is arguably Italy's most famous club, thanks to its record twenty-seven Italian championships and triumphs at the 1985 and 1996 European Cups and 1977, 1990, and 1993 UEFA Cups. The club long ago unseated Torino as the king of Turin, and Juve's black-and-white-striped jerseys and white shorts make it one of the game's most recognizable teams.

There is a dark secret in the club's past, however: when SC Juventus was founded in 1897 by high school and gymnasium students, the players wore . . . pink jerseys.

This exercise in very bad taste went on for six long years until the club ordered a new set of uniforms from England. The order was botched and a shipment of uniforms intended for Notts County of England, featuring Notts' zebra shirts, was erroneously sent to Juventus. Perhaps seeing the light, Juve kept them. A legendary look was launched in northern Italy and a sports fashion disaster was brought to a merciful end in 1903.

Or was it? In December 2003 Juve marked one hundred pink-less years by donning pink once again for a game against Lazio. The players of Lazio rubbed their eyes and later rolled to a 2–0 win.

Meanwhile, wearing black and white stripes has done precious little for Notts County. Founded in 1862 and an original member of the English Football League, the world's oldest soccer club has done no better than third-place finishes in the first division in 1891 and 1901. Since then the Magpies have done nothing but spin their wheels, racking up a record twenty-six promotions and relegations.

Pop Less than Thrilled by Son's Game-winning Goal

With his father looking on, FC Utrecht's Ricky Kruys, age nineteen, entered a November 2004 Dutch first-division match in the eighty-first minute and, with his first touch of the game, blasted a shot that beat De Graafschap, 1–0.

Dad, however, wasn't cheering. Gert Kruys was the De Graafschap coach.

"We did well, and then suddenly such a tiny tot comes onto the pitch and shoots in the top corner with a terrific drive," said the elder Kruys. "I have told him that he will not be allowed to come home for a while."

Young Ricky's brilliant strike left Dad's club winless after fourteen games and mired in last place.

A Matter of Priorities

Perhaps the best soccer-inspired quote—author unknown—was the by-product of the generations of British fans who have turned football wagering into an extra reason for living. It saw print in 1914 at the end of an article headlined "Do Work," in an issue of Britain's *Football Mail*:

"And I met a manufacturer on Tuesday who was seriously considering the closing of his mill on Saturday morning simply because the men were so busy discussing the coming matches on the afternoons that he could get no work done. It was bad enough, he thought, to have a great deal of time wasted on Mondays in discussing Saturday's matches, and more on Fridays canvassing prospects, organizing sweepstakes and filling up coupons.

"There is no wonder that employers of labour regard any increase in football fixtures with apprehension, for so many workmen act up to the motto, 'If your work interferes with your football, give it up.'"

Obscure Root Fuels Peruvian Club's Championship

As secret weapons go, it's not much to look at. But Cienciano, a club based in the Andean city of Cuzco that has never won a Peruvian championship, swears by it.

Cienciano defeated mighty River Plate of Argentina in the 2003 Copa Sudamerica final after a steady diet of fresh maca, a root first eaten by the Incas to help them cope with life at high altitude. Maca, related to turnips and cabbage, is high in calcium, phosphorus, protein, iron, mineral salts, fiber, and an antioxidant that is not banned by any sports organization. The players ate the root three times a day, and the results were positively stimulating as Cienciano became the first Peruvian club to win a major international honor.

First to fall was Santos of Brazil, followed by Universidad Catolica of Chile and Atlético Nacional of Colombia. In the final, the upstarts survived the Buenos Aires leg, holding on for a 3–3 tie with River Plate before a Monumental Stadium crowd of fifty thousand. In the second leg, Cienciano, urged on by forty-four thousand in Arequipa, eked out a 1–0 victory on a seventy-seventh-minute goal by Carlos Lugo to take the series. And the Peruvians did it despite having two men sent off in the second half.

Cienciano's triumph was a tremendous advertisement for Hersil, the company that supplied the club with its daily dose of maca. Hersil next planned to donate supplies of the root to the Peruvian National Team, which hasn't appeared in a World Cup since 1982.

Lions, Red Devils, Socceroos, and Other Creatures

For every expansion team in American pro sports given an antiseptic nickname through a fan survey or focus group, there are dozens and dozens of soccer clubs throughout the world that proudly boast colorful monikers that have nothing to do with cold calculation or the conclusion of a faceless marketing firm.

England's Aston Villa is known, of course, as the Villains, while Arsenal, a club founded by South London munitions workers, is known as the Gunners. West Ham United's foundry, er, founding fathers came from the nineteenth-century team known as Thames Ironworks FC and is known as the Hammers.

Fearsome nicknames indeed in a country where other clubs have been dubbed the Tykes (Barnsley), Trotters (Bolton), Cherries (the all-red-clad Bournemouth), Robins (Bristol City and Swindon Town), Shakers (Bury), Quakers (Darlington), Toffees (Everton, which shared a Liverpool neighborhood with two popular confectioners), Red Imps (Lincoln City), Hatters (Luton Town and Stockport County), Magpies (Newcastle United and Notts County, for their black-and-white-striped jerseys), Cobblers (Northampton Town), Canaries (the yellow plumage of Norwich City), Posh (Petersborough United), Pilgrims (Plymouth Argyle), Lilywhites (Preston North End), Merry Millers (Rotherham United), Saints (Southampton), Shrimpers (Southend United), and Potters (Stoke City).

Then it gets much stranger.

There's the Go Ahead Eagles of Holland. And FC Boom of Belgium—great name except when one considers that the team represents the city of Boom, near Antwerp, and *boom* simply means "tree" in Dutch.

Switzerland has Young Boys Berne, Old Boys Basle, and Grasshoppers Zurich, not to mention Neuchatel Xamax FC, whose name is a palindrome based on the first name of star striker and team cofounder Max "Xam" Abegglen, an early Swiss international.

Norway gives us Odd—Odd SK Skien, that is—winner of four of its first five national cups, finalist in eight of its first nine, and, oddly enough, winner of nothing else since 1931. Argentina offers Club Deportivo Moron, from the Buenos Aires district of Moron, where, it is presumed, the team's opponents consider their supporters morons.

Ghana presents the King Faisal Babies, Hearts of Oak, Cape Coast Dwarfs, Eleven Wise FC and—what must've been a favorite of real gridiron football fan Rush Limbaugh—Real Republicans, who won four straight Ghanan Cups in the 1960s before folding. Far to the southeast is Botswana and more unusual names: Miscellaneous FC, Killer Giants, and Naughty Boys.

Is there a more cocksure name than Liberia's Invincible Eleven? It might be The Strongest of Bolivia, a country that also boasts clubs like Destroyer and Always Ready.

And it must be the Caribbean climate that has inspired the likes of the populist Joe Public FC (Trinidad and Tobago), fanciful Robin Hood (Surinam), conflicted Playtime Tigers (Bermuda), and bucolic Boys Town (Jamaica). The U.S. Virgin Islands alone can claim clubs named Skills and Unique (both in St. Croix), and Positive Vibes and New Vibes (both in St. Thomas).

National teams also have nicknames. Some are inspired by the team's colors, some by an indigenous product, some by overly enthusiastic or whimsical members of the press. Africa leads in nicknames, with nearly all of its national teams sporting a moniker based on a favorite home-based animal. In Africa and elsewhere, lions, tigers, eagles, hawks, stars, dragons, and devils figure prominently. A sampling:

EUROPE

Austria. Rot-Weiss-Roten (Red, White, and Red, in German), Wunderteam (at its height in the 1930s).

Azerbaijan. Odlar Yurdu Komandasi (the Team from the Land of Fire).

Belgium. Diables Rouges (Red Devils, in French), Rode Duivels (Red Devils, in Flemish).

Croatia. Vatreni (Fiery Ones).

Czech Republic. Reprezentace (the Representation), Cesti Ivi (Czech Lions).

Denmark. Danish Dynamite (inspired by a major victory for the Danes over England in a 1984 European Championship qualifier).

England. The Three Lions.

France. Les Bleus (the Blues).

Georgia. Jvarosnebi (the Crusaders).

Germany. Nationalmannschaft (National Team).

Greece. To Peiratiko (the Pirate Ship, inspired by the Greeks' unlikely seizure of the 2004 European Championship trophy).

Holland. Oranje (the Orange, for the team's jerseys; the national flag's red, white, and blue colors aside, orange is the color of the royal family, the House of Oranje-Nassau, which dates to William of Orange).

Hungary. The Magic Magyars (but particularly the team from the 1950s).

Ireland. The Boys in Green.

Italy. Squadra Azzurra (Blue Team; Italy was clad in white for its first two internationals, in 1910, and the following year it donned blue shirts in honor of the House of Savoy, the ruling dynasty at the time. The familiar red, white, and green of the present Italian flag— Il Tricolore—wasn't adopted until 1948).

Kazakhstan. Kazakhstanskie barsy (Snow Leopards, in Russian).

Malta. Kavallieri Ta Malta (Knights of Malta).

Poland. Polskie Orly (Polish Eagles).

Portugal. Seleçao das Quinas (Selection of the Five, for the five escutcheons on the shield on the Portuguese flag).

San Marino. La Serenissima (the Most Serene, in Italian; not quite appropriate for a team that has never won a competitive international match).

Scotland. The Tartan Army (also the nickname for the team's fans).

Serbia. Plavi (Blues).

Spain. La Furia Roja (Red Fury).

Sweden. Blagult (the Blue and Yellow).

Switzerland. Nati (short for National Selection).

Turkey. Ay Yildiz (the Team of the Moon and Star).

Wales. Red Lions, the Dragons.

SOUTH AMERICA

Argentina. La Albicelestes (White and Sky Blues).

Brazil. Seleçao (the Selection), Canarinhos (Canaries), Verdeamarelos (Green and Yellows), Auriverdes (Gold and Green), Pentacampeoes (Five-Time Champs).

Bolivia. Verde (Green).

Chile. Roja (Red).

Colombia. La Selección Cafetera (the Coffee-Makers Team).

Ecuador. Amarillos (Yellows).

Paraguay. Albirrojos (Red and Whites, for its striped jersey).

Peru. Blanquirroja (White and Red, for its white jersey with diagonal red stripe).

Uruguay. La Celeste (the Sky Blues).

Venezuela. Vinotinto (Wine-colored, for its burgundy jerseys).

NORTH AMERICA, CENTRAL AMERICA, AND THE CARIBBEAN

Costa Rica. Ticos (slang for Costa Rican Natives).

Grenada. Spice Boyz (a nod to the country's nutmeg production).

Guatemala. Chapines (slang for Guatemalan Natives).

El Salvador. La Selecta or Cuscatlecos (slang for Salvadoran Natives).

Jamaica. Reggae Boyz (home of Bob Marley).

Mexico. El Tricolores or El Tri (for the red, white, and green of the nation's flag).

Panama. Canaleros.

St. Kitts and Nevis. Sugar Boyz (for the islands' sugar industry).

Trinidad and Tobago. Soca Warriors (a play on soccer and the name of a local genre of music).

AFRICA

Algeria. Les Fennecs (Desert Foxes, in French).

Angola. Palancas Negras (Black Antelopes, in Portuguese).

Benin. Squirrels.

Botswana. Zebras (although the team jersey is sky blue, not black and white stripes).

Burkina Faso. Stallions.

Burundi. Swallows.

Cameroon. Indomitable Lions.

Cape Verde. Tubaroes Azuis (Blue Sharks, in Portuguese).

Central African Republic. Le Faons d'Ubangui (the Fawns of Ubangui, after the tributary of the Congo River, in French).

Congo DR. Simbas (Lions, in Swahili. Known as the Leopards when the country was Zaire).

Egypt. Pharoahs.

Ghana. Black Stars (from the nation's flag; refers to the Black Star Line shipping corporation created by Jamaican activist Marcus Garvey to return Africans in the Caribbean to their ancestral continent).

Guinea. Syli (nickname for an indigenous elephant).

Ivory Coast. Elephants.

Kenya. Harambee Stars (*harambee* means "We will work together"—the national motto—in Swahili).

Mali. Eagles.

Morocco. Atlas Lions.

Mozambique. Mambas.

Nigeria. Super Eagles (the national women's team is called the Super Falcons).

Senegal. Lions of Teranga (*teranga* means "hospitality" in the Wolof language).

South Africa. Bfana Bfana (the Boys, in Zulu).

Sudan. Nile Crocodiles.

Tanzania. Kilimanjaro Stars.

Togo. Sparrowhawks.

Tunisia. Carthage Eagles.

Zambia. Chipolopolo (Copper Bullets, in the Bemba language).

Zimbabwe. Warriors.

ASIA

Australia. Socceroos (the national women's team is known as the Matildas, the youth team as the Joeys).

Bhutan. Druk XI (the Eleven Dragons, in Dzongkha).

India. The Bhangra Boys (based on the Bhangra dance popular in the Punjab region).

Iraq. The Babylon Lions, or Osod Al Rafideen (the Lions of the Two Rivers, in Arabic).

Iran. Shirants Perse (Persian Lions, in Persian).

Japan. Blue Samurais.

Lebanon. Al Aarz (the Team of Cedars, in Arabic).

North Korea. Chollima (mythical Korean horse).

Philippines. Azkals (Stray Dogs, in Filipino).

Saudi Arabia. Ouilad Al Sahraa (Sons of the Desert, in Arabic).

Turkmenistan. Akhal-Teke (the Dark Horses).
Yemen. Al Yemen al Saeed (Happy Yemen, in Arabic).
South Korea. Taeguk Warriors.

OCEANIA

New Caledonia. Les Cagous (the Kagu Birds, in French).
New Zealand. All Whites (the national rugby team is known as the All Blacks).

Pelé the Popular

Just how popular was the immortal Pelé at the peak of his playing career?

In January 1969, during the worst of the five-year Biafran War, Pelé and his club, Santos of Brazil, came to Nigeria to play a friendly against the Nigerian National Team. The federal government and rebels of Biafra declared a three-day cease-fire to mark the occasion. The game was played, and Santos, behind two goals by Pelé, tied Nigeria, 2–2. Pelé and Santos left the country, and the war resumed.

Years later, Pelé told this one on himself: At an August 2001 press conference in Rio de Janeiro called to announce that the retired superstar had become a spokesman for Coca-Cola, a journalist ingratiatingly said, "There are three things known all over the world: Coca-Cola, Pelé, and Jesus Christ."

Replied Pele, "I remember going to a small island off the coast of Japan once, and everyone knew who I was. But, as most of the inhabitants were Buddhists, not all of them had heard of Jesus Christ."

He added quickly, "Unfortunately, there are large parts of the world where Jesus Christ is not so well known."

And then there's what the media thinks of the player known as the Black Pearl. Pelé and the rise of the Brazilian National Team was the top pick as the international sports story of the century in a poll of Associated Press subscribers worldwide conducted in December 1999. Trailing, in order, were the 1972 Munich Olympics massacre, the career of Muhammad Ali, Jesse Owens's performance at the 1936 Berlin Olympics, and the exploits of basketball's Michael Jordan. Sports editors and broadcasters from more than thirty nations took part.

One country missing from that poll was the United States, where

Pelé is seen as merely mortal. A sixteen-member panel determined the United States' version of the top one hundred athletes of the century, and Babe Ruth finished first, followed by Jordan, Jim Thorpe, Ali, and Wayne Gretzky. Pelé, who was far down the list at number fifteen, was the only soccer player named.

Pelé, two more times: In October 1999 the Brazilian legend and his wife, Assyria, were in a chauffeur-driven Mercedes Benz. They were stopped at a traffic light in São Paulo's Itaim Bibi district when a gunman approached on foot.

The would-be holdup man demanded money and jewelry . . . then recognized Pelé. He apologized and fled. Nothing was taken, and Pelé did not report the incident to authorities.

Less than nine years later, things had changed. Pelé was riding in a chauffeur-driven car in Guaruja, near his vacation home at Pernambuco Beach, when a band of ten youths armed with knives and guns took advantage of a traffic jam to rob El Rey of a gold necklace, his cell phone, and an expensive wristwatch.

The thieves, who robbed the occupants of other vehicles stuck in the snarl, were said to have recognized the three-time World Cup winner before fleeing.

Once again, Pelé did not report the incident to police.

Seeing Triple in Glasgow

Rangers appeared to have pulled the ultimate coup on bitter crosstown rival Celtic in June 2004 with the signing of thirteen-year-old triplets Kyle, Sheldon, and Devon Jacobs—Celtic fans to a man, or boy.

"The three boys signing for Rangers is a dream come true," said proud mother Irene, whose children were born in South Africa and raised in Livingston, Scotland, "although down deep they are Celtic supporters. But it is all about football, and wherever they get an opportunity they have to take it."

Paving the way was the triplets' older brother, Keaghan, who two years earlier signed at age twelve with hometown Livingston. Though Kyle, Sheldon, and Devon eventually left Rangers, the Jacobs brothers were reunited on the field in 2007 when all four started for Livingston in an under-19 match.

The closest thing to an international hat trick of brothers came November 1933 in a Home International Championship match between Northern Ireland and Wales in Belfast. Samuel Jones, who scored in the 1–1 draw, was joined on the Northern Irish halfback line by his brother, Jack, and his brother-in-law, William Mitchell.

It's Time for a Substitution or Two . . . or Eleven

There's nothing like the ol' vote of confidence from the boss—something the starting lineup of Selkirk, a team in the Border Amateur League's "W" Division, did *not* receive during its darkest hour, a Scottish Cup first-round match in December 1984 played before hundreds at Stirling Albion.

Though Stirling was a first-division side, no one was anticipating a double-digit blowout. Still, the hosts took a 5–0 lead at the half, inspiring their bloodthirsty fans to chant "We want ten." That milestone was reached after an hour, and late in the game the chant was inflated to "We want twenty."

With David Thompson leading the parade with seven goals and Willie Irvine not far behind with five, Stirling won, 20–0.

Late in the game Selkirk officials on the sidelines were beyond mortified and could only laugh at the situation. They collected as many numeral signs as possible from the fourth official and held them up in a mock signal to the referee that they wanted to substitute all eleven of their players at once.

Fans Help English Players Weather a Storm

Rain and football go hand in hand in all but the most arid parts of the world, but early in the game's history there was a day when a couple of players decided that enough was enough.

In the 1890s a tremendous downpour arrived while Aston Villa was playing Sheffield United in an English first division game. Among the soaked players was Villa's right winger, Charlie Athersmith, an English international. Athersmith suffered along with the rest of his teammates until a sympathetic spectator handed him an umbrella, which he gratefully accepted and held over his head on his runs up and down the wing.

That inspired Villa's John Devey, also an England international, to borrow a raincoat from a fan, and the two forwards played through the remainder of the deluge in greater comfort while the crowd roared its approval.

Arab/Jewish Club Wins Israeli Cup

Arab teams have won their share of Asian club competitions, but they have never captured a European title—for obvious reasons. Leave it to Israel, then, to give Arabs hope of European glory.

Bnei Sakhnin qualified for the UEFA Cup as winner of the 2004 Israeli Cup. The club was based in the village of Ilut outside Nazareth, the country's largest Arab city with a population of seventy thousand. The Bnei Sakhnin roster wasn't exclusively Arab; the club included local Jews, Muslims, and Christians and a contingent of Africans of various faiths. However, the club won praise for its seizing the opportunity to serve as an example of Arab-Israeli cooperation.

Bnei Sakhnin cleared its first hurdle by finishing off Partizani Tirana of Albania by a 6–1 aggregate in the qualifiers in August to earn passage to the eighty-club first round. There, it was brought back to earth by England's Newcastle United, 2–0 and 5–1.

Those Dunces in the Front Office

Len Shackleton, a star center forward for Sunderland in the late 1940s and '50s, wrote his autobiography upon his retirement and in it made clear his opinion of club management.

Known as the clown prince of English soccer, Shackleton exacted his revenge on the suits in Chapter 8, "The Football Knowledge of the Average Director." The chapter's six pages were left blank.

Shackleton was a physical comedian as well. He mocked opposing fullbacks by playing one-twos with the corner flag. And in one game against Arsenal, with his side ahead, 2–1, and five minutes remaining, Shackleton dribbled into the Gunners' penalty area, stopped, stood on the ball, and pretended to comb his hair while alternately checking his imaginary watch.

Obviously, in light of such antics, the committee that selected the English National Team at that time limited Shackleton's international career to just five games. One committee member once explained Shackleton's rejections thus: "Because we play at Wembley Stadium, not the London Palladium."

Freedom Isn't Free, Except When Mexico Wins

There are celebrations, and then there's the celebration carried out during the 1970 World Cup by Mexican Augusto Mariaga, warden of a maximum security prison in Chilpancingo, Guerrero.

After his beloved Mexico edged Belgium, 1–0, in Mexico City to advance to the final eight for the first time ever, Mariaga raced around his prison compound, shouting "Viva Mexico" as he shot his pistol into the air. Not done, he then unlocked every cell, releasing 142 men of questionable character.

Later, after Mexico fell to eventual finalist Italy, 4–1, in the quarterfinals, Mariaga was acquitted by a sympathetic court. The verdict: Mariaga had "acted in patriotic exaltation."

Goalkeepers Rarely Stay in Center during PKS

It's the "Why not?" of soccer: a player lines up a penalty kick, approaches the ball, and chips it high into the center of the net while the opposing goalkeeper flings himself toward one post or the other. The British would call it "cheeky," and it's rare, but why don't more shooters do it?

Perhaps more penalty-kick takers would choose to become straight shooters if they knew the results of a 2005 study, "Action Bias Among Elite Soccer Goalkeepers: The Case of Penalty Kicks," conducted by five Israeli professors. They found that while "the utility-maximizing behavior of goalkeepers is to stay in the goal's center during the kick, in 93.7 percent of the kicks the goalkeepers chose to jump right or left."

That means "when in doubt, do nothing" was the choice of top goalkeepers on just 6.3 percent of PK attempts they faced.

"According to the norm theory," the study continued, "people have stronger feelings associated with outcomes when they come from abnormal causes. Consequently, because the norm is that goalkeepers jump to one of the sides, the disutility associated with missing a ball might be greater following a non-common behavior (staying in the center) than following normal behavior (jumping to the side)."

Of course, remaining in the center on every penalty kick would hardly earn a 'keeper the plaudits of the crowd.

Uruguay and the First Lap of Victory

The trophy presentation at the end of a major soccer competition has become formulaic, what with the quick erection of a stage at midfield, the crush of photographers, the handing out of medals to the somber losing players and jubilant winning players, and, finally, the hoisting of the gleaming cup by the triumphant team captain to the burst of confetti pop guns.

What happens next is a less contrived moment as the winning players run the trophy around the floor of the stadium, each of them showing it off to fans for a few yards along the perimeter before passing it along to a teammate. No matter how often it's played out, this demonstration of joy continues to give the impression of being spontaneous as the players—stumbling and leaping, many of them shirtless, some of them millionaires, some teens or even amateurs—pass the hardware like tipsy waiters.

The first such "victory lap" or "lap of honor" was indeed a spontaneous demonstration, performed first by the Uruguay players moments after they won the 1924 Olympic soccer tournament. Though holders of the Copa America, the Uruguayans came to Paris—via third-class passage—as something of a mystery team, but their dazzling skills and a midfield known as *la costilla metallica* ("the iron curtain") quickly made them the darlings of the tournament.

After beating Yugoslavia, 7–0; the United States, 3–0; host France, 5–1; and Holland, 2–1, Uruguay easily rolled over Switzerland, 3–0, in the final before a sellout crowd of forty-one thousand at the Olympic Stadium of Colombes (another ten thousand were turned away). Thoroughly won over, the frenzied spectators urged the new gold medalists to circle the field so they could be properly saluted, and a tradition, once called the "Olympic turn," was born.

(The organizers of the Paris Games probably would have liked to have joined them. More than one-third of all '24 Olympic income came from the two dozen matches of the soccer competition; the final alone accounted for one-twelfth.)

Di Stéfano Plays for Three Countries

In the mid-nineteenth century there was literature's Philip Nolan, the title character in Edward Everett Hale's *The Man Without a Country*.

A hundred years later there was soccer's Alfredo Di Stéfano, soccer's man with three countries.

Before FIFA tightened the rules limiting players to play internationally on the senior level for no more than one nation, the world's first true global soccer superstar, Di Stéfano, wore the colors of three different national teams.

The deep-lying center forward, who would go on to lead Real Madrid in its run of consecutive European Cups from 1956 to 1960, was born in Argentina in 1926 to Italian parents. After becoming an overnight sensation with River Plate, in 1947 he made the first of seven international appearances for Argentina, scoring six goals.

Future FIFA statues would have prevented Di Stéfano from ever playing for another country, regardless of how many times he changed his citizenship. But given the rules at the time, he was far from finished.

In 1950 Di Stéfano jumped River Plate and joined several of his fellow Argentines in Colombia, where a cash-rich rebel league had been formed. The "Blond Arrow" was signed by the free-spending Bogota club known as Millonarios and quickly led it to two championships. In the meantime, this former Argentine international made four appearances for Colombia. No problem.

Di Stéfano's 259 goals in 292 games for Millonarios brought him to the attention of Spanish giant Real Madrid, which signed him in 1955. His acquisition was not without dispute: while Real Madrid bought Di Stéfano from Millonarios, Real's hated rival FC Barcelona worked out a separate deal with River Plate. A Spanish court made the bizarre ruling that Di Stéfano would alternate seasons between Real and Barca, but Barcelona ultimately sold its share of the world's greatest Argentine/Colombian goal scorer to Real.

Known as perhaps the most complete player of his time, Di Stéfano was the toast of Europe for the next eleven years, scoring 405 goals in 624 matches for Real, leading the Spanish first division in scoring five of six seasons and playing on six European Cup–winning teams.

Di Stéfano also made it a hat trick of national teams, playing thirty-one times—and scoring twenty-three goals—for his third and final country, Spain. (By obtaining Spanish citizenship, Di Stéfano made himself eligible for the newly created European Footballer of the Year award, which he won in 1957 and 1959.)

Despite appearing in three different national team uniforms, Di

Stéfano never played in a World Cup. He came closest with Chile '62, when he would have teamed with his Real Madrid strikemate, Ferenc Puskás, the Hungarian legend who was playing for his second country, and a third star forward in the twilight of his career, FC Barcelona's Ladislao Kubala, who was playing for *his* third country.

But Di Stéfano sat out the tournament with an injury, as did Kubala, who earlier represented Czechoslovakia and his native Hungary. Spain, minus two parts of what would have been a three-man front line for the ages, scored twice in its three matches and limped out of Chile last in its first-round group.

God Shoots, and You Know the Rest

The players from Hungary had to be fearing the worst when they lined up to face Poland in the opening round of the 1936 Berlin Olympics and found that the opposition's inside left forward was, well, God.

Sure enough, God scored twice and the Poles cruised to a 3–0 victory, which carried them into the quarterfinals. There, God took his foot off the pedal a bit, scoring once, but it helped Poland to a 5–4 win over Great Britain.

There would be no divine intervention in the semifinals. Oh, God scored again all right, but it wasn't enough as Poland lost to Austria, 3–1. In the bronze medal game two days later Poland was completely forsaken: God, far from almighty, went scoreless and Norway, on a hat trick by Arne Brustad, won, 3–2.

Italy took the gold in a 2–1 thriller over the Austrians, and God's four goals got him a very mortal-like tie for fifth place among the tournament's leading scorers.

For the record, God was Hubert God, whose name was also spelled "Gad." A temporary replacement in Berlin for star inside left Ernest Wilimowski, God played only a handful of games for Poland, including four after the Olympics. He died while swimming in a lake just weeks before the German invasion of Poland; God's pallbearers included several star Poland teammates.

Goalkeeper Is Lost in a Fog

A most dedicated goalkeeper for an English Sunday league team found himself lost in a fog—literally—during an early winter match played in South Yorkshire in 2002. The UniBond League first-division contest between Stocksbridge Steels of Sheffield and Witton Albion was thirty minutes old when fog reduced visibility to half the length of the field, so the referee decided to abandon the match while the ball was on the Witton half of the field. The players retired to their respective dressing rooms, but after a few minutes the members of Stocksbridge realized that their goalkeeper, Richard Siddall, was missing.

A quick search was conducted and the ever-vigilant Siddall was found on the field, still poised between the Stocksbridge posts, unaware of the abandonment and quite pleased that his side apparently had managed to keep the ball far from his goal for so long.

"I didn't have a clue," Siddall told the *Independent*, a national newspaper. "I just stood there waiting for a player to come through the mist."

Some would praise Siddall's extraordinary focus. BBC Radio One, however, named the twenty-year-old its "Clown of the Week."

Soccer, Before It Was a Business

Manchester United, boasting 50 million fan club members worldwide, is the most valuable sports franchise on earth. First listed on the London stock exchange in 1991, the club's worth, according to *Forbes* magazine, was $1.8 billion in 2008, nearly double its price tag in 2002.

The Red Devils' revenue for the year was $394 million, second only to Real Madrid, whose value was $1.28 billion. Also on *Forbes'* list were Arsenal ($1.20 billion), Liverpool ($1.05 billion), Bayern Munich ($917 million), AC Milan ($798 million), FC Barcelona ($784 million), Chelsea ($764 million), Juventus ($510 million), and Schalke 04 ($470 million).

On-field success and tradition combined with shrewd management, to be sure. However, there was a time, at least in England, when football teams were considered hobbies, not businesses, by those in charge. The board members—prominent members of the community, all—served on a part-time basis and were not allowed to draw a salary. Many of the shareholders were average fans from the working class, their stock certificates held as a concrete symbol of their support for the team, like a souvenir scarf.

Just how quaint was the arrangement? In 1980 Arsenal, an eight-time English League champion to that point, had a share issue totaling just 5,849 pounds. The club decided not to pay a dividend because the cost of mailing checks to the thousands of people who owned only one share would have exceeded the actual dividend.

Here Comes the Groom . . . to Score a Hat Trick

In February 1922, with Leeds United limping to a fourteenth-place finish in the English second division, Welsh inside forward Bill Poyntz, who earlier in the month became the first Leeds player ever sent off, got married in the morning, then celebrated his nuptials by scoring three goals in a victory that afternoon against Leicester City.

It is assumed it was the greatest day of his life.

A Spanish Cup Final Not to Be Missed

It was a long time in coming, so Deportivo La Coruña, founded in 1906, wasn't about to let Mother Nature interfere in the celebration of the club's first-ever honor as it closed in on victory in the 1995 Spanish Cup.

Deportivo and Valencia were tied, 1–1, late in the final at Santiago Bernabeu Stadium in Madrid, but a freak thunderstorm brought the game to a halt in the seventy-ninth minute. With the remaining eleven minutes of the match scheduled to be played three days later, Deportivo management paid for thirty-five thousand of the club's fans to make the ten-hour trip back to Madrid, where they saw Alfredo score the goal that gave their heroes a 2–1 triumph.

Brazil and Its One-name Wonders

Brazil is known for its galaxy of stars so great that they need only one name: Bebeto, Careca, Junior, Oscar, Jarizinho, Clodoaldo, Tostao, Garrincha, Ademir, Tim—the list is as long as the Amazon. Many are nicknames. Some are inspired by a player's appearance, like Dunga (a Portuguese variation of "Dopey"). Others come from a player's similarity to a star from the past (Ronaldinho, or "Little Ronaldo").

And some come out of thin air. That's how Edson Arantes do Nascimento became Pelé. He says his boyhood playmates hung that moniker on him, and no one knew what it meant. (The poor children of the small village of Tres Coracoes couldn't possibly have been familiar with Pele, the mythical Hawaiian goddess of volcanoes.)

Hence the icon known as Pelé—that's peh-LAY, not the "PAY-LAY" preferred by more than two generations of American sportscasters.

As Pelé wrote in his autobiography, *My Life and the Beautiful Game*:

Names, of course, are the cheapest thing around, so even the most poverty-stricken Brazilian can afford to be generous with them. And he is. He is equally generous with nicknames, possibly for the same reason, and very few of the nicknames have any meaning. "Dico" [still Pelé's nickname among immediate family members] is a common nickname for Edson, although I would not be surprised to discover 10 other nicknames for the same name. Nor do I know why Zoca was the nickname my brother earned when his baptised name was Jair. I sometimes have a strong feeling that nicknames—especially short nicknames—were either invented, or at least encouraged, by radio announcers. A Brazilian radio announcer, describing an important football game, sounds like a hysterical machine gun with the stutters gone mad. It helps him a good deal, of course, to have players called Pelé, Didi, Vavá, or Pepe. I can hardly picture a radio announcer using the full imaginative range of the average Brazilian father in his broadcast:

" . . . Edson Arantes do Nascimento receives the ball from Sebastião da Silva Tenorio Texeira Araujo and passes it to Valdemar João Mendes de Morais, Filho, who dribbles it past Artur Ribeiro Carvalho José Brito to pass it to Ruy Moreira Acácio Guimarães, who heads it . . ."

With that in mind, here's a very small sampling of Brazilian player nicknames (all internationals, most of them prominent figures at one time or another):

Zé.
Zezé.
Zico.
Zito.
Zinho.
Zizinho.
Zozimo.

Pelé.
Lelé.
Branco.
Chico.
Doca.
Rinaldo.
Rivaldo.
Ronaldo.
Ronaldao.
Ronaldinho.
Edu.
Cafú.
Tatú.
Lula.
Dida.
Tita.
Didí.
Mimi.
Vavá.
Baba.
Kaká.
Dudu.
Dunga.
Pinga.
Juvenal.
Júnior.
Juninho.
Roberto Dinamite.
And the best of all, Hércules, Sócrates, Milton, Romeo, and . . .
Larry and Fred.

BIBLIOGRAPHIC ESSAY

There would be no *Soccer Stories: Anecdotes, Oddities, Lore and Amazing Feats* were it not for *The Encyclopedia of World Soccer* by Richard Henshaw (Washington DC: New Republic Books, 1979). As one embarking on a career as a soccer writer, editor, and publicist, it was important to go beyond how the game was played to get a thorough understanding of its overall structure, milestones, and leading figures. It was read cover to cover, and discovered buried within its 828 pages were what would become several of the remarkable tales that were included in this book.

The Encyclopedia of World Soccer was comprehensive, authoritative, and, unfortunately, ahead of its time: Henshaw's book, released to an American public just coming to appreciate soccer, was out of print by the early 1980s. There were, however, several other outstanding resources that helped bring *Soccer Stories* to completion.

The most invaluable tool was, without question, *The Guinness Book of World Soccer* by Guy Oliver (London: Guinness Publishing, 1995). The first edition, published in 1992, lists basic information on every nation affiliated with FIFA; for every country in Europe and South America, plus the United States, Mexico, and Canada, the book offers a soccer history, club directory, top honors won, year-by-year league and cup results, and scores of every international match played. The second edition unscrambled international soccer in the post-Soviet world, providing entries on Bosnia-Herzegovina, Estonia, Ukraine, and other new states. Without Oliver's work, this book would be half finished. A third edition of *The Guinness Book of World Soccer* is sorely overdue.

Although this is a book written by an American for American readers, Oliver's wasn't the only English work that proved to be highly useful. The World Cup is the game's quadrennial high point, and three valuable sources in explaining this phenomenon were *The World Cup: A Complete Record* by Ian Morrison (Derby, England: Breedon Books Sport, 1990), *Superstars of the World Cup* by Jon Palmer (Bristol, England: Parragon, 1998), and *The History of the World Cup* by the dean of British soccer scribes, Brian Glanville (Plymouth, England: Latimer Trend & Co. Ltd., 1984).

Two sources closer to home were especially useful in presenting information on U.S. soccer from the not-too-distant past. *U.S. Soccer vs. the World* by Tony Cirino (Leonia NJ: Damon Press, Inc., 1983) was a useful history of the U.S. national and Olympic teams program from the USA's first international match in 1886 to the beginning of the NASL's ill-fated Team America experiment; unfortunately, it misses out on the later successes of the U.S. men, the U.S. women's national and Olympic teams, and American youth teams. *NASL: A Complete Record of the North American Soccer League* by the Canadian-based soccer author and historian Colin Jose (Derby, England: Breedon Books Sport, 1989) features bios and statistics of notable NASL players and coaches and lists every team roster and results over the league's tortured seventeen-year history.

Henshaw's encyclopedia and most of these sources were written before the rise of the United States on the international soccer stage, America's hosting of the 1994 World Cup, and, in the case of Palmer's gallery of profiles, the latest wave of star players and shifts in the balance of power around the soccer-playing world. The Internet and reliable Web sites, then, played a part in the writing of some of the more current items. The most trustworthy of the Web sites visited— frequently—was Rec.Sport.Soccer Statistics Foundation (www.rsssf

.com), a treasure trove of national league and cup results, standings and stats, some dating to the late nineteenth century.

Other resources include leading international newspapers and magazines (Italy's *Guerin Sportivo*, Spain's *Don Balon*, Brazil's *Placar*, England's *World Soccer* and *Four-Two-Four*, Germany's *Kicker*); media guides from the U.S. Soccer Federation, NASL, American Soccer League, and Major Indoor Soccer League; and annuals such as Mike Hammond's *The European Football Yearbook* (Smethwick, England: Sports Projects Ltd.) and Jock Rollin's *Rothmans Football Yearbook*, now known as Sky Sports Football Yearbook (London: Queen Anne Press).